Sources for
Western Society

Since 1300

Sources for
Western Society

Since 1300

Third Edition

The Companion Reader for
A History of Western Society

Eleventh Edition

John P. McKay
Clare Haru Crowston
Merry E. Wiesner-Hanks
Joe Perry

BEDFORD/ST. MARTIN'S   Boston ◆ New York

For Bedford/St. Martin's

Publisher for History: Mary V. Dougherty
Executive Editor for History: Traci M. Crowell
Director of Development for History: Jane Knetzger
Developmental Editor: Annette Fantasia
Publishing Services Manager: Andrea Cava
Senior Production Supervisor: Dennis J. Conroy
Executive Marketing Manager: Sandra McGuire
Editorial Assistant: Emily DiPietro
Project Management: Books By Design, Inc.
Senior Art Director: Anna Palchik
Text Design: Lily Yamamoto, LMY Studio, Inc.
Cover Design: Billy Boardman
Cover Photo: The Little English Shoeshine, 1882, Bastien-Lepage, Jules (1848–1884)/Musée des Arts
   Décoratifs Paris/Scala/White Images/Art Resource, NY
Composition: Jouve
Printing and Binding: RR Donnelley and Sons

President, Bedford/St. Martin's: Denise B. Wydra
Director of Marketing: Karen R. Soeltz
Production Director: Susan W. Brown
Director of Rights and Permissions: Hilary Newman

Manufactured in the United States of America.
8 7 6 5 4 3
f e d c b a

For information, write: Bedford/St. Martin's, 75 Arlington Street, Boston, MA 02116
   (617-399-4000)

ISBN 978-1-4576-1521-4

Acknowledgments
*Acknowledgments and copyrights appear on pages xxi–xxiii, which constitute an extension of the
copyright page. It is a violation of the law to reproduce these selections by any means whatsoever
without the written permission of the copyright holder.*

PREFACE

Thoroughly revised and expanded, *Sources for Western Society* gathers a diverse array of primary sources from Western history that brings the past to life for students. Recognizing that history is shaped by the many as much as it is shaped by the few, *Sources for Western Society* includes the voices of men and women from across the social spectrum, each offering their own unique perspective on the events and developments of their times. Designed specifically to be used with all versions of *A History of Western Society*, Eleventh Edition, the collection mirrors and complements each chapter of the parent textbooks, encouraging students to place the viewpoints of individual authors and artists in the context of the changing world in which they lived.

With input from current instructors of the Western civilization survey course, these documents have been compiled with one goal foremost in mind: to make history's most compelling voices accessible to students, from the most well-known thinkers of their times to the galvanized or introspective commoner. This emphasis on accessibility is crucial, since the reader is designed to challenge students to put aside their own preconceptions and to see history from the point of view of the people of the past. In Chapter 14, for example, students have the opportunity to look at the African slave trade from the perspective of an Italian trader writing in the mid-fifteenth century and an African king writing some seventy years later. Written from different perspectives and at different points in time, these documents help students to develop a nuanced, multi-sided picture of this seminal development in Western history.

To allow instructors flexibility in assigning individual sources while providing opportunities for students to focus on a document-based issue through analysis of multiple sources, each chapter provides a selection of individual documents that illuminate the variety of major developments and themes from the textbook, as well as a "Sources in Conversation" feature that allows students to examine an issue from multiple perspectives. Selections range widely in length to allow for a range of class assignments.

This companion reader steps back from drawing conclusions and instead provides just enough background to facilitate students' own analyses of the sources at hand. Chapter introductions set the context of the documents that follow within the framework of the corresponding textbook chapter. A concise headnote for each document provides key information about the author and the circumstances surrounding the document's creation, while helpful gloss notes aid comprehension of unfamiliar terms and references. Each document is followed by Reading Questions that promote understanding and critical analysis of the material, while chapter-concluding Comparative and Discussion Questions encourage students to contemplate the harmony and discord among the sources within and across the chapters.

New to This Edition

For the third edition of *Sources*, almost every aspect of the collection has been revised to include fresh and exciting sources that align with the new edition of the parent textbook and aid students' interpretation of the evidence. More than fifty new documents—including several compelling images—have been added, broadening the scope of this edition and offering increased representation of women and minority perspectives. To name just a few, Chapter 9 now includes a Jewish account of the anti-Semitic violence that accompanied the Crusades, Chapter 12 features two paintings by Artemisia Gentileschi that offer insight into a young woman's experience of gender and power in Renaissance Italy, and Chapter 30 provides a photograph of a Tunisian woman casting her vote in the elections that followed the series of uprisings during the Arab Spring. To help students better grasp the historical conditions in which the documents were produced, as well as key details in each selection, the chapter introductions, source headnotes, and questions have all been reworked and improved, providing the sources with a stronger contextual framework and highlighting the connections between them and the major themes of the textbook.

To the same end, one of the most significant changes in the new edition is the revision of the "Viewpoints" feature from the previous edition. Retitled "Sources in Conversation," each feature now begins with a brief introduction that provides a contextual framework for students to analyze and synthesize a set of two or more documents touching on a central theme. As the feature's title suggests, students are encouraged to find connections between the documents and to "join in the conversation" that the sources initiate about the nature and meaning of historical events and developments. In many cases, the features utilize brand-new sources. For example, "World War I in the Trenches and in the Air" in Chapter 25 focuses on two new photographs, one of an anonymous French soldier preparing for a gas attack and the other of Baron Manfred von Richthofen, offering students an opportunity to reflect on the implications of these conflicting images of individual combatants in the Great War. In other cases, the features build on documents included in the previous edition. For example, the feature entitled "Challenging the Prewar Social and Political Order" in Chapter 28 uses the writings of Frantz Fanon and Simone de Beauvoir to prompt students to explore the role of World War II in sparking both anticolonial activity and the postwar feminist movement. All "Sources in Conversation" features are designed to give students the tools they need to use multiple sources to build complex and nuanced pictures of the past.

Finally, new multiple-choice questions based on documents from each chapter of this sourcebook are available to users of the parent textbook's interactive e-book. Perfect for homework assignments or as preparation for discussions, these auto-graded questions provide instant feedback and help students build document-analysis skills.

Acknowledgments

Thanks to the instructors whose insightful comments and thoughtful suggestions helped shape the third edition: LeNie Adolphson, Sauk Valley Community College; Angela L. Ash, Owensboro Community and Technical College; Megan Boimann-Hennies, Highlands High School; David J. Chordas, Orange High School; Rebecca Favorito, The Ohio State University; David M. Gallo, College of Mount Saint Vincent; James Garcia, Centennial High School; Robert H. Greene, University of Montana; Justin Horton, Thomas Nelson Community College; Jodie A. Kreider, Colorado State University; Lisa Leff, American University; Kate Martin, Cape Cod Community College; Jennifer McNabb, Western Illinois University; Larry Myers, Butler Community College; Daniel Newman, Loyola Marymount University; Matthew Pehl, Augustana College; Judith Szapor, McGill University; George W. Whitton, State University of New York Institute of Technology at Utica/Rome.

Special thanks go to John Reisbord for his excellent and substantive contributions to this reader. Many thanks also to development editor Annette Fantasia, editorial assistant Emily DiPietro, and publishing services manager Andrea Cava of Bedford/St. Martin's, and to freelance development editor Danielle Slevens, Nancy Benjamin of Books By Design, Inc., and Laura Urling Moore of Creative Compliance.

CONTENTS

Acknowledgments (*continued from page iv*)

Chapter 11

11-4 Kupferstichkabinett, Staatliche Museen, Berlin, Germany / Jorg P. Anders / Art Resource, N.Y.

Chapter 12

12-4 Desiderius Erasmus, *The Education of a Christian Prince*, by Desiderius Eramsmus, translated by Lester K. Born. Copyright © 1936 Columbia University Press. Reprinted with permission of the publisher.

12-5 Christine de Pizan, *The Book of the City of Ladies*, by Christine de Pizan, translated by Earl Jeffrey Richards. Copyright © 1982 by Persea Books, Inc. Reprinted by permission of Persea Books, Inc. New York. All rights reserved.

Chapter 13

13-2 akg-images.

13-3 Jean Bodin, *On the Demon-Mania of Witches*, trans. Randy Scott, intro. Jonathan L. Pearl (Toronto: Centre for Reformation and Renaissance Studies, 1995.) Reprinted by permission of Victoria University Centre for Reformation and Renaissance Studies.

13-4 Charles Williams, "Confessions of the Chelmsford Witches." From *Witchcraft* by Charles Williams. Copyright © 2005 by Watkins/Loomis Agency. Reprinted by permission of the estate of Charles Williams and the Watkins/Loomis Agency.

Chapter 14

14-1 Oliver Dunn and James E. Kelly, Jr., *The Diario of Christopher Columbus's First Voyage to America, 1492–1493*, translated by Oliver Dunn and James E. Kelly, Jr. Copyright © 1989 by Oklahoma University Press. Reprinted with permission.

14-4 King Kzinga Mbemba Affonso of Congo, "Letters on the Slave Trade." From *The African Past* by Basil Davidson (Longmans, 1964), pp. 191–193. Reissued by Africa World Press 1990 as *African Civilization Revisited: From Antiquity to Modern Times* by Basil Davidson.

Chapter 17

17-4 "Olaudah Equiano, A Description of the Middle Passage." From *The Interesting Narrative of the Life of Olaudah Equiano Written by Himself*, edited by Robert J. Allison, pp. 67–68. Copyright © 2007 by Bedford/St. Martin's. Reprinted with permission.

Chapter 19

19-2 Abbé Sieyès, "What Is the Third Estate?" From *The French Revolution and Human Rights: A Brief Documentary History*, edited and translated by Lynn Hunt, pp. 65–70. Copyright © 1996 by Bedford/St. Martin's. Reprinted with permission.

19-5 Napoleon Bonaparte, *The Napoleonic Code*. From *A Documentary Survey of Napoleonic France*, edited and translated by E. A. Arnold (University Press of America, 1993), pp. 151–164. Reprinted with permission of the publisher.

19-7 François Dominique Toussaint L'Ouverture, "A Black Revolutionary Leader in Haiti." From C. L. R. James, *The Black Jacobins*, 2nd edition, edited by C. L. R. James (New York: Vintage Books, 1963), pp. 195–197. Reproduced with permission of Curtis Brown Group Ltd. London on behalf of the Estate of C. L. R. James. Copyright © C. L. R. James 1983.

Chapter 20

20-6 ca. 1842, French School (19th century) / Bibliothèque des Arts Decoratifs, Paris, France / Archives Charmet / The Bridgeman Art Library.

Chapter 22

22-4 Cregmile, Kate R. (1891–1923) / Cincinnati Art Museum, Ohio, USA / The Bridgeman Art Library.

22-4 Cregmile, Kate R. (1891–1923) / Cincinnati Art Museum, Ohio, USA / The Bridgeman Art Library.

Chapter 23

23-1 De Agostini Picture Library / G. Dagli Orti / The Bridgeman Art Library.

23-2 Martin Clark, *The Italian Risorgiment*, edited by Martin Clark. Copyright © 2009 by Pearson Education. Reprinted with permission.

23-3 Jan Goldstein, "Otto von Bismarck, Speech Before the Reichstag: On the Law for Workmen's Compensation" from *Readings in Western Civilization*, vol. 8, edited by Jan Goldstein and translated by John W. Boyer. Copyright © 1988 by University of Chicago Press. Reprinted with permission.

Chapter 24

24-2 Jules Ferry, "Speech Before the French Chamber of Deputies, March 28, 1884." From *Discours et Opinions de Jules Ferry*, edited by Paul Robiquet (Paris: Armand Colin & Cie, 1897), vol. 5, pp. 199–201, 210–211, 215–218. Translation by Ruth Kleinman is reprinted from *The Shaping of the Modern World: Core Curriculum 2.2 Readings*, 4th ed. (Boston: Pearson Custom Publishing, 2007), pp. 260–263, by permission of the Brooklyn College Department of History.

24-3 From *Punch*, 10 December 1892, English School (19th century) / Private Collection / The Bridgeman Art Library.

Chapter 25

25-1 Louis L. Snyder. *Documents of German History* by Louis L. Snyder. Copyright © 1958 by Louis L. Snyder. Reprinted with permission of Rutgers University Press.

25-2 Illustration from *The Illustrated War News*, 24 January 1917, French photographer (20th century) / Private Collection / The Stapleton Collection / The Bridgeman Art Library.

25-3 German photographer (20th century) / Private Collection / Peter Newark Military Pictures / The Bridgeman Art Library.

Chapter 26

26-1 Sigmund Freud, *The Interpretation of Dreams*. From *The Interpretation of Dreams* by Sigmund Freud, pp. 613–621, translated by James Strachey, published by Basic Books c/o Perseus Books Group and the Hogarth Press c/o The Random House Group Ltd. Translation copyright © 1955 by James Strachey. Reprinted by permission of the publishers. Electronic rights administered in the USA by Basic Books.

26-2 Cassatt, Mary Stevenson (1844–1926) / Private Collection / Photo © Christie's Images / The Bridgeman Art Library.

26-4 Universal History Archive/ UIG / The Bridgeman Art Library.

26-7 Courtesy of CCI I The Art Archive at Art Resource, N.Y.

Chapter 28

28-1 George C. Marshall, "An American Plan to Rebuild a Shattered Europe." "The Address of Secretary Marshall at Harvard," *The New York Times*, Friday June 6, 1947, is reprinted courtesy of the George C. Marshall Research Library, Lexington, VA: http://www.marshallfoundation.org.

28-2 Alexander Solzhenitsyn, *One Day in the Life of Ivan Denisovich*: "The Stalinist Gulag." From *One Day in the Life of Ivan Denisovich*, by Alexander Solzhenitsyn, pp. 17–25, translated by Ralph Parker, copyright © 1963 by E. P. Dutton and Victor Gollancz, Ltd. Copyright renewed by © 1991 by Penguin USA and Victor Gollancz, Ltd. Used by permission of Dutton, a division of Penguin Group (USA) Inc., and Victor Gollancz, an imprint of The Orion Publishing Group, London.

28-4 Frantz Fanon, *The Wretched of the Earth*. From "Conclusion" in *The Wretched of the Earth* by Frantz Fanon, translated by Constance Farrington (Grove Press, 1963) pp. 311–316, copyright © 1963 by *Présence Africaine*. Used by permission of Grove/Atlantic, Inc.

11

The Later Middle Ages
1300–1450

Calamity followed calamity over the course of the fourteenth century. The High Middle Ages had been a period of slow but sustained population growth. That trend began to reverse itself at the beginning of the fourteenth century, when Europe's climate took a turn for the worse. As Europe grew colder and wetter, crop yields fell and famine followed. Thus, Europe's population was already weakened by malnutrition when plague struck in 1347, introduced into Europe through the same trade routes that had fueled the prosperity of the previous century. In the wake of the plague, peasant uprisings were frequent, as were uprisings of the urban poor. Between 1337 and 1453, the Hundred Years' War—in actuality a series of wars and civil wars—wreaked havoc on France. Finally, the papacy experienced a period of sharp decline in prestige and power, as the political rivalries of secular rulers led to schism within the Church. The documents included in this chapter examine these catastrophes and their consequences. As you read the documents, think about the impact of war, disease, and religious strife on medieval social, religious, and political institutions. What changes in European society were made possible by the destruction of the fourteenth century?

11-1 | The Psychological and Emotional Impact of the Plague
GIOVANNI BOCCACCIO, *The Decameron: The Plague Hits Florence* (ca. 1350)

The first wave of the Black Death began in the late 1340s. The disease spread rapidly, and contemporaries understood very little about it, although they did associate it with rats. The only effective countermeasures were quarantine and isolation. The infection, which spread

From *The Decameron, or Ten Days' Entertainment of Boccaccio* (Chicago: Stewart & Kidd Company, 1920), pp. xix–xxii.

along trade routes from Central Asia, killed some 75 million people. Even after the first incidence receded, plague returned to Europe in many subsequent outbreaks until the 1700s, with varying mortality rates. In this document, excerpted from his famous collection of novellas, the Italian writer Giovanni Boccaccio (JEE-oh-VAH-nee buh-CAH-chee-oh) details the chaos unleashed in Florence as a result of the plague.

In the year then of our Lord 1348, there happened at Florence, the finest city in all Italy, a most terrible plague; which, whether owing to the influence of the planets, or that it was sent from God as a just punishment for our sins, had broken out some years before in the Levant[1]; and after passing from place to place, and making incredible havoc all the way, had now reached the west; where, in spite of all the means that art and human foresight could suggest, such as keeping the city clear from filth, and excluding all suspected persons, notwithstanding frequent consultations what else was to be done; nor omitting prayers to God in frequent processions: in the spring of the forgoing year, it began to show itself in a sad and wonderful[2] manner; and, different from what it had been in the east, where bleeding from the nose is the fatal prognostic, here there appeared certain tumors in the groin, or under the armpits, some as big as a small apple, others as an egg; and afterwards purple spots in most parts of the body; in some cases large and but few in number, in others smaller and more numerous, both sorts the usual messengers of death. . . .

These accidents, and others of the like sort, occasioned various fears and devices amongst those people who survived, all tending to the same uncharitable and cruel end; which was to avoid the sick, and everything that had been near them, expecting by that means to save themselves. And some holding it best to live temperately, and to avoid excesses of all kinds, made parties, and shut themselves up from the rest of the world; eating and drinking moderately of the best, and diverting themselves with music, and such other entertainments as they might have within doors; never listening to anything from without, to make them uneasy. Others maintained free living to be a better preservative, and would balk no passion or appetite they wished to gratify, drinking and revelling incessantly from tavern to tavern, or in private houses; which were frequently found deserted by the owners, and therefore common to every one, yet avoiding, with all this irregularity, to come near the infected. And such at that time was the public distress, that the laws, human and divine, were not regarded; for the officers, to put them in force, being either dead, sick, or in want of persons to assist them, every one did just as he pleased. A third sort of people chose a method between these two: not confining themselves to rules of diet like the former, and yet avoiding the intemperance of the latter; but eating and drinking what their appetites required, they walked everywhere with odors and nosegays[3] to smell

---

[1]**the Levant**: The eastern Mediterranean.
[2]**wonderful**: Astonishing.
[3]**odors and nosegays**: Perfumes and small bunches of flowers.

to; as holding it best to corroborate the brain: for they supposed the whole atmosphere to be tainted with the stink of dead bodies, arising partly from the distemper itself, and partly from the fermenting of the medicines within them. Others of a more cruel disposition, as perhaps the more safe to themselves, declared that the only remedy was to avoid it: persuaded, therefore, of this, and taking care for themselves only, men and women in great numbers left the city, their houses, relations, and effects, and fled into the country; as if the wrath of God had been restrained to visit those only within the walls of the city. . . . I pass over the little regard that citizens and relations showed to each other; for their terror was such that a brother even fled from his brother, a wife from her husband, and, what is more uncommon, a parent from its own child.

READING QUESTIONS

1. According to this account, how did civil order break down during the plague?

2. How does the narrator try to explain why the plague happened?

3. What are some of the things people thought might save them from the plague?

11-2 | A Town Chronicler Describes the Black Death
ANGELO DI TURA, *Sienese Chronicle* (1348–1351)

Densely populated and closely connected to the Mediterranean trade routes that brought the plague to Europe, Italian cities were among the hardest hit communities. Angelo di Tura was the town chronicler for the Tuscan town of Siena when the Black Death struck in the spring of 1348. According to di Tura, more people died in Siena in the first few months following the arrival of plague than had died in the previous twenty years. As you read his account of the devastation, reflect on the impact of the plague on the town's ability to function. With more than half the population wiped out, how did the Sienese community keep from falling into anarchy?

The mortality, which was a thing horrible and cruel, began in Siena in the month of May [1348]. I do not know from where came this cruelty or these pitiless ways, which were painful to see and stupefied everyone. There are not words to describe how horrible these events have been and, in fact, whoever can say that they have not lived in utterly horrid conditions can truly consider themselves lucky. The infected die almost immediately. They swell beneath the armpits and in the groin, and fall over while talking. Fathers abandon their sons, wives their husbands, and one brother the other. In the end, everyone escapes and abandons anyone who might be infected. Moreover, it appears that this plague can be

From John Aberth, *The Black Death: The Great Mortality of 1348–1350: A Brief History with Documents* (Boston: Bedford/St. Martin's, 2005), pp. 81–82.

communicated through bad breath and even by just seeing one of the infected. In these ways, they die and no one can be found who would want to bury them, not even for money or in the name of friendship. Those who get infected in their own house, they remove them the best way they can and they bury them without the supervision of a priest. No one controls anything and they do not even ring the church bells anymore. Throughout Siena, giant pits are being excavated for the multitudes of the dead and the hundreds that die every night. The bodies are thrown into these mass graves and are covered bit by bit. When those ditches are full, new ditches are dug. So many have died that new pits have to be made every day.

And I, Agnolo di Tura, called the Fat, have buried five of my sons with my own hands. Yet still I do not steal from those who were poorly buried like the dogs that eat them and litter them about the city. There is no one who weeps for any of the dead, for instead everyone awaits their own impending death. So many have died that everyone believes it is the end of the world. Medicine and other cures do not work. In fact, the more medicine people are given the quicker they die. The leaders of the city have elected three citizens that have been given 1,000 florins for the expense of taking care of the homeless and for burying them. These conditions have been so horrible that I do not reflect as often as I used to about the situation. I have thought so much about these events that I cannot tell the stories any longer. This is how the people lived until September [1348], and it would be too much for me to write the whole story. One would find that in this period of time more people died than in twenty years or more. In Siena alone, 36,000 people have died. If you count the elderly and others, the number could be 52,000 in total. In all of the boroughs, the number could be as high as 30,000 more. So it can be seen that in total the death toll may be as high as 80,000. There are only about 10,000 people left in the city and those that live on are hopeless and in utter despair. They leave their homes and other things. Gold, silver, and copper lay scattered about. In the countryside, even more died, so many that farms and agricultural lands are left without people to work them. I cannot write about the cruelties that existed in the countryside: that wolves and other wild beasts eat the improperly buried and other horrors that are too difficult for anyone who would read this account. . . .

The city of Siena appeared uninhabited because almost no one was found there. The pestilence remained and everyone who survived celebrated his or her fate. Of the monks, priests, nuns, women, and others from the secular community, they didn't worry about their expenses or games. Everyone appeared to be rich because they had survived and regained value in life. Now, no one knows how to put their life back in order.

READING QUESTIONS

1. How would you characterize di Tura's reaction to the plague?

2. What explanation, if any, did di Tura offer for the terrible events he described?

3. What signs of social breakdown did he note? What do they suggest about the full extent of the impact of the plague on late medieval life?

11-3 | Social and Economic Unrest in England

The Anonimalle Chronicle: The English Peasants' Revolt (1381)

Agricultural labor was traditionally carried out by serfs, who were bound by tradition to fulfill their obligations to their lords. The high mortality rate of the plague, however, resulted in a labor shortage across Europe. Some peasants tried to act on this advantage and force the lords to end their serfdom. When their demands were not satisfied, peasants often rose up against their lords. In England in 1381, an unpopular tax on all adult males prompted thousands of peasants to revolt. As you read this account of the revolt, pay particular attention to the targets of the peasants' anger. What distinction did the rebels make between the nobility and the king?

And on that Thursday, the said feast of Corpus Christi, the King, being in the Tower [of London] very sad and sorry, mounted up into a little turret towards St. Catherine's, where were lying a great number of the commons, and had proclamation made to them that they all should go peaceably to their homes, and he would pardon them all manner of their trespasses. But all cried with one voice that they would not go before they had captured the traitors who lay in the Tower, nor until they had got charters to free them from all manner of serfdom, and had got certain other points which they wished to demand. And the King benevolently granted all, and made a clerk write a bill in their presence in these terms: "Richard, King of England and France, gives great thanks to his good commons, for that they have so great a desire to see and to keep their king, and grants them pardon for all manner of trespasses and misprisions and felonies done up to this hour, and wills and commands that every one should now return to his own home, and wills and commands that each should put his grievances in writing, and have them sent to him; and he will provide, with the aid of his loyal lords and his good council, such remedy as shall be profitable both to him and to them, and to all the kingdom." On this document he sealed his signet in presence of them all, and sent out the said bill by the hands of two of his knights to the folks before St. Catherine's. And he caused it to be read to them, and the knight who read it stood up on an old chair before the others so that all could hear. All this time the King was in the Tower in great distress of mind. And when the commons had heard the Bill, they said that this was nothing but trifles and mockery. Therefore they returned to London and had it cried around the City that all lawyers, and all the clerks of the Chancery and the

From Charles Oman, *The Great Revolt of 1381* (Oxford, U.K.: Clarendon Press, 1906), pp. 196–203.

Exchequer and every man who could write a brief or a letter should be beheaded, whenever they could be found. At this time they burnt several more houses in the City, and the King himself ascended to a high garret of the Tower and watched the fires. Then he came down again, and sent for the lords to have their counsel, but they knew not how they should counsel him, and all were wondrous abashed. . . .

And by seven o'clock the King [went to meet the peasants]. And when he was come the commons all knelt down to him, saying "Welcome our Lord King Richard, if it pleases you, and we will not have any other king but you." And Wat Tighler [Wat Tyler], their leader and chief, prayed in the name of the commons that he would suffer them to take and deal with all the traitors against him and the law, and the King granted that they should have at their disposition all who were traitors, and could be proved to be traitors by process of law. The said Walter and the commons were carrying two banners, and many pennons and pennoncels,[1] while they made their petition to the King. And they required that for the future no man should be in serfdom, nor make any manner of homage or suit to any lord, but should give a rent of 4d. an acre for his land. They asked also that no one should serve any man except by his own good will, and on terms of regular covenant.

And at this time the King made the commons draw themselves out in two lines, and proclaimed to them that he would confirm and grant it that they should be free, and generally should have their will, and that they might go through all the realm of England and catch all traitors and bring them to him in safety, and then he would deal with them as the law demanded.

[Meanwhile, fighting between the nobles and peasants continued, and many lords lost their heads to the commoners.]

And when he was summoned, . . . Wat Tighler of Maidstone, he came to the King with great confidence, mounted on a little horse, that the commons might see him. And he dismounted, holding in his hand a dagger which he had taken from another man, and when he had dismounted he half bent his knee, and then took the King by the hand, and shook his arm forcibly and roughly, saying to him, "Brother, be of good comfort and joyful, for you shall have, in the fortnight that is to come, praise from the commons even more than you have yet had, and we shall be good companions." And the King said to Walter, "Why will you not go back to your own country?" But the other answered, with a great oath, that neither he nor his fellows would depart until they had got their charter such as they wished to have it, and had certain points rehearsed, and added to their charter which they wished to demand. And he said in a threatening fashion that the lords of the realm would rue it bitterly if these points were not settled to their pleasure. Then the King asked him what were the points which he

---

[1]**pennons and pennoncels:** Small banners attached to lances.

wished to have revised, and he should have them freely, without contradiction, written out and sealed. Thereupon the said Walter rehearsed the points which were to be demanded; and he asked that . . . there should be equality among all people save only the King, and that the goods of Holy Church should not remain in the hands of the religious, nor of parsons and vicars, and other churchmen; but that clergy already in possession should have a sufficient sustenance from the endowments, and the rest of the goods should be divided among the people of the parish.

[The King agreed to these terms, and after he left, the Mayor of London captured Wat Tighler and killed him.]

READING QUESTIONS

1. Who did the peasants blame for their troubles? Why?

2. What demands did the peasants make? What do these demands reveal about their social and political beliefs?

3. Is it plausible that the Mayor of London would have Wat Tighler killed without the king's consent? What does this tell you about the king's true attitude toward the rebellion?

11-4 | A Simple Social World?

PETRARCA-MEISTER, *The Social Order* (ca. 1515)

At first glance, this German woodcut seems to be a straightforward depiction of the traditional medieval social and political hierarchy, with peasants at the bottom, merchants and craftsmen at the next level, secular and clerical elites one level higher, and the pope and emperor at the top. That interpretation is challenged, however, by the peasants perched at the top of tree, one with his foot on the pope's shoulder and the other enjoying a nap. Moreover, instead of presenting the various social groups as part of a collective, with each group playing its own distinct and necessary role, the branches create clear separations between the groups, giving the impression that each group occupies a world of its own. As you examine the woodcut, come up with your own interpretation. What connections can you make between the woodcut and the social and economic developments of the fourteenth century?

Kupferstichkabinett, Staatliche, Museen, Berlin, Germany/Jorg P. Anders/Art Resource, N.Y.

READING QUESTIONS

1. How would you characterize the peasants at the bottom of the tree? What about the peasants at the top?

2. How would you describe the society depicted in the woodcut? What are its defining attributes?

3. Do you see this as a conservative or a subversive image? Why?

SOURCES IN CONVERSATION

Women and Power

Power politics in the Late Middle Ages was a man's game. The medieval vision of government and society was profoundly patriarchal, and assumptions of male superiority shaped almost every aspect of medieval life. There were, however, women who were exceptions to the rule. For the most part, such women enjoyed the advantages of wealth and status. Less common were women, such as Catherine of Siena (1347–1380) and Joan of Arc (ca. 1412–1431), who gained power through their reputation for holiness. Catherine, a nun of humble background who claimed to have experienced mystical visions, was an important participant in the religious and political debates of her day. Joan of Arc, a young woman from a small farming community, convinced many of France's leaders that God had chosen her to guide the French to victory in the Hundred Years' War. As you read the documents relating to these two women, ask yourself what made their rise to prominence possible. What precedents could they draw on to help legitimize their participation in arenas usually reserved for men? What special dangers did they face as women who claimed divine authority for their actions?

11-5 | CATHERINE OF SIENA, *Letter to Gregory XI* (1372)

In the early 1300s, the papacy moved its capital to Avignon, inside French territory. Because the pope was the bishop of Rome, it seemed wrong to move the head of the church away from his rightful home—and to a place where he could be easily influenced by the French king. Many people blamed the Avignon papacy for the plague and warfare across Europe. Still more linked the Avignon papacy to a general decline in the reputation and prestige of the

From Vida D. Scudder, trans. and ed., *Catherine of Siena as Seen in Her Lives and Letters* (London: J. M. Dent, 1906), pp. 131–132.

Church. In the 1370s, Catherine joined the effort to persuade Pope Gregory XI to return to Rome. As you read her letter to the pope, consider how her gender and spiritual reputation might have influenced the pope's reaction to her message.

Alas, what confusion is this, to see those who ought to be a mirror of voluntary poverty, meek as lambs, distributing the possessions of Holy Church to the poor: and they appear in such luxury and state and pomp and worldly vanity, more than if they had turned them to the world a thousand times! Nay, many seculars put them to shame who live a good and holy life. . . . For ever since [the Church] has aimed more at temporal than at spiritual, things have gone from bad to worse. See therefore that God, in judgment, has allowed much persecution and tribulation to befall her. But comfort you, father, and fear not for anything that could happen, which God does to make her state perfect once more, in order that lambs may feed in that garden, and not wolves who devour the honor that should belong to God, which they steal and give to themselves. Comfort you in Christ sweet Jesus; for I hope that His aid will be near you, plenitude[1] of divine grace, aid and support divine in the way that I said before. Out of war you will attain greatest peace; out of persecution, greatest unity; not by human power, but by holy virtue, you will discomfit those visible demons, wicked men, and those invisible demons who never sleep around us.

But reflect, sweet father, that you could not do this easily unless you accomplished the other two things which precede the completion of the other: that is, your return to Rome and uplifting of the standard of the most holy Cross. Let not your holy desire fail on account of any scandal or rebellion of cities which you might see or hear; nay, let the flame of holy desire be more kindled to wish to do swiftly. Do not delay, then, your coming.

READING QUESTIONS

1. What did Catherine want the pope to do, and why did she want him to do it?

2. According to Catherine, what happened to the Church when the pope left Rome for Avignon?

3. What authority did Catherine have to make demands of the pope? How would you explain her prominence in the effort to persuade the pope to return to Rome?

---

[1]**plenitude**: Full supply.

11-6 | *The Debate Over Joan of Arc's Clothes* (1429)

The public debate over Joan of Arc's status began almost as soon as she presented herself to the French court. Even after Joan had been accepted by the Dauphin and joined the French in battle, supporters and opponents clashed over her claims to divine inspiration. In the spring of 1429, one of Joan's supporters circulated a treatise entitled *De mirabili victoria*. Later that same year, an anonymous member of the University of Paris countered with *De bono et malo spiritu*. One important point of contention between the two authors was Joan's decision to wear men's clothing. As you read the excerpts from these treatises, think about how female models and stereotypes shaped each author's argument.

De mirabili victoria

Here follow three truths in justification of the wearing of male clothing by the Pucelle,[1] chosen while following her sheep.

I. The old law [of the Old Testament], prohibiting the woman from using the clothing of a man and the man from the clothing of a woman [Deuteronomy 22: 5], is purely judicial and does not carry any obligation under the new law [of the New Testament]. [This is] because it is a constant and necessary truth for salvation that the judicial precepts of the ancient law [Old Testament] are quashed and, as such, do not bind the new one, unless they have been instituted again and confirmed by superiors.

II. This law [of the Old Testament] included a moral dimension that must remain in all law. It can be expressed as a prohibition on indecent clothing both for the man and for the woman, [as this is] contrary to the requirement of virtue. This should affect all circumstances bound by law, so that the wise person will judge when, where, to whom and how it is appropriate, and in this way the rest. This [law of the Old Testament] on these things is not confined to that one situation.

III. This law [of the Old Testament], whether judicial or moral, does not condemn the wearing of the clothing of a man and a warrior by our Pucelle, manly and a warrior, whom God in heaven has chosen through certain signs as his standard-bearer for those fighting the enemies of justice and to raise up his friends, so that he might overthrow by the hand of a woman, a young girl [*puellaris*] and a virgin, the powerful weapons of iniquity, with the help of the angels. By her virginity, she is loved and known, according to St. Jerome; and this frequently appears in the histories of saints, such as Cecilia,[2] visibly with a crown of roses and lilies. On the other hand, through this she is safeguarded from the [consequences of the] cutting of her hair, which the Apostle prohibits from being seen on a woman.

From Craig Taylor, trans. and ed., *Joan of Arc: La Pucelle* (Manchester, U.K.: Manchester University Press, 2006), pp. 82–83, 125–127.

[1]**the Pucelle**: The maid.
[2]**Cecilia**: Catholic saint, martyred by the Romans in the second century C.E.

Therefore may the inquitious talk be put to an end and cease. For, when divine virtue operates, it establishes the means according to its aim; hence, it is not safe to disparage or to find fault, out of rash bravado, with those things which are from God, according to the Apostle.

Finally many details and examples from sacred and secular history could be added; for example those of Camilla and the Amazons,[3] and moreover in cases either of necessity or evident utility, or where approved by custom, or by the authority and dispensation of superiors. But these are sufficient for brevity and for the truth. The party having just cause should be on close guard unless, through disbelief and ingratitude, or some injustices, they might render the divine help useless, that has begun so patiently and miraculously; just as [happened] for Moses and the sons of Israel, after having received such divine promises, as we read contained [in the scriptures]. For even if God does not change His advice, He does change his opinion according to what people deserve.

De bono et malo spiritu

Regarding the preceding, I mean to deduce from canon law a small number of issues, in praise of all-mighty God, and in exaltation of the holy catholic faith.

And first, we have a duty to adhere firmly to the catholic faith, following the chapter *Firmiter* of the title *De Summa Trinitate*, without giving in any manner our approval to superstitious innovations, seeing that they engender discords, as one reads in the chapter *Cum consuetudinis* of the title *De consuetudine*.

Item, to give his support so easily to a young girl that was not known, without the support of a miracle or on the testimony of the holy scriptures, is to undermine this truth and this unchanging force of the catholic faith: wise men and canonists would not have any doubt about this. The proof is in the chapter *Cum ex injuncto* of the title *De hæreticis*.

Item, if those who approve of the matter of this Pucelle say that she has been sent by God in an invisible, and in some sense inspired way, and that such an invisible mission is much more worthy than a visible mission, just as a divine mission is more worthy than a human mission, it is reasonable to reply to them that as this entirely inner mission escapes observation, it is not enough that someone claims purely and simply to be sent from God—this is the claim of all heretics—but it is necessary that he proves this invisible mission to us through a miraculous work or by a precise testimony drawn from the holy scripture. All this is demonstrated in the chapter cited above, *Cum ex injuncto*.

Item, as this Pucelle has not proved in any of these ways that she has been sent from God, there is no room to believe in her on her word, but there is room to proceed against her as if suspected of heresy.

Added to this, if she has really been sent from God, she would not take clothing prohibited by God and forbidden for women by cannon law under penalty of anathema, according to the chapter *Si qua mulier*. . . .

---

[3]**Camilla and the Amazons**: Examples of female warriors from Classical mythology.

Moreover, in the case where those who let themselves be deceived by this Pucelle attempt to excuse and to justify her clothing in consideration of the matter for which she was supposedly sent, such niceties are useless; these are rather those excuses of which the Psalmist speaks, that one searches for to excuse sins (Psalm 140: 4), and they accuse more than they excuse, as it says in chapter *Quanto* of the title *De consuetudine*. In this case, one might do lots of evil things under the appearance of good. And yet it is necessary to refrain not only from evil, but from all appearance of evil, as one reads in the chapter *Cum ab omni* of the title *De vita et honestate clericorum*.

Item, if a women [*sic*] could put on male clothing as she liked with impunity, women would have unrestrained opportunities to fornicate and to practice manly acts which are legally forbidden for them according to doctrine, etc., [as this is] against the canonical teaching contained in the chapter *Nova quædam* of the title *De pœnitentiis et remissionibus*.

Item, in general, all masculine duties are forbidden to women, for example, to preach, to teach, to bear arms, to absolve, to excommunicate, etc., as one sees in that chapter *Nova quædam* and in the Digest, in the [second] law of the title *De regulis juris*.

READING QUESTIONS

1. On what grounds did the author of *De mirabili victoria* support Joan's insistence on wearing men's clothing?

2. Why did the author of *De bono et malo spiritu* believe that Joan's clothes supported his position that she was, in all likelihood, a heretic?

3. What do these treatises tell you about late medieval ideas about women's nature and their proper role in society?

▪ COMPARATIVE AND DISCUSSION QUESTIONS ▪

1. Consider the account of the English Peasants' Revolt and *The Social Order*. What light do they shed on social change and continuity in late medieval Europe?

2. What do the writings of Boccaccio and di Tura reveal about the range of reactions to the devastation produced by the Black Death?

3. What do Catherine and Joan have in common? What kind of power did they have, and how did they use it?

12

European Society in the Age of the Renaissance

1350–1550

The Renaissance began in the Italian city-states of the fourteenth century and spread throughout Europe. Renaissance scholars, artists, and philosophers articulated a new vision of human possibility inspired by the Classical past. Standing on the shoulders of the giants of Greco-Roman culture, they believed that their own society could match, or even exceed, the achievements of their ancestors. The commercial and political dynamism of the Italian city-states played a key role in fostering the Renaissance. Italian cities were primary beneficiaries of the commercial revival of the High Middle Ages, and competition, both within cities and between cities, spurred individuals and communities to pour their resources into cultural activity. Competition between city-states had a darker side, however, and often escalated into conflict; endemic warfare left Italy weak and divided. As you explore the sources, consider what the Renaissance meant to these authors and artists. How would they describe the movement in which they were participants? What hopes and fears did they have for their own society?

12-1 | An Italian Admirer of the Classical Past
PETRARCH, *Letter to Livy* (1350)

Around 1350, Italian scholar and poet Francesco Petrarca, or Petrarch (1304–1374), proposed a new kind of education that centered on the study and emulation of the works of ancient Roman authors. In his view, the implementation of this program would produce a generation

From Marco Emilio Cosenza, trans., *Petrarch's Letters to Classical Authors* (Chicago: University of Chicago Press, 1910), pp. 100–103.

of young men capable of achievements unmatched in Europe for a thousand years. Petrarch and his followers came to be known as humanists, and their intellectual agenda had a profound influence on the art and ideas of their age. We get a sense of the intensity of Petrarch's regard for Classical culture in a letter addressed to the ancient Roman historian Livy. As you read it, think about what it tells you about the aspirations of Petrarch and his fellow humanists.

I should wish (if it were permitted from on high) either that I had been born in thine age or thou in ours; in the latter case our age itself, and in the former I personally should have been the better for it. I should surely have been one of those pilgrims who visited thee. For the sake of seeing thee I should have gone not merely to Rome, but indeed, from either Gaul or Spain I should have found my way to thee as far as India. . . . We know that thou didst write one hundred and forty-two books on Roman affairs. With what fervor, with what unflagging zeal must thou have labored; and of that entire number there are now extant scarcely thirty. . . . It is over these small remains that I toil whenever I wish to forget these regions, these times, and these customs. Often I am filled with bitter indignation against the morals of today, when men value nothing except gold and silver, and desire nothing except sensual, physical pleasures. If these are to be considered the goal of mankind, then not only the dumb beasts of the field, but even insensible and inert matter has a richer, a higher goal than that proposed to itself by thinking man. But of this elsewhere.

It is now fitter that I should render thee thanks, for many reasons indeed, but for this in especial: that thou didst so frequently cause me to forget the present evils, and transfer me to happier times. . . .

Pray greet in my behalf thy predecessors Polybius and Quintus Claudius and Valerius Antias, and all those whose glory thine own greater light has dimmed; and of the later historians, give greeting to Pliny the Younger, of Verona, a neighbor of thine, and also to thy former rival Crispus Sallustius. . . . Farewell forever, thou matchless historian!

Written in the land of the living, in that part of Italy and in that city in which I am now living and where thou were once born and buried, . . . and in view of thy very tombstone; on the twenty-second of February, in the thirteen hundred and fiftieth year from the birth of Him whom thou wouldst have seen, or of whose birth thou couldst have heard, hadst thou lived a little longer.

READING QUESTIONS

1. Why did Petrarch admire Livy?
2. What implicit contrast did Petrarch draw between Livy's time and his own?
3. In what ways does Petrarch's wish to bring Livy into his world encapsulate the humanist program?

12-2 | Power Politics During the Italian Renaissance
NICCOLÒ MACHIAVELLI, *The Prince* (1513)

Niccolò Machiavelli (Nee-koh-LOH mah-key-ah-VEL-ee) (1469–1527) was a political philosopher and diplomat who had represented the Italian republic of Florence on numerous diplomatic missions. In 1512, when the powerful Medici family regained control of Florence, the anti-Medici Machiavelli was arrested and tortured. In 1513, he wrote *The Prince*, a guide to gaining and consolidating political power, and dedicated it to Lorenzo de Medici, perhaps as a way to curry favor with the new rulers. The cynicism of *The Prince* stands in stark contrast to the idealism exhibited in the excerpt from Petrarch included in this chapter. Here, Machiavelli argued that a willingness to engage in deception and violence were critical to a ruler's success.

Every one understands how praiseworthy it is in a prince to keep faith, and to live uprightly and not craftily. Nevertheless we see, from what has taken place in our own days, that princes who have set little store by their word, but have known how to overreach men by their cunning, have accomplished great things, and in the end got the better of those who trusted to honest dealing.

Be it known, then, that there are two ways of contending,—one in accordance with the laws, the other by force; the first of which is proper to men, the second to beasts. But since the first method is often ineffectual, it becomes necessary to resort to the second. A prince should, therefore, understand how to use well both the man and the beast. . . . But inasmuch as a prince should know how to use the beast's nature wisely, he ought of beasts to choose both the lion and the fox; for the lion cannot guard himself from the toils, nor the fox from wolves. He must therefore be a fox to discern toils, and a lion to drive off wolves.

To rely wholly on the lion is unwise; and for this reason a prudent prince neither can nor ought to keep his word when to keep it is hurtful to him and the causes which led him to pledge it are removed. If all men were good, this would not be good advice, but since they are dishonest and do not keep faith with you, you in return need not keep faith with them; and no prince was ever at a loss for plausible reasons to cloak a breach of faith. Of this numberless recent instances could be given, and it might be shown how many solemn treaties and engagements have been rendered inoperative and idle through want of faith among princes, and that he who has best known how to play the fox has had the best success.

It is necessary, indeed, to put a good color on this nature, and to be skilled in simulating and dissembling. But men are so simple, and governed so absolutely by their present needs, that he who wishes to deceive will never fail in finding willing dupes. One recent example I will not omit. Pope Alexander VI had no care or thought but how to deceive, and always found material to work on. No

From Niccolò Machiavelli, *The Prince*, trans. N. H. Thomson, in James Harvey Robinson, ed., *Readings in European History*, 2 vols. (Boston: Ginn, 1906), 2:10–13.

man ever had a more effective manner of asseverating, or made promises with more solemn protestations, or observed them less. And yet, because he understood this side of human nature, his frauds always succeeded. . . .

In his efforts to aggrandize his son the duke [Cesare Borgia], Alexander VI had to face many difficulties, both immediate and remote. In the first place, he saw no way to make him ruler of any state which did not belong to the Church. Yet, if he sought to take for him a state of the Church, he knew that the duke of Milan and the Venetians would withhold their consent, Faenza and Rimini [towns in the province of Romagna] being already under the protection of the latter. Further, he saw that the forces of Italy, and those more especially of which he might have availed himself, were in the hands of men who had reason to fear his aggrandizement,—that is, of the Orsini, the Colonnesi [Roman noble families] and their followers. These, therefore, he could not trust. . . .

And since this part of his [Cesare Borgia's] conduct merits both attention and imitation, I shall not pass it over in silence. After the duke had taken Romagna, finding that it had been ruled by feeble lords, who thought more of plundering than of governing their subjects,—which gave them more cause for division than for union, so that the country was overrun with robbery, tumult, and every kind of outrage,—he judged it necessary, with a view to rendering it peaceful, and obedient to his authority, to provide it with a good government. Accordingly he set over it Messer Remiro d'Orco, a stern and prompt ruler, who, being entrusted with the fullest powers, in a very short time, and with much credit to himself, restored it to tranquility and order. But afterwards the duke, apprehending that such unlimited authority might become odious, decided that it was no longer needed, and established [at] the center of the province a civil tribunal, with an excellent president, in which every town was represented by its advocate. And knowing that past severities had generated ill feeling against himself, in order to purge the minds of the people and gain their good will, he sought to show them that any cruelty which had been done had not originated with him, but in the harsh disposition of this minister. Availing himself of the pretext which this afforded, he one morning caused Remiro to be beheaded, and exposed in the market place of Cesena with a block and bloody ax by his side. The barbarity of this spectacle at once astounded and satisfied the populace.

READING QUESTIONS

1. Why must a prince be both a lion and a fox? What qualities do these animals represent?

2. What light does *The Prince* shed on the realities of Italian politics?

3. How might a Renaissance critic of Machiavelli have responded to his work? What objections might such a person have raised to *The Prince*? How might Machiavelli have countered his critics' arguments?

12-3 | A Description of the Ideal Courtier

BALDASSARE CASTIGLIONE, *The Book of the Courtier* (1528)

Baldassare Castiglione (ball-duh-SAH-ray kahs-teel-YOH-nay) (1478–1529) was an Italian diplomat who spent many years traveling through the courts of Europe. Based on his experiences, he wrote *The Book of the Courtier* as a manual on the proper education, manners, dress, and skills of a companion to and defender of royalty. The book was written in the form of a conversation among some of the leading nobility in Italy and was a bestseller in its time. As you read this excerpt, think about the models upon which Castiglione might have drawn. To what extent does his courtier resemble the ideal medieval knight? To what extent does he seem to be a product of humanist education and training?

I wish then, that this Courtier of ours should be nobly born. I am of the opinion that the principal and true profession of the courtier ought to be that of arms;[1] which I would have him follow actively above all else, and be known among others as bold and strong, and loyal to whomsoever he serves. . . .

Therefore let the man we are seeking be very bold, stern, and always among the first, where the enemy are to be seen; and in every other place, gentle, modest, reserved, above all things avoiding ostentation and that impudent self-praise by which men ever excite hatred and disgust in all who hear him. . . .

And so I would have him well built and shapely of limb, and would have him show strength and lightness and suppleness, and know all bodily exercises that befit a man of war: whereof I think the first should be to handle every sort of weapon well on foot and on horse. . . .

There are also many other exercises, which although not immediately dependent upon arms, yet are closely connected therewith, and greatly foster manly sturdiness; and one of the chief among these seems to me to be the chase,[2] because it bears a certain likeness to war; and truly it is an amusement for great lords and befitting a man at court, and furthermore it is seen to have been much cultivated among the ancients. It is fitting also to know how to swim, to leap, to run, to throw stones, for besides the use that may be made of this in war, a man often has occasion to show what he can do in such matters; whence good esteem is to be won, especially with the multitude, who must be taken into account withal. Another admirable exercise, and one fitting a man at court, is the game of tennis, in which are well shown the disposition of the body. . . .

I think that the conversation, which the Courtier ought most to try in every way to make acceptable, is that which he holds with his prince; and although this word "conversation" implies a certain equality that seems impossible between a

From Baldassare Castiglione, *The Book of the Courtier*, trans. Leonard Opdycke (New York: Charles Scribner's Sons, 1903), pp. 22, 26, 29, 31, 93–94.

[1]**arms**: Weaponry.
[2]**chase**: Hunting.

lord and his inferior, yet we will call it so for the moment. Therefore, besides daily showing everyone that he possesses the worth we have already described, I would have the Courtier strive, with all the thoughts and forces of his mind, to love and almost adore the prince whom he serves, above every other thing, and mold his ways to his prince's liking. . . .

Moreover it is possible without flattery to obey and further the wishes of him we serve, for I am speaking of those wishes that are reasonable and right, or of those that in themselves are neither good not evil, such as would be a liking for a play or devotion to one kind of exercise above another. And I would have the Courtier bend himself to this even if he be by nature alien to it, so that on seeing him his lord shall always feel that he will have something agreeable to say. . . . He will not be an idle or untruthful tattler, nor a boaster nor pointless flatterer, but modest and reserved, always and especially in public showing the reverence and respect which befit the servant towards the master.

READING QUESTIONS

1. What are the characteristics of a good courtier? How would you explain the stress Castiglione places on military aptitude and training?

2. What role does the courtier play in royal government? How does he facilitate his master's success?

3. Would you describe Castiglione's courtier as a medieval or a Renaissance figure? Why?

12-4 | A Humanist Prescription for the Education of Princes

DESIDERIUS ERASMUS, *The Education of a Christian Prince* (1516)

Desiderius Erasmus (1462–1536) of Rotterdam was the foremost northern humanist. A priest, theologian, and teacher, Erasmus placed humanist scholarship in the service of religious reform. His work combines a humanist's respect for reason and the value of the individual with an equally profound commitment to his faith. In this excerpt from *The Education of a Christian Prince*, Erasmus begins by discussing a classical metaphor for the relationship of the ruler to the state, and then uses this as a starting point for exploring the relationship between a Christian prince, his subjects, and God. As you read it, pay particular attention to the way in which he mixes classical and Christian concepts.

[R]emember this idea also, which was known and handed down by the pagan philosophers, that the rule of a prince over his people is no different from that of the mind over the body. The mind dominates the body because it knows more than

From Desiderius Erasmus, *The Education of a Christian Prince*, trans. Lester K. Born (New York: Columbia University Press, 1936), pp. 175–178.

the physical body, but it does so to the great advantage of the latter rather than to itself. The blessed fortune of the physical form is this rule of the mind. What the heart is in the body of a living creature, that the prince is in the state. If the heart is sound, it imparts life to the whole body, since it is the fountain of the blood and life spirit; but if it has been infected, it brings utter collapse to every part of the body. The heart is the last part of a living body to be broken down, and the very last traces of life are thought to survive in it. Consequently the prince should keep himself clean and undefiled from all corrupting folly whenever any such disease lays hold of the people. In a man it is the finely organized part (namely, the mind) that exercises the control. Likewise, in the mind it is its finest element, reason, that asserts itself. And God, who rules the universe, is the very essence of all things. Therefore, whosoever assumes the functions of rule in a state, as in a sort of great body, should excel all others in goodness, wisdom, and watchfulness. The prince should be superior to his officers in the same degree that they are to the common people. If there is any evil in the mind it springs from infection, and contact with the body, which is subject to the passions. Any good that the body possesses is drawn from the mind as from a fountain. How unbelievable it would be and how contrary to nature, if ills should spread from the mind down into the body, and the health of the body be corrupted by the viscious habits of the mind. It would be just as absurd for wars, seditious uprisings, profligate morals, debased laws, corrupt officials, and every similar curse to a state, to spring from the prince whose wisdom should lay the storms stirred up by the folly of the common folk. But we often see states (*civitates*), well established and flourishing under the diligent activity of the people, overthrown by mismanagement of the princes. How unlike a Christian it is to take pleasure in the title "Master," which many who were not in the fold of Christ have shunned; that which in their ambition they desire to be but do not want to be called because of the odium attached to the name. Yet will a Christian prince think it just in the eyes of God for him to be the same [sort of man] and be called "The Magnificent"? The emperor Augustus, even though he had gained the imperial throne through foul intrigue, considered it an insult to be called "Master;" and when this title was used by an actor before all the people, he showed his disapproval by his facial expression and his remarks, as if it were a term of reproach applied to tyrants. And shall the Christian prince not imitate this propriety of the pagan? If you are master of all your subjects, they must of necessity be your slaves. Then have a care that you do not fulfill the ancient proverb: "You have as many enemies as you have slaves."

Nature created all men equal, and slavery was superimposed on nature, which fact the laws of even the pagans recognized. Now stop and think how out of proportion it is for a Christian to usurp full power over other Christians, whom the laws did not design to be slaves, and whom Christ redeemed from all slavery. Recall the instance when Paul called Onesimus (who was born a slave) the brother of his former master Philemon, from the time of his baptism. How incongruous it is to consider them slaves whom Christ redeemed with the same blood [as He did you]; whom He declared free along with all others; whom He fostered with the same sacraments as He did you; whom He calls to the same heritage of immortality! And over them, who have the same Master as you, the Prince, Jesus Christ, will you impose the yoke of slavery?

There is only one Master of Christian men. Why, then, do those who assume His functions, prefer to take their pattern of government from anyone except Him, who alone is in all ways to be imitated? It is proper enough to gather from others whatever virtues they have; but in Him is the perfect example of all virtue and wisdom. This seems the [essence of] foolishness to those outside the faith, but to us, if we are really faithful, He is the goodness of God and the wisdom of God. Now I do not want you to think that this means that you should be a slave, not a ruler. On the contrary, it illustrates the finest way to rule, unless, of course, you think God is only a bondsman because He governs the whole universe without recompense, because everyone and everything has felt His kindness, although they give Him nothing in return, and unless the mind seems a slave because it looks out so zealously for the welfare of the body, which it does not need, or unless you think the eye is a slave to all the other parts of the body because it sees for them all. You may well consider this: if someone should turn all these men whom you call your own into swine and asses by the art of Circe,[1] would you not say your ruling power had been reduced to a lower level? I think you would. And yet you may exercise more authority over swine and asses than over men. You may treat them as you please, divide them off as you will, and even kill them. Surely he who has reduced his free subjects to slaves has put his power on a meaner level. The loftier the ideal to which you fashion your authority, the more magnificently and splendidly will you rule. Whoever protects the liberty and standing of your subjects is the one that helps your sovereign power. God gave the angels and men free will so that He would not be ruling over bondsmen, and so that He might glorify and add further grandeur to His kingdom. And who, now, would swell with pride because he rules over men cowed down by fear, like so many cattle?

READING QUESTIONS

1. What metaphors did Erasmus use to describe the relationship of a prince to his people?

2. In Erasmus's view, what qualities should a Christian prince embody? Why?

3. Erasmus argued that the ideal Christian prince ruled over a "free" people. How might he have explained this apparent contradiction? What similarities and differences do you see between his understanding of the meaning of freedom and your own?

---

[1]**Circe**: An enchantress who turned the legendary Greek hero Odysseus and his men into pigs.

12-5 | A Female Author Argues for the Education of Women

CHRISTINE DE PIZAN, *The Book of the City of Ladies: Against Those Men Who Claim It Is Not Good for Women to Be Educated* (1404)

Christine de Pizan (ca. 1363–1434) may have been the first European woman to earn her living as a writer. The daughter of a Venetian nobleman and scholar, de Pizan grew up in the court of Charles V of France, where her father had accepted a position as royal astrologer and physician. There, de Pizan was given the opportunity to develop her intellectual interests and abilities. In 1390, when her husband died in an epidemic and left her with three children, de Pizan began her literary career. Her works were popular among the French nobility, and she even enjoyed the financial support of the French queen. Humanists were divided in their opinions on the education of women. Some thought women were simply not capable of learning. Others thought a limited form of education in good morals was sufficient. De Pizan challenged both of these ideas, and some scholars now regard her as one of the first Western feminists.

I realize that women have accomplished many good things and that even if evil women have done evil, it seems to me, nevertheless, that the benefits accrued and still accruing because of good women—particularly the wise and literary ones and those educated in the natural sciences whom I mentioned above—outweigh the evil. Therefore, I am amazed by the opinion of some men who claim that they do not want their daughters, wives, or kinswomen to be educated because their mores would be ruined as a result.

Here you can clearly see that not all opinions of men are based on reason and that these men are wrong. For it must not be presumed that mores necessarily grow worse from knowing the moral sciences, which teach the virtues, indeed, there is not the slightest doubt that moral education amends and ennobles them. How could anyone think or believe that whoever follows good teaching or doctrine is the worse for it? Such an opinion cannot be expressed or maintained. I do not mean that it would be good for a man or a woman to study the art of divination or those fields of learning which are forbidden—for the holy Church did not remove them from common use without good reason—but it should not be believed that women are the worse for knowing what is good.

Quintus Hortensius, a great rhetorician and consummately skilled orator in Rome, did not share this opinion. He had a daughter, named Hortensia, whom he greatly loved for the subtlety of her wit. He had her learn letters and study the science of rhetoric, which she mastered so thoroughly that she resembled her father Hortensius not only in wit and lively memory but also in her excellent delivery and order of speech—in fact, he surpassed her in nothing. . . . That is, during the time when Rome was governed by three men, this Hortensia began to support the cause of women and to undertake what no man dared to undertake. There was a question whether certain taxes should be levied on women and on their jewelry during a

From Christine de Pizan, *The Book of the City of Ladies*, trans. Earl Jeffrey Richards (New York: Persea Books, 1982), pp. 153–155.

needy period in Rome. This woman's eloquence was so compelling that she was listened to, no less readily than her father would have been, and she won her case.

Similarly, to speak of more recent times, without searching for examples in ancient history, Giovanni Andrea, a solemn law professor in Bologna not quite sixty years ago, was not of the opinion that it was bad for women to be educated. He had a fair and good daughter, named Novella, who was educated in the law to such an advanced degree that when he was occupied by some task and not at leisure to present his lectures to his students, he would send Novella, his daughter, in his place to lecture to the students from his chair. And to prevent her beauty from distracting the concentration of her audience, she had a little curtain drawn in front of her. In this manner she could on occasion supplement and lighten her father's occupation. . . .

Thus, not all men (and especially the wisest) share the opinion that it is bad for women to be educated. But it is very true that many foolish men have claimed this because it displeased them that women knew more than they did. [My] father, who was a great scientist and philosopher, did not believe that women were worth less by knowing science; rather, as you know, he took great pleasure from seeing your inclination to learning.

READING QUESTIONS

1. How does de Pizan defend a woman's ability to learn?
2. What examples of learned women does she provide?
3. According to de Pizan, why do some men not want to see women educated?

SOURCES IN CONVERSATION

A Female Painter Tells Stories About Women

Renaissance and Early Modern artists drew heavily for their inspiration on Christianity and the Classical past, but this does not mean that they were uninterested in the present. In the hands of a skilled artist, the past became a vehicle for commenting on what was important to the artist, his or her patron, and the community to which they both belonged. The work of the Roman painter Artemisia Gentileschi (1593–ca. 1656) is a case in point. The daughter of painter Orazio Gentileschi, Artemisia was perhaps the most successful female artist of her day. Her paintings *Susannah and the Elders* and *Judith and Holofernes*, both depicting scenes from the Old Testament, demonstrate how deeply personal such works could be. *Susannah and the Elders*, Artemisia's first work, was completed in 1610 when she was seventeen. Between that time and the completion of *Judith and Holofernes* in 1612, Artemisia was raped

by one of her father's colleagues, Agostino Tassi. As you examine these two
works, consider the connections between the content and themes of the paintings and Gentileschi's own experiences. How did she use these paintings to
comment on the power dynamics that shaped women's lives?

12-6 | ARTEMISIA GENTILESCHI, *Susannah and the Elders* (1610)

Taken from the Book of Daniel, the story of *Susannah and the Elders* centers on a false accusation of adultery. As Susannah, a young wife, bathes in her garden, two elders of her community watch secretly. Filled with lust, the two men threaten to denounce her as an adulteress if
she refuses to have sex with them. When she resists their attempts at blackmail, they follow
through on their threat. Only the intervention of Daniel, who exposes inconsistencies in their
story, saves Susannah from execution. As you examine the painting, pay particular attention
to the way Gentileschi composed it. How does the placement of the three figures help to
amplify its message?

Susannah and the Elders, ca. 1610 (oil on canvas), Gentileschi, Artemisia (1597–ca. 1651) / Private
Collection / The Bridgeman Art Library.

READING QUESTIONS

1. How would you describe Gentileschi's Susannah? How does the position of her arms and head help to convey her reaction to the unwanted advances of the elders?

2. How would you characterize the two elders? How does their placement in the painting reflect their power? What might explain Gentileschi's decision to depict them whispering to one another at the very moment they accost Susannah?

12-7 | ARTEMISIA GENTILESCHI, *Judith and Holofernes* (1610)

Like *Susannah and the Elders*, *Judith and Holofernes* depicts a scene from the Old Testament, this time from the Book of Judith. In order to save Israel from Assyrian domination, Judith seduces the Assyrian general Holofernes. After he falls asleep drunk, Judith and her maid servant cut off his head. The personal importance of the story to Gentileschi is underscored by the fact that she chose to depict herself as Judith and Agostino Tassi, her rapist, as Holofernes. As you examine the painting, compare its composition to that of *Susannah and the Elders*. In what ways does this painting invert the power relationships of the earlier work?

Judith and Holofernes (panel), Gentileschi, Artemisia (1597–ca. 1651) / Museo e Gallerie Nazionali di Capodimonte, Naples, Italy / The Bridgeman Art Library.

READING QUESTIONS

1. How would you describe Gentileschi's Judith? How would you characterize her facial expression?

2. What might explain Gentileschi's decision to focus attention on Judith's arms and those of her maid?

3. Compare this work to *Susannah and the Elders*. Taken together, what do the two paintings tell us about the connections Gentileschi made between gender, power, and violence?

■ COMPARATIVE AND DISCUSSION QUESTIONS ■

1. Compare and contrast Petrarch and Machiavelli. Should they both be considered humanists? Why or why not?

2. Compare and contrast Erasmus's depiction of the successful prince with Machiavelli's. How does each one envision the Renaissance state? What does each think is necessary for a government to function well?

3. What light do the works of Christine de Pizan and Artemisia Gentileschi shed on the challenges faced by women of their day? How would you explain the success of each in male-dominated fields?

4. What marks Erasmus's *Education of a Christian Prince* as a work of the northern Renaissance? How does it differ from some of the other works included in this chapter?

13

Reformations and Religious Wars

1500–1600

Even before Martin Luther posted his "Ninety-five Theses on the Power of Indulgences," numerous Catholic practices had come under widespread criticism. The specific political situation in the Holy Roman Empire enabled Luther and other reformers to spread their ideas. Strong local governments and high nobles, who exercised more power in their territories than did the central government of the Holy Roman Empire, welcomed Lutheran ideas and offered safe havens to the Protestants. Protestant reform extended to social thought as well—for example, priests were no longer required to remain celibate in the Protestant tradition. Some reformers adopted beliefs that were far more radical than those of Luther or other reformers and were condemned by Protestants and Catholics alike. Meanwhile, the Catholic Church developed its own plans for reform, both to counter Protestant attacks and to revitalize the church. The age of Reformation was also an age of religious violence, as religious and political conflicts merged and overlapped, fueling war, riots, and the persecution of dissenters and outsiders.

13-1 | Martin Luther Takes a Stand

MARTIN LUTHER, *Ninety-five Theses on the Power of Indulgences* (1517)

Martin Luther (1483–1546) composed his *Ninety-five Theses* in response to Pope Leo X's decision to raise funds for the construction of a new cathedral in Rome through the sale of indulgences in Germany. An indulgence was a document issued by the Catholic Church lessening a person's penance or time in purgatory. Many believed that the purchase of an indulgence was an effective substitute for genuine repentance, a belief papal agents did little or nothing to discourage. Luther's attack on this practice went far beyond a simple accusation of papal corruption. Instead, it struck directly at the power of the Church, suggesting that priests had no necessary role in salvation.

1. Our Lord and Master Jesus Christ in saying "Repent ye" etc., intended that the whole life of believers should be penitence.
2. This word cannot be understood as sacramental penance, that is, of the confession and satisfaction which are performed under the ministry of priests.
3. It does not, however, refer solely to inward penitence; nay such inward penitence is naught, unless it outwardly produces various mortifications of the flesh.
4. The penalty thus continues as long as the hatred of self (that is, true inward penitence); namely, till our entrance into the kingdom of heaven.
5. The pope has neither the will nor the power to remit any penalties except those which he has imposed by his own authority, or by that of the canons.
6. The pope has no power to remit any guilt, except by declaring and warranting it to have been remitted by God; or at most by remitting cases reserved for himself; in which cases, if his power were despised, guilt would certainly remain.
7. Certainly God remits no man's guilt without at the same time subjecting him, humbled in all things, to the authority of his representative the priest. . . .
20. Therefore the pope, when he speaks of the plenary remission of all penalties, does not mean really of all, but only of those imposed by himself.
21. Thus those preachers of indulgences are in error who say that by the indulgences of the pope a man is freed and saved from all punishment.
22. For in fact he remits to souls in purgatory no penalty which they would have had to pay in this life according to the canons.
23. If any entire remission of all penalties can be granted to any one it is certain that it is granted to none but the most perfect, that is to very few.

From Martin Luther, "Ninety-five Theses," in *Translations and Reprints from the Original Sources of European History* (Philadelphia: University of Pennsylvania Press, 1898), 2/6:12–18.

24. Hence, the greater part of the people must needs be deceived by this indiscriminate and high-sounding promise of release from penalties. . . .

26. The pope acts most rightly in granting remission to souls not by the power of the keys (which is of no avail in this case) but by the way of intercession.[1]

27. They preach man [rather than God] who say that the soul flies out of Purgatory as soon as the money thrown into the chest rattles.[2]

28. It is certain that, when the money rattles in the chest, avarice and gain may be increased, but the effect of the intercession of the Church depends on the will of God alone. . . .

30. No man is sure of the reality of his own contrition, much less of the attainment of plenary remission. . . .

35. They preach no Christian doctrine who teach that contrition is not necessary for those who buy souls [out of purgatory] or buy confessional licenses.

36. Every Christian who feels true compunction has of right plenary remission of punishment and guilt even without letters of pardon.

37. Every true Christian, whether living or dead, has a share in all the benefits of Christ and of the Church, given him by God, even without letters of pardon. . . .

38. The remission, however, imparted by the pope is by no means to be despised, since it is, as I have said, a declaration of the divine remission.

39. It is a most difficult thing, even for the most learned theologians, to exalt at the same time in the eyes of the people the ample effect of pardons and the necessity of true contrition.

40. True contrition seeks and loves punishment; while the ampleness of pardons relaxes it, and causes men to hate it, or at least gives occasion for them to do so. . . .

43. Christians should be taught that he who gives to a poor man, or lends to a needy man, does better than if he bought pardons.

44. Because by works of charity, charity increases, and the man becomes better; while by means of pardons, he does not become better, but only freer from punishment. . . .

49. Christians should be taught that the pope's pardons are useful if they do not put their trust in them, but most hurtful if through them they lose the fear of God. . . .

54. Wrong is done to the Word of God when, in the same sermon, an equal or longer time is spent on pardons than on it.

55. The mind of the pope necessarily is that, if pardons, which are a very small matter, are celebrated with single bells, single processions, and single

---

[1]**intercession**: Prayer to God on another's behalf.

[2]**They preach . . . rattles**: This was the claim being made by the indulgence seller Tetzel in Luther's Saxony.

ceremonies, the Gospel, which is a very great matter, should be preached with a hundred bells, a hundred processions, and a hundred ceremonies.

56. The treasures of the Church, whence the pope grants indulgences, are neither sufficiently named nor known among the people of Christ.

57. It is clear that they are at least not temporal treasures, for these are not so readily lavished, but only accumulated, by many of the preachers. . . .

67. Those indulgences, which the preachers loudly proclaim to be the greatest graces, are seen to be truly such as regards the promotion of gain.

68. Yet they are in reality most insignificant when compared to the grace of God and the piety of the cross. . . .

75. To think that the papal pardons have such power that they could absolve a man even if—by an impossibility—he had violated the Mother of God, is madness.

76. We affirm on the contrary that papal pardons cannot take away even the least of venial sins, as regards its guilt. . . .

79. To say that the cross set up among the insignia of the papal arms is of equal power with the cross of Christ, is blasphemy.

80. Those bishops, priests, and theologians who allow such discourses to have currency among the people will have to render an account. . . .

82. As for instance: Why does not the pope empty purgatory for the sake of most holy charity and of the supreme necessity of souls—this being the most just of all reasons—if he redeems an infinite number of souls for the sake of that most fatal thing, money, to be spent on building a basilica—this being a very slight reason?

83. Again; why do funeral masses and anniversary masses for the deceased continue, and why does not the pope return, or permit the withdrawal of, the funds bequeathed for this purpose, since it is a wrong to pray for those who are already redeemed?

84. Again; what is this new kindness of God and the pope, in that, for money's sake, they permit an impious man and an enemy of God to redeem a pious soul which loves God, and yet do not redeem that same pious and beloved soul out of free charity on account of its own need?

85. Again; why is it that the penitential canons, long since abrogated and dead in themselves, in very fact and not only by usage, are yet still redeemed with money, through the granting of indulgences, as if they were full of life?

86. Again; why does not the pope, whose riches are at this day more ample than those of the wealthiest of the wealthy, build the single Basilica of St. Peter with his own money rather than with that of poor believers? . . .

89. Since it is the salvation of souls, rather than money, that the pope seeks by his pardons, why does he suspend the letters and pardons granted long ago, since they are equally efficacious? . . .

91. If all these pardons were preached according to the spirit and mind of the pope, all these questions would be resolved with ease; nay, would not exist.

READING QUESTIONS

1. In Thesis 36, Luther writes, "Every Christian who feels true compunction has of right plenary remission of punishment and guilt even without letters of pardon." Why would many interpret this as an attack on the papacy?

2. According to the theses, in what ways have the leaders of the church failed to teach true Christian doctrine?

3. Based on your reading of Theses 82–91, how would you classify the sorts of reform that Luther would like to see within the church?

13-2 | Reformation Propaganda

HANS HOLBEIN THE YOUNGER, *Luther as the German Hercules* (ca. 1519)

One of Martin Luther's greatest assets was the printing press. Print technology facilitated the rapid dissemination of Lutheran ideas to a wide variety of audiences. The propaganda campaign waged by Luther's supporters included inexpensive print versions of his tracts, pamphlets, and treatises. It also included images aimed at the illiterate and semi-literate. A majority of sixteenth-century Europeans could not read, and woodcuts like this one, created by Hans Holbein the Younger (1498–1543), served as vehicles for their inclusion in the religious debates that dominated much of the century. Here, Luther is depicted as the Greek hero Hercules, who killed the hydra, a beast with nine heads. The artist has replaced the hydra with nine churchmen, including the theologian Thomas Aquinas (see Document 10-6), monks, and priests. The strangled pope, identifiable by his triple crown, dangles from the rope in Luther's mouth.

READING QUESTIONS

1. How would you describe the way Luther is depicted here? What about the church leaders?

2. How would you sum up the intended message of this image in a single sentence? What group or groups might it have been meant to influence?

3. What light does this image shed on the nature of religious conflict during the Reformation? What room, if any, did such images leave for compromise between Protestants and Catholics?

SOURCES IN CONVERSATION

The War on Witches

Starting around 1560, prosecutions of alleged witches rose dramatically. The next century would see between one hundred thousand and two hundred thousand people tried for witchcraft, which resulted in forty thousand to sixty thousand executions. Possible explanations for this phenomenon include changes in legal procedures, the religious upheaval of the Reformation, the social and economic dislocation created by a changing agricultural economy, the efforts of early modern states to assert greater control over their subjects, and new definitions of witchcraft. It should be stressed, however, that each witchcraft trial was different and that a different combination of factors was in play in each case. While shaped by larger social and cultural trends, witchcraft trials were, in the end, local events, and the relationships and personal histories of the individuals involved were at the heart of each outbreak of accusations.

13-3 | JEAN BODIN, *On the Demon-Mania of Witches* (1580)

Jean Bodin (1529/30–1596) was one of the foremost political theorists of his time. A professor of law and adviser to kings, he is best known for his *Six livres de la République* (1576), in which he developed a case for royal absolutism that rested on a belief in the divine right of kings. It might be surprising that a man of such erudition and international status was also a leading proponent of aggressive efforts to detect and punish witchcraft. For Bodin, however, concern about witchcraft was a natural extension of his interest in politics and government. As he saw it, the "status and greatness of the state" depended on the "punishment of the bad," and there was no greater evil than witchcraft.

From Alan Kors and Edward Peters, eds., *Witchcraft in Europe, 400–1700: A Documentary History*, 2d ed. (Philadelphia: University of Pennsylvania, 2001), pp. 291–293.

Now if ever there was a way to appease the anger of God, to obtain His blessing, to dismay some by the punishment of others, to preserve some from the infection of others, to reduce the number of the wicked, to secure the safety of the good, and to punish the most despicable wickednesses that the human mind can imagine, it is to chastise witches with the utmost rigour. However, the word "rigour" is a misnomer, since there is no penalty cruel enough to punish the evils of witches, since all their wickednesses, blasphemies, and all their designs rise up against the majesty of God to vex and offend Him in a thousand ways. . . . Some people raise objections to burning witches, even witches who have a formal pact with Satan. For it is principally against those witches that one must seek vengeance with the greatest diligence and utmost rigour, in order to bring an end to the wrath of God, and His vengeance upon us. And especially since those who have written on it interpret a magic spell as heresy, and nothing more—although true heresy is the crime of treason against God, and punishable by the fire. It is necessary, however, to note the difference between this crime and simple heresy. For we showed initially that the first occupation of witches is to deny God and all religion. The law of God condemns that person who has left the true God for another to be stoned, which all the Hebrew commentators say is the most terrible form of execution. This point is very significant. For the witch whom I have described does not just deny God in order to change and take up another religion, but he renounces all religion, either true or superstitious, which can keep men in the fear of committing offence.

The second crime of witches is, after having renounced God, to curse, blaspheme and scorn Him, and any other god or idol which he feared. Now the law of God declares as follows, "Whoever curses his God shall bear his sin. He who blasphemes the name of the Lord shall be put to death." . . .

For it seems that God wants to show that those who blaspheme what they think is God, do blaspheme God, with respect to their intention, which is the foundation of the hearts and minds of men: like the witches described above who broke the arms and legs on crucifixes, which they thought were gods. They also offered toads the host[1] to feed on. One sees then a double outrage of impiety with witches who blaspheme the true God, and anything they think has some divinity, so as to uproot all pious conviction and fear of offence.

The third crime is even more abominable. Namely, they do homage to the Devil, worship him, offer sacrifice, and the most despicable make a trench and put their face in the ground praying and worshiping him with all their heart. . . . This abomination surpasses any penalty that man can conceive, considering the formal text of the law of God, which requires that one who only bows down to pay honour to images, which the Greeks call "idols," be put to death. . . . Now witches are not content to worship, or only to bow down before Satan, but they offer themselves to Satan, pray to him and invoke him.

---

[1]**the host**: The sanctified bread that signifies the body of Christ.

The fourth crime is even greater: many witches have been convicted, and have confessed to promising their children to Satan. The fifth is even worse; that is, that witches are frequently convicted by their confession of having sacrificed to the Devil their infant children before they are baptised. They raise them in the air, and then insert a large pin into their head, which causes them to die and is a crime more bizarre than the one before. In fact Sprenger[2] relates that he had one burned who had killed forty-one of them in this way.

The sixth crime is even more horrible. For witches are not satisfied to offer their own children to the Devil and burn them as a sacrifice . . . but they even dedicate them right from the mother's womb . . . which is a double parricide with the most abominable idolatry imaginable.

The seventh and the most common is that witches make an oath and promise the Devil to lure as many as they can into his service, which they customarily do, as we showed earlier. Now the law of God states that that person who is called this way, must stone the one who tried to entice him.

The eighth crime is to call upon and swear by the name of the Devil as a mark of honour, as witches do having it always on their lips, and swearing only by him, except when they renounce God. This is directly against the law of God, which forbids swearing by anything other than the name of God. This, Scripture says, gives glory to God. Thus judges said in taking the oath of parties or witnesses, "Glory be to God."

The ninth is that witches are incestuous, which is the crime they have been charged with and convicted of from earliest times. For Satan gives them to understand that there was never a perfect sorcerer or enchanter who was not born from father and daughter, or mother and son. . . . All these impieties are directly against God and His honour, which judges must avenge with the utmost rigour, and bring an end to God's wrath against us. As for the other crimes of witches, they concern injuries done to men, which they will avenge whenever they can. Now there is nothing so displeasing to God as to see judges avenge the smallest offences committed against themselves or others, but dissemble the horrible blasphemies against the majesty of God, such as those I have cited about witches.

Let us continue then with the other crimes. The tenth is that witches make a profession of killing people, and worse of murdering little children, then boiling them to render their humours and flesh drinkable, which Sprenger says he learned from their confessions; and the Neopolitan Battista della Porta[3] writes about it in his book on magic. And still another fact to underline, is that they put children to death before they are baptised. These are four circumstances which make the murder very much worse.

---

[2]**Sprenger**: Jacob Sprenger (1436–1495). A Dominican inquisitor and coauthor with Heinrich Kramer of the *Malleus Maleficarum,* or *The Hammer of Witches* (1487), an influential handbook for the investigation of witchcraft.

[3]**Battista della Porta**: Giambattista della Porta (1535–1615). Italian natural philosopher and author of *Magiae Naturalis,* or *Natural Magic* (1558).

The eleventh crime is that witches eat human flesh, especially of little children, and of course drink their blood. . . . But one sees that it is a vile belief the Devil puts into the hearts of men in order to make them kill and devour each other, and destroy the human race. Again it must be noted that all witches customarily make poisons, which is enough to justify the death sentence. . . .

Now murder, according to the law of God and the laws of men, merits death. And those who eat human flesh, or have others eat it, also deserve death: as for example, a baker in Paris who made a business of making pies from the flesh of people hanged. He was burned, and his house razed to the ground. . . .

The twelfth is particular, killing with poisons or spells, which is distinct from simple homicide. . . . For it is a much more serious offence to kill with poison than with overt violence, as we shall presently point out; and even more serious to cause death by sorcery than by poison. . . .

The thirteenth crime of witches is to kill livestock, something which is customary. . . . The fourteenth is common, and recognised by law, namely, killing crops and causing famine and sterility in an entire region. The fifteenth is that witches have carnal copulation with the Devil, (and very often near their husbands, as I remarked earlier), a wickedness they all confess to.

There then are fifteen detestable crimes, the least of which merits a painful death. This does not mean that all witches are guilty of such evils, but it has been well established that witches who have a formal compact with the Devil are normally guilty of all or of most of these evil deeds.

READING QUESTIONS

1. What crimes does Bodin attribute to witches?

2. Why does Bodin believe that it was essential for the state to aggressively pursue witchcraft allegations?

3. What does Bodin's discussion of witchcraft tell us about his religious views? What about his political views?

13-4 | *Elizabeth Francis Confesses to Witchcraft* (1566)

In 1563, a new witchcraft law was enacted in England. It is notable for its introduction of the death penalty for individuals convicted of murder by witchcraft. This provision was put into effect for the first time at the conclusion of a 1566 trial involving three women from Chelmsford in Essex. The confession of one of the women, Elizabeth Francis, is included here. As you read it, consider how prevalent ideas about women factored into witchcraft trials. What fears about women's alleged moral and spiritual weakness are "confirmed" by Francis's confession?

From Alan Kors and Edward Peters, eds., *Witchcraft in Europe, 400–1700: A Documentary History*, 2d ed. (Philadelphia: University of Pennsylvania, 2001), pp. 304–305.

Elizabeth Francis, the first to be examined, deposed as follows:

"First she learned this art of witchcraft at the age of twelve years of her grandmother, whose name was Mother Eve of Hatfield Peverel, deceased. Item, when she taught it her, she counselled her to renounce God and his word and to give of her blood to Satan (as she termed it), which she delivered her in the likeness of a white spotted cat, and taught her to feed the said cat with bread and milk, and she did so, also she taught her to call it by the name of Satan and to keep it in a basket.

"When this Mother Eve had given her the Cat Satan, then this Elizabeth desired first of the said Cat (calling it Satan) that she might be rich and to have goods, and he promised her she should—asking her what she would have, and she said sheep (for this Cat spake to her as she confessed in a strange hollow voice, but such as she understood by use) and this Cat forthwith brought sheep into her pasture to the number of eighteen, black and white, which continued with her for a time, but in the end did all wear away she knew not how.

"Item, when she had gotten these sheep, she desired to have one Andrew Byles to her husband, which was a man of some wealth, and the Cat did promise she should, but that he said she must first consent that this Andrew should abuse her, and she so did.

"And after when this Andrew had thus abused her he would not marry her, wherefore she willed Satan to waste his goods, which he forthwith did, and yet not being contented with this, she willed him to touch his body which he forthwith did whereof he died.

"Item, that every time that he did anything for her, she said that he required a drop of blood, which she gave him by pricking herself, sometime in one place and then in another, and where she pricked herself there remained a red spot which was still to be seen.

"Item, when this Andrew was dead, she doubting herself with child, willed Satan to destroy it, and he bade her take a certain herb and drink it, which she did, and destroyed the child forthwith.

"Item, when she desired another husband he promised her another, naming this Francis whom she now hath, but said he is not so rich as the other, willing her to consent unto that Francis in fornication which she did, and thereof conceived a daughter that was born within a quarter of a year after they were married.

"After they were married they lived not so quietly as she desired, being stirred (as she said) to much unquietness and moved to swearing and cursing, wherefore she willed Satan her Cat to kill the child, being about the age of half a year old, and he did so, and when she yet found not the quietness that she desired, she willed it to lay a lameness in the leg of this Francis her husband, and it did in this manner. It came in a morning to this Francis' shoe, lying in it like a toad, and when he perceived it putting on his shoe, and had touched it with his foot, he being suddenly amazed asked of her what it was, and she bad[e] him kill it and he was forthwith taken with a lameness whereof he cannot be healed.

"After all this when she had kept this Cat by the space of fifteen or sixteen years, and as some say (though untruly) being weary of it, she came to one Mother Waterhouse her neighbour (a poor woman) when she was going to the oven and desired her to give her a cake, and she would give her a thing that she should be the better for so long as she lived, and this Mother Waterhouse gave her a cake, whereupon she brought her this cat in her apron and taught her as she was instructed before by her grandmother Eve, telling her that she must call him Satan and give him of her blood and bread and milk as before, and at this examination would confess no more."

READING QUESTIONS

1. To what crimes did Francis confess? How did Satan allegedly assist her in these crimes? What might explain Francis's decision to confess to crimes that she did not commit?

2. What does Francis's confession suggest about the ways in which knowledge of witchcraft allegedly spread? What importance should we attach to the fact that Francis's grandmother is referred to as "Mother Eve"?

3. What connections does the confession suggest between fears about witchcraft and fears about female sexuality?

13-5 | Calvin Defines His Protestant Vision

JOHN CALVIN, *The Institutes of Christian Religion* (1559)

Martin Luther may have initiated the Protestant Reformation, but once it began it quickly moved beyond his control. Over the course of the sixteenth century, Protestantism splintered into numerous sects, some largely conforming to Luther's views, others deviating from them in important ways. The most important alternative to Lutheranism was developed by the French theologian John Calvin (1509–1564). At the core of Calvin's theology was a belief in the omnipotence of God and the utter powerlessness of human beings. It was on this foundation that he built the principle of predestination, the idea that the salvation or damnation of every person is foreordained by God and there is nothing any individual can do to alter his or her ultimate fate. In this excerpt from *The Institutes of Christian Religion*, Calvin defined predestination and offered the history of the Jews as evidence of its veracity.

From Hans J. Hillerbrand, *The Protestant Reformation* (New York: Harper and Row, 1968), pp. 184–185.

When we attribute foreknowledge to God, we mean that all things always were, and perpetually remain, under His eyes, so that to His knowledge there is nothing future or past, but all things are present. And they are present in such a way that He not only conceives them through ideas, as we have before us those things which our minds remember, but He truly looks upon them and discerns them as things placed before Him. And this foreknowledge is extended throughout the universe to every creature. We call predestination God's eternal decree, by which He determined with Himself what He willed to become of each man. For all are not created in equal condition; rather, eternal life is foreordained for some, eternal damnation for others. Therefore, as any man has been created to one or the other of these ends, we speak of him as predestined to life or to death.

God has attested this not only in individual persons but has given us an example of it in the whole offspring of Abraham, to make it clear that in His choice rests the future condition of each nation. "When the Most High divided the nations, and separated the sons of Adam . . . the people of Israel were His portion, . . . the cord of His inheritance" [Deut. 32:8–9]. The separation is apparent to all men: in the person of Abraham, as in a dry tree trunk, one people is peculiarly chosen, while the others are rejected; but the cause does not appear except that Moses, to cut off from posterity any occasion to boast, teaches that they excel solely by God's freely given love. For he declares this the cause of their deliverance: that God loved the patriarchs, "and chose their seed after them" [Deut. 4:37].

More explicitly, in another chapter: "Not because you surpassed all other peoples in number did He take pleasure in you to choose you, . . . but because He loved you" [Deut. 7:7–8]. . . . Believers also proclaim this with one voice: "He chooses our heritage for us, the glory of Jacob, whom He has loved" [Psalms 47:4]. For all who have been adorned with gifts by God credit them to His freely given love because they knew not only that they had not merited them but that even the holy patriarch himself was not endowed with such virtue as to acquire such a high honor for himself and his descendants. And in order more effectively to crush all pride, he reproaches them as deserving no such thing, since they were a stubborn and stiff-necked people [Ex. 32:9; cf. Deut. 9:6]. Also, the prophets often confront the Jews with this election, to the latters' displeasure and by way of reproach, since they had samefully fallen away from it [cf. Amos 3:2].

Be this as it may, let those now come forward who would bind God's election either to the worthiness of men or to the merit of works. Since they see one nation preferred above all others, and hear that God was not for any reason moved to be more favorably inclined to a few, ignoble—indeed, even wicked and stubborn—men, will they quarrel with Him because He chose to give such evidence of His mercy? But they shall neither hinder His work with their clamorous voices nor strike and hurt His righteousness by hurling the stones of their insults toward heaven. Rather, these will fall back on their own heads!

READING QUESTIONS

1. How did Calvin define predestination? What about foreknowledge?

2. Why did Calvin believe that the history of the Jews provided evidence in support of predestination?

3. Why did Calvin believe it was a mistake to "bind God's election either to the worthiness of men or to the merit of works"?

13-6 | Training the Soldiers of Christ

IGNATIUS OF LOYOLA, *Rules for Right Thinking* (1548)

While recovering from an injury, the Spanish soldier Ignatius (ig-NAY-shus) of Loyola (1491–1556) had a religious experience that inspired him to found a new monastic order unlike most others. Conceived as front-line troops in the battle against Protestantism, members of this order, which became known as the Society of Jesus, or the Jesuits, rejected monastic isolation and instead served as teachers and missionaries. Loyola's *Rules for Right Thinking* was designed to help individuals prepare to serve as Catholic soldiers in the Counter-Reformation. As you read this excerpt, consider what it reveals about how Loyola saw the conflict between Protestantism and Catholicism. Why did he believe that strict obedience to Church teachings was critical to the ultimate triumph of Catholicism?

First Rule. The first: All judgment laid aside, we ought to have our mind ready and prompt to obey, in all, the true Spouse of Christ our Lord, which is our holy Mother the Church. . . .

Fifth Rule. The fifth: To praise vows of Religion, of obedience, of poverty, of chastity, and of other perfections. . . .

Sixth Rule. To praise relics of the Saints, giving veneration to them and praying to the Saints; and to praise . . . pilgrimages, indulgences, . . . and candles lighted in the churches. . . .

Eighth Rule. To praise the ornaments and the buildings of churches; likewise images, and to venerate them according to what they represent.

Ninth Rule. Finally, to praise all precepts of the Church, keeping the mind prompt to find reasons in their defense and in no manner against them.

Tenth Rule. We ought to be more prompt to find good and praise as well the . . . recommendations as the ways of our Superiors. Because, although some are not or have not been [upright], to speak against them, whether preaching in public or discoursing before the common people, would rather give rise to fault-finding and scandal than profit; and so the people would be incensed

From Father Elder Mullen, S.J., trans., *The Spiritual Exercises of St. Ignatius of Loyola* (New York: P. J. Kennedy & Sons, 1914), p. 39. Christian Classics Ethereal Library. Web. February 24, 2010.

against their Superiors, whether temporal or spiritual. So that, as it does harm to speak evil to the common people of Superiors in their absence, so it can make profit to speak of the evil ways to the persons themselves who can remedy them. . . .

Twelfth Rule. We ought to be on our guard in making comparison of those of us who are alive to the blessed passed away, because error is committed not a little in this; that is to say, in saying, this one knows more than St. Augustine; he is another, or greater than, St. Francis; he is another St. Paul in goodness, holiness, etc.

Thirteenth Rule. To be right in everything, we ought always to hold that the white which I see, is black, if the Church so decides it, believing that between Christ our Lord, . . . and the Church, . . . there is the same Spirit which governs and directs us for the salvation of our souls. Because by the same Spirit and our Lord Who gave the ten Commandments, our holy Mother the Church is directed and governed.

Fourteenth Rule. Although there is much truth in the assertion that no one can save himself without being predestined and without having faith and grace; we must be very cautious in the manner of speaking and communicating with others about all these things.

Fifteenth Rule. We ought not, by way of custom, to speak much of predestination; but if in some way and at some times one speaks, let him so speak that the common people may not come into any error, as sometimes happens, saying: Whether I have to be saved or condemned is already determined, and no other thing can now be, through my doing well or ill; and with this, growing lazy, they become negligent in the works which lead to the salvation and the spiritual.

Sixteenth Rule. In the same way, we must be on our guard that by talking much and with much insistence of faith, without any distinction and explanation, occasion be not given to the people to be lazy and slothful in works, whether before faith is formed in charity or after.

READING QUESTIONS

1. What rules should the Jesuits follow in order to be faithful to the church?

2. What should a Jesuit do if he disagrees with the church?

3. What things should not be spoken of to the people? Why?

■ COMPARATIVE AND DISCUSSION QUESTIONS ■

1. In what ways did Luther's and Calvin's versions of Protestantism differ? Which version might have seemed more threatening to secular rulers? Why?

2. Review Loyola's comments on predestination, as well as Calvin's explanation of the term. Why did Loyola consider it wise for Jesuits to remain silent on this subject?

3. What connections can you make between religious upheaval and the surge in witchcraft prosecutions that began in the mid-sixteenth century?

4. Compare and contrast the image of the pope in the woodcut (c. 1519) with what Luther said of him in his "Ninety-five Theses" (1517). How would you explain the differences you note?

14

European Exploration and Conquest
1450–1650

In the mid-1400s, western Europe faced a rapidly expanding Muslim power in the east. The Ottoman Empire captured Constantinople in 1453 and over time came to rule, directly or indirectly, much of eastern Europe. Now cut off from direct access to Asian trade via the eastern Mediterranean, Europeans turned south and west in search of new trade routes to India and China. Portugal led the way in the fifteenth century, launching expeditions to explore the west coast of Africa and eventually rounding the tip of Africa and reaching India. After Columbus's voyages, Spain and Portugal began to explore and conquer the Americas. Portuguese exploration of Africa combined with the establishment of colonial empires in the Americas led to a new era of worldwide trade in African slaves. Through trade, travel, and missionary work, Europeans increasingly came into contact with peoples of whom they had previously had little or no knowledge. For many Europeans, this only reinforced their sense of cultural and religious superiority. For others, it prompted a re-evaluation of basic assumptions about their own society and its place in the world.

14-1 | Columbus Sets the Context for His Voyage
CHRISTOPHER COLUMBUS, *Diario* (1492)

The year 1492 was a momentous one in Spanish history. With the fall of the Muslim state of Granada, Ferdinand of Aragon and Isabella of Castille completed the Christian *reconquista* (reconquest) of the Iberian Peninsula. Having driven the "infidel" from its last stronghold, they

---

From *The Diario of Christopher Columbus's First Voyage to America*, trans. Oliver Dunn and James E. Kelly, Jr. (Norman: University of Oklahoma Press, 1989), pp. 17, 19, 21.

turned to the "enemy within," issuing a proclamation expelling all Jews from their lands. It was at this moment, fired with a crusading spirit and eager to gain access to the wealth of Asia, that Ferdinand and Isabella chose to sponsor the exploratory westward voyage of Christopher Columbus. As you read the introduction from Columbus's *Diario* (diary), compiled at the request of his sponsors, notice the connections Columbus makes between the events described above and his own voyage. What does his introduction suggest about the role of religion in sparking Spain's involvement in westward expansion?

Whereas, Most Christian and Very Noble and
Very Excellent and Very Powerful Princes, King
and Queen of the Spains and of the Islands of
the Sea, our Lords: This present year of 1492,
after Your Highnesses had brought to an end
the war with the Moors who ruled in Europe and
had concluded the war in the very great city
of Granada, where this present year on the
second day of the month of January I saw the
Royal Standards of Your Highnesses placed by
force of arms on the towers of the Alhambra,
which is the fortress of the said city; and I
saw the Moorish King come out to the gates of
the city and kiss the Royal Hands of Your
Highnesses and of the Prince my Lord; and
later in that same month, because of the
report that I had given to Your Highnesses about
the lands of India and about a prince who is
called "Grand Khan," which means in our
Spanish language "King of Kings"; how, many times,
he and his predecessors had sent to Rome to
ask for men learned in our Holy Faith in order
that they might instruct him in it and how the
Holy Father had never provided them; and thus
so many peoples were lost, falling into idolatry
and accepting false and harmful religions;
and Your Highnesses, as Catholic Christians
and Princes, lovers and promoters of the Holy
Christian Faith, and enemies of the false
doctrine of Mahomet and of all idolatries and
heresies, you thought of sending me, Christóbal
Colón, to the said regions of India to see
the said princes and the peoples and the lands,
and the characteristics of the lands and of
everything, and to see how their conversion to
our Holy Faith might be undertaken. And you
commanded that I should not go to the East by
land, by which way it is customary to go, but

by the route to the West, by which route we do
not know for certain that anyone previously
has passed. So, after having expelled all the
Jews from all of your Kingdoms and Dominions,
in the same month of January Your Highnesses
commanded me to go, with a suitable fleet, to
the said regions of India. And for that you
granted me great favors and ennobled me so
that from then on I might call myself "Don"
and would be Grand Admiral of the Ocean Sea
and Viceroy and perpetual Governor of all the
islands and lands that I might discover and
gain and [that] from now on might be discovered
and gained in the Ocean Sea; and likewise my
eldest son would succeed me and his son him,
from generation to generation forever. And I
left the city of Granada on the twelfth day of
May in the same year of 1492 on Saturday, and
I came to the town of Palos, which is a seaport,
where I fitted out three vessels very
well suited for such exploits; and I left the
said port, very well provided with supplies
and with many seamen, on the third day of
August of the said year, on a Friday, half an
hour before sunrise; and I took the route to
Your Highnesses' Canary Islands, which are in
the said Ocean Sea, in order from there to
take my course and sail so far that I would
reach the Indies and give Your Highnesses'
message to those princes and thus carry out
that which you had commanded me to do. And
for this purpose I thought of writing on this
whole voyage, very diligently, all that I
would do and see and experience, as will be
seen further along. Also, my Lord Princes,
besides writing down each night whatever I
experience during the day and each day what I
sail during the night, I intend to make a new
sailing chart. In it I will locate all of the
sea and the lands of the Ocean Sea in their
proper places under their compass bearings
and, moreover, compose a book and similarly
record all of the same in a drawing, by latitude
from the equinoctial line and by longitude
from the west; and above all it is very

important that I forget sleep and pay much
attention to navigation in order thus to carry
out these purposes, which will be great labor.

READING QUESTIONS

1. How did Columbus explain Ferdinand and Isabella's decision to sponsor his voyage?

2. What does the document suggest about the Spanish monarchs' motives for sponsoring Columbus? What does it suggest about Columbus's motives for conducting the expedition?

3. What might explain Columbus's decision to focus on the *reconquista* and the expulsion of the Jews in the introduction to the *Diario*?

14-2 | Cortés Describes the Conquest of the Aztecs

HERNANDO CORTÉS, *Two Letters to Charles V: On the Conquest of the Aztecs* (1521)

Hernando Cortés (1485–1547) described his conquest of the Aztec Empire of Mexico in a number of letters to his sovereign and king of Spain, the Holy Roman Emperor Charles V. While Cortés was surprised, even impressed, by the advanced culture he encountered, his conquests were not without considerable violence. In one incident, one of his men ordered the massacre of thousands of unarmed members of the Aztec nobility who had assembled peaceably. Under examination, Cortés claimed that this act was done to instill fear and prevent future treachery. Some contemporaries speculated that Cortés embellished his accounts in order to retain the favor of the king.

[Second Letter]

This great city of Tenochtitlan is built on the salt lake. . . . It has four approaches by means of artificial causeways. . . . The city is as large as Seville or Cordoba. Its streets . . . are very broad and straight, some of these, and all the others, are one half land, and the other half water on which they go about in canoes. . . . There are bridges, very large, strong, and well constructed, so that, over many, ten horsemen can ride abreast. . . . The city has many squares where markets are held. . . . There is one square, twice as large as that of Salamanca, all surrounded by arcades, where there are daily more than sixty thousand souls, buying and selling . . . in the service and manners of its people, their fashion of living was almost the same as in Spain, with just as much harmony and order; and considering that these people were barbarous, so cut off from the knowledge of God and

From *Letters of Cortés*, trans. Francis A. MacNutt (New York: 1908), 1:256–257, 2:244.

other civilized peoples, it is admirable to see to what they attained in every respect.

[Fifth Letter]

It happened . . . that a Spaniard saw an Indian . . . eating a piece of flesh taken from the body of an Indian who had been killed. . . . I had the culprit burned, explaining that the cause was his having killed that Indian and eaten him which was prohibited by Your Majesty, and by me in Your Royal name. I further made the chief understand that all the people . . . must abstain from this custom. . . . I came . . . to protect their lives as well as their property, and to teach them that they were to adore but one God . . . that they must turn from their idols, and the rites they had practiced until then, for these were lies and deceptions which the devil . . . had invented. . . . I, likewise, had come to teach them that Your Majesty, by the will of Divine Providence, rules the universe, and that they also must submit themselves to the imperial yoke, and do all that we who are Your Majesty's ministers here might order them.

READING QUESTIONS

1. Although Cortés described the people of Tenochtitlán as "barbarous" and lamented that they are "cut off from the knowledge of God and other civilized peoples," what positive qualities did he attribute to the city and its people?

2. Why do you think Cortés chose to describe an act of cannibalism? Why might he have believed that such an account would find favor with his royal reader?

3. What different images of Mexico was Cortés trying to impress upon Charles V?

The Slave Trade in Africa

Slavery and the slave trade existed in West Africa long before the arrival of Europeans in the fifteenth and sixteenth centuries. For centuries, Africans had enslaved other Africans, both to use as slaves in Africa and to sell to Muslim merchants as part of the international trade that connected Africa to the Arab world. Nonetheless, European participation altered the African slave trade in profound ways. Most important, it resulted in a surge in demand for African slaves. As European empires in the New World grew, so too did the demand for slave labor. Over time, the combined efforts of Africans and Europeans to meet that demand would distort and destabilize African societies and economies.

14-3 | ALVISE DA CA' DA MOSTO, *Description of Capo Bianco and the Islands Nearest to It: Fifteenth-Century Slave Trade in West Africa* (1455–1456)

Alvise da Ca' da Mosto (ca. 1428–1483) was an Italian trader and explorer. After his father was banished from Venice, Ca' da Mosto took up service with Prince Henry of Portugal, a key promoter of Portuguese exploration of the West African coast. In 1455, he traveled to the Canary and Madeira Islands and sailed past Cape Verde to the Gambia River. During another voyage in 1456, Ca' da Mosto discovered islands off Cape Verde and sailed sixty miles up the Gambia River. In the excerpt that follows, Ca' da Mosto describes the African Muslims who served as middlemen in the Atlantic slave trade. As you read it, notice both the details he chose to include and those he chose to leave out. What do these choices tell you about the nature of his interest in the communities he visited? What does it tell you about his readers' interests?

You should also know that behind this Cauo Bianco[1] on the land, is a place called Hoden,[2] which is about six days inland by camel. This place is not walled, but is frequented by Arabs, and is a market where the caravans arrive from Tanbutu [Timbuktu], and from other places in the land of the Blacks, on their way to our nearer Barbary. The food of the peoples of this place is dates, and barley, of which there is sufficient, for they grow in some of these places, but not abundantly. They drink the milk of camels and other animals, for they have no wine. They also have cows and goats, but not many, for the land is dry. Their oxen and cows, compared with ours, are small.

They are Muhammadans, and very hostile to Christians. They never remain settled, but are always wandering over these deserts. These are the men who go to the land of the Blacks, and also to our nearer Barbary. They are very numerous, and have many camels on which they carry brass and silver from Barbary and other things to Tanbutu and to the land of the Blacks. Thence they carry away gold and pepper, which they bring hither. They are brown complexioned, and wear white cloaks edged with a red stripe: their women also dress thus, without shifts. On their heads the men wear turbans in the Moorish fashion, and they always go barefooted. In these sandy districts there are many lions, leopards, and ostriches, the eggs of which I have often eaten and found good.

You should know that the said Lord Infante of Portugal [the crown prince, Henry the Navigator] has leased this island of Argin to Christians [for ten years], so that no one can enter the bay to trade with the Arabs save those who hold the license. These have dwellings on the island and factories where they buy and sell

---

From Alvise da Ca' da Mosto, "Description of Capo Bianco and the Islands Nearest to It," in *European Reconnaissance: Selected Documents*, ed. J. H. Parry (New York: Walker, 1968), pp. 59–61.

[1]**Cauo Bianco**: West African port.

[2]**Hoden**: Wadan, an important desert market about 350 miles east of Arguim. Later, in 1487, when the Portuguese sought to penetrate the interior, they attempted to establish a trading factory at Wadan that acted as a feeder to Arguim, tapping the northbound caravan traffic and diverting some of it to the west coast.

with the said Arabs who come to the coast to trade for merchandise of various kinds, such as woollen cloths, cotton, silver, and "alchezeli," that is, cloaks, carpets, and similar articles and above all, corn, for they are always short of food. They give in exchange slaves whom the Arabs bring from the land of the Blacks, and gold tiber [gold dust]. The Lord Infante therefore caused a castle to be built on the island to protect this trade for ever. For this reason, Portuguese caravels are coming and going all the year to this island.

These Arabs also have many Berber horses, which they trade, and take to the land of the Blacks, exchanging them with the rulers for slaves. Ten or fifteen slaves are given for one of these horses, according to their quality. The Arabs likewise take articles of Moorish silk, made in Granata and in Tunis of Barbary, silver, and other goods, obtaining in exchange any number of these slaves, and some gold. These slaves are brought to the market and town of Hoden; there they are divided: some go to the mountains of Barcha, and thence to Sicily, [others to the said town of Tunis and to all the coasts of Barbary], and others again are taken to this place, Argin, and sold to the Portuguese leaseholders. As a result every year the Portuguese carry away from Argin a thousand slaves. Note that before this traffic was organized, the Portuguese caravels, sometimes four, sometimes more, were wont to come armed to the Golfo d'Argin, and descending on the land by night, would assail the fisher villages, and so ravage the land. Thus they took of these Arabs both men and women, and carried them to Portugal for sale: behaving in a like manner along all the rest of the coast, which stretches from Cauo Bianco to the Rio di Senega and even beyond.

READING QUESTIONS

1. Why do you think Ca' da Mosto wrote this account?

2. What were the principal patterns of commerce in northern Africa?

3. What groups were involved in the various facets of the slave trade?

4. In what ways did the arrival of the Portuguese change West African slavery and the slave trade?

14-4 | KING NZINGA MBEMBA AFFONSO OF CONGO, *Letters on the Slave Trade* (1526)

In 1491, the Portuguese granted the right to send merchants and missionaries into the West African kingdom of Congo. King Affonso, the king of Congo, converted to Christianity, and the trading relationship between Portugal and Congo created many lucrative opportunities

From Basil Davidson, *The African Past: Chronicles from Antiquity to Modern Times* (Boston: Little, Brown and Company, 1964), pp. 191–193; reissued by Africa World Press in 1990 as *African Civilization Revisited: From Antiquity to Modern Times.*

for merchants from both countries. By the 1520s, however, Affonso had grown increasingly concerned about the negative impact that the slave trade was having on his kingdom. The following selection contains two letters from Affonso to the king of Portugal, written in July and October 1526.

[First Letter]

Sir, Your Highness should know how our Kingdom is being lost in so many ways that it is convenient to provide for the necessary remedy, since this is caused by the excessive freedom given by your agents and officials to the men and merchants who are allowed to come to this Kingdom to set up shops with goods and many things which have been prohibited by us, and which they spread throughout our Kingdoms and Domains in such an abundance that many of our vassals, whom we had in obedience, do not comply because they have the things in greater abundance than we ourselves; and it was with these things that we had them content and subjected under our vassalage and jurisdiction, so it is doing a great harm not only to the service of God, but the security and peace of our Kingdoms and State as well.

And we cannot reckon how great the damage is, since the mentioned merchants are taking every day our natives, sons of the land and the sons of our noblemen and vassals and our relatives, because the thieves and men of bad conscience grab them wishing to have the things and wares of this Kingdom which they are ambitious of; they grab them and get them to be sold; and so great, Sir, is the corruption and licentiousness that our country is being completely depopulated, and Your Highness should not agree with this nor accept it as in your service. And to avoid it we need from those [your] Kingdoms no more than some priests and a few people to teach in schools, and no other goods except wine and flour for the holy sacrament. That is why we beg of Your Highness to help and assist us in this matter, commanding your factors that they should not send here either merchants or wares, because it is *our will that in these Kingdoms there should not be any trade of slaves nor outlet for them. . . .*

[Second Letter]

Moreover, Sir, in our Kingdoms there is another great inconvenience which is of little service to God, and this is that many of our people, keenly desirous as they are of the wares and things of your Kingdoms, which are brought here by your people, and in order to satisfy their voracious appetite, seize many of our people, freed and exempt men, and very often it happens that they kidnap even noblemen and the sons of noblemen, and our relatives, and take them to be sold to the white men who are in our Kingdoms; and for this purpose they have concealed them; and others are brought during the night so that they might not be recognized.

And as soon as they are taken by the white men they are immediately ironed and branded with fire, and when they are carried to be embarked, if they are caught by our guards' men the whites allege that they have bought them but they cannot say from whom, so that it is our duty to do justice and to restore to the freemen their freedom, but it cannot be done if your subjects feel offended, as they claim to be.

And to avoid such a great evil we passed a law so that any white man living in our Kingdoms and wanting to purchase goods in any way should first inform three of our noblemen and officials of our court whom we rely upon in this matter, and these are Dom Pedro Manipanza and Dom Manuel Manissaba, our chief usher, and Gonçalo Pires our chief freighter, who should investigate if the mentioned goods are captives or free men, and if cleared by them there will be no further doubt nor embargo for them to be taken and embarked. But if the white men do not comply with it they will lose the aforementioned goods. And if we do them this favor and concession it is for the part Your Highness has in it, since we know that it is in your service too that these goods are taken from our Kingdom, otherwise we should not consent to this.

READING QUESTIONS

1. What negative effects did King Affonso argue that the slave trade was having on his kingdom?

2. In the king's view, who profited from the slave trade? Who bore the social and economic costs of that trade?

3. What did King Affonso propose to do about the slave trade in the first letter? In the second letter? Why do you think he changed his plan?

14-5 | The Jesuits Bring Christianity to Asia

SAINT FRANCIS XAVIER, *Missionaries in Japan* (1552)

The Society of Jesus was founded to stop the spread of Protestantism and reinforce the authority of the church in Catholic countries. Soon after the order's founding, the Jesuit mission expanded to include the spread of Catholicism around the world. Among the first Jesuit missionaries was Francis Xavier (1506–1552). Xavier devoted most of his life to missionary work, travelling throughout Asia in an effort to advance the Catholic cause. This excerpt from his letters describes his activities in Japan. As you read it, consider what it tells us about the Jesuits' missionary strategy.

From Henry James Coleridge, ed., *The Life and Letters of St. Francis Xavier*, 3d ed. (London: Burns & Oates, 1876), 2:331–348.

But to return to what we did in Japan. In the first place, we landed, as I told you, at Cagoxima,[1] Paul's[2] native place, where by his constant instructions he converted all his family to Jesus Christ, and where, but for the opposition of the bonzes,[3] he would easily have converted the whole town also. The bonzes persuaded the King, whose authority extends over a good part of the country, that, if he were to sanction the introduction of the divine law into his dominions, the result would infallibly be the ruin, not only of his entire kingdom, but also of the worship of the gods and of the institutions of his ancestors; and that he ought for the future to forbid any one becoming a Christian, on pain of death.

After the lapse of a year, seeing this prince openly opposed to the progress of the Gospel, we bade farewell to our [converts] at Cagoxima, and to Paul, in whose care we left them, and went on thence to a town in the kingdom of Amanguchi.[4] . . . I myself went on to . . . the capital of the kingdom, an immense city containing more than ten thousand houses. Here we preached the Gospel to the people in the public streets, to the princes and nobles in their own residences. Many heard us eagerly, others with reluctance. We did not always escape unhurt, having many insults offered us by the boys and the crowds in the streets. The King of the country summoned us to his presence, and, having asked the reason of our coming, invited us of his own accord to explain the law of God to him; he listened to us with deep attention for a whole hour while we spoke to him of religion. . . .

The king was made favorable to us by the letters and presents sent by the Bishop and the Governors from India and Malacca, and we obtained from him without difficulty the publication of edicts declaring his approval of the promulgation of the divine law in the cities of his dominions, and permitting such of his subjects as pleased to embrace it. When he had done us this favor he also assigned a monastery to us for a residence. Here by means of daily sermons and disputes with the bonzes, the sorcerers, and other such men, we converted to the religion of Jesus Christ a great number of persons, several of whom were nobles. Amongst them we found some able to inform us, and we made it our business to gain acquaintance with the various sects and opinions of Japan, and so know how to refute them by arguments and proofs prepared for the purpose.

READING QUESTIONS

1. What was the Jesuits' goal in Japan?
2. How did the Japanese respond to the missionaries' preaching of Christianity?
3. Why was the king so important to the Jesuits? What might explain the king's decision to change his mind about allowing the Jesuits to operate in his territory?

---

[1]**Cagoxima**: Region in southwestern Japan.
[2]**Paul**: A Japanese convert to Christianity.
[3]**bonzes**: Buddhist monks.
[4]**Amanguchi**: Yamaguchi, in southwestern Japan.

14-6 | A Critique of European "Superiority"
MICHEL DE MONTAIGNE, *Of Cannibals* (1580)

Michel de Montaigne (duh mahn-TAYN) (1533–1592), a French lawyer and government official, wrote about his personal experiences and travels in his *Essays* of 1580. Writing during a
period of religious warfare in Europe and the expansion of the European presence around the
world, Montaigne offered a critique of European assumptions of social and cultural superiority. In his essay "Of Cannibals," Montaigne pointed out the virtues of Native American society
as he saw them. As you read this excerpt from the essay, consider how Montaigne's own
assumptions and cultural commitments shaped his view of Native American society. How did
Montaigne's diagnosis of the ills of his own society affect his perception of the peoples of the
Americas?

When King Pyrrhus[1] invaded Italy, having viewed and considered the order of
the army the Romans sent out to meet him; "I know not," said he, "what kind of
barbarians" (for so the Greeks called all other nations) "these may be; but the
disposition of this army that I see has nothing of barbarism in it." . . . By which it
appears how cautious men ought to be of taking things upon trust from vulgar
opinion, and that we are to judge by the eye of reason, and not from common
report.

I long had a man in my house that lived ten or twelve years in the New
World, discovered in these latter days, and in that part of it where Villegaignon
landed, which he called Antarctic France.[2] This discovery of so vast a country
seems to be of very great consideration. I cannot be sure, that hereafter there may
not be another, so many wiser men than we having been deceived in this. I am
afraid our eyes are bigger than our bellies, and that we have more curiosity than
capacity; for we grasp at all, but catch nothing but wind. . . .

This man that I had was a plain ignorant fellow, and therefore the more
likely to tell truth: for your better-bred sort of men are much more curious in
their observation; . . . they never represent things to you simply as they are, but
rather as they appeared to them, or as they would have them appear to you. . . . I
would have every one write what he knows, and as much as he knows, but no
more; and that not in this only but in all other subjects. . . .

Now, to return to my subject, I find that there is nothing barbarous and savage in this nation, by anything that I can gather, excepting, that every one gives

---

From *Essays of Montaigne*, trans. Charles Cotton, ed. William Carew Hazlitt (London: Reeves and
Turner, 1902), I:237–252.

[1]**Pyrrhus**: Greek king of Sicily (319–272 B.C.E.) who attempted to prevent Roman armies
from advancing into southern Italy.

[2]**and in that part . . . Antarctic France**: Nicolas Durand de Villegaignon (1510–1571) was an
officer in the French navy who in 1555 captured the region surrounding what is now Rio de
Janeiro, Brazil, from the Portuguese. In addition to creating new trading opportunities, his goal
was to build a refuge for the French Calvinists to escape religious persecution in France. Portugal
retook the colony in 1567.

the title of barbarism to everything that is not in use in his own country. As, indeed, we have no other level of truth and reason than the example and idea of the opinions and customs of the place wherein we live: there is always the perfect religion, there the perfect government, there the most exact and accomplished usage of all things. . . .

These nations then seem to me to be so far barbarous, as having received but very little form and fashion from art and human invention, and consequently to be not much remote from their original simplicity. The laws of nature, however, govern them still, not as yet much [corrupted] with any mixture of ours: but 'tis in such purity, that I am sometimes troubled we were not sooner acquainted with these people, and that they were not discovered in those better times, when there were men much more able to judge of them than we are. . . . To my apprehension, what we now see in those nations, does not only surpass all the pictures with which the poets have adorned the golden age, and all their inventions in feigning a happy state of man, but, moreover, the fancy and even the wish and desire of philosophy itself; so native and so pure a simplicity, as we by experience see to be in them, could never enter into their imagination, nor could they ever believe that human society could have been maintained with so little artifice and human patchwork. I should tell Plato[3] that it is a nation wherein there is no manner of traffic, no knowledge of letters, no science of numbers, no name of magistrate or political superiority; no use of service, riches or poverty, no contracts, no successions, no dividends, no properties, no employments, but those of leisure, no respect of kindred, but common, no clothing, no agriculture, no metal, no use of corn or wine; the very words that signify lying, treachery, dissimulation, avarice, envy, detraction, pardon, never heard of. How much would he find his imaginary Republic short of his perfection? . . .

As to the rest, they live in a country very pleasant and temperate, so that, as my witnesses inform me, 'tis rare to hear of a sick person, and they moreover assure me, that they never saw any of the natives, either paralytic, bleary-eyed, toothless, or crooked with age. The situation of their country is along the seashore. . . . They have great store of fish and flesh that have no resemblance to those of ours: which they eat without any other cookery, than plain boiling, roasting, and broiling. The first that rode a horse thither, though in several other voyages he had contracted an acquaintance and familiarity with them, put them into so terrible a fright, with his centaur[4] appearance, that they killed him with their arrows before they could come to discover who he was. Their buildings are very long, and of capacity to hold two or three hundred people. . . . They have wood so hard, that they cut with it, and make their swords of it, and their grills of it to broil their meat. Their beds are of cotton, hung swinging from the roof, like our seamen's hammocks, every man his own, for the wives lie apart from their

---

[3]**Plato**: Greek philosopher (427–347 B.C.E.) and author of *The Republic*, who wrote about an ideal city in which people were ruled by philosophers.

[4]**centaur**: Half-human, half-horse creature from Greek mythology.

husbands. They rise with the sun, and so soon as they are up, eat for all day, for they have no more meals but that; they do not then drink, . . . but drink very often all day after, and sometimes to a rousing pitch. . . . The whole day is spent in dancing. Their young men go a-hunting after wild beasts with bows and arrows; one part of their women are employed in preparing their drink the while, which is their chief employment. One of their old men, in the morning before they fall to eating, preaches to the whole family, walking from the one end of the house to the other, and several times repeating the same sentence, till he has finished the round, for their houses are at least a hundred yards long. Valor towards their enemies and love towards their wives, are the two heads of his discourse. . . . They believe in the immortality of the soul, and that those who have merited well of the gods are lodged in that part of heaven where the sun rises, and the accursed in the west. . . .

They have continual war with the nations that live further within the mainland, beyond their mountains, to which they go naked, and without other arms than their bows and wooden swords, fashioned at one end like the head of our javelins. The obstinacy of their battles is wonderful, and they never end without great effusion of blood: for as to running away, they know not what it is. Every one for a trophy brings home the head of an enemy he has killed, which he fixes over the door of his house. After having a long time treated their prisoners very well, and given them all the regales they can think of, he to whom the prisoner belongs, invites a great assembly of his friends. They being come, he ties a rope to one of the arms of the prisoner, of which, at a distance, out of his reach, he holds the one end himself, and gives to the friend he loves best the other arm to hold after the same manner; which being done, they two, in the presence of all the assembly, dispatch him with their swords. After that, they roast him, eat him amongst them, and send some chops to their absent friends. They do not do this, as some think, for nourishment, . . . but as a representation of an extreme revenge; as will appear by this: that having observed the Portuguese, who were in league with their enemies, to inflict another sort of death upon any of them they took prisoners, which was . . . to shoot at [them] till [they were] stuck full of arrows, and then to hang them, they thought those people of the other world . . . did not exercise this sort of revenge without a meaning, and that it must needs be more painful than theirs, they began to leave their old way, and to follow this. I am not sorry that we should here take notice of the barbarous horror of so cruel an action, but that, seeing so clearly into their faults, we should be so blind to our own. I conceive there is more barbarity in eating a man alive, than when he is dead; in tearing a body limb from limb by racks and torments, that is yet in perfect sense; in roasting it by degrees; in causing it to be bitten and worried by dogs and swine (as we have not only read, but lately seen, not amongst inveterate and mortal enemies, but among neighbors and fellow-citizens, and, which is worse, under color of piety and religion), than to roast and eat him after he is dead. . . .

We may then call these people barbarous, in respect to the rules of reason: but not in respect to ourselves, who in all sorts of barbarity exceed them. Their wars are throughout noble and generous, and carry as much excuse and fair pretence, as that human malady is capable of; having with them no other foundation than the sole jealousy of valor. Their disputes are not for the conquest of new lands, for these they already possess are so fruitful by nature, as to supply them without labor or concern, with all things necessary, in such abundance that they have no need to enlarge their borders. And they are, moreover, happy in this, that they only covet so much as their natural necessities require: all beyond that is superfluous to them. . . . If their neighbors pass over the mountains to assault them, and obtain a victory, all the victors gain by it is glory only, and the advantage of having proved themselves the better in valor and virtue: for they never meddle with the goods of the conquered, but presently return into their own country, where they have no want of anything necessary, nor of this greatest of all goods, to know happily how to enjoy their condition and to be content. And those in turn do the same; they demand of their prisoners no other ransom, than acknowledgment that they are overcome. . . . There is not a man amongst them who had not rather be killed and eaten, than so much as to open his mouth to entreat he may not. They use them with all liberality and freedom, to the end their lives may be so much the dearer to them; but frequently entertain them with menaces of their approaching death, of the torments they are to suffer, of the preparations making in order to it, of the mangling of their limbs, and of the feast that is to be made, where their carcass is to be the only dish. All which they do, to no other end, but only to extort some gentle or submissive word from them, or to frighten them so as to make them run away, to obtain this advantage that they were terrified, and that their constancy was shaken; and indeed, if rightly taken, it is in this point only that a true victory consists. . . .

But to return to my story: these prisoners are so far from discovering the least weakness, for all the terrors that can be represented to them, that, on the contrary, during the two or three months they are kept, they always appear with a cheerful countenance; importune their masters to make haste to bring them to the test, defy, rail at them, and reproach them with cowardice, and the number of battles they have lost against those of their country. I have a song made by one of these prisoners, wherein he bids them "come all, and dine upon him, and welcome, for they shall withal eat their own fathers and grandfathers, whose flesh has served to feed and nourish him. These muscles," says he, "this flesh and these veins, are your own: poor silly souls as you are, you little think that the substance of your ancestors' limbs is here yet; notice what you eat, and you will find in it the taste of your own flesh:" in which song there is to be observed an invention that nothing relishes of the barbarian. Those that paint these people dying after this manner, represent the prisoner spitting in the faces of his executioners and making wry mouths at them. And 'tis most certain, that to the very last gasp, they never cease to brave and defy them both in word and gesture. In plain truth, these men are very savage in comparison of us; of necessity, they must either be absolutely so or else we are savages; for there is a vast difference betwixt their manners and ours.

READING QUESTIONS

1. Why does Montaigne write that the words of a "plain ignorant fellow" are more reliable than the words of someone who has been educated? Why does he think it important that reason should be the guide to understanding?

2. How does Montaigne use the word *barbarian* in this essay? To him, what makes someone a barbarian, and why?

3. On what points does Montaigne compare and contrast Native American society with Portuguese society? In what ways does he find the Portuguese to be more barbarous than the cannibals? Why?

■ COMPARATIVE AND DISCUSSION QUESTIONS ■

1. What light do Cortés and Columbus shed on the motives behind Spanish exploration and colonization of the Americas?

2. Compare and contrast the two documents on the African slave trade (Documents 14-3 and 14-4). What do these documents reveal about the nature of Portuguese participation?

3. Based on your reading of the documents in these chapters, which distinctions among peoples seem most important for Europeans of the fifteenth and sixteenth centuries? How do the attitudes of the Jesuits toward non-Europeans compare to Montaigne's?

15

Absolutism and Constitutionalism
ca. 1589–1725

Sixteenth- and seventeenth-century Europe witnessed a prolonged struggle between monarchs seeking to consolidate and extend their power, and social groups and institutions opposing those efforts. Many factors — political, social, and economic — influenced the course of this struggle, and the outcome varied from country to country. France's kings managed to suppress some of the opposition to royal power and thus are termed "absolutist" monarchs, although even the greatest of them, Louis XIV, lacked the power and authority to exert his unchallenged will over all of his subjects, in particular the great nobles. Eastern European rulers in Prussia, Austria, and Russia also augmented their power and authority, although there were significant differences from state to state, and none matched Louis XIV's achievement. Still, all experienced greater success in expanding royal authority than did their counterparts in the Netherlands and England. Two English kings, Charles I and James II, lost their thrones as a consequence of political revolutions, and the former was also tried and executed for crimes against his subjects.

15-1 | A French King Establishes Limited Religious Toleration
HENRY IV, *Edict of Nantes* (1598)

Prince Henry of Navarre (1553–1610) was a Huguenot, or Protestant, in an overwhelmingly Roman Catholic country. He ascended to the French throne as Henry IV in 1589 in the midst of the French Wars of Religion. A pragmatist, Henry realized that the country's Catholic majority

---

From King Henry of Navarre, "Edict of Nantes," in *Readings in European History*, ed. James Harvey Robinson, 2 vols. (Boston: Ginn, 1906), 2:183–185.

would never accept a Protestant as their legitimate ruler, so he converted to Catholicism. However, in order to protect the Huguenots against religiously motivated attacks, as well as to establish peace among the people he was determined to rule, he issued the Edict of Nantes. In so doing, Henry legally sanctioned a degree of religious tolerance in a Europe previously characterized by the formula "one king, one people, one faith."

Among the infinite benefits which it has pleased God to heap upon us, the most signal and precious is his granting us the strength and ability to withstand the fearful disorders and troubles which prevailed on our advent in this kingdom. The realm was so torn by innumerable factions and sects that the most legitimate of all the parties[1] was fewest in numbers. God has given us strength to stand out against this storm; we have finally surmounted the waves and made our port of safety,—peace for our state. For which his be the glory all in all, and ours a free recognition of his grace in making use of our instrumentality in the good work. . . . We implore and await from the Divine Goodness the same protection and favor which he has ever granted to this kingdom from the beginning. . . .

We have, by this perpetual and irrevocable edict, established and proclaimed and do establish and proclaim:

I. First, that the recollection of everything done by one party or the other between March, 1585, and our accession to the crown, and during all the preceding period of troubles, remain obliterated and forgotten, as if no such things had ever happened. . . .

III. We ordain that the Catholic Apostolic and Roman religion shall be restored and reestablished in all places and localities of this our kingdom and countries subject to our sway, where the exercise of the same has been interrupted, in order that it may be peaceably and freely exercised, without any trouble or hindrance; forbidding very expressly all persons, of whatsoever estate, quality, or condition, from troubling, molesting, or disturbing ecclesiastics in the celebration of divine service, in the enjoyment or collection of tithes, fruits, or revenues of their benefices, and all other rights and dues belonging to them; and that all those who during the troubles have taken possession of churches, houses, goods, or revenues, belonging to the said ecclesiastics, shall surrender to them entire possession and peaceable enjoyment of such rights, liberties, and sureties as they had before they were deprived of them. . . .

VI. And in order to leave no occasion for troubles or differences between our subjects, we have permitted, and herewith permit, those of the said religion called Reformed [Protestant] to live and abide in all the cities and places of this our kingdom and countries of our sway, without being annoyed, molested, or compelled

---

[1]**the most legitimate of all the parties**: Faction supporting Valois King Henry III (r. 1574–1589) during the French Wars of Religion (1561–1598). Henry's subsequent reference to "one party or the other" refers to the three factions, two of them Catholic, one of them Protestant, that struggled for control of the French throne.

to do anything in the matter of religion contrary to their consciences, . . . upon conditions that they comport themselves in other respects according to that which is contained in this our present edict.

VII. It is permitted to all lords, gentlemen, and other persons making profession of the said religion called Reformed, holding the right of high justice [or a certain feudal tenure], to exercise the said religion in their houses. . . .

IX. We also permit those of the said religion to make and continue the exercise of the same in all villages and places of our dominion where it was established by them and publicly enjoyed several and divers times in the year 1597, up to the end of the month of August, notwithstanding all decrees and judgments to the contrary. . . .

XIII. We very expressly forbid to all those of the said religion its exercise, either in respect to ministry, regulation, discipline, or the public instruction of children, or otherwise, in this our kingdom and lands of our dominion, otherwise than in the places permitted and granted by the present edict.

XIV. It is forbidden as well to perform any function of the said religion on our court or retinue, or in our lands and territories beyond the mountains, or in our city of Paris, or within five leagues of the said city. . . .

XVIII. We also forbid all our subjects, of whatever quality and condition, from carrying off by force or persuasion, against the will of their parents, the children of the said religion, in order to cause them to be baptized or confirmed in the Catholic Apostolic and Roman Church; and the same is forbidden to those of the said religion called Reformed, upon penalty of being punished with special severity. . . .

XXI. Books concerning the said religion called Reformed may not be printed and publicly sold, except in cities and places where the public exercise of the said religion is permitted.

XXII. We ordain that there shall be no difference or distinction made in respect to the said religion, in receiving pupils to be instructed in universities, colleges, and schools; or in receiving the sick and poor into hospitals, retreats and public charities.

XXIII. Those of the said religion called Reformed shall be obliged to respect the laws of the Catholic Apostolic and Roman Church, recognized in this our kingdom, for the consummation of marriages contracted, or to be contracted, as regards to the degrees of consanguinity and kinship.

READING QUESTIONS

1. Why was Henry so intent on "obliterating" the memory of "everything done by one party or the other" in the years immediately prior to his coronation as king of France?

2. Is the Edict of Nantes consistent with Henry's aim of increasing the monarchy's and the state's power? Why or why not?

3. Why might Henry's son, Louis XIII, have regarded the Huguenots as "a state within a state"?

4. Based on the details of the edict regarding ceremonies, property, literature, and education, what sorts of practices defined a religion before and during Henry's reign? What, if any, practices did he consider irreligious, or purely civil?

15-2 | An Argument for the Divine Right of Kings

JACQUES-BÉNIGNE BOSSUET, *Politics Drawn from the Very Words of Holy Scripture* (1679)

The French cleric Jacques-Bénigne Bossuet (1627–1704) was a staunch advocate of the divine right of kings and a favorite of Louis XIV. He preached to the court regularly from 1660 to 1669 and was especially renowned for his funeral orations. In 1670 he was appointed tutor to Louis's eldest son, and thus had the weighty task of instructing the heir to the throne on the duties of a king. The work from which the following excerpts are taken was composed in 1679 for the Dauphin's guidance. As you read the excerpts, think about the implications of Boussuet's position. What powers did kings have as God's chosen ruler? What obligations did that status carry with it?

All power is of God. The ruler, [states] St. Paul, "is the minister of God to thee for good. But if thou do that which is evil, be afraid; for he beareth not the sword in vain: for he is the minister of God, a revenger to execute wrath upon him that doeth evil." Rulers then act as the ministers of God and as his lieutenants on earth. It is through them that God exercises his empire. . . . Consequently, as we have seen, the royal throne is not the throne of a man, but the throne of God himself. The Lord "hath chosen Solomon my son to sit upon the throne of the kingdom of the Lord over Israel." And again, "Solomon sat on the throne of the Lord."

Moreover, that no one may assume that the Israelites were peculiar in having kings over them who were established by God, note what is said in Ecclesiasticus: "God has given to every people its ruler, and Israel is manifestly reserved to him." He therefore governs all peoples and gives them their kings, although he governed Israel in a more intimate and obvious manner.

It appears from all this that the person of the king is sacred, and that to attack him in any way is sacrilege. God has the kings anointed by his prophets with the holy unction in like manner as he has bishops and altars anointed. But even without the external application in thus being anointed, they are by their very office the representatives of the divine majesty deputed by Providence for the execution of his purposes. Accordingly God calls Cyrus his anointed. "Thus saith the Lord to his anointed, to Cyrus, whose right hand I have holden, to subdue nations before him." . . . Kings should be guarded as holy things, and whosoever neglects to protect them is worthy of death. . . .

From James Harvey Robinson, ed. *Readings in European History*, 2 vols. (Boston: Ginn, 1906), 2:273–277.

There is something religious in the respect accorded to a prince. The service of God and the respect for kings are bound together. St. Peter unites these two duties when he says, "Fear God. Honor the king." . . .

But kings, although their power comes from on high, as has been said, should not regard themselves as masters of that power to use it at their pleasure . . . they must employ it with fear and self-restraint, as a thing coming from God and of which God will demand an account. "Hear, O kings, and take heed, understand, judges of the earth, lend your ears, ye who hold the peoples under your sway, and delight to see the multitude that surround you. It is God who gives you the power. Your strength comes from the Most High, who will question your works and penetrate the depths of your thoughts, for, being ministers of his kingdom, ye have not given righteous judgments nor have ye walked according to his will. He will straightway appear to you in a terrible manner, for to those who command is the heaviest punishment reserved. The humble and the weak shall receive mercy, but the mighty shall be mightily tormented. For God fears not the power of any one, because he made both great and small and he has care for both." . . .

Kings should tremble then as they use the power God has granted them; and let them think how horrible is the sacrilege if they use for evil a power which comes from God. We behold kings seated upon the throne of the Lord, bearing in their hand the sword which God himself has given them. What profanation, what arrogance, for the unjust king to sit on God's throne to render decrees contrary to his laws and to use the sword which God has put in his hand for deeds of violence and to slay his children! . . .

The royal power is absolute. With the aim of making this truth hateful and insufferable, many writers have tried to confound absolute government with arbitrary government. But no two things could be more unlike, as we shall show when we come to speak of justice.

The prince need render account of his acts to no one. "I counsel thee to keep the king's commandment, and that in regard of the oath of God. Be not hasty to go out of his sight: stand not on an evil thing for he doeth whatsoever pleaseth him. Where the word of a king is, there is power: and who may say unto him, what doest thou? Whoso keepeth the commandment shall feel no evil thing." Without this absolute authority the king could neither do good nor repress evil. It is necessary that his power be such that no one can hope to escape him, and, finally, the only protection of individuals against the public authority should be their innocence.

This conforms with the teaching of St. Paul: "Wilt thou then not be afraid of the power? Do that which is good."

I do not call majesty that pomp which surrounds kings or that exterior magnificence which dazzles the vulgar. That is but the reflection of majesty and not majesty itself. Majesty is the image of the grandeur of God in the prince.

God is infinite, God is all. The prince, as prince, is not regarded as a private person: he is a public personage, all the state is in him; the will of all the people is included in his. As all perfection and all strength are united in God, so all the power of individuals is united in the person of the prince. What grandeur that a single man should embody so much!

The power of God makes itself felt in a moment from one extremity of the earth to another. Royal power works at the same time throughout all the realm. It holds all the realm in position, as God holds the earth. Should God withdraw his hand, the earth would fall to pieces; should the king's authority cease in the realm, all would be in confusion.

Look at the prince in his cabinet. Thence go out the orders which cause the magistrates and the captains, the citizens and the soldiers, the provinces and the armies on land and on sea, to work in concert. He is the image of God, who, seated on his throne high in the heavens, makes all nature move. . . .

Finally, let us put together the things so great and so august which we have said about royal authority. Behold an immense people united in a single person; behold this holy power, paternal and absolute; behold the secret cause which governs the whole body of the state, contained in a single head: you see the image of God in the king, and you have the idea of royal majesty. God is holiness itself, goodness itself, and power itself. In these things lies the majesty of God. In the image of these things lies the majesty of the prince.

So great is this majesty that it cannot reside in the prince as in its source; it is borrowed from God, who gives it to him for the good of the people, for whom it is good to be checked by a superior force. Something of divinity itself is attached to princes and inspires fear in the people. The king should not forget this. "I have said," — it is God who speaks, — "I have said, Ye are gods; and all of you are children of the Most High. But ye shall die like men, and fall like one of the princes." "I have said, Ye are gods"; that is to say, you have in your authority, and you bear on your forehead, a divine imprint. "You are the children of the Most High"; it is he who has established your power for the good of mankind. But, O gods of flesh and blood, gods of clay and dust, "ye shall die like men, and fall like princes." Grandeur separates men for a little time, but a common fall makes them all equal at the end.

O kings, exercise your power then boldly, for it is divine and salutary for human kind, but exercise it with humility. You are endowed with it from without. At bottom it leaves you feeble, it leaves you mortal, it leaves you sinners, and charges you before God with a very heavy account.

READING QUESTIONS

1. If, as Bossuet argued, kings were "the representatives of the divine majesty deputed by Providence for the execution of his purposes," then what need was there for clergymen like him?

2. Bossuet admits that "many writers have tried to confound absolute government with arbitrary government." How does he distinguish between the two, if, as he also claims, the "prince need render account of his acts to no one"?

3. Does Bossuet admit to *any* constraints on royal power?

4. According to Bossuet, the "only protection of individuals against the public authority should be their innocence." What sort of protection would that have been against "absolute" royal power?

15-3 | The English Place Limits on Monarchical Power
The Bill of Rights (1689)

Almost a century of struggle between the forces of constitutionalism and absolutism in England culminated in the Bill of Rights. The Bill of Rights was an unequivocal statement that Parliament, not the monarch, was the source of English law and that all Englishmen, including the monarch, were subject to the law. Acceptance of the Bill of Rights was a non-negotiable condition of the ascendency of William and Mary to the English throne. Thus, the very first act of the new monarchs was an acknowledgment of the limits of their power. As you read this excerpt, think about what it reveals about late-seventeenth-century notions of freedom and tyranny. What kinds of abuses of power did Parliament fear? What rights and liberties did it seek to protect?

Whereas the late King James the Second, by the assistance of divers evil counsellors, judges and ministers employed by him, did endeavour to subvert and extirpate the Protestant religion and the laws and liberties of this kingdom;

By assuming and exercising a power of dispensing with and suspending of laws and the execution of laws without consent of Parliament;

By committing and prosecuting divers worthy prelates for humbly petitioning to be excused from concurring to the said assumed power;

By issuing and causing to be executed a commission under the great seal for erecting a court called the Court of Commissioners for Ecclesiastical Causes;

By levying money for and to the use of the Crown by pretence of prerogative for other time and in other manner than the same was granted by Parliament;

By raising and keeping a standing army within this kingdom in time of peace without consent of Parliament, and quartering soldiers contrary to law;

By causing several good subjects being Protestants to be disarmed at the same time when papists were both armed and employed contrary to law;

By violating the freedom of election of members to serve in Parliament;

By prosecutions in the Court of King's Bench for matters and causes cognizable only in Parliament, and by divers other arbitrary and illegal courses;

And whereas of late years partial corrupt and unqualified persons have been returned and served on juries in trials, and particularly divers jurors in trials for high treason which were not freeholders;

And excessive bail hath been required of persons committed in criminal cases to elude the benefit of the laws made for the liberty of the subjects;

And excessive fines have been imposed;

http://avalon.law.yale.edu/17th_century/england.asp.

And illegal and cruel punishments inflicted;

And several grants and promises made of fines and forfeitures before any conviction or judgment against the persons upon whom the same were to be levied;

All which are utterly and directly contrary to the known laws and statutes and freedom of this realm;

And whereas the said late King James the Second having abdicated the government and the throne being thereby vacant, his Highness the prince of Orange (whom it hath pleased Almighty God to make the glorious instrument of delivering this kingdom from popery and arbitrary power) did (by the advice of the Lords Spiritual and Temporal and divers principal persons of the Commons) cause letters to be written to the Lords Spiritual and Temporal being Protestants, and other letters to the several counties, cities, universities, boroughs and cinque ports, for the choosing of such persons to represent them as were of right to be sent to Parliament, to meet and sit at Westminster upon the two and twentieth day of January in this year one thousand six hundred eighty and eight [old-style date], in order to such an establishment as that their religion, laws and liberties might not again be in danger of being subverted, upon which letters elections having been accordingly made;

And thereupon the said Lords Spiritual and Temporal and Commons, pursuant to their respective letters and elections, being now assembled in a full and free representative of this nation, taking into their most serious consideration the best means for attaining the ends aforesaid, do in the first place (as their ancestors in like case have usually done) for the vindicating and asserting their ancient rights and liberties declare

That the pretended power of suspending the laws or the execution of laws by regal authority without consent of Parliament is illegal;

That the pretended power of dispensing with laws or the execution of laws by regal authority, as it hath been assumed and exercised of late, is illegal;

That the commission for erecting the late Court of Commissioners for Ecclesiastical Causes, and all other commissions and courts of like nature, are illegal and pernicious;

That levying money for or to the use of the Crown by pretence of prerogative, without grant of Parliament, for longer time, or in other manner than the same is or shall be granted, is illegal;

That it is the right of the subjects to petition the king, and all commitments and prosecutions for such petitioning are illegal;

That the raising or keeping a standing army within the kingdom in time of peace, unless it be with consent of Parliament, is against law;

That the subjects which are Protestants may have arms for their defence suitable to their conditions and as allowed by law;

That election of members of Parliament ought to be free;

That the freedom of speech and debates or proceedings in Parliament ought not to be impeached or questioned in any court or place out of Parliament;

That excessive bail ought not to be required, nor excessive fines imposed, nor cruel and unusual punishments inflicted;

That jurors ought to be duly impanelled and returned, and jurors which pass upon men in trials for high treason ought to be freeholders;

That all grants and promises of fines and forfeitures of particular persons before conviction are illegal and void;

And that for redress of all grievances, and for the amending, strengthening and preserving of the laws, Parliaments ought to be held frequently.

READING QUESTIONS

1. According to the authors, in what ways did James II abuse his power?

2. What steps did the authors take to protect the power of Parliament? To ensure the impartial application of the law?

3. What restrictions did the Bill of Rights place on the rights of Catholics? How might the authors have justified their inclusion of discriminatory provisions in a law meant to protect the rights of the English people?

15-4 | A Tsar Imposes Western Styles on the Russians
PETER THE GREAT, *Edicts and Decrees* (1699–1723)

Peter the Great's reign (1682–1725) marked Russia's emergence as a major European power. Russia defeated Sweden in the grueling Great Northern War (1700–1721) and acquired a "window on Europe" at the head of the Gulf of Finland, where Peter built a new capital, St. Petersburg. In order to defeat the Swedes, who had routed his ill-trained army at Narva in 1700, Peter had reformed and modernized his military along western European lines. His enthusiasm for western technology and tactics extended also to other realms, including education, dress, and economic programs, as can be seen from the following excerpts. As you read them, ask yourself why the west was of such interest to Peter. What did he hope to accomplish through his program of "westernization"?

Decree on the New Calendar, 1699

It is known to His Majesty that not only many European Christian lands, but also Slavic nations which are in total accord with our Eastern Orthodox Church . . . agree to count their years from the eighth day after the birth of Christ, that is from the first day of January, and not from the creation of the world,[1] because of

---

From Marthe Blinoff, *Life and Thought in Old Russia* (University Park: Pennsylvania State University Press, 1961), pp. 49–50; Eugene Schuyler, *Peter the Great*, vol. 2 (New York: Charles Scribner's Sons, 1884), pp. 176–177; L. Jay Oliva, *Peter the Great* (Englewood Cliffs, N.J.: Prentice-Hall, 1970), p. 50; George Vernadsky et al., *A Source Book for Russian History from Early Times to 1917*, vol. 2 (New Haven and London: Yale University Press, 1972), pp. 329, 347, 357.

[1]**agree to count their years . . . world**: Before January 1, 1700, the Russian calendar started from the date of the creation of the world, which was reckoned at 5508 B.C.E. The year began on September 1.

the many difficulties and discrepancies of this reckoning. It is now the year 1699 from the birth of Christ, and from the first of January will begin both the new year 1700 and a new century; and so His Majesty has ordered, as a good and useful measure, that from now on time will be reckoned in government offices and dates be noted on documents and property deeds, starting from the first of January 1700. And to celebrate this good undertaking and the new century . . . in the sovereign city of Moscow . . . let the reputable citizens arrange decorations of pine, fir, and juniper trees and boughs along the busiest main streets and by the houses of eminent church and lay persons of rank. . . . Poorer persons should place at least one shrub or bough on their gates or on their house. . . . Also . . . as a sign of rejoicing, wishes for the new year and century will be exchanged, and the following will be organized: when fire-works are lit and guns fired on the great Red Square, let the boyars [nobles], the Lords of the Palace, of the Chamber, and the Council, and the eminent personages of Court, Army, and Merchant ranks, each in his own grounds, fire three times from small guns, if they have any, or from muskets and other small arms, and shoot some rockets into the air.

Decree on the Invitation of Foreigners, 1702

Since our accession to the throne all our efforts and intentions have tended to govern this realm in such a way that all of our subjects should, through our care for the general good, become more and more prosperous. For this end we have always tried to maintain internal order, to defend the state against invasion, and in every possible way to improve and to extend trade. With this purpose we have been compelled to make some necessary and salutary changes in the administration, in order that our subjects might more easily gain a knowledge of matters of which they were before ignorant, and become more skillful in their commercial relations.

We have therefore given orders, made dispositions, and founded institutions indispensable for increasing our trade with foreigners, and shall do the same in the future. Nevertheless we fear that matters are not in such a good condition as we desire, and that our subjects cannot in perfect quietness enjoy the fruits of our labors, and we have therefore considered still other means to protect our frontier from the invasion of the enemy, and to preserve the rights and privileges of our State, and the general peace of all Christians. . . .

To attain these worthy aims, we have endeavored to improve our military forces, which are the protection of our State, so that our troops may consist of well-drilled men, maintained in perfect order and discipline. In order to obtain greater improvement in this respect, and to encourage foreigners, who are able to assist us in this way, as well as artisans profitable to the State, to come in numbers to our country, we have issued this manifesto, and have ordered printed copies of it to be sent throughout Europe. . . . And as in our residence of Moscow, the free exercise of religion of all other sects, although not agreeing with our church, is already allowed, so shall this be hereby confirmed anew in such manner that we, by the power granted to us by the Almighty, shall exercise no compulsion over the consciences of men, and shall gladly allow every Christian to care for his own salvation at his own risk.

An Instruction to Russian Students Abroad Studying Navigation, 1714

1. Learn how to draw plans and charts and how to use the compass and other naval indicators.
2. Learn how to navigate a vessel in battle as well as in a simple maneuver, and learn how to use all appropriate tools and instruments; namely, sails, ropes, and oars, and the like matters, on row boats and other vessels.
3. Discover . . . how to put ships to sea during a naval battle. . . . Obtain from foreign naval officers written statements, bearing their signatures and seals, of how adequately you are prepared for naval duties.
4. If, upon his return, anyone wishes to receive from the Tsar greater favors, he should learn, in addition to the above enumerated instructions, how to construct those vessels [aboard] which he would like to demonstrate his skills.
5. Upon his return to Moscow, every foreign-trained Russian should bring with him at his own expense, for which he will later be reimbursed, at least two experienced masters of naval science. They [the returnees] will be assigned soldiers, one soldier per returnee, to teach them what they have learned abroad. . . .

Decree on Western Dress, 1701

Western ["German"] dress shall be worn by all the boyars, okol'nichie,[2] members of our councils and of our court . . . gentry of Moscow, secretaries . . . provincial gentry, boiarskie,[3] gosti,[4] government officials, strel'tsy,[5] members of the guilds purveying for our household, citizens of Moscow of all ranks, and residents of provincial cities . . . excepting the clergy (priests, deacons, and church attendants) and peasant tillers of the soil. The upper dress shall be of French or Saxon cut, and the lower dress—[including] waistcoat, trousers, boots, shoes, and hats—shall be of the German type. They shall also ride German saddles. [Likewise] the womenfolk of all ranks, including the priests', deacons', and church attendants' wives, the wives of the dragoons, the soldiers, and the strel'tsy and their children, shall wear Western ["German"] dresses, hats, jackets, and underwear—undervests and petticoats—and shoes. From now on no one [of the abovementioned] is to wear Russian dress or Circassian coats,[6] sheepskin coats, or Russian peasant

---

[2]**boyars, okol'nichie**: Nobles of the highest and second-highest rank, respectively.
[3]**boiarskie**: Sons of boyars.
[4]**gosti**: Merchants who often served the tsar in some capacity.
[5]**strel'tsy**: Members of the imperial guard stationed in Moscow.
[6]**Circassian coats**: Traditional outer garments worn by the people of Circassia, a Russian territory between the Caspian and Black Seas. The style was evidently adopted by the nobility.

coats, trousers, boots, and shoes. It is also forbidden to ride Russian saddles, and the craftsmen shall not manufacture them or sell them at the marketplaces.

Decree on Shaving, 1705

A decree to be published in Moscow and in all the provincial cities: Henceforth, in accordance with this, His Majesty's decree, all court attendants . . . provincial service men, government officials of all ranks, military men, all the gosti, members of the wholesale merchants' guild, and members of the guilds purveying for our household must shave their beards and moustaches. But, if it happens that some of them do not wish to shave their beards and moustaches, let a yearly tax be collected from such persons. . . . Special badges shall be issued to them from the Administrator of Land Affairs [of Public Order] . . . which they must wear. . . . As for the peasants, let a toll of two half-copecks[7] per beard be collected at the town gates each time they enter or leave a town; and do not let the peasants pass the town gates, into or out of town, without paying this toll.

Decree on Promotion to Officer's Rank, 1714

Since there are many who promote to officer rank their relatives and friends—young men who do not know the fundamentals of soldiering, not having served in the lower ranks—and since even those who serve [in the ranks] do so for a few weeks or months only, as a formality; therefore . . . let a decree be promulgated that henceforth there shall be no promotion [to officer rank] of men of noble extraction or of any others who have not first served as privates in the Guards. This decree does not apply to soldiers of lowly origin who, after long service in the ranks, have received their commissions through honest service or to those who are promoted on the basis of merit, now or in the future; it applies exclusively to those who have remained in the ranks for a short time, only as a formality, as described above.

Statute for the College of Manufactures, 1723

His Imperial Majesty is diligently striving to establish and develop in the Russian Empire such manufacturing plants and factories as are found in other states, for the general welfare and prosperity of his subjects. He [therefore] most graciously charges the College of Manufactures[8] to exert itself in devising the means to introduce, with the least expense, and to spread in the Russian Empire these and other ingenious arts, and especially those for which materials can be found

---

[7]**half-copecks**: One-twentieth of a ruble, the basic unit of Russian money.
[8]**College of Manufactures**: One of several administrative boards created by Peter in 1717, modeled on Swedish practice.

within the empire; [the College of Manufactures] must also consider the privileges that should be granted to those who might wish to found manufacturing plants and factories.

His Imperial Majesty gives permission to everyone, without distinction of rank or condition, to open factories wherever he may find suitable. . . .

Factory owners must be closely supervised, in order that they have at their plants good and experienced [foreign] master craftsmen, who are able to train Russians in such a way that these, in turn, may themselves become masters, so that their produce may bring glory to the Russian manufactures. . . .

By the former decrees of His Majesty commercial people were forbidden to buy villages [i.e., to own serfs], the reason being that they were not engaged in any other activity beneficial for the state save commerce; but since it is now clear to all that many of them have started to found manufacturing establishments and build plants, both in companies and individually, which tend to increase the welfare of the state . . . therefore permission is granted both to the gentry and to men of commerce to acquire villages for these factories without hindrance. . . .

In order to stimulate voluntary immigration of various craftsmen from other countries into the Russian Empire, and to encourage them to establish factories and manufacturing plants freely and at their own expense, the College of Manufactures must send appropriate announcements to the Russian envoys accredited at foreign courts. The envoys should then, in an appropriate way, bring these announcements to the attention of men of various professions, urge them to come to settle in Russia, and help them to move.

READING QUESTIONS

1. Why do you think Peter decreed that the nobles, merchants, and townspeople wear German, rather than French, clothes, seeing as the French kings and their palaces were objects of emulation throughout Europe?

2. What does Peter's decree encouraging foreign soldiers and artisans to emigrate to Russia and his Statute for the College of Manufactures suggest about the state of its military forces and economy as of the early 1700s?

3. Why didn't Russia have a navy prior to 1700?

4. What, according to Peter, was wrong with the system of promotion in the Russian army, and how did he intend to redress it? What does his decree on promotion suggest about the power and benefits granted to the Russian nobility?

SOURCES IN CONVERSATION

The Commonwealth and the State of Nature

Over the course of the seventeenth century, England experienced two civil wars, the execution of a king, and the forced abdication of another. These dramatic events raised fundamental political questions, such as: What limitations exist on monarchical authority? What rights do subjects enjoy, and under what conditions can those rights be abridged? What means of redress, if any, do subjects have if their leaders abuse their power? The political philosophers Thomas Hobbes and John Locke developed the two most important theoretical responses to these questions. While their answers differed, they framed their analyses in similar ways. Both addressed two overarching questions: How and why do governments form, and what are the implications of the origins of the state for contemporary political conflicts?

15-5 | THOMAS HOBBES, *Leviathan* (1651)

Thomas Hobbes (1588–1679), the son of a Church of England clergyman, was educated at Oxford University and spent the years between 1608 and 1637 chiefly as a tutor to aristocratic families. Rising religious and political tensions in England drove Hobbes to flee to Paris in 1640, and there he remained until the publication of *Leviathan*, which aroused so much anger among English royalists that he was forced to seek protection from Cromwell's republican government. Leviathan originally referred to a biblical sea monster, but Hobbes used it as a synonym for the commonwealth; the frontispiece to his book depicts a gargantuan human figure made up of smaller people (members of the commonwealth) with the head of a monarch. *Leviathan* itself is based on the premise that without a sovereign authority invested with absolute power, human society is in a state of perpetual violence. Faced with such a prospect, he argued, individuals voluntarily relinquish their personal rights and liberties in return for protection.

Nature hath made men so equal, in the faculties of body and mind, as that though there be found one man sometimes manifestly stronger in body, or of quicker mind than another; yet when all is reckoned together, the difference between man and man is not so considerable, as that one man can thereupon claim to himself any benefit, to which another may not pretend, as well as he. For as to the strength of body, the weakest has strength enough to kill the strongest, either by secret machination or by confederacy with others that are in the same danger with himself. . . .

From Thomas Hobbes, *Leviathan, or the Matter, Form, and Power of a Commonwealth, Ecclesiastical and Civil* (London: George Routledge and Sons, 1886), pp. 64–66, 82, 84–85.

From this equality of ability, ariseth equality of hope in the attaining of our ends. And therefore if any two men desire the same thing, which nevertheless they cannot both enjoy, they become enemies, and in the way to their end, . . . endeavor to destroy, or subdue one another. . . .

So that in the nature of man, we find three principal causes of quarrel. First, competition; secondly, diffidence; thirdly, glory.

The first maketh men invade for gain; the second, for safety; and the third, reputation. The first use violence to make themselves masters of other men's persons, wives, children, and cattle; the second, to defend them; the third, for trifles, as a word, a smile, a different opinion, and any other sign of undervalue, either direct in their persons, or by reflection in their kindred, their friends, their nation, their profession, or their name.

Hereby it is manifest, that during the time men live without a common power to keep them all in awe, they are in that condition which is called war; and such a war, as is of every man, against every man. . . .

[On "the state of nature":]

Whatsoever therefore is consequent to a time of war, where every man is enemy to every man; the same is consequent to the time wherein men live without other security, than what their own strength and their own invention shall furnish them withall. In such condition, there is no place for industry, because the fruit thereof is uncertain, and consequently no culture of the earth; no navigation, nor use of the commodities that may be imported by sea; no commodious building; no instruments of moving and removing such things as require much force; no knowledge of the face of the earth; no account of time; no arts; no letters; no society; and, which is worst of all, continual fear, and danger of violent death; and the life of man, solitary, poor, nasty, brutish, and short. . . .

The passions that incline men to peace, are fear of death; desire of such things as are necessary to commodious living; and a hope by their industry to obtain them. And reason suggesteth convenient articles of peace, upon which men may be drawn to agreement. . . .

And because the condition of man, as hath been declared in the precedent chapter, is a condition of war of everyone against everyone; in which case everyone is governed by his own reason, and there is nothing he can make use of, that may not be a help unto him, in preserving his life against his enemies; It followeth that, in such a condition, every man has a right to every thing, even to one another's body. And therefore, as long as this natural right of every man to everything endureth, there can be no security to any man, how strong or wise soever he be, of living out the time, which Nature ordinarily alloweth men to live. . . .

If there be no power erected, or not great enough for our security, every man will and may lawfully rely on his own strength and art, for caution against all other men. . . .

The only way to erect such a common power, as may be able to defend them from the invasion of foreigners, and the injuries of one another, and thereby to secure them in such sort as that by their own industry and by the fruits of the earth they may nourish themselves and live contentedly, is to confer all their power and strength upon one man, or upon one assembly of men, that may reduce all their wills, by plurality of voices, unto one will: which is as much as to say, to appoint one man, or assembly of men, to bear their person; and every one to own and acknowledge himself to be author of whatsoever he that so beareth their person shall act, or cause to be acted, in those things which concern the common peace and safety; and therein to submit their wills, every one to his will, and their judgments to his judgment. This is more than consent, or concord; it is a real unity of them all in one and the same person, made by covenant of every man with every man, in such manner as if every man should say to every man: "I authorize and give up my right of governing myself to this man, or to this assembly of men, on this condition, that thou give up thy right to him, and authorize all his actions in like manner." This done, the multitude so united in one person is called a "commonwealth," in Latin, *civitas*. This is the generation of that great "leviathan," or rather, to speak more reverently, of that "mortal god," to which we owe under the "immortal God," our peace and defense. For by this authority, given him by every particular man in the commonwealth, he hath the use of so much power and strength conferred on him that by terror thereof, he is enabled to perform the wills of them all, to peace at home, and mutual aid against their enemies abroad. And in him consisteth the essence of the commonwealth; which, to define it, is "one person, of whose acts a great multitude, by mutual covenants one with another, have made themselves every one the author, to the end he may use the strength and means of them all as he shall think expedient, for their peace and common defense."

And he that carryeth this person is called "sovereign," and said to have "sovereign power"; and every one besides, his "subject." . . .

They that have already instituted a commonwealth, being thereby bound by covenant to own the actions and judgments of one, cannot lawfully make a new covenant, amongst themselves, to be obedient to any other, in anything whatsoever, without his permission. And therefore, they that are subjects to a monarch cannot without his leave cast off monarchy, and return to the confusion of a disunited multitude; nor transfer their person from him that beareth it to another man, other assembly of men . . . [he] that already is their sovereign shall do and judge fit to be done: so that any one man dissenting, all the rest should break their covenant made to that man, which is injustice: and they have also every man given the sovereignty to him that beareth their person; and therefore if they depose him, they take from him that which is his own, and so again it is injustice. . . . And whereas some men have pretended for their disobedience to their sovereign, a new covenant, made not with men but with God; this also is unjust: for there is no covenant with God but by mediation of somebody that representeth God's person; which none doth but God's lieutenant, who hath the sovereignty under God. But this pretence of covenant with God is so evident a lie, even in the pretenders' own consciences, that it is not only an act of an unjust, but also of a vile and unmanly disposition. . . .

Consequently none of [the sovereign's] subjects, by any pretence of forfeiture, can be freed from his subjection.

READING QUESTIONS

1. How does Hobbes characterize human existence without the peace and order afforded by a ruler vested with absolute authority?
2. What is Hobbes's view of religious or divine justifications for absolute power?
3. Having placed themselves under the sovereign power of a ruler, what freedom of action do individuals have to govern their own affairs?
4. What options, according to Hobbes, do a sovereign's subjects have in the event that he abuses his power?

15-6 | JOHN LOCKE, *Second Treatise of Civil Government: Vindication for the Glorious Revolution* (1690)

John Locke (1632–1704) was, along with Thomas Hobbes, one of the two greatest English political theorists of the seventeenth century. Unlike Hobbes, however, who provided a justification for monarchical absolutism, Locke's *Second Treatise of Government*, published anonymously in 1690, argued that government is an agreement between governors and the governed. The people submit to governmental authority in return for protection of their life, liberty, and property, and the governors' fundamental task is to provide those essential protections. According to Locke, a government that failed to do so or became tyrannical lost its claim to legitimacy, and could therefore be cast off by the governed.

87. Man being born, as has been proved, with a title to perfect freedom and an uncontrolled enjoyment of all the rights and privileges of the law of Nature, equally with any other man, or number of men in the world, hath by nature a power not only to preserve his property—that is, his life, liberty and estate against the injuries and attempts of other men; but to judge of and punish the breaches of that law in others, as he is persuaded the offense deserves, even with death itself, in crimes where the heinousness of the fact, in his opinion, requires it. But because no political society can be, nor subsist, without having in itself the power to preserve the property, and in order thereunto punish the offenses of all those of that society, there, and there only is political society where every one of the members hath quitted this natural power, resigned it up into the hands of the community in all cases that exclude him not from appealing for protection to the

From John Locke, *Two Treatises on Civil Government* (London: George Routledge and Sons, 1887), pp. 234–38.

law established by it. And thus all private judgment of every particular member being excluded, the community comes to be umpire, and by understanding indifferent rules and men authorized by the community for their execution, decides all the differences that may happen between any members of that society concerning any matter of right, and punishes those offenses which any member hath committed against the society with such penalties as the law has established; whereby it is easy to discern, who are, and are not, in political society together. Those who are united into one body, and have a common established law and judicature to appeal to, with authority to decide controversies between them and punish offenders, are in civil society one with another; but those who have no such common appeal, I mean on earth, are still in the state of Nature, each being where there is no other, judge for himself and executioner; which is, as I have before showed it, the perfect state of Nature.

88. And thus the commonwealth comes by a power to set down what punishment shall belong to the several transgressions they think worthy of it, committed amongst the members of that society (which is the power of making laws) as well as it has the power to punish any injury done unto any of its members by any one that is not of it (which is the power of war and peace); and all this for the preservation of the property of all the members of that society, as far as is possible. But though every man entered into society has quitted his power to punish offenses against the law of Nature in prosecution of his own private judgment, yet with the judgment of offenses which he has given up to the legislative, in all cases where he can appeal to the magistrate, he has given up a right to the commonwealth to employ his force, for the execution of the judgments of the commonwealth whenever he shall be called to it, which, indeed, are his own judgments, they being made by himself or his representative. And herein we have the original of the legislative and executive power of civil society, which is to judge by standing laws how far offenses are to be punished when committed within the commonwealth; and also by occasional judgments founded on the present circumstances of the fact, how far injuries from without are to be vindicated; and in both these to employ all the force of all the members when there shall be need.

89. Wherever, therefore, any number of men so unite into one society as to quit every one his executive power of the law of Nature, and to resign it to the public, there and there only is a political or civil society. And this is done wherever any number of men, in the state of nature, enter into society to make one people one body politic under one supreme government; or else when any one joins himself to, and incorporates with any government already made. For hereby he authorizes the society, or which is all one, the legislative thereof, to make laws for him as the public good of the society shall require; to the execution whereof his own assistance (as to his own decrees) is due. And this puts men out of a state of Nature into that of a commonwealth, by setting up a judge on earth with authority to determine all the controversies and redress the injuries that may happen to any member of the commonwealth; which judge is the legislative or magistrates appointed by it. And wherever there are any number of men,

however associated, that have no such decisive power to appeal to, there they are still in the state of Nature.

90. And hence it is evident that absolute monarchy, which by some men is counted for the only government in the world, is indeed inconsistent with civil society, and so can be no form of civil government at all. For the end of civil society being to avoid and remedy those inconveniencies of the state of nature which necessarily follow from every man's being judge in his own case by setting up a known authority to which every one of that society may appeal upon any injury received, or controversy that may arise, and which every one of the society ought to obey. Wherever any persons are who have not such an authority to appeal to, and decide any difference between them there, those persons are still in the state of Nature. And so is every absolute prince in respect of those who are under his dominion.

91. For he being supposed to have all, both legislative and executive, power in himself alone, there is no judge to be found, no appeal lies open to any one, who may fairly and indifferently, and with authority decide, and from whence relief and redress may be expected of any injury or inconveniency that may be suffered from him, or by his order. So that such a man, however entitled, Czar, or Grand Signior, or how you please, is as much in the state of Nature, with all under his dominion, as he is with the rest of mankind. For wherever any two men are, who have no standing rule and common judge to appeal to on earth, for the determination of controversies of right betwixt them, there they are still in the state of Nature, and under all the inconveniencies of it, with only this woeful difference to the subject, or rather slave of an absolute prince. That whereas, in the ordinary state of nature, he has a liberty to judge of his right, and according to the best of his power to maintain it; but whenever his property is invaded by the will and order of his monarch, he has not only no appeal, as those in society ought to have, but as if he were degraded from the common state of rational creatures, is denied a liberty to judge of, or to defend his right, and so is exposed to all the misery and inconveniencies that a man can fear from one, who being in the unrestrained state of Nature, is yet corrupted with flattery and armed with power.

92. For he that thinks absolute power purifies men's bloods, and corrects the baseness of human nature, need read but the history of this, or any other age, to be convinced of the contrary.

READING QUESTIONS

1. What, according to Locke, distinguishes "political, or civil society" from "a state of nature"?

2. What, in Locke's opinion, led to the creation of "political, or civil society"?

3. Why does he argue that "absolute monarchy, which by some men is counted the only government in the world, is indeed inconsistent with civil society, and so can be no form of civil government at all"?

4. Why do you think Locke published this work anonymously, rather than publicly claiming credit for what is now generally regarded as one of the classics of Western political theory?

■ COMPARATIVE AND DISCUSSION QUESTIONS ■

1. What would Hobbes say of Bossuet's justification for absolute royal authority? What would Bossuet say of Hobbes's?
2. How does Hobbes's "social contract" theory differ from Locke's? How do Hobbes and Locke use "the state of nature" to further their arguments?
3. In what ways are Locke's views reflected in the English Bill of Rights?
4. What do Henry IV's and Peter the Great's edicts tell you about their attitudes toward monarchy and their roles in the lives of their subjects?

16

Toward a New Worldview
1540–1789

For the most part, medieval scholars turned to authoritative texts for information and ideas about the natural world. Placing their faith in the Bible and in the insights of ancient scholars, they forged a vision of the universe and its workings that infused classical models with Christian implications. Those models were first challenged and then overturned over the course of the sixteenth and seventeenth centuries, as direct observation and experiment combined with increasingly sophisticated mathematics to produce a revolution in the study of the natural world. This process culminated at the end of the seventeenth century in the discoveries of Isaac Newton, whose work would provide the fundamental framework for Western physics well into the twentieth century. By the eighteenth century, the spirit of this "scientific revolution" had spread to human affairs. Philosophers and scientists of the European Enlightenment, particularly in France, began to question traditional forms of social and political organization. Some thinkers rejected the legitimacy of absolutism and divine right. Others challenged the authority of the Roman Catholic Church. In the climate of the age, even absolutist monarchs saw advantages to embracing aspects of Enlightenment thought, though with varying degrees of enthusiasm and success.

16-1 | A New Model of the Solar System

NICOLAUS COPERNICUS, *On the Revolutions of the Heavenly Spheres* (1542)

There was nothing revolutionary about Polish cleric and astronomer Nicolaus Copernicus's (1473–1543) motives for developing a heliocentric (sun-centered) model of the universe. Frustrated by the cumbersome calculations and inaccuracies of the Ptolemaic model, Copernicus sought an alternative that overcame these limitations and, in his view, offered a better reflection of the perfection of God's creation. Moreover, he retained many elements of earlier systems. For example, Copernicus still imagined the stars embedded in crystalline spheres. For all the conservatism of his approach, however, Copernicus was well aware of the stir his work might produce. Fearful of the response of Church authorities, Copernicus waited to publish his findings until 1542, more than a decade after his work was complete and shortly before his death. As you read this excerpt, consider its mix of traditional and revolutionary ideas. In what ways does Copernicus seem like a medieval scholar? In what ways does he seem closer to what we think of as a scientist?

That the Universe Is Spherical

First we must remark that the universe is globe-shaped, either because that is the most perfect shape of all, needing no joint, an integral whole; or because that it is the most capacious of shapes, which is most fitting because it is to contain and preserve all things; or because the most finished parts of the universe, I mean the Sun, Moon, and stars, are observed to have that shape, or because everything tends to take on this shape, which is evident in drops of water and other liquid bodies, when they take on their natural shape. There should therefore be no doubt that this shape is assigned to the heavenly bodies.

That the Earth Is Also Spherical

The Earth is also globe-shaped, because every part of it tends towards its center. Although it is not immediately apparent that it is a perfect sphere, because the mountains project so far and the valleys are so deep, they produce very little variation in the complete roundness of the Earth. That is evident from the fact that as one moves northward from any point that pole [the North Pole] of the diurnal [daily] rotation rises little by little, while the other pole on the contrary sinks to the same extent, and several stars round the North Pole seem not to set, while some in the South no longer rise. . . .

From Nicolaus Copernicus, *De Revolutionibus Orbium Celestium,* trans. A. M. Duncan (Newton Abbot, Devonshire: David and Charles, 1976), pp. 36, 37, 40–41, 43–44, 45–46.

Whether the Earth Has a Circular Motion, and Concerning the Location of the Earth

As it has now been shown that the Earth also has the shape of a globe, I believe we must consider whether its motion too follows its shape, and what place it holds in the universe, without which it is impossible to find a reliable explanation of celestial phenomena. Among the authorities it is generally agreed that the Earth is at rest in the middle of the universe, and they regard it as inconceivable and even ridiculous to hold the opposite opinion. However, if we consider it more closely the question will be seen to be still unsettled, and so decidedly not to be despised. For every apparent change in respect of position is due to motion of the object observed, or of the observer, or indeed to an unequal change of both. (Between objects which move equally in the same direction no motion is perceived, I mean between that which is observed and the observer.) Now the Earth is the point from which the rotation of the heavens is observed, and brought into our view. If therefore some motion is imputed to the Earth, the same motion will appear in all that is external to the Earth, but in the opposite direction, as if it were passing by. The first example of this is the diurnal rotation. This seems to whirl round the whole universe, except the Earth and the things on it. But if you grant that the heaven has no part in this motion, but that the Earth revolves from west to east, as far as the apparent rising and setting of the Sun, Moon, and stars is concerned, if you consider the point seriously, you will find that this is the way of it. And as the heaven is that which contains and cloaks all things, where everything has its place, it is not at once apparent why motion is attributed to that which is contained rather than to the container, to that which is located rather than that which locates it. . . . If this assumption is made there follows another and no lesser problem about the position of the Earth, although almost everyone admits and believes the Earth to be the center of the universe. For if one argues that the Earth does not occupy the center or middle of the universe, not claiming that its distance is great enough to be comparable with the sphere of the fixed stars, but that it is appreciable and significant compared with the orbits of the Sun and other stars,[1] and believing that on this account their motion seems to be variable, as if they were regular with respect to [i.e., revolved around] some center other than the center of the Earth, he would perhaps be able to put forward a not unreasonable account of the apparently variable motion. For the fact that the wandering stars are observed to be sometimes nearer to the Earth and sometimes further away from it necessarily shows that the center of the Earth is not the center of their orbits. It is also undecided whether the Earth veers toward them and away from them or they towards and away from the Earth. It would also not be

---

[1]**not claiming . . . other stars**: Copernicus is arguing here that the diameter of the earth's orbit is insignificant compared to the distance of the earth from the "fixed stars," which he, like his contemporaries, believed to be embedded in an invisible crystalline sphere, but is comparable to that of the "wandering stars," i.e., the visible planets.

surprising if in addition to this daily revolution another motion should be supposed for the Earth. Indeed that the Earth revolves, wanders with several motions, and is one of the stars [i.e., planets] is said to have been the opinion of Philolaus the Pythagorean,[2] no mean mathematician. . . .

Refutation of the Arguments Quoted, and Their Insufficiency[3]

From this and similar arguments, then, they say that the Earth is at rest in the middle of the universe, and that such is undoubtedly the state of affairs. Yet if anyone should hold the opinion that the Earth revolves, he will surely assert that its motion is natural, not violent. What is natural produces contrary effects to what is violent. For objects to which force or impulse is applied must necessarily be destroyed and cannot long subsist; but objects which exist naturally are in their proper state, and continue in their perfect form. There is therefore no need for Ptolemy to fear the scattering of the Earth and of all terrestrial objects in a revolution brought about through the workings of nature, which is far different from artifice, or what can be achieved by human abilities. Further, why is not the same question raised even more strongly about the universe, the motion of which must be much swifter in proportion as the heaven is greater than the Earth? Or has heaven become so immense, because it is drawn outwards from the middle by a motion of ineffable strength [i.e., centrifugal force], that it would collapse if it were not at rest? Certainly if this reasoning were to be accepted, the magnitude of the heaven will rise to infinity. For in proportion it is thrown higher by the impulse of the motion, so the motion will be swifter, on account of the continual increase in the circumference which it must traverse in the space of twenty-four hours; and on the other hand as the motion increased, so would the immensity of the heaven. So the velocity would increase the magnitude, and the magnitude the velocity, to infinity. But according to that axiom in physics, that what is infinite cannot be traversed, nor moved by any means, the heaven will necessarily be at rest. But they say that outside the heaven there is no body, no place, no empty space, in fact nothing whatsoever, and therefore there is nothing to which the heaven can go out. In that case it is remarkable indeed if something can be restrained by nothing. But if the heaven is infinite, and finite only in its hollow interior, perhaps it will be more clearly proved that there is nothing outside the heaven, since every single thing will be within, whatever amount of space it occupies, but the heaven will remain immovable. For the strongest argument by which they try to establish that the universe is finite, is its motion. Therefore let us leave the question whether the universe is finite or infinite for the natural philosophers[4] to

---

[2]**Philolaus the Pythagorean**: Greek mathematician and philosopher (ca. 470–385 B.C.E.).

[3]**the arguments quoted . . . insufficiency**: Arguments by ancient authorities, maintaining that "the Earth was at rest in the middle of the universe as if it was the center."

[4]**natural philosophers**: Scientists.

argue. What we do know for certain is that the Earth is limited by its poles and bounded by a globular surface. . . .

Surely Aristotle's division of simple motion into three types, away from the middle, towards the middle, and round the middle, will be regarded merely as an intellectual division; just as we distinguish between a line, a point, and a surface, although one cannot exist without the other, and none of them without a body. A further point is that immobility is considered a more noble and divine state than that of change and instability, which is for that reason more appropriate to the Earth than to the universe. I also add that it would seem rather absurd to ascribe motion to that which contains and locates, and not rather to that which is contained and located, that is the Earth. Lastly, since it is evident that the wandering stars are sometimes nearer, sometimes further from the Earth, this will also be an example of motion of a single body which is both round the middle, by which they mean the center, away from the middle, and towards it. Motion round the midpoint must therefore be accepted more generally, and as satisfactory, provided that each motion is motion about its own midpoint. You will see then that from all these arguments the mobility of the Earth is more probable than its immobility, especially in the daily revolution, as that is particularly fitting for the Earth.

READING QUESTIONS

1. What justification does Copernicus offer for his opening premise that the universe is spherical? What is his justification for the premise that the earth, too, is spherical?

2. Why does Copernicus accuse Ptolemy of logical inconsistency?

3. On what grounds does Copernicus argue that the heavens (or universe) are of finite extent? Does his logic on this score convince you? Why or why not?

4. Why does Copernicus argue that the earth, like the other planets, is in motion? Why did scientists before him accept the idea that the earth was stationary?

16-2 | A Defense of Science

FRANCIS BACON, *On Superstition and the Virtue of Science* (1620)

Trained as a lawyer, Sir Francis Bacon (1561–1626) served in the court of the English king James I (r. 1603–1625) and conducted numerous experiments designed to explain the natural world. Bacon's most important contribution was to the scientific method itself. Bacon was a

From Francis Bacon, "Aphorisms Concerning the Interpretation of Nature and the Kingdom of Man," in *The Works of Francis Bacon: Popular Edition, Based Upon the Complete Edition of Spedding, Ellis, and Heath*, vol. 1 (New York: Hurd and Houghton, 1877), pp. 70–71, 124–126.

proponent of inductive reasoning, the arrival at general principles though the collection and analysis of empirical evidence. He contrasted his method with deductive reasoning, the use of general principles to interpret particular events and phenomena. In this excerpt from his writing, Bacon laid out his general method and sought to defend it against critics who saw in his work a threat to religion.

There is no soundness in our notions, whether logical or physical. Substance, quality, action, passion, essence itself are not sound notions; much less are heavy, light, dense, rare, moist, dry, generation, corruption, attraction, repulsion, element, matter, form, and the like; but all are fantastical and ill-defined. . . .

The discoveries which have hitherto been made in the sciences are such as lie close to vulgar notions, scarcely beneath the surface. In order to penetrate into the inner and further recesses of nature, it is necessary that both notions and axioms [be] derived from things by a more sure and guarded way, and that a method of intellectual operation be introduced altogether better and more certain. . . .

There are and can be only two ways of searching into and discovering truth. The one flies from the senses and particulars to the most general axioms, and from these principles, the truth of which it takes for settled and immovable, proceeds to judgment and the discovery of middle axioms. And this way is now in fashion. The other derives axioms from the senses and particulars, rising by a gradual and unbroken ascent, so that it arrives at the most general axioms last of all. This is the true way, but as yet untried. . . .

It is not to be forgotten that in every age natural philosophy has had a troublesome adversary and hard to deal with—namely, superstition and the blind and immoderate zeal of religion. For we see among the Greeks that those who first proposed to man's uninitiated ears the natural causes for thunder and for storms were thereupon found guilty of impiety. Nor was much more forbearance shown by some of the ancient fathers of the Christian Church to those who, on most convincing grounds (such as no one in his senses would now think of contradicting), maintained that the earth was round and, of consequence, asserted the existence of the antipodes.[1]

Moreover, as things now are, to discourse of nature is made harder and more perilous by the summaries and systems of the schoolmen; who, having reduced theology into regular order as well as they were able, and fashioned it into the shape of an art, ended in incorporating the contentious and thorny philosophy of Aristotle, more than was fit, with the body of religion. . . .

Lastly . . . some are weakly afraid lest a deeper search into nature should transgress the permitted limits of sobermindedness; wrongfully wresting and

---

[1]**maintained that the earth was round . . . antipodes**: Bacon refers to an ancient debate relating to the shape of the earth; if the earth was round, some Greek theorists argued, then there would be lands (or ocean) on the side of the world directly opposite the one they inhabited. The debate was largely resolved by the fifteenth-century voyages of European explorers, culminating in the 1492 discovery of the New World, when the theorists were proven correct.

transferring what is said in Holy Writ [the Christian Bible] against those who pry into sacred mysteries to the hidden things of nature, which are barred by no prohibition. Others, with more subtlety, surmise and reflect that if secondary causes are unknown everything can be more readily referred to the divine hand and rod,—a point in which they think religion greatly concerned; which is, in fact, nothing else but to seek to gratify God with a lie. Others fear from past example that movements and changes in philosophy will end in assaults on religion; and others again appear apprehensive that in the investigation of nature something may be found to subvert, or at least shake, the authority of religion, especially with the unlearned. But these two last fears seem to me to savor utterly of carnal wisdom; as if men in the recesses and secret thoughts of their hearts doubted and distrusted the strength of religion, and the empire of faith over the senses, and therefore feared that the investigation of truth in nature might be dangerous to them. But if the matter be truly considered, natural philosophy is, after the word of God, at once the surest medicine against superstition and the most approved nourishment for faith; and therefore she is rightly given to religion as her most faithful handmaid, since the one displays the will of God, the other his power.

READING QUESTIONS

1. In Bacon's view, what was, and had always been, the most important adversary of the natural philosopher?

2. Why, according to Bacon, did some observers see natural philosophy as a threat to religion? How did Bacon counter this criticism?

3. What do Bacon's assertions about natural philosophy suggest about the larger relationship between science and faith in the seventeenth century?

SOURCES IN CONVERSATION

Monarchical Power and Responsibility

Enlightenment reformers offered critiques of almost all aspects of European society, from education, to religion, to economics. For the most part, however, *philosophes* were not revolutionaries. In the determined application of rational thought, they saw a tool for the improvement of human life, not a weapon for destroying all that had come before. Thus, most *philosophes* supported monarchical government, the European norm in the eighteenth century. Certainly, they saw countless ways in which such governments could be made more efficient, less arbitrary, and more productive of the common good. They did not, however, want to do away with kings.

16-3 | FREDERICK THE GREAT, *Essay on the Forms of Government* (ca. 1740)

Frederick II of Prussia (r. 1740–1786) worked hard to associate himself with the Enlightenment. He was a patron of the arts and learning, modernized Prussia's bureaucracy and educational system in accordance with Enlightenment principles, abolished torture and corporal punishment, and favored religious tolerance. He also corresponded with French philosophe Jean d'Alembert and had a long, if at times stormy, friendship with Voltaire. For all of this, he was, nonetheless, a staunch advocate of absolute monarchy whose fundamental goal was to strengthen the Prussian state and enhance its military might. Enlightenment principles were only of interest to him insofar as they advanced this agenda. As you read this excerpt from Frederick's writings, consider what it tells you about Frederick's vision of good government. In what ways, if any, did Frederick depart from traditional ideas of kingship?

Princes, sovereigns, and king have not been given supreme authority in order to live in luxurious self-indulgence and debauchery. They have not been elevated by their fellow-men to enable them to strut about and to insult with their pride the simple-mannered, the poor, and the suffering. They have not been placed at the head of the State to keep around themselves a crowd of idle loafers whose uselessness drives them towards vice. The bad administration which may be found in monarchies springs from many different causes, but their principal cause lies in the character of the sovereign. A ruler addicted to women will become a tool of his mistresses and favorites, and these will abuse their power and commit wrongs of every kind, will protect vice, sell offices, and perpetrate every infamy. . . .

The sovereign is the representative of his State. He and his people form a single body. Ruler and ruled can be happy only if they are firmly united. The sovereign stands to his people in the same relation in which the head stands to the body. He must use his eyes and his brain for the whole community, and act on its behalf to the common advantage. If we wish to elevate monarchical above republican government, the duty of sovereigns is clear. They must be active, hard-working, upright and honest, and concentrate all their strength upon filling their office worthily. That is my idea of the duties of sovereigns.

A sovereign must possess an exact and detailed knowledge of the strong and of the weak points of his country. He must be thoroughly acquainted with its resources, the character of the people, and the national commerce. . . .

Rulers should always remind themselves that they are men like the least of their subjects. The sovereign is the foremost judge, general, financier, and minister of his country, not merely for the sake of his prestige. Therefore, he should perform with care the duties connected with these offices. He is merely the principal servant of the State. Hence, he must act with honesty, wisdom, and complete disinterestedness in such a way that he can render an account of his

From *The Foundations of Germany*, trans. J. Ellis Barker (New York: E. P. Dutton, 1916), pp. 22–23.

stewardship to the citizens at any moment. Consequently, he is guilty if he wastes the money of the people, the taxes which they have paid, in luxury, pomp, and debauchery. He who should improve the morals of the people, be the guardian of the law, and improve their education should not pervert them by his bad example.

READING QUESTIONS

1. In what ways do you think Enlightenment principles informed Frederick's views on the duties of rulers?

2. How did traditional models of kingship inform Frederick's views? How did he modify such models to accommodate Enlightenment ideas?

3. What limits, if any, did Frederick place on the power and authority of the king? In what ways, if any, did Frederick believe monarchs were accountable to their subjects?

16-4 | CHARLES DE SECONDAT, BARON DE MONTESQUIEU, From *The Spirit of Laws: On the Separation of Governmental Powers* (1748)

The writings of Frenchman Charles de Secondat (1689–1755), better known as Baron Montesquieu (mahn-tuhs-KYOO), were composed as the spirit of the Enlightenment swept over Europe in the early eighteenth century. Montesquieu's political writings, excerpted here, were concerned with the makeup of the state and the effect of a government on the lives of those it ruled. In this excerpt from *The Spirit of Laws*, Montesquieu argued for the importance of the separation of powers, or the assignment of executive, legislative, and judicial powers to different individuals or political bodies. As you read, consider the implications for political reform. Why, despite Montesquieu's avowed support of European monarchies, might monarchs have seen his work as a threat?

In every government there are three sorts of power: the legislative; the executive in respect to things dependent on the law of nations; and the executive in regard to matters that depend on the civil law.

By virtue of the first, the prince or magistrate enacts temporary or perpetual laws, and amends or abrogates those that have been already enacted. By the second, he makes peace or war, sends or receives embassies, establishes the public security, and provides against invasions. By the third, he punishes criminals, or determines the disputes that arise between individuals. The latter we shall call the judiciary power, and the other simply the executive power of the state.

From Baron de Montesquieu, *The Spirit of Laws*, trans. T. Nugent (New York: Hafner, 1949), pp. 151–152.

The political liberty of the subject is a tranquility of mind arising from the opinion each person has of his safety. In order to have this liberty, it is requisite the government be so constituted as one man need not be afraid of another.

When the legislative and executive powers are united in the same person, or in the same body of magistrates, there can be no liberty; because apprehensions may arise, lest the same monarch or senate should enact tyrannical laws, to execute them in a tyrannical manner.

Again, there is no liberty, if the judiciary power be not separated from the legislative and executive. Were it joined with the legislative, the life and liberty of the subject would be exposed to arbitrary control; for the judge would be then the legislator. Were it joined to the executive power, the judge might behave with violence and oppression.

There would be an end of everything, were the same man or the same body, whether of the nobles or of the people, to exercise those three powers, that of enacting laws, that of executing the public resolutions, and of trying the causes of individuals.

Most kingdoms in Europe enjoy a moderate government because the prince who is invested with the two first powers leaves the third to his subjects. In Turkey, where these three powers are united in the Sultan's person, the subjects groan under the most dreadful oppression.

In the republics of Italy, where these three powers are united, there is less liberty than in our monarchies. Hence their government is obliged to have recourse to as violent methods for its support as even that of the Turks; witness the state inquisitors, and the lion's mouth into which every informer may at all hours throw his written accusations.

What a situation must the poor subject be in, under those republics! The same body of magistrates are possessed, as executors of the laws, of the whole power they have given themselves in quality of legislators. They may plunder the state by their general determinations; and as they have likewise the judiciary power in their hands, every private citizen may be ruined by their particular decisions.

The whole power is here united in one body; and though there is no external pomp that indicates a despotic sway, yet the people feel the effects of it every moment.

Hence it is that many of the princes of Europe, whose aim has been levelled at arbitrary power, have constantly set out with uniting in their own persons, all the branches of magistracy, and all the great offices of state.

READING QUESTIONS

1. How did Montesquieu define liberty? Why did he believe that a separation of powers was crucial to the protection of liberty?

2. In Montesquieu's view, under what circumstances could liberty be obtained under a monarchy? Under what circumstances could a republic produce tyranny?

3. How might opponents of absolute monarchy have used Montesquieu's ideas to support their position?

16-5 | JEAN-JACQUES ROUSSEAU, *The Social Contract: On Popular Sovereignty and the General Will* (1762)

Jean-Jacques Rousseau (1712–1778) was born in Swiss Geneva—not France—and came from the common, not the aristocratic, class. He left Geneva at the age of sixteen; after spending years living on charity and the income from odd jobs, he traveled to Paris seeking to make a name for himself. Rousseau's poverty and origins, combined with his prickly personality, made him something of an outsider in Enlightenment social circles. His 1762 work on political theory, *The Social Contract*, was part of an extended argument in the seventeenth and eighteenth centuries over the sources of governmental power and the conditions, if any, under which one form of government could be replaced with another.

Since no man has any natural authority over his fellowmen, and since force is not the source of right, conventions remain as the basis of all lawful authority among men. [Book I, Chapter 4].

Now, as men cannot create any new forces, but only combine and direct those that exist, they have no other means of self-preservation than to form by aggregation a sum of forces which may overcome the resistance, to put them in action by a single motive power, and to make them work in concert.

This sum of forces can be produced only by the combination of many; but the strength and freedom of each man being the chief instruments of his preservation, how can he pledge them without injuring himself, and without neglecting the cares which he owes to himself? This difficulty, applied to my subject, may be expressed in these terms.

"To find a form of association which may defend and protect with the whole force of the community the person and property of every associate, and by means of which each, coalescing with all, may nevertheless obey only himself, and remain as free as before." Such is the fundamental problem of which the social contract furnishes the solution. . . .

If then we set aside what is not of the essence of the social contract, we shall find that it is reducible to the following terms: "Each of us puts in common his person and his whole power under the supreme direction of the general will, and in return we receive every member as an indivisible part of the whole." [Book I, Chapter 6].

But the body politic or sovereign, deriving its existence only from the contract, can never bind itself, even to others, in anything that derogates from the

From Jean-Jacques Rousseau, *The Social Contract*, in *Translations and Reprints from the Original Sources of European History* (Philadelphia: University of Pennsylvania Press, 1898), 5/1:14–16.

original act, such as alienation of some portion of itself, or submission to another sovereign. To violate the act by which it exists would be to annihilate itself, and what is nothing produces nothing. [Book I, Chapter 7].

It follows from what precedes, that the general will is always right and always tends to the public advantage; but it does not follow that the resolutions of the people have always the same rectitude. Men always desire their own good, but do not always discern it; the people are never corrupted, though often deceived, and it is only then that they seem to will what is evil. [Book II, Chapter 3].

The public force, then, requires a suitable agent to concentrate it and put it in action according to the directions of the general will, to serve as a means of communication between the state and the sovereign, to effect in some manner in the public person what the union of soul and body effects in a man. This is, in the State, the function of government, improperly confounded with the sovereign of which it is only the minister.

What, then, is the government? An intermediate body established between the subjects and the sovereign for their mutual correspondence, charged with the execution of the laws and with the maintenance of liberty both civil and political. [Book III, Chapter 1].

It is not sufficient that the assembled people should have once fixed the constitution of the state by giving their sanction to a body of laws; it is not sufficient that they should have established a perpetual government, or that they should have once for all provided for the election of magistrates. Besides the extraordinary assemblies which unforeseen events may require, it is necessary that there should be fixed and periodical ones which nothing can abolish or prorogue; so that, on the appointed day, the people are rightfully convoked by the law, without needing for that purpose any formal summons. [Book III, Chapter 13].

So soon as the people are lawfully assembled as a sovereign body, the whole jurisdiction of the government ceases, the executive power is suspended, and the person of the meanest citizen is as sacred and inviolable as that of the first magistrate, because where the represented are, there is no longer any representative. [Book III, Chapter 14].

These assemblies, which have as their object the maintenance of the social treaty, ought always to be opened with two propositions, which no one should be able to suppress, and which should pass separately by vote. The first: "Whether it pleases the sovereign to maintain the present form of government." The second: "Whether it pleases the people to leave the administration to those at present entrusted with it."

I presuppose here what I believe I have proved, viz., that there is in the State no fundamental law which cannot be revoked, not even this social compact; for if all the citizens assembled in order to break the compact by a solemn agreement, no one can doubt that it could be quite legitimately broken. [Book III, Chapter 18].

READING QUESTIONS

1. What might Rousseau mean when he says "force is not the source of right"?

2. From where does Rousseau see a government deriving its legitimacy, and on what basis?

3. How does Rousseau's concept of the "general will" relate to the concept of majority rule in a representative government?

4. In what way might the concept of dissolving an unrepresentative government be a dangerous one, particularly in a world of hereditary monarchs?

16-6 | A Philosophe Argues for Religious Toleration

VOLTAIRE, *A Treatise on Toleration* (1763)

François-Marie Arouet (1694–1778), who used the pen name Voltaire, was arguably the greatest of the Enlightenment philosophes. He was an astonishingly prolific author whose output amounted to hundreds of books and pamphlets. In some respects he was unrepresentative of the general currents of Enlightenment thought, being skeptical of both human rationality and human progress. Like virtually all the philosophes, however, he was an unceasing critic of religious dogma and intolerance. The following excerpts from Voltaire's *Treatise on Toleration* (1763) present the essential components of his argument in favor of religious toleration. As you read, consider what core assumptions form the foundation of his position. How did Voltaire's beliefs about the fundamental equality of human beings and the limits of human knowledge shape his views on religion?

Chapter XXI. Universal Toleration

It does not require any great art or studied eloquence, to prove, that Christians should tolerate each other. I shall go further, and say, that we should regard all men as our brethren. What! a Turk my brother? a Chinese my brother? a Jew? a Siamese? my brother? Yes, without doubt; for are we not all children of the same father, and creatures of the same God?

But these people despise us and treat us as idolaters! It may be so; but I shall only tell them, they are to blame. It seems to me, I should stagger the

---

From Voltaire, *A Treatise on Toleration; The Ignorant Philosopher; and A Commentary on the Marquis of Becaria's [sic] Treatise on Crimes and Punishments,* trans. David Williams (London: Fielding and Walker, 1779), pp. 118–123.

haughty obstinacy of an Iman,[1] or a Talapoin,[2] if I spoke to them in the following manner:

This little globe, which is but a point, rolls in universal space, in the same manner as other globes, and we are lost in the immensity. Man, a being about five feet in height, is assuredly a thing of no great importance in the creation. One of those beings, called men, and who are hardly perceptible, says to some of his neighbors in Arabia or in the country of the Cafres:[3] "Attend to what I say, for the God of all these worlds has enlightened me. There are about nine hundred millions of little ants, such as we are, on this earth, but my ant-hill alone is [in] the care of God, all the rest have been hateful to him from [i.e., for] all eternity; we only shall be happy; all others will be eternally wretched."

They would stop me, and ask, who is this madman, who utters such folly? I should be obliged to answer each of them, It is you. I might then take occasion to meliorate their dispositions into something like humanity; but that I should find difficult.

I will now address myself to Christians; and venture to say to a Dominican,[4] who is an inquisitor, "My brother, you know, that every province of Italy has its jargon; that they do not speak at Venice and Bergamo as they do at Florence. The Academy de la Crusca[5] has fixed the general disposition and construction of the language; its dictionary is a rule from which no deviations are allowed; and the grammar of Buon mattei's[6] is an infallible guide, which must be followed. But do you think that the consul, president of the Academy, or in his absence, Buon mattei, could have the conscience, to order the tongues of all the Venetians and Bergamese to be cut out, who should persist in their provincial dialects?"

The inquisitor would answer me: "The cases are very different. The question here is the salvation of your soul; it is for your good, that the court of inquisition ordains, that you should be seized, on the deposition of a single person, though he be infamous, and in the hands of justice; that you have no advocate[7] to plead for you; that the very name of your accuser should be unknown to you; that the inquisitor should promise you mercy, and afterwards condemn you; that he apply five different kinds of torture to you, and that afterwards you should be whipt [i.e., whipped] or sent to the galleys, or burnt [at the stake] as a spectacle in

---

[1]**Iman**: Imam; a Muslim religious leader.

[2]**Talapoin**: Buddhist priest or monk.

[3]**Cafres**: Kaffirs; South Africa.

[4]**Dominican**: The Dominicans were a Roman Catholic religious order who, as Voltaire suggests, conducted the Inquisition.

[5]**Academy de la Crusca**: Accademia della Crusca; an Italian learned society founded in 1582. Its members were chiefly linguists and philologists. In 1612 it sponsored publication of a dictionary of the Italian language.

[6]**Buon mattei**: Benedetto Buommattei (1581–1647), also rendered as *Boum mattei* and *Buonmattei*; Florentine lexicographer, author of *Della Lingua Toscana*.

[7]**advocate**: Lawyer.

a religious ceremony.[8] Father Ivonet, [and] Doctor[s] Cuchalon, Zarchinus, Campegius, Royas, Telinus, Gomarus, Diabarus, and Gemelinus[9] lay down these things as laws, and this pious practice must not be disputed. "I would take the liberty to answer, "My brother, perhaps you are right; I am convinced of the good you wish to do me; but, without all this, is it not possible to be saved?"

It is true that these absurd horrors do not always deform the face of the earth; but they have been very frequent; and we might collect materials to compose a volume on these practices, much larger than the gospels which condemn them. It is not only cruel to persecute in this short life those who do not think as we do, but it is audacious to pronounce their eternal damnation. It seems to me, that it little becomes the atoms of a moment [i.e., such insignificant, ephemeral creatures], such as we are, thus to anticipate the decrees of the Creator. I am very far from opposing that opinion, "that out of [i.e., outside] the church there is no salvation." I respect it, as well as everything taught by the church: but, in truth, are we acquainted with all the ways of God, and the whole extent of his mercy? Is it not permitted that we should hope in him, as well as fear him? Is it not sufficient that we are faithful to the church? Is it necessary that every individual should usurp the power of the Deity, and decide, before him, the eternal lot of all mankind?

When we wear mourning for a king of Sweden, Denmark, England, or Prussia, do we say that we mourn for a reprobate who will burn eternally in hell? There are in Europe forty millions of inhabitants, who are not [members] of the Church of Rome; shall we say to each of them, "Sir, as you are to be infallibly damned, I would neither eat, deal, or converse with you."

Is it to be supposed, that an ambassador of France, presented to the Grand Seignior,[10] would say to himself, His highness will be burnt to all eternity, because he has submitted to circumcision? If he really thought that the Grand Seignior was a mortal enemy to God, and the object of his vengeance, could he have spoken to him? Should he have been sent to him? With whom could we have dealings in trade? What duty of civil life could we ever fulfill, if we were in fact possessed with the idea, that we were conversing with persons eternally reprobated?

O ye followers of a merciful God! if you have cruel hearts. If, in adoring him, whose whole law consists in these words, "Love God and your neighbor," you have encumbered that pure and holy law with sophisms, and incomprehensible disputes! If you have lighted the fires of discord, sometimes for a new word, sometimes for a letter of the alphabet! If you have annexed eternal torments to the omission of some words, or some ceremonies, which other people cannot be [i.e., are not] acquainted with—I must say, while shedding tears for mankind: "Transport yourselves with me to that day, in which all men will be judged, and when God will render to every one according to his works."

---

[8]Here Voltaire inserted a footnote instructing his readers to "See that excellent book, intitled [sic], *The Manual of the Inquisition.*"

[9]**Father Ivonet, . . . Gemelinus**: Roman Catholic theologians.

[10]**Grand Seignior**: Grand Signeur; the Ottoman Sultan.

"I see all the dead, of past and present ages, appearing in his presence. Are you very sure that our Creator and Father will say to the wise and virtuous Confucius, to the legislator Solon, to Pythagoras, Zaleucus, Socrates, Plato, the divine Antonini, the good Trajan, to Titus the delight of mankind, to Epictetus,[11] and to many others who have been the models of human nature: Go, monsters! Let your punishments be as eternal as my being!—and you, my well-beloved, Jean Châtel, Ravaillac, Damiens, Cartouche,[12] &c. who have died according to the forms which are enjoined, sit at my right hand and partake of my dominion, and of my felicity!"

You shrink with horror at these words; and after they have escaped me, I have nothing more to say to you.

Chapter XXII. Prayer to God

I no longer then look up to men; it is to thee, the God of all beings, of all worlds, and of all ages, I address myself—If weak creatures, lost in immensity and imperceptible to the rest of the universe, may dare to ask any thing of thee, who hast given [us] all things, and whose decrees are immutable and eternal! Deign to regard with pity the errors inseparable from our nature; let not these errors prove our calamities! Thou hast not given us hearts to hate, and hands to destroy each other; dispose us to mutual assistance, in supporting the burden of a painful and transitory life! Let the little differences in the garments which cover our frail bodies; in all our imperfect languages, in our ridiculous customs, our imperfect laws, our idle opinions, in our ranks and conditions, so unequal in our eyes, and so equal in thine: let all those little shades which distinguish the atoms called *men*, be no more signals of hatred and persecution! Let those who light tapers [i.e., candles] at noon-day, to glorify thee—bear with those who content themselves with the light of thy sun! Let not those who throw over their garments a white surplice, while they say it is the duty of men to love thee, hate those who say the same thing in a black woolen cloak! Let it be equal, to adore thee in a jargon formed from an ancient, or from a modern language! May those whose

---

[11]**Confucius, Solon, . . . Titus, Epictetus**: Confucius (551–479 B.C.E.), Chinese philosopher; Solon (638–558 B.C.E.), Athenian statesman and lawgiver; Pythagoras (ca. 570–495 B.C.E.), Greek philosopher, theologian, and mathematician; Zaleucus, (seventh century B.C.E.), Greek lawgiver; Socrates, (ca. 469–399 B.C.E.), Greek philosopher; Plato (428–348 B.C.E.), Greek philosopher and mathematician; Antoninus Pius (r. 138–161), Roman emperor, and Marcus Aurelius Antoninus (r. 161–180), Roman emperor and Stoic philosopher; Trajan (r. 98–117), Roman emperor; Titus Pomponius Atticus (ca. 112–ca. 35 B.C.E.), Roman editor and man of letters; Epictetus (55–135), Greek Stoic philosopher.

[12]**Jean Châtel, Ravaillac, Damiens, Cartouche**: Jean Châtel (1575–1594), tortured and executed for attempting to assassinate Henry IV of France; François Ravaillac (1578–1610), tortured and drawn and quartered for assassinating Henry IV of France; Robert-François Damiens (1715–1757), tortured and drawn and quartered for attempting to assassinate Louis XV of France; Louis Dominique Bourguignon, known as Cartouche (1693–1721), French highwayman tortured to death.

vestments are dipped in scarlet, or in purple who domineer over a small parcel of the small heap of the dirt and mud of this world; and those who possess a few round fragments of a certain metal, enjoy without pride, what they call grandeur and riches; and may others regard them without envy: for thou knowest, there is nothing in these things to inspire envy or pride!

May all men remember that they are brethren! May they regard in horror tyranny, the tyranny exercised over the mind, as they do rapine, which carries away by force the fruits of peaceable labor and industry! If the scourges of war be inevitable, let us not hate and destroy each other in the bosom of peace; let us employ the instant of our existence to praise, in a thousand different languages, from Siam to California, thy goodness which hath granted us that instant!

READING QUESTIONS

1. In Voltaire's view, what important differences, if any, exist between individual human beings? Between different human societies? How did Voltaire's answers to these questions shape his view of religion?

2. What does Voltaire's argument in favor of religious toleration tell you about his beliefs about the limits of human understanding?

3. Do you find Voltaire's argument in favor of universal religious toleration persuasive? Why or why not?

■ COMPARATIVE AND DISCUSSION QUESTIONS ■

1. Nicolaus Copernicus and Francis Bacon were separated by a lifetime. (Copernicus died almost twenty years before Bacon was born.) What similarities do you note between their modes of thinking? In what ways did they differ?

2. What differences do you note between Montesquieu's and Rousseau's theories about the nature of government and how it ought to interact with its citizens? Where do they seem to be in agreement?

3. Frederick the Great ruled a state in which "the legislative and executive powers [were] united in the same person." What would Montesquieu say to such an arrangement? How do you think Frederick would reply to Montesquieu's charge that under those conditions, "there can be no liberty"?

4. How did the new vision of the universe created by participants in the Scientific Revolution shape Voltaire's view of human beings and their societies?

5. What would Frederick think of Bossuet's divine-right monarchical theory (Document 15-2), and why? How would Rousseau respond to Frederick's and Bossuet's views on the monarchy?

The Expansion of Europe
1650–1800

European overseas expansion in the early modern era (ca. 1500–1800) had profound social and economic consequences, both for Europe and for the rest of the world. European expansion accelerated the integration of the world's regional economies, changed the global balance of wealth and power, and led to the movement, both voluntary and forced, of vast numbers of people from one part of the world to another. It also led to the first true world wars, as competition for colonies and profits around the world fueled a prolonged imperial conflict between France and Great Britain. The two rivals fought over North America, the Caribbean sugar islands, control of the Atlantic slave trade, and trade with India. The eventual outcome was the establishment of British rule over most of North America and much of India. The documents included in this chapter explore early modern efforts to describe and understand the dynamic global economy that emerged during this period. As you examine them, think about the ways in which European expansion changed both how Europeans lived and how they saw themselves and their place in the world.

17-1 | The Domestic Economy
The Guild System in Germany (1704–1719)

While overseas expansion produced considerable economic change within Europe in the early modern period, most European manufacturing remained guild based for much of the era. The images included below demonstrate an important fact about the early modern guild system. While, with few exceptions, only male heads of a household were guild members, the family

From Franciscus Philippus Florinus, *Oeconomus prudens et legalis, oder Allgemeiner Klug- und Rechts-verständiger Haus-Vatter* (Nuremberg, Frankfurt, and Leipzig: Christoph Riegel, 1704–1719), pp. 528, 1191.

was the fundamental unit of the early modern economy, with wives, children, and servants all participating in the family's economic activity.

The first image depicts bakers at work; the male in the background is kneading dough, the woman in the center is adding water to the dough, and the woman on the left is hauling a basket containing baked loaves. The oven is visible to the left, and loaves line the shelves behind. The second image shows basket makers, where again, both sexes are depicted at work at similar tasks. The woman in the background to the left appears to be churning butter.

READING QUESTIONS

1. What do these illustrations suggest about the sexual division of labor in preindustrial households?

2. Judging by these pictures, what sorts of limitations might be inherent in the guild system of production?

17-2 | Defining and Defending Mercantilism

THOMAS MUN, *England's Treasure by Foreign Trade* (1664)

The overseas trade and colonization policies adopted by early modern European countries were shaped, to a considerable degree, by the economic theory known as mercantilism. Mercantilists saw global wealth as finite and measured its movement from one nation to another exclusively in reference to the balance of trade. Since new wealth could not be created, one nation's gain was always another nation's loss. Thus, in the mercantilist view, the goal of government economic policy should be to maximize exports while minimizing imports. This goal had implications that went far beyond trade policy itself. Mercantilist governments attempted to stimulate economic activities at home that would produce goods with ready foreign markets. At the same time, they sought to acquire colonies abroad which would eliminate the need to purchase raw materials from foreign competitors. In the excerpt below, Thomas Mun (1571–1641), an influential English merchant and economic theorist, laid out the basic premise of mercantilism. As you read it, think about the kinds of policies that might follow from Mun's assumptions.

Although a Kingdom may be enriched by gifts received, or by purchase taken from some other Nations, yet these are things uncertain and of small consideration when they happen. The ordinary means therefore to encrease our wealth and treasure is by *Foreign Trade*, wherein we must ever observe this rule; to sell more to strangers yearly than we consume of theirs in value. For suppose that when this Kingdom is plentifully served with the Cloth, Lead, Tinn, Iron, Fish and other native commodities, we do yearly export the overplus to foreign Countries to the value of twenty two hundred thousand pounds; by which means we are enabled beyond the Seas to buy and bring in foreign wares for our use and Consumptions, to the value of twenty hundred thousand pounds; By this order duly kept in our trading, we may rest assured that the Kingdom shall be enriched yearly two hundred thousand pounds, which must be brought to us in so much Treasure; because that part of our stock which is not returned to us in wares must necessarily be brought home in treasure.

From Thomas Mun, *England's Treasure by Foreign Trade* (Cambridge, U.K.: Economic History Society, 1664), pp. 5–6.

For in this case it cometh to pass in the stock of a Kingdom, as in the estate of a private man; who is supposed to have one thousand pounds yearly revenue and two thousand pounds of ready money in his Chest. If such a man through excess shall spend one thousand five hundred pounds *per annum*, all his ready money will be gone in four years; and in the like time his said money will be doubled if he take a Frugal course to spend but five hundred pounds *per annum*; which rule never faileth likewise in the Commonwealth, but in some cases (of no great moment) which I will hereafter declare, when I shall shew by whom and in what manner this balance of the Kingdoms account ought to be drawn up yearly, or so often as it shall please the State to discover how much we gain or lose by trade with foreign Nations. But first I will say something concerning those ways and means which will encrease our exportations and diminish our importations of wares; which being done, I will then set down some other arguments both affirmative and negative to strengthen that which is here declared, and thereby to shew that all the other means which are commonly supposed to enrich the Kingdom with Treasure are altogether insufficient and mere fallacies.

READING QUESTIONS

1. According to Mun, what rule must England follow if it was to increase its wealth?

2. What analogy did Mun use to prove his point? Do you find it convincing? Why or why not?

3. What connections can you draw between mercantilism and the trade wars of the early modern period?

17-3 | Critiquing Mercantilism
ADAM SMITH, *The Wealth of Nations* (1776)

Adam Smith (1723–1790) is widely regarded as the father of modern economics. His most famous work, *An Inquiry into the Nature and Causes of the Wealth of Nations* (1776), from which the following excerpts are drawn, was a sustained critique of mercantilism. Smith was not the first economist to advocate free trade, but he was certainly the most famous and persuasive. At the time *The Wealth of Nations* appeared, government policies throughout Europe were still firmly mercantilistic, but over the following decades his arguments gained more adherents, especially in Britain, and his theories formed the basis for classical liberal economics.

From Adam Smith, *An Inquiry into the Nature and Causes of the Wealth of Nations*, vol. 1, ed. James E. Thorold Rodgers (Oxford, U.K.: Clarendon Press, 1869), pp. 5–7, 9, 12, 14–15, 30–31, 57–59, 62–65, 125, 128, 136.

Book I, Chapter 1. *Of the Division of Labor*

The greatest improvement in the productive powers of labor, and the greater part of the skill, dexterity, and judgment with which it is anywhere directed, or applied, seem to have been the effects of the division of labor. . . .

To take an example, . . . the trade of the pin-maker; a workman not educated to this business, . . . nor acquainted with the use of the machinery employed in it . . . , could scarce, perhaps, with his utmost industry, make one pin in a day, and certainly could not make twenty. But in the way in which this business is now carried on, not only the whole work is a peculiar trade, but it is divided into a number of branches, of which the greater part are likewise peculiar trades. One man draws out the wire, another straights it, a third cuts it, a fourth points it, a fifth grinds it at the top for receiving, the head; to make the head requires two or three distinct operations; to put it on is a peculiar business, to whiten the pins is another; it is even a trade by itself to put them into the paper [container in which they are sold]; and the important business of making a pin is, in this manner, divided into about eighteen distinct operations, which, in some manufactories, are all performed by distinct hands, though in others the same man will some-times perform two or three of them. I have seen a small manufactory of this kind where ten men only were employed, and where some of them consequently per-formed two or three distinct operations. But though they were very poor, and therefore but indifferently accommodated with the necessary machinery, they could, when they exerted themselves, make among them about twelve pounds of pins in a day. There are in a pound upwards of four thousand pins of a middling size. Those ten persons, therefore, could make among them upwards of forty-eight thousand pins in a day. Each person, therefore, making a tenth part of forty-eight thousand pins, might be considered as making four thousand eight hundred pins in a day. But if they had all wrought separately and independently, and without any of them having been educated to this peculiar business, they certainly could not each of them have made twenty, perhaps not one pin in a day; that is, certainly, not the two hundred and fortieth, perhaps not the four thousand eight hundredth part of what they are at present capable of perform-ing, in consequence of a proper division and combination of their different operations. . . .

The division of labor, so far as it can be introduced, occasions, in every art, a proportionable increase of the productive powers of labor. The separation of dif-ferent trades and employments from one another seems to have taken place in consequence of this advantage. This separation, too, is generally called furthest in those countries which enjoy the highest degree of industry and improvement; what is the work of one man in a rude state of society being generally that of sev-eral in an improved one. . . .

This great increase of the quantity of work which, in consequence of the divi-sion of labor, the same number of people are capable of performing, is owing to three different circumstances; first, to the increase of dexterity in every particular workman; secondly, to the saving of the time which is commonly lost in passing from one species of work to another; and lastly, to the invention of a great number of machines which facilitate and abridge labor, and enable one man to do the work of many....

It is the great multiplication of the productions of all the different arts, in consequence of the division of labor, which occasions, in a well-governed society, that universal opulence which extends itself to the lowest ranks of the people. Every workman has a great quantity of his own work to dispose of beyond what he himself has occasion for; and every other workman being exactly in the same situation, he is enabled to exchange a great quantity of his own goods for a great quantity, or, what comes to the same thing, for the price of a great quantity of theirs. He supplies them abundantly with what they have occasion for, and they accommodate him as amply with what he has occasion for, and a general plenty diffuses itself through all the different ranks of the society....

Book I, Chapter 2. *Of the Principle Which Gives Occasion to the Division of Labor*

This division of labor, from which so many advantages are derived, is not originally the effect of any human wisdom, which foresees and intends that universal opulence to which it gives occasion. It is the necessary, though very slow and gradual consequence of a certain propensity in human nature which has in view no such extensive utility; the propensity to truck, barter, and exchange one thing for another....

Man has almost constant occasion for the help of his brethren, and it is in vain for him to expect it from their benevolence only. He will be more likely to prevail if he can interest their self-love in his favor, and show them that it is for their own advantage to do for him what he requires of them. Whoever offers to another a bargain of any kind, proposes to do this. Give me that which I want, and you shall have this which you want, is the meaning of every such offer; and it is in this manner that we obtain from one another the far greater art of those good offices which we stand in need of. It is not from the benevolence of the butcher, the brewer, or the baker that we expect our dinner, but from their regard to their own interest....

Book I, Chapter 5. *Of the Real and Nominal Price of Commodities, or Their Price in Labor, and Their Price in Money*

Every man is rich or poor according to the degree in which he can afford to enjoy the necessaries, conveniences, and amusements of human life. But after the division of labor has once thoroughly taken place, it is but a very small part of these with which a man's own labor can supply him. The far greater part of them he must derive from the labor of other people, and he must be rich or poor according to the quantity of that labor which he can command, or which he can afford to purchase. The value of any commodity, therefore, to the person who possesses it, and who means not to use or consume it himself, but to exchange it for other commodities, is equal to the quantity of labor which it enables him to purchase or command. Labor, therefore, is the real measure of the exchangeable value of all commodities.

The real price of everything, what everything really costs to the man who wants to acquire it, is the toil and trouble of acquiring it. What everything is really worth to the man who has acquired it, and who wants to dispose of it or exchange it for something else, is the toil and trouble which it can save to himself, and which it can impose upon other people. What is bought with money or with goods is purchased by labor as much as what we acquire by the toil of our own body. That money or those goods indeed save us this toil. . . .

Book I, Chapter 7. *Of the Natural and Market Price of Commodities*

There is in every society or neighborhood an ordinary or average rate both of wages and profit in every different employment of labor and stock. This rate is naturally regulated, as I shall show hereafter, partly by the general circumstances of the society, their riches or poverty, their advancing, stationary, or declining condition; and partly by the particular nature of each employment.

There is likewise in every society or neighborhood an ordinary or average rate of rent, which is regulated too, as I shall show hereafter, partly by the general circumstances of the society or neighborhood in which the land is situated, and partly by the natural or improved fertility of the land.

These ordinary or average rates may be called the natural rates of wages, profit, and rent, at the time and place in which they commonly prevail.

When the price of any commodity is neither more nor less than what is sufficient to pay the rent of the land, the wages of the labor, and the profits of the stock employed in raising, preparing, and bringing it to market, according to their natural rates, the commodity is then sold for what may be called its natural price. . . .

Though the price, therefore, which leaves him this profit is not always the lowest at which a dealer may sometimes sell his goods, it is the lowest at which he is likely to sell them for any considerable time; at least where there is perfect liberty, or where he may change his trade as often as he pleases.

The actual price at which any commodity is commonly sold is called its market price. It may either be above, or below, or exactly the same with its natural price. . . .

When the quantity of any commodity which is brought to market falls short of the effectual demand, all those who are willing to pay the whole value of the rent, wages, and profit, which must be paid in order to bring it thither, cannot be supplied with the quantity which they want. Rather than want it altogether, some of them will be willing to give more. . . .

When the quantity brought to market exceeds the effectual demand, it cannot be all sold to those who are willing to pay the whole value of the rent, wages, and profit, which must be paid in order to bring it thither. Some part must be sold to those who are willing to pay less, and the low price which they give for it must reduce the price of the whole. . . .

When the quantity brought to market is just sufficient to supply the effectual demand, and no more, the market price naturally comes to be either exactly, or as nearly as can be judged of, the same with the natural price. The whole quantity upon hand can be disposed of for this price, and cannot be disposed of for more. . . .

Such fluctuations affect both the value and the rate either of wages or of profit, according as the market happens to be either overstocked or understocked with commodities or with labor; with work done, or with work to be done. . . .

When by an increase in the effectual demand, the market price of some particular commodity happens to rise a good deal above the natural price, those who employ their stocks in supplying that market are generally careful to conceal this change. If it was commonly known, their great profit would tempt so many new rivals to employ their stocks in the same way that, the effectual demand being fully supplied, the market price would soon be reduced to the natural price, and perhaps for some time even below it. If the market is at a great distance from the residence of those who supply it, they may sometimes be able to keep the secret for several years together, and may so long enjoy their extraordinary profits without any new rivals. Secrets of this kind, however, it must be acknowledged, can seldom be long kept; and the extraordinary profit can last very little longer than they are kept. . . .

A monopoly granted either to an individual or to a trading company has the same effect as a secret in trade or manufactures. The monopolists, by keeping the market constantly understocked, by never fully supplying the effectual demand, sell their commodities much above the natural price, and raise their emoluments, whether they consist in wages or profit, greatly above their natural rate. . . .

The exclusive privileges of corporations, statutes of apprenticeship, and all those laws which restrain in particular employments the competition to a smaller number than might otherwise go into them, have the same tendency, though in a less degree. They are a sort of enlarged monopolies, and may frequently, for ages together, and in whole classes of employments, keep up the market price of particular commodities above the natural price, and maintain both the wages of the labor and the profits of the stock employed about them somewhat above their natural rate.

Such enhancements of the market price may last as long as the regulations of policy which give occasion to them. . . .

Book I, Chapter 10. *Of Wages and Profit in the Different Employments of Labor and Stock*

First the policy of Europe occasions a very important inequality in the whole of the advantages and disadvantages of the different employments of labor and stock, by restraining the competition in some employments to a smaller number than might otherwise be disposed to enter into them.

The exclusive privileges of corporations, or guilds, are the principal means it makes use of for this purpose. . . .

The property which every man has in his own labor, as it is the original foundation of all other property, so it is the most sacred and inviolable. The patrimony of a poor man lies in the strength and dexterity of his hands; and to hinder him from employing this strength and dexterity of his hands; and to hinder him from employing this strength and dexterity in what manner he thinks proper without injury to his neighbor is a plain violation of this most sacred property. It is a manifest encroachment upon the just liberty both of the workman and of those who might be disposed to employ him. . . .

The pretense that corporations are necessary for the better government of the trade is without any foundation. The real and effectual discipline which is exercised over a workman is not that of his corporation, but that of his customers. It is the fear of losing their employment which restrains his frauds and corrects his negligence. An exclusive corporation necessarily weakens the force of this discipline.

READING QUESTIONS

1. On what grounds does Smith extol the division of labor? Can you think of any drawbacks that might result from such a form of labor organization?

2. What, according to Smith, motivates human activity? What are the consequences of this motive?

3. What, according to Smith, gives goods and services their value?

4. Explain what Smith means by "natural" and "market" prices. Why are the two often not the same?

5. What is Smith's attitude toward monopolies and why?

SOURCES IN CONVERSATION

The Moral Implications of Expansion

By the end of the eighteenth century, Europeans had built considerable overseas empires. Britain, in particular, stood out, controlling vast territories in both Asia and the Americas. As Britain's empire grew, and the British and colonial economies grew ever more entwined, some British observers began to question the morality of unrestrained exploitation of non-Europeans. The emergence of the antislavery movement in the late eighteenth century is, perhaps, the most notable example of this trend. More broadly, many in Britain came to believe that the British Empire could be sustained only if it operated according to "British values."

17-4 | OLAUDAH EQUIANO, *A Description of the Middle Passage* (1789)

African American slavery was key to the economic development of not only the southern colonies of British North America but also the sugar industry in the West Indies and Brazil. Indeed, most of the slaves transported to the Americas during the period 1620–1850 went to those destinations (rather than to North America) due chiefly to the appalling mortality rate among slaves engaged in sugar production. As enslaved Africans died, more were imported to replenish the labor force. In the second half of the eighteenth century, organized opposition to slavery began to form in Britain. Olaudah Equiano (1745–1797), a former slave, was an important participant in that opposition. In the passage from his memoirs included here, Equiano describes the "Middle Passage," the horrific transatlantic crossing made by African slaves on their way to the Americas. As you read it, think about who Equiano might have hoped to influence. What groups might have been most susceptible to his appeal?

The closeness of the place, and the heat of the climate, added to the number in the ship, which was so crowded that each had scarcely room to turn himself, almost suffocated us. This produced copious perspirations, so that the air soon became unfit for respiration, from a variety of loathsome smells, and brought on a sickness among the slaves, of which many died, thus falling victims to the improvident avarice, as I may call it, of their purchasers. This wretched situation was again aggravated by the galling of the chains, now become insupportable; and the filth of the necessary tubs, into which the children often fell, and were almost suffocated. The shrieks of the women, and the groans of the dying, rendered the whole a scene of horror almost inconceivable. Happily perhaps for myself I was soon reduced so low here that it was thought necessary to keep me almost always on deck; and from my extreme youth I was not put in fetters. In this situation I expected every hour to share the fate of my companions, some of whom were almost daily brought upon deck at the point of death, which I began to hope would soon put an end to my miseries. Often did I think many of the inhabitants of the deep much more happy than myself. I envied them the freedom they enjoyed, and as often wished I could change my condition for theirs. Every circumstance I met with served only to render my state more painful, and heighten my apprehensions, and my opinion of the cruelty of the whites. One day they had taken a number of fishes; and when they had killed and satisfied themselves with as many as they thought fit, to our astonishment who were on the deck, rather than give any of them to us to eat as we expected, they tossed the remaining fish into the sea again, although we begged and prayed for some as well as we could, but in vain; and some of my countrymen, being pressed by hunger, took an opportunity, when they thought no one saw them, of trying to get a little privately; but they were discovered, and the attempt procured

From Robert J. Allison, ed., *The Interesting Narrative of the Life of Olaudah Equiano Written by Himself* (Boston: Bedford/St. Martin's, 2007), pp. 67–68.

them some very severe floggings. One day, when we had a smooth sea and moderate wind, two of my wearied countrymen who were chained together (I was near them at the time), preferring death to such a life of misery, somehow made through the nettings and jumped into the sea: immediately another quite dejected fellow, who, on one account of his illness, was suffered to be out of irons, also followed their example; and I believe many more would very soon have done the same if they had not been prevented by the ship's crew, who were instantly alarmed. Those of us that were the most active were in a moment put down under the deck, and here was such a noise and confusion amongst the people of the ship as I never heard before, to stop her, and get the boat out to go after the slaves. However two of the wretches were drowned, but they got the other, and afterwards flogged him unmercifully for thus attempting to prefer death to slavery. In this manner we continued to undergo more hardships than I can now relate, hardships which are inseparable from this accursed trade. Many a time we were near suffocation from the want of fresh air, which we were often without for whole days together. This, and the stench of the necessary tubs, carried off many.

READING QUESTIONS

1. According to Equiano, what were conditions like aboard a slave ship?

2. How did the crew treat their cargo? What seems to have been their highest priorities with respect to the slaves?

3. What does Equiano's account tell you about the psychological impact of enslavement and transportation overseas?

17-5 | ROBERT, FIRST BARON CLIVE, *Speech in the House of Commons on India* (1772)

Robert Clive (1725–1774) was born into an English minor gentry family. Apprenticed as a "writer" (clerk) in the British East India Company, he arrived in India in 1744, in the midst of the War of the Austrian Succession. The conflict offered opportunities for bold and ambitious men like Clive, and his bravery won him a commission in the company's army. In 1757 he defeated an Indian army at the Battle of Plassey, and in 1765 received as a gift from the Mughal emperor the province of Bengal, one of the richest and most populous in India. Clive was thus responsible for transforming the East India Company from a trading entity into a governmental one that directly ruled Indian territory. In the following passage from his writings, Clive defended himself against charges of greed and corruption. As you read it, pay

From "Speech Given in the House of Commons, March 30, 1772," in *The Parliamentary History of England from the Earliest Period to the Year 1803*, vol. 17 (London: T. C. Hansard, 1806–1820), pp. 354–357.

particular attention to the way in which Clive used the alleged moral failings of the Indians to justify his own actions.

Indostan [India] was always an absolute despotic government. The inhabitants, especially of Bengal, in inferior stations, are servile, mean [poor], submissive, and humble. In superior stations, they are luxurious, effeminate, tyrannical, treacherous, venal, cruel. The country of Bengal is called, by way of distinction, the paradise of the earth. It not only abounds with the necessaries of life to such a degree, as to furnish a great part of India with its superfluity, but it abounds in very curious and valuable manufactures, sufficient not only for its own use, but for the use of the whole globe. The silver of the west and the gold of the east have for many years been pouring into that country, and goods only have been sent out in return. This has added to the luxury and extravagance of Bengal.

From time immemorial it has been the custom of that country, for an inferior never to come into the presence of a superior without a present. It begins at the nabob,[1] and ends at the lowest man that has an inferior. The nabob has told me, that the small presents he received amounted to £300,000 a year; and I can believe him; because I know that I might have received as much during my last government. The Company's servants have ever been accustomed to receive presents. Even before we took part in the country troubles, when our possessions were very confined and limited, the governor and others used to receive presents; and I will take upon me to assert, that there has not been an officer commanding his Majesty's fleet; nor an officer commanding his Majesty's army; not a governor, not a member of council, not any other person, civil or military, in such a station as to have connection with the country government, who has not received presents. With regard to Bengal, there they flow in abundance indeed. Let the House figure to itself a country consisting of 15 millions of inhabitants, a revenue of four millions sterling, and a trade in proportion. By progressive steps the Company have become sovereigns of that empire. Can it be supposed that their servants will refrain from advantages so obviously resulting from their situation? The Company's servants, however, have not been the authors of those acts of violence and oppression, of which it is the fashion to accuse them. Such crimes are committed by the natives of the country acting as their agents and for the most part without their knowledge. . . . Let us for a moment consider the nature of the education of a young man who goes to India. The advantages arising from the Company's service are now very generally known; and the great object of every man is to get his son appointed a writer to Bengal; which is usually at the age of 16. His parents and relations represent to him how certain he is of making a fortune; that my lord such a one, and my lord such a one, acquired so much money in such a time; and Mr. such a one, and Mr. such a one, so much in such a time. Thus are their principles corrupted at their very setting out, and as they generally go a good many together, they inflame one another's expectations to such a

---

[1]**nabob**: More properly, nawab; a provincial ruler.

degree, in the course of the voyage, that they fix upon a period for their return[2] before their arrival.

Let us now take a view of one of these writers arrived in Bengal, and not worth a groat.[3] As soon as he lands, a banyan,[4] worth perhaps £100,000 desires he may have the honor of serving this young gentleman, at 4s. 6d.[5] per month. The Company has provided chambers for him, but they are not good enough: the banyan finds better. The young man takes a walk about the town, he observes that other writers, arrived only a year before him, live in splendid apartments or have houses of their own, ride upon fine prancing Arabian horses, and in palanqueens[6] and chaises; that they keep seraglios,[7] make entertainments, and treat with champagne and claret. When he returns he tells the banyan what he has observed. The banyan assures him he may soon arrive at the same good fortune; he furnishes him with money; he is then at his mercy. The advantages of the banyan advance with the rank of his master, who in acquiring one fortune generally spends three. But this is not the worst of it: he is in a state of dependence under the banyan, who commits acts of violence and oppression, as his interest prompts him to, under the pretended sanction and authority of the Company's servant. Hence, Sir, arises the clamor against the English gentlemen in India. But look at them in a retired situation, when returned to England, when they are no longer nabobs and sovereigns of the east: see if there be any thing tyrannical in their disposition towards their inferiors: see if they are not good and humane masters: Are they not charitable? Are they not benevolent? Are they not generous? Are they not hospitable? If they are, thus far, not contemptible members of society, and if in all their dealings between man and man, their conduct is strictly honorable: if, in short, there has not yet been one character found amongst them sufficiently flagitious[8] for Mr. Foote[9] to exhibit on the theatre in the Haymarket, may we not conclude, that if they have erred, it has been because they were men, placed in situations subject to little or no control?

READING QUESTIONS

1. What does Clive's description of Indian character suggest about his racial attitudes?

---

[2]**they fix upon a period for their return**: In other words, the date by which they expect to return to Britain, fortune in hand.

[3]**groat**: Four pence.

[4]**banyan**: Indian merchant or trader.

[5]**4s. 6d.**: Four shillings, six pence; a modest sum.

[6]**palanqueen**: More properly, *palanquin*: an enclosed litter, seating one, carried by four or six servants.

[7]**seraglio**: Harem.

[8]**flagitious**: Wicked, villainous.

[9]**Mr. Foote**: Playwright and theater impresario Samuel Foote (1721–1777), who in 1772 staged a play at Haymarket Theater titled *The Nabob*, a satire about the East India Company.

2. How does Clive justify out-and-out bribery and corruption in Indian government, and the East India Company's enrichment by that means?

3. How does Clive excuse the behavior of East India Company employees and exonerate them of "flagitious" actions?

■ COMPARATIVE AND DISCUSSION QUESTIONS ■

1. What do you think Smith's attitude was toward guilds like those depicted in the German guild illustrations, and why?

2. How did Smith undermine mercantilist arguments like the one put forward by Mun?

3. How did the activities described by Equiano and Clive contribute to the growth of British wealth and power?

Life in the Era of Expansion
1650–1800

For the social historian, the task of understanding how the "ordinary people" of early modern Europe lived—to say nothing of what they thought—is quite challenging. Most of the non-elite in the seventeenth and eighteenth centuries were illiterate and thus left no self-composed evidence of their existence. Historians studying the period have to rely on the limited writings left by common people or try to interpret their lives through the lens of the better-off classes. Nonetheless, careful attention to the available sources is rewarded with glimpses of a variety of aspects of the changing social and cultural world of the eighteenth century. The documents included in this chapter offer an opportunity to explore eighteenth-century attitudes about mortality, religious belief, children and education, and the state of medical knowledge.

18-1 | The Dangers of Eighteenth-Century Life

EDMOND WILLIAMSON, *Births and Deaths in an English Gentry Family* (1709–1720)

Little is known of Edmond Williamson. He lived in Bedfordshire, one of the "Home Counties" surrounding London. The mere fact that he was literate and kept a diary suggests that he was a man of means, as does his mention of the servants present at his wife's childbirths. Despite their brevity, his diary entries reveal that proximity of death was a central fact of life, even in the lives of the relatively affluent. Three of Williamson's seven children died at birth or shortly afterward, and a fourth succumbed to smallpox before the age of three. Williamson's wife died as well, just a month after the birth of her last child. As you read the diary excerpts, think about the light they shed on eighteenth-century family life.

From Edmond Williamson, "An Account of the Birth of My Children by My Second Wife (1709–1720)," in *The Past Speaks*, 2d ed., ed. Walter Arnstein (Lexington, Mass.: D. C. Heath, 1993), 2:33–34.

1709

March 29. My wife fell into labor and a little after 9 in the morning was delivered of a son. Present: aunt Taylor, cousin White, sister Smith, cousin Clarkson, widow Hern, Mrs. Howe, midwife, Mr[s]. Wallis, nurse, Mrs. Holms, Eleanor Hobbs, servants.

   April 4. He was baptised by Doctor Battle by the name of John. . . .

   [April] 16. The child died about 1 o'clock in the morning.

1711

Sept. 17. My said wife was delivered of a son just before 4 in the morning. Present: Mrs. Thomas Molyneux's lady and maid, Mrs. Mann, midwife, Margaret Williamson, nurse, Susan Nuthall, servant.

   Oct. 4. He was baptised by Mr. Trabeck by the name of Talbot after my grandmother's name. Sir John Talbot and John Pulteny esquire were gossips [godfathers], with my sister Smith godmother. . . .

1713

June 9. About 8 at night my said wife began her labor.

   [June] 10. Half an hour after 1 in the morning was brought to bed of a son. Present: Mrs. Molyneux, Mrs. Bisset, Mrs. Mann, midwife, Nurse Williamson, Susan Nuthall and Betty Ginger, servants.

   [June] 30. Baptised by Mr. Mompesson of Mansfield by the name of Edmond. . . .

1715

March 7. My said wife was brought to bed of a daughter 10 minutes before 6 in the morning. Present: Mrs. Molyneux, Mrs. Mann, midwife, Nurse Williamson, Mary Evans, Mary Cole and Mary Wheeler, servants.

   [March] 29. Was baptised by Dr. Mandivel, chancellor of Lincoln, by the name of Christian.

1716

March 9. My wife was delivered of a daughter at 7 at night. Present: aunt Taylor, Mrs. Molyneux, Mrs. Oliver, Mrs. Mann, midwife, Mary Smith, nurse, Jane Kensey, and Mary Wheeler, servants.

   [March] 31. Was baptised by Mr. Widmore, the reader of St. Margaret's, by the name of Elizanna. . . . Registered in St. Margaret's, Westminster, as all the rest were.

   April 27. Died, was buried in the new chapel yard in the Broadway.

1718

Jan. 21. [Mrs. Williamson:] I was brought to bed of a son about 2 in the morning, Mrs. Mann, midwife, nurse Chatty, dry-nurse, present; Mrs. Taylor, Mrs. White and Mrs. Molyneux, Jane Beadle; servants: Mary Wells, Jane Griffith, Edmond Kinward. He was baptised by Mr. Widmore, reader of St. Margaret's, Westminster, by the name of Francis. . . .

1719

Feb. 21. [Mrs. Williamson:] I was brought to bed of a son between 6 and 7 in the evening, Mrs. Mann, midwife, nurse Chatty, dry-nurse; present: aunt Taylor, Mrs. Molyneux and Jane Beadle; servants: Rebecca Shippy, Betty Hall and Mathew Dowect.

March 7. He was baptised by Mr. Widmore, reader of St. Margaret's, Westminster, by the name of William. . . .

[Undated]. Died and buried at Hadley.

1720

June. My wife brought to bed of a daughter, but the child did not live a minute.

July 21. My wife died and was buried at Isleworth.

Sept. 9. [Francis] died of the smallpox at Nurse Ward's.

READING QUESTIONS

1. What does the Williamsons' account of the births of their children suggest about pregnancy in early-eighteenth-century England? What factors would account for this?

2. What does Williamson's record of the deaths of his children suggest about the incidence of infant mortality in early modern Europe?

3. Apart from labor, births, and deaths, what else did Williamson record, and what does this tell us?

4. In what ways did the ritual of childbirth in early-eighteenth-century England differ from that in modern developed countries? What could account for the differences?

18-2 | Embracing Innovation in Medicine

MARY WORTLEY MONTAGU, *On Smallpox Inoculations* (ca. 1717)

While medical progress in the eighteenth century was slow, there were some notable break-throughs, as the combined impact of the Scientific Revolution and the Enlightenment led some to challenge medical orthodoxy. Such breakthroughs did not always come from within the medical profession. Mary Wortley Montagu (1689–1762) is a case in point. The daughter of an English aristocrat and an unusually well-educated woman, Montagu narrowly survived smallpox, an often fatal disease, in 1715. A year later, while accompanying her diplomat husband in Constantinople, Montagu witnessed what was a common practice in that part of the world, inoculation against smallpox. She subsequently had both of her children inoculated, and, upon returning to England, championed the procedure despite strong anti-"Oriental" sentiment against it. The following letter was written to a close friend; its substance was made public in the 1720s.

A propos of distempers, I am going to tell you a thing, that will make you wish yourself here. The small-pox, so fatal, and so general amongst us, is here entirely harmless, by the invention of engrafting, which is the term they give it. There is a set of old women, who make it their business to perform the operation, every autumn, in the month of September, when the great heat is abated. People send to one another to know if any of their family has a mind to have the small-pox; they make parties for this purpose, and when they are met (commonly fifteen or sixteen together) the old woman comes with a nut-shell full of the matter of the best sort of smallpox, and asks what vein you please to have opened. She immediately rips open that you offer to her, with a large needle (which gives you no more pain than a common scratch) and puts into the vein as much matter as can lie upon the head of her needle, and after that, binds up the little wound with a hollow bit of shell, and in this manner opens four or five veins. The Grecians have commonly the superstition of opening one in the middle of the forehead, one in each arm, and one on the breast, to mark the sign of the Cross; but this has a very ill effect, all these wounds leaving little scars, and is not done by those that are not superstitious, who choose to have them in the legs, or that part of the arm that is concealed. The children or young patients play together all the rest of the day, and are in perfect health to the eighth [day]. Then the fever begins to seize them, and they keep their beds two days, very seldom three. They have very rarely above twenty or thirty [pockmarks] in their faces, which never mark [i.e., leave scars] and in eight days time they are as well as before their illness. Where they are wounded [i.e., where pock marks appear], there remains running sores during the distemper, which I don't doubt is a great relief to it. Every year, thousands undergo this operation, and the French Ambassador says pleasantly,

---

From Lady Mary Wortley Montagu, *Letters of the Right Honourable Lady M—y W—y M—e: Written During Her Travels in Europe, Asia and Africa . . .* , vol. 1 (Aix: Anthony Henricy, 1796), pp. 167–169.

that they take the small-pox here by way of diversion, as they take the waters[1] in other countries. There is no example of any one that has died in it, and you may believe I am well satisfied of the safety of this experiment, since I intend to try it on my dear little son. I am patriot enough to take the pains to bring this useful invention into fashion in England, and I should not fail to write to some of our doctors very particularly about it, if I knew any one of them that I thought had virtue enough to destroy such a considerable branch of their revenue, for the good of mankind. But that distemper is too beneficial to them, not to expose to all their resentment, the hardy weight that should undertake to put an end to it. Perhaps if I live to return, I may, however, have courage to war with them. Upon this occasion, admire the heroism in the heart of

Your friend, etc. etc.

READING QUESTIONS

1. According to Montagu, who administered smallpox inoculations in Constantinople? What does this suggest about Turkish popular medicine in the eighteenth century?

2. What might explain Montagu's skepticism about the willingness of English doctors to adopt the practice of inoculation?

3. What does Montagu's letter suggest about upper-class women's education and empowerment in early modern English society? Do you think she was representative of all women? Of all upper-class women? Why or why not?

4. What are some of the likely reasons English doctors dismissed the smallpox inoculation that was so successful abroad?

18-3 | Shaping Young Minds and Bodies

JOHN LOCKE, *Some Thoughts Concerning Education* (1693)

John Locke's (1632–1704) intellectual curiosity and influence ranged wide, from political theory to the nature of human consciousness, from economics to, in this piece, education. Originally composed as a series of letters to a friend who had sought Locke's advice concerning his son's education, "Some Thoughts" constitutes a companion piece to his "Essay Concerning Human Understanding" (1690), in which he argued that the mind at birth was a "blank slate" upon which ideas were imprinted, and that all knowledge was derived from sensory experience and reasoning. As you read the excerpt, ask yourself why education was so

From *English Philosophers of the Seventeenth and Eighteenth Centuries* (New York: P. F. Collier & Son, 1910), pp. 6–7, 9, 11, 28–29, 33–36, 39, 53–54, 111, 123, 136, 179, 184–185.

[1]**take the waters**: Upper-class men and women across Europe routinely visited spas with mineral waters or hot springs, like Bath in England, to "take the waters." Such trips combined medicinal and recreational motives.

important to Locke and, indeed, to so many of the participants in the Enlightenment. What connections can you make between Locke's philosophical positions and his ideas about education?

The well educating of their children is so much the duty and concern of parents, and the welfare and prosperity of the nation so much depends on it, that I would have every one lay it seriously to heart; and after having well examined and distinguished what fancy, custom, or reason advises in the case, set his helping hand to promote everywhere that way of training up youth, with regard to their several conditions, which is the easiest, shortest, and likeliest to produce virtuous, useful, and able men in their distinct callings; tho' that most to be taken care of is the gentleman's calling. For if those of that rank are by their education once set right, they will quickly bring all the rest into order. . . .

A sound mind in a sound body, is a short, but full description of a happy state in this world. He that has these two, has little more to wish for; and he that wants either of them, will be but little the better for anything else. Men's happiness or misery is most part of their own making. He, whose mind directs not wisely, will never take the right way; and he, whose body is crazy and feeble, will never be able to advance in it. I confess, there are some men's constitutions of body and mind so vigorous, and well framed by nature, that they need not much assistance from others; but by the strength of their natural genius, they are from their cradles carried towards what is excellent; and by the privilege of their happy constitutions, are able to do wonders. But examples of this kind are but few; and I think I may say, that of all the men we meet with, nine parts of ten are what they are, good or evil, useful or not, by their education. 'Tis that which makes the great difference in mankind. The little, or almost insensible impressions on our tender infancies, have very important and lasting consequences: and there 'tis, as in the fountains of some rivers, where a gentle application of the hand turns the flexible waters in channels, that make them take quite contrary courses; and by this direction given them at first in the source, they receive different tendencies, and arrive at last at very remote and distant places. . . .

I have said he here [as opposed to "she" or "they"], because the principal aim of my discourse is, how a young gentleman should be brought up from his infancy, which in all things will not so perfectly suit the education of daughters; though where the difference of sex requires different treatment, 'twill be no hard matter to distinguish. . . .

[Locke provides extensive advice on healthy eating and drinking habits for children.]

As the strength of the body lies chiefly in being able to endure hardships, so also does that of the mind. And the great principle and foundation of all virtue and worth is placed in this: that a man is able to deny himself his own desires, cross his own inclinations, and purely follow what reason directs as best, tho' the appetite lean the other way.

The great mistake I have observed in people's breeding their children, has been, that this has not been taken care enough of in its due season: that the mind has not been made obedient to discipline, and pliant to reason, when at first it was most tender, most easy to be bowed. Parents being wisely ordained by nature to love their children, are very apt, if reason watch not that natural affection very warily, are apt, I say, to let it run into fondness. They love their little ones and it is their duty; but they often, with them, cherish their faults too. . . .

It seems plain to me, that the principle of all virtue and excellency lies in a power of denying ourselves the satisfaction of our own desires, where reason does not authorize them. This power is to be got and improved by custom, made easy and familiar by an early practice. If therefore I might be heard, I would advise, that, contrary to the ordinary way, children should be used to submit their desires, and go without their longings, even from their very cradles. The first thing they should learn to know, should be, that they were not to have anything because it pleased them, but because it was thought fit for them. If things suitable to their wants were supplied to them, so that they were never suffered to have what they once cried for, they would learn to be content without it, would never, with bawling and peevishness, contend for mastery, nor be half so uneasy to themselves and others as they are, because from the first beginning they are not thus handled. If they were never suffered to obtain their desire by the impatience they expressed for it, they would no more cry for another thing, than they do for the moon. . . .

Those therefore that intend ever to govern their children, should begin it while they are very little, and look that they perfectly comply with the will of their parents. Would you have your son obedient to you when past a child; be sure then to establish the authority of a father as soon as he is capable of submission, and can understand in whose power he is. If you would have him stand in awe of you, imprint it in his infancy; and as he approaches more to a man, admit him nearer to your familiarity; so shall you have him your obedient subject (as is fit) while he is a child, and your affectionate friend when he is a man. For methinks they mightily misplace the treatment due to their children, who are indulgent and familiar when they are little, but severe to them, and keep them at a distance, when they are grown up: for liberty and indulgence can do no good to children; their want of judgment makes them stand in need of restraint and discipline; and on the contrary, imperiousness and severity is but an ill way of treating men, who have reason of their own to guide them; unless you have a mind to make your children, when grown up, weary of you, and secretly to say within themselves, When will you die, father? . . .

This being laid down in general, as the course that ought to be taken, 'tis fit we now come to consider the parts of the discipline to be used, a little more particularly. I have spoken so much of carrying a strict hand over children, that perhaps I shall be suspected of not considering enough, what is due to their tender age and constitutions. But that opinion will vanish, when you have heard me a little farther: for I am very apt to think, that great severity of punishment does but very little good, nay, great harm in education; and I believe it will be found that . . . those children who have been most chastised, seldom make the best men. All that I have hitherto contended for, is, that whatsoever rigor is necessary, it is more to be used, the younger children are; and having by a due application wrought its effect, it is to be relaxed, and changed into a milder sort of government. . . .

Beating them, and all other sorts of slavish and corporal punishments, are not the discipline fit to be used in the education of those we would have wise, good, and ingenuous men; and therefore very rarely to be applied, and that only in great occasions, and cases of extremity. On the other side, to flatter children by rewards of things that are pleasant to them, is as carefully to be avoided. He that will give to his son apples or sugar-plumbs, or what else of this kind he is most delighted with, to make him learn his book, does but authorize his love of pleasure, and cocker up that dangerous propensity, which he ought by all means to subdue and stifle in him. . . .

[Locke warns against the bad influence of servants upon children.]

Having named company, I am almost ready to throw away my pen, and trouble you no farther on this subject: for since that does more than all precepts, rules, and instructions, methinks 'tis almost wholly in vain to make a long discourse of other things, and to talk of that almost to no purpose. For you will be ready to say, what shall I do with my son? If I keep him always at home, he will be in danger to be my young master; and if I send him abroad, how is it possible to keep him from the contagion of rudeness and vice, which is everywhere so in fashion? In my house he will perhaps be more innocent, but more ignorant too of the world; wanting there change of company, and being used constantly to the same faces, he will, when he comes abroad, be a sheepish or conceited creature.

I confess both sides have their inconveniences. Being abroad, 'tis true, will make him bolder, and better able to bustle and shift among boys of his own age; and the emulation of school-fellows often puts life and industry into young lads. But still you can find a school, wherein it is possible for the master to look after the manners of his scholars, and can show as great effects of his care of forming their minds to virtue, and their carriage to good breeding, as of forming their tongues to the learned languages. . . .

Virtue is harder to be got than a knowledge of the world; and if lost in a young man, is seldom recovered. Sheepishness and ignorance of the world, the faults imputed to a private education, are neither the necessary consequences of being bred at home, nor if they were, are they incurable evils. Vice is the more stubborn, as well as the more dangerous evil of the two; and therefore in the first place to be fenced against. If that sheepish softness which often enervates those who are bred like fondlings [fools] at home, be carefully to be avoided, it is principally so for virtue's sake; for fear lest such a yielding temper should be too susceptible of vicious impressions, and expose the novice too easily to be corrupted. A young man before he leaves the shelter of his father's house, and the guard of a tutor, should be fortified with resolution, and made acquainted with men, to

secure his virtues, lest he should be led into some ruinous course, or fatal preci-
pice, before he is sufficiently acquainted with the dangers of conversation, and
has steadiness enough not to yield to every temptation. Were it not for this, a
young man's bashfulness and ignorance in the world, would not so much need
an early care. Conversation would cure it in a great measure; or if that will not do
it early enough, it is only a stronger reason for a good tutor at home. For if pains
be to be taken to give him a manly air and assurance betimes, it is chiefly as a
fence to his virtue when he goes into the world under his own conduct. . . .

[Locke urges parents to choose tutors for their children discriminately, as children learn by
example.]

Curiosity in children . . . ought to be encouraged in them, not only as a good sign,
but as the great instrument nature has provided to remove that ignorance they
were born with; and which, without this busy inquisitiveness, will make them
dull and useless creatures. . . .

That which every gentleman . . . desires for his son, besides the estate he
leaves him, is contained . . . in these four things, virtue, wisdom, breeding, and
learning. . . .

I place virtue as the first and most necessary of those endowments that
belong to a man or a gentleman; as absolutely requisite to make him valued and
beloved by others, acceptable or tolerable to himself. Without that, I think, he
will be happy neither in this nor the other world.

You will wonder, perhaps, that I put learning last, especially if I tell you I
think it the least part. This may seem strange in the mouth of a bookish man; and
this making usually the chief, if not only bustle and stir about children, this being
almost that alone which is thought on, when people talk of education, makes it
the greater paradox. When I consider, what ado is made about a little Latin and
Greek, how many years are spent in it, and what a noise and business it makes to
no purpose, I can hardly forbear thinking that the parents of children still live in
fear of the school-master's rod, which they look on as the only instrument of education; as a language or two to be its whole business. How else is it possible that a
child should be chained to the oar seven, eight, or ten of the best years of his life,
to get a language or two, which, I think, might be had at a great deal cheaper rate
of pains and time, and be learned almost in playing? . . .

Reading and writing and learning I allow to be necessary, but yet not the
chief business. I imagine you would think him a very foolish fellow, that should
not value a virtuous or a wise man infinitely before a great scholar. . . .

To conclude this part . . . , his tutor should remember, that his business is not
so much to teach him all that is knowable, as to raise in him a love and esteem of
knowledge; and to put him in the right way of knowing and improving himself
when he has a mind to it. . . .

Teach him to get a mastery over his inclinations, and submit his appetite to
reason. This being obtained, and by constant practice settled into habit, the hardest part of the task is over. To bring a young man to this, I know nothing which so

much contributes as the love of praise and commendation, which should therefore be instilled into him by all arts imaginable. Make his mind as sensible of credit and shame as may be; and when you have done that, you have put a principle into him, which will influence his actions when you are not by, to which the fear of a little smart of a rod is not comparable, and which will be the proper stock whereon afterwards to graft the true principles of morality and religion.

READING QUESTIONS

1. Why does Locke advocate beginning a child's education at the earliest possible age?

2. What is Locke's opinion on the education of young women? What in the letter suggests his beliefs on sexual difference and gender roles?

3. What are Locke's views about the need for disciplining children and the nature of discipline to be used?

4. What were Locke's highest priorities for a childhood education? What sort of person might he have hoped a good education to produce?

SOURCES IN CONVERSATION

The Challenge to Established Religion in the 1700s

By the eighteenth century, established churches in both Catholic and Protestant lands had evolved into extensions of state bureaucracies. Closely tied to the interests of ruling political elites, their purpose was more the preservation of the social and political status quo than it was a true engagement with the spiritual needs of ordinary people. To many Europeans, Christianity promoted by such churches was comprised of empty gestures and routines with no real substance. For some Enlightenment thinkers, the ossification of established churches was an indictment of organized religion as a whole, and deism, a rational theology that rejected divine intervention in everyday life, gained popularity in certain circles. Perhaps more important, however, was the challenge to established religion from sincere believers eager for the emergence of a new, more emotionally satisfying form of Christianity. If the eighteenth century was the Age of Enlightenment, it was also an age of popular religious revival, and our understanding of the religious life of the period is incomplete if we do not incorporate both developments.

18-4 | JOHN WESLEY, *The Ground Rules for Methodism* (1749)

John Wesley (1703–1791), the son of an Anglican clergyman, was himself trained to the ministry. He found little solace in the Anglicanism of his youth, however, and endured years of spiritual yearning until, in 1738, he had a religious awakening. His resulting theological message was quite simple: salvation was possible for all. The appeal of Wesley's message, coupled with his tireless preaching, often to huge crowds outdoors, quickly brought him a large following. These followers became known as "Methodists," after a Bible study group Wesley attended while at Oxford University.

The Nature, Design, and General Rules of the United Societies

1. About ten years ago my brother [Charles Wesley] and I were desired to preach in many parts of London. We had no view therein but, so far as we were able (and we knew God could work by whomsoever it pleased Him) to convince those who would hear, what true Christianity was, and to persuade them to embrace it.

2. The points we chiefly insisted upon were four: First, that orthodoxy or right opinions is, at best, but a very slender part of religion, if it can be allowed to be any part of it at all; that neither does religion consist in negatives, in bare harmlessness of any kind, nor merely in externals in doing good or using the means of grace, in works of piety (so called) or of charity: that it is nothing short of or different from the mind that was in Christ, the image of God stamped upon the heart, inward righteousness attended with the peace of God and joy in the Holy Ghost.

Secondly, that the only way under heaven to this religion is to repent and believe the gospel, of (as the apostle words it) repentance toward God and faith in our Lord Jesus Christ.

Thirdly, that by this faith, he that worketh not, but believeth in Him that justifieth the ungodly, is justified freely by His grace, through the redemption which is in Jesus Christ.

And lastly, that being justified by faith we taste of the heaven to which we are going; we are holy and happy; we tread down sin and fear, and sit in heavenly places with Christ Jesus.

3. Many of those who heard this, began to cry out, that we brought strange things to their ears: that this was doctrine which they never heard before, or, at least, never regarded. They searched the scriptures, whether these things were so, and acknowledged the truth as it is in Jesus. Their hearts also were influenced as well as their understandings, and they determined to follow Jesus Christ and Him crucified.

From John Wesley, "A Plain Account of the People Called Methodists" (1749), in *The Past Speaks*, 2d ed., ed. Walter Arnstein (Lexington, Mass.: D. C. Heath, 1993), 2:87–89.

4. Immediately [those who accepted this new way] were surrounded with difficulties. All the world rose up against them; neighbors, strangers, acquaintances, relations, friends began to cry out amain, "Be not righteous overmuch: why shouldst thou destroy thyself? Let not much religion make thee mad." . . .

Directions Given to the Band Societies

You are supposed to have the faith that "overcometh the world." To you, therefore, it is not grievous:

I. Carefully to abstain from doing evil; in particular:
1. Neither to buy nor sell anything at all on the Lord's day.
2. To taste no spiritous liquor, no dram of any kind, unless prescribed by a physician.
3. To be at a word [i.e., to be honest] both in buying and selling.
4. To pawn nothing, no, not to save life.
5. Not to mention the fault of any behind his back, and to stop those short that do.
6. To wear no needless ornaments, such as rings, earrings, necklaces, lace, ruffles.
7. To use no needless self-indulgence, such as taking snuff or tobacco, unless prescribed by a physician.
II. Zealously to maintain good works; in particular:
1. To give alms of such things as you possess, and that to the uttermost of your power.
2. To reprove all that sin in your sight, and that in love and meekness of wisdom.
3. To be patterns of diligence and frugality, of self-denial, and taking up the cross daily.
III. Constantly to attend on all the ordinances of God; in particular:
1. To be at church and at the Lord's table every week, and at every public meeting of the bands.
2. To attend the ministry of the word every morning unless distance, business or sickness prevent.
3. To use private prayer every day; and family prayer, if you are at the head of a family.
4. To read the scriptures, and meditate therein, at every vacant hour. And
5. To observe, as days of fasting or abstinence, all Fridays in the year.

READING QUESTIONS

1. What, according to Wesley, is the *only* means of obtaining salvation? What is the true nature of religion?
2. What kinds of criticism did Wesley anticipate? What might explain the hostility with which Methodism was sometimes met?

3. Given Wesley's insistence that external behavior has little to do with true religion, what should we make of the detailed directions he laid out for Methodist societies? Why insist on certain behaviors and practices, if they are not part of the essential experience of Christianity?

4. What might explain the appeal of Methodism? How did it differ from other more established forms of Christianity?

18-5 | THOMAS PAINE, *The Age of Reason* (1794)

Thomas Paine (1737–1809) is best known for *Common Sense* (1776), an enormously influential pamphlet in which Paine argued for American independence. *The Age of Reason*, excerpted here, was produced in reaction to another revolution, the French Revolution of 1789. Paine rejoiced in the revolutionary government's dismantling of the established church, and was certain that events in France would usher in a new age in European spiritual life, one in which reason, and not revelation, would be the foundation of religious thought and practice. As you read the excerpt, pay particular attention to Paine's views on the relationship between church and state. Why did he see close ties between secular and religious authorities as evil?

It has been my intention, for several years past, to publish my thoughts upon religion; I am well aware of the difficulties that attend the subject, and from that consideration, had reserved it to a more advanced period of life. I intended it to be the last offering I should make to my fellow-citizens of all nations, and that at a time when the purity of the motive that induced me to it could not admit of a question, even by those who might disapprove the work.

The circumstance that has now taken place in France, of the total abolition of the whole national order of priesthood, and of everything appertaining to compulsive systems of religion, and compulsive articles of faith, has not only precipitated my intention, but rendered a work of this kind exceedingly necessary, lest, in the general wreck of superstition, of false systems of government, and false theology, we lose sight of morality, of humanity, and of the theology that is true.

As several of my colleagues, and others of my fellow-citizens of France, have given me the example of making their voluntary and individual profession of faith, I also will make mine; and I do this with all that sincerity and frankness with which the mind of man communicates with itself.

I believe in one God, and no more; and I hope for happiness beyond this life.

I believe the equality of man, and I believe that religious duties consist in doing justice, loving mercy, and endeavouring to make our fellow-creatures happy.

From Thomas Paine, *The Age of Reason*, ed. Moncure Daniel Conway (New York: G. P. Putnam's Sons, 1924), pp. 21–23.

But, lest it should be supposed that I believe many other things in addition to these, I shall, in the progress of this work, declare the things I do not believe, and my reasons for not believing them.

I do not believe in the creed professed by the Jewish church, by the Roman church, by the Greek church, by the Turkish church, by the Protestant church, nor by any church that I know of. My own mind is my own church.

All national institutions of churches, whether Jewish, Christian, or Turkish, appear to me no other than human inventions set up to terrify and enslave mankind, and monopolize power and profit.

I do not mean by this declaration to condemn those who believe otherwise; they have the same right to their belief as I have to mine. But it is necessary to the happiness of man, that he be mentally faithful to himself. Infidelity does not consist in believing, or in disbelieving; it consists in professing to believe what he does not believe.

It is impossible to calculate the moral mischief, if I may so express it, that mental lying has produced in society. When a man has so far corrupted and prostituted the chastity of his mind, as to subscribe his professional belief to things he does not believe, he has prepared himself for the commission of every other crime. He takes up the trade of a priest for the sake of gain, and, in order to qualify himself for that trade, he begins with a perjury. Can we conceive anything more destructive to morality than this?

Soon after I had published the pamphlet COMMON SENSE, in America, I saw the exceeding probability that a revolution in the system of government would be followed by a revolution in the system of religion. The adulterous connection of church and state, wherever it had taken place, whether Jewish, Christian, or Turkish, had so effectually prohibited, by pains and penalties, every discussion upon established creeds, and upon first principles of religion, that until the system of government should be changed, those subjects could not be brought fairly and openly before the world; but that whenever this should be done, a revolution in the system of religion would follow. Human inventions and priest-craft would be detected; and man would return to the pure, unmixed, and unadulterated belief of one God, and no more.

READING QUESTIONS

1. What did Paine believe? What did he *not* believe?

2. How did Paine characterize organized religions? What might explain the intensity of his views?

3. Why did Paine believe that a "revolution in the system of government" would almost certainly produce a "revolution in the system of religion"? What light does this shed on Paine's understanding of the nature of established churches?

■ COMPARATIVE AND DISCUSSION QUESTIONS ■

1. What can be gleaned from Williamson's and Wesley's accounts about the prevalence and nature of religious belief in eighteenth-century England?

2. What do Williamson's and Montagu's accounts suggest about the state and extent of medical knowledge in eighteenth-century Europe?

3. What can be learned from Williamson's, Locke's, and Montagu's accounts about attitudes toward children in the late seventeenth and eighteenth centuries?

4. On which aspects of religious belief and practice might Paine and Wesley agree? On which would they disagree?

19

Revolutions in Politics
1775–1815

The revolution that erupted in France in 1789, and would, in time, engulf all of Europe in political upheaval and war, was sparked by a financial crisis that had been brewing for more than a century. Over the course of the seventeenth and eighteenth centuries, the cost of warfare rose dramatically, and France was at war for almost all of that time. Under Louis XIV (1638–1715), France launched one war after another in an effort to cement French dominance in Europe. Louis XV (r. 1715–1774) inherited Louis XIV's ambitions and spent much of the eighteenth century unsuccessfully battling Britain for a world empire. By 1789 France's finances had reached the crisis point. With no options left, Louis XVI (r. 1774–1792) gave in to noble pressure to summon the Estates General, the French representative body that had last met in 1614. Louis hoped to use the Estates General as a vehicle for limited financial reform, but events quickly spun out of his control. What had begun as a financial crisis became a far-ranging debate over rights, liberty, and equality, the implications of which would reverberate around the world. While France would return to conservative government, first under Napoleon's dictatorship and then under a restored monarchy, the French Revolution would remain a potent symbol of the possibility of dramatic social and political change for centuries to come.

19-1 | The Third Estate Speaks
COMMISSIONERS OF THE THIRD ESTATE OF THE CARCASSONNE, *Notebooks of Grievances* (1789)

Assuming the throne in 1774, Louis XVI inherited a bankrupt government that spent half its income just to pay the interest on the national debt. The *Cahiers de Doleances (Notebooks of*

From Commissioners of Carcassonne, in *Readings in European History*, ed. James Harvey Robinson, 2 vols. (Boston: Ginn, 1904), 2:397–399.

Grievances) were an attempt to discover and catalogue the issues the king would need to resolve at the meeting of the Estates General in order to get approval for new taxes. Long denied any formal avenue of complaint, the third estate—everyone who was not a member of the nobility or clergy—responded with a flood of complaints and suggestions that surprised Louis and his advisers. While phrased in respectful language, the *Cahiers* illuminate a society at odds with the absolutism of Louis XVI's predecessors. As you read this example from the district of Carcassonne, ask yourself what kind of state would result from the reforms the authors propose. What rights would they claim for the people? What limits would they place on monarchial power?

The third estate of the electoral district of Carcassonne,[1] desiring to give to a beloved monarch, and one so worthy of our affection, the most unmistakable proof of its love and respect, of its gratitude and fidelity, desiring to cooperate with the whole nation in repairing the successive misfortunes which have overwhelmed it, and with the hope of reviving once more its ancient glory, declares that the happiness of the nation must, in their opinion, depend upon that of its king, upon the stability of the monarchy, and upon the preservation of the orders which compose it and of the fundamental laws which govern it.

Considering, too, that a holy respect for religion, morality, civil liberty, and the rights of property, a speedy return to true principles, a careful selection and due measure in the matter of the taxes, a strict proportionality in their assessment, a persistent economy in government expenditures, and indispensable reforms in all branches of the administration, are the best and perhaps the only means of perpetuating the existence of the monarchy;

The third estate of the electoral district of Carcassonne very humbly petitions his Majesty to take into consideration these several matters, weigh them in his wisdom, and permit his people to enjoy, as soon as may be, fresh proofs of that benevolence which he has never ceased to exhibit toward them and which is dictated by his affection for them.

In view of the obligation imposed by his Majesty's command that the third estate of this district should confide to his paternal ear the causes of the ills which afflict them and the means by which they may be remedied or moderated, they believe that they are fulfilling the duties of faithful subjects and zealous citizens in submitting to the consideration of the nation, and to the sentiments of justice and affection which his Majesty entertains for his subjects, the following:

1. Public worship should be confined to the Roman Catholic apostolic religion,[2] to the exclusion of all other forms of worship; its extension should be

---

[1]**Carcassonne**: Town in southern France, near the Mediterranean coast.

[2]**apostolic religion**: "Apostolic" meant that the leaders of the Roman Catholic Church claimed to have received their authority in succession from one of the original twelve apostles, specifically Peter. Of the Protestant churches, only the Church of England could claim apostolic succession.

promoted and the most efficient measures taken to reestablish the discipline of the Church and increase its prestige.

2. Nevertheless the civil rights of those of the king's subjects who are not Catholics should be confirmed, and they should be admitted to positions and offices in the public administration, without however extending this privilege— which reason and humanity alike demand for them—to judicial or police functions or to those of public instruction.

3. The nation should consider some means of abolishing the annates[3] and all other dues paid to the holy see, to the prejudice and against the protests of the whole French people. . . .

[The holding of multiple church positions should be prohibited, monasteries reduced in numbers, and holidays suppressed or decreased.]

7. The rights which have just been restored to the nation should be consecrated as fundamental principles of the monarchy, and their perpetual and unalterable enjoyment should be assured by a solemn law, which should so define the rights both of the monarch and of the people that their violation shall hereafter be impossible.

8. Among these rights the following should be especially noted: the nation should hereafter be subject only to such laws and taxes as it shall itself freely ratify.

9. The meetings of the Estates General of the kingdom should be fixed for definite periods, and the subsidies judged necessary for the support of the state and the public service should be voted for no longer a period than to the close of the year in which the next meeting of the Estates General is to occur.

10. In order to assure to the third estate the influence to which it is entitled in view of the number of its members, the amount of its contributions to the public treasury, and the manifold interests which it has to defend or promote in the national assemblies, its votes in the assembly should be taken and counted by head.

11. No order, corporation, or individual citizen may lay claim to any pecuniary exemptions. . . . All taxes should be assessed on the same system throughout the nation.

12. The due exacted from commoners holding fiefs[4] should be abolished, and also the general or particular regulations which exclude members of the third estate from certain positions, offices, and ranks which have hitherto been bestowed on nobles either for life or hereditarily. A law should be

---

[3]**annates**: Refers to the practice of claiming the first year's profits from a church district, or see, for the bishop who oversaw that district.

[4]**fiefs**: Medieval gifts of land in return for military service. With the rise of professional armies, many fief holders were expected to make cash payments instead.

passed declaring members of the third estate qualified to fill all such offices for which they are judged to be personally fitted.

13. Since individual liberty is intimately associated with national liberty, his Majesty is hereby petitioned not to permit that it be here-after interfered with by arbitrary orders for imprisonment. . . .

14. Freedom should be granted also to the press, which should however be subjected, by means of strict regulations, to the principles of religion, morality, and public decency. . . .

60. The third estate of the district of Carcassonne places its trust, for the rest, in the zeal, patriotism, honor, and probity of its deputies in the National Assembly in all matters which may accord with the beneficent views of his Majesty, the welfare of the kingdom, the union of the three estates, and the public peace.

READING QUESTIONS

1. What implications would this document have for a system of government based on absolute royal authority?

2. What position do the commissioners take toward the relationship of government and religion?

3. What economic reforms does the *Cahier* propose, and how might those affect the social structure of France?

4. How do the suggested reforms take the rights of the individual into account?

19-2 | Redefining Society and the Nation
ABBÉ SIEYÈS, *What Is the Third Estate?* (1789)

The Estates General was a representative body in only the most limited sense of the term. Organized around the traditional division of French society into the clergy, the nobility, and the commoners, its procedures reflected and reinforced the power of the privileged classes. While the clergy and nobility made up only a very small percentage of France's population, together they controlled two-thirds of the voting power of the Estates General. From the moment of its convening, delegates of the Third Estate, along with allies from the clerical and noble ranks, agitated for a change in this arrangement. Abbé Sieyès's pamphlet entitled "What Is the Third Estate?" embodied the position of many such delegates. As you read this excerpt from the pamphlet, pay particular attention to the way Sieyès defined the French nation. How did his definition challenge the traditional social vision embodied in the Estates General?

From Lynn Hunt, ed. and trans., *The French Revolution and Human Rights: A Brief Documentary History* (Boston: Bedford/St. Martin's, 1996), pp. 65–70.

The plan of this work is quite simple. We must ask ourselves three questions.

1. What is the Third Estate? Everything.
2. What has it been until now in the political order? Nothing.
3. What does it want? To become something. . . .

What does a Nation require to survive and prosper? *Private* employment and *public* offices.

Private employment includes four classes of work:

1. Since the land and water provide the raw material for the needs of mankind, the first class, in logical order, includes all those families attached to work in the countryside.

2. Between the initial sale of raw materials and their consumption or usage as finished goods, labor of various sorts adds more value to these goods. In this way human industry manages to improve on the blessings of Nature and to multiply the value of the raw materials two, ten, or a hundredfold. Such is the second class of work.

3. Between production and consumption, as also between the different stages of production, there are a host of intermediary agents, useful both to producers and consumers; these are the merchants and wholesale traders. Wholesale traders constantly weigh demand according to place and time and speculate on the profit that they can make on storage and transport; merchants actually sell the goods on the markets, whether wholesale or retail. This type of utility designates the third class of work.

4. Besides these three classes of hard-working and useful Citizens who occupy themselves with the *things* fit to be consumed or used, society also needs a multitude of private occupations and services *directly* useful or agreeable to the *person*. This fourth class embraces all those occupations from the most distinguished scientific and liberal professions down to the least esteemed domestic servants.

These are the kinds of work that sustain society. Who carries them out? The Third Estate.

In the present state of affairs public offices can also be ranked in four well-known categories: the Sword [the army], the Robe [the courts], the Church, and the Administration. Detailed analysis is not necessary to show that the Third Estate makes up everywhere 19/20ths of their number, except that it is charged with all the really hard work, all the work that the privileged order refuses to perform. Only the lucrative and most honored places are taken by the members of the privileged order. Should we praise them for this? We could do so only if the Third [Estate] was unwilling or unable to fill these offices. We know the truth of the matter, but the Third Estate has nonetheless been excluded. They are told, "Whatever your services, whatever your talents, you will only go so far and no further. Honors are not for your sort." A few rare exceptions, noteworthy as they are bound to be, are only a mockery, and the language encouraged on these exceptional occasions is but an additional insult.

If this exclusion is a social crime committed against the Third Estate, can we say at least that it is useful to the public good? Ah! Are the effects of monopoly not known? If it discourages those whom it pushes aside, does it not also render those it favors less competent? Is it not obvious that every piece of work kept out of free competition will be made more expensively and less well?

. . . It suffices here to have made the point that the supposed usefulness of a privileged order to the public service is nothing but a mirage; that without that order, all that is most arduous in this service is performed by the Third Estate; that without the privileged the best places would be infinitely better filled; that such places should naturally be the prize and reward for recognized talents and services; and that if the privileged have succeeded in usurping all the lucrative and honored posts, this is at once an odious iniquity committed against the vast majority of the citizenry and an act of treason against the public good.

Who therefore dares to say that the Third Estate does not contain within itself all that is needed to form a complete Nation? The Third Estate is like a strong and robust man with one arm still in chains. If we remove the privileged order, the Nation will not be something less but something more. Thus, what is the Third Estate? All, but an all that is shackled and oppressed. What would it be without the privileged order? All, but an all that is free and flourishing. Nothing can be done without it [the Third Estate]; everything would be infinitely better without the other two orders.

It does not suffice to have demonstrated that the privileged, far from being useful to the Nation, can only weaken and harm it; it must be proved further that the noble order is not even part of society itself: It may very well be a burden for the Nation but it cannot be a part of it. . . .

What is a Nation? A body of associates living under a *common* law and represented by the same *legislature*.

Is it not more than certain that the noble order has privileges, exemptions, and even rights that are distinct from the rights of the great body of citizens? Because of this, it does not belong to the common order, it is not covered by the law common to the rest. Thus its civil rights already make it a people apart inside the great Nation. It is truly *imperium in imperio* [a law unto itself].

As for its *political* rights, the nobility also exercises them separately. It has its own representatives who have no mandate from the people. Its deputies sit separately, and even when they assemble in the same room with the deputies of the ordinary citizens, the nobility's representation still remains essentially distinct and separate: it is foreign to the Nation by its very principle, for its mission does not emanate from the people, and by its purpose, since it consists in defending, not the general interest, but the private interests of the nobility.

The Third Estate therefore contains everything that pertains to the Nation and nobody outside of the Third Estate can claim to be part of the Nation. What is the Third Estate? EVERYTHING. . . .

By Third Estate is meant the collectivity of citizens who belong to the common order. Anybody who holds a legal privilege of any kind leaves that common order, stands as an exception to the common law, and in consequence does not belong to the Third Estate. . . . It is certain that the moment a citizen acquires privileges contrary to common law, he no longer belongs to the common order. His new interest is opposed to the general interest; he has no right to vote in the name of the people. [Thus nobles should not be allowed to represent the Third Estate in the Estates General.] . . .

In vain can anyone's eyes be closed to the revolution that time and the force of things have brought to pass; it is none the less real. Once upon a time the Third Estate was in bondage and the noble order was everything that mattered. Today the Third is everything and nobility but a word. Yet under the cover of this word a new and intolerable aristocracy has slipped in, and the people has every reason to no longer want aristocrats. . . .

What is the will of a Nation? It is the result of individual wills, just as the Nation is the aggregate of the individuals who compose it. It is impossible to conceive of a legitimate association that does not have for its goal the common security, the common liberty, in short, the public good. No doubt each individual also has his own personal aims. He says to himself, "protected by the common security, I will be able to peacefully pursue my own personal projects, I will seek my happiness where I will, assured of encountering only those legal obstacles that society will prescribe for the common interest, in which I have a part and with which my own personal interest is so usefully allied." . . .

Three kinds of interests can be found in the hearts of men: 1) that which makes them all alike; it marks the boundaries of the common interest, 2) that which unites an individual to only some others; this is the interest of a body or group; and finally, 3) that which isolates each person and makes him think only of himself; this is a personal interest. The interest whereby a man comes to an agreement with all of his associates is obviously the purpose toward which everyone's will and that of the common assembly both tend. The influence of personal interest ought to count for nothing in this domain. That is in fact what happens, for the diversity of interest is its own remedy. The great difficulty comes from that interest whereby a citizen agrees with only some others. This permits them to connive and conspire to devise schemes that are dangerous for the community interest; this kind of interest creates the most formidable enemies of the people. History presents countless examples of this truth.

It is therefore not surprising that social order rigorously demands that ordinary citizens refrain from constituting themselves in *corporations* [such as guilds]; it even requires that public officials, who of necessity from true *corps* or official bodies, renounce the possibility of being elected to the legislature as long as they are so employed.

Thus and not otherwise is the common interest assured of dominating over personal interests. Only under these conditions can one accept the possibility of founding human associations for the general advantage of those so associated and as a result grant the *legitimacy* of political societies or clubs. . . .

Advantages which differentiate citizens from one another lie outside the purview of citizenship. Inequalities of wealth or ability are like the inequalities of age, sex, size, etc. In no way do they detract from the *equality* of citizenship. These individual advantages no doubt benefit from the protection of the law; but it is not the legislator's task to create them, to give privileges to some and refuse them to others. The law grants nothing; it protects what already exists until such time that what exists begins to harm the common interest. These are the only limits on individual freedom. I imagine the law as being at the center of a large globe; we the citizens, without exception, stand equidistant from it on the surface and occupy equal places; all are equally dependent on the law, all present it with their liberty and their property to be protected; and this is what I call the *common rights* of citizens, by which they are all alike. All these individuals communicate with each other, enter into contracts, negotiate, always under the common guarantee of the law. If in this general activity somebody wishes to get control over the person of his neighbor or usurp his property, the common law goes into action to repress this criminal attempt and puts everyone back in their place at the same distance from the law. . . .

It is impossible to say what place the two privileged orders ought to occupy in the social order: this is the equivalent of asking what place one wishes to assign to a malignant tumor that torments and undermines the strength of the body of a sick person. It must be *neutralized*. We must re-establish the health and working of all the organs so thoroughly that they are no longer susceptible to these fatal schemes that are capable of sapping the most essential principles of vitality.

READING QUESTIONS

1. How did Sieyès answer his own question posed in the title of his pamphlet?

2. What did he mean when he said that the Third Estate was a "complete nation"?

3. What productive role, if any, did he imagine the clergy and the nobility playing in national government?

4. What were the political implications of Sieyès's claim that the Third Estate was "everything"?

Imagining a New France

Each phase in the French Revolution was marked by the emergence of a new vision of France's future, of the kind of nation that would embody the French people's essential principles and core qualities. During the first phase, the emphasis of reformers was on equality before the law. Drawing on Enlightenment thought, the members of the National Assembly who drafted the *Declaration of the Rights of Man and of the Citizen* concentrated on identifying the rights shared by all French citizens and on eliminating legal distinctions that privileged one group within French society over another.

During the Second Revolution, leaders such as Robespierre aimed for a far more radical remaking of France, seeking to change not only France's laws, but its social and cultural values as well. Under the Directory and later under Napoleon, a conservative backlash set in, as French elites sought to reinforce traditional social and economic hierarchies, even as elements of the revolution were incorporated into the new French state.

19-3 | NATIONAL ASSEMBLY OF FRANCE, *Declaration of the Rights of Man and of the Citizen* (1789)

After the fall of the Bastille, rumors that the nobility were plotting to use foreign mercenaries to suppress the Revolution swept through the French countryside. In an effort to quell the "great fear," the National Assembly abolished feudalism and released the "Declaration of the Rights of Man," which laid out the basic principles upon which their government would be founded. While Enlightenment thinkers had used reason to critique social practices and customs but rarely produced actual reforms, the French revolutionaries applied the spirit of reason to practical politics. It is a measure of their success that their ideas about a citizen's relationship with their government no longer seem so radical.

The representatives of the French people, organized as a National Assembly, believing that the ignorance, neglect, or contempt of the rights of man are the sole cause of public calamities and of the corruption of governments, have determined to set forth in a solemn declaration the natural, inalienable, and sacred rights of man, in order that this declaration, being constantly before all the members of the social body, shall remind them continually of their rights and duties; in order that the acts of the legislative power, as well as those of the executive power, may be compared at any moment with the objects and purposes of all political institutions and may thus be more respected; and, lastly, in order that the grievances of the citizens, based hereafter upon simple and incontestable principles, shall tend to the maintenance of the constitution and redound to the happiness of all. Therefore the National Assembly recognizes and proclaims, in the presence and under the auspices of the Supreme Being, the following rights of man and of the citizen:

ARTICLE 1. Men are born and remain free and equal in rights. Social distinctions may be founded only upon the general good.

2. The aim of all political association is the preservation of the natural and imprescriptible rights of man. These rights are liberty, property, security, and resistance to oppression.

From James Harvey Robinson, ed., *Readings in European History*, 2 vols. (Boston: Ginn, 1904), 2:409–411.

3. The principle of all sovereignty resides essentially in the nation. No body nor individual may exercise any authority which does not proceed directly from the nation.

4. Liberty consists in the freedom to do everything which injures no one else; hence the exercise of the natural rights of each man has no limits except those which assure to the other members of the society the enjoyment of the same rights. These limits can only be determined by law.

5. Law can only prohibit such actions as are hurtful to society. Nothing may be prevented which is not forbidden by law, and no one may be forced to do anything not provided for by law.

6. Law is the expression of the general will. Every citizen has a right to participate personally, or through his representative, in its formation. It must be the same for all, whether it protects or punishes. All citizens, being equal in the eyes of the law, are equally eligible to all dignities and to all public positions and occupations, according to their abilities, and without distinction except that of their virtues and talents.

7. No person shall be accused, arrested, or imprisoned except in the cases and according to the forms prescribed by law. Any one soliciting, transmitting, executing, or causing to be executed, any arbitrary order, shall be punished. But any citizen summoned or arrested in virtue of the law shall submit without delay, as resistance constitutes an offense.

8. The law shall provide for such punishments only as are strictly and obviously necessary, and no one shall suffer punishment except it be legally inflicted in virtue of a law passed and promulgated before the commission of the offense.

9. As all persons are held innocent until they shall have been declared guilty, if arrest shall be deemed indispensable, all harshness not essential to the securing of the prisoner's person shall be severely repressed by law.

10. No one shall be disquieted on account of his opinions, including his religious views, provided their manifestation does not disturb the public order established by law.

11. The free communication of ideas and opinions is one of the most precious of the rights of man. Every citizen may, accordingly, speak, write, and print with freedom, but shall be responsible for such abuses of this freedom as shall be defined by law.

12. The security of the rights of man and of the citizen requires public military forces. These forces are, therefore, established for the good of all and not for the personal advantage of those to whom they shall be intrusted.

13. A common contribution is essential for the maintenance of the public forces and for the cost of administration. This should be equitably distributed among all the citizens in proportion to their means.

14. All the citizens have a right to decide, either personally or by their representatives, as to the necessity of the public contribution; to grant this freely; to know to what uses it is put; and to fix the proportion, the mode of assessment and of collection and the duration of the taxes.

15. Society has the right to require of every public agent an account of his administration.

16. A society in which the observance of the law is not assured, nor the separation of powers defined, has no constitution at all.

17. Since property is an inviolable and sacred right, no one shall be deprived thereof except where public necessity, legally determined, shall clearly demand it, and then only on condition that the owner shall have been previously and equitably indemnified.

READING QUESTIONS

1. Who, according to the authors of this document, make up the "nation"? What is the basis of the government they propose?

2. In what ways is this declaration revolutionary, and in what ways does it continue the status quo?

3. What sort of balance does the declaration attempt to strike between the rights and responsibilities of citizens?

19-4 | *The Law of 22 Prairial* (1794)

The Terror took place against a backdrop of war with Austria and Prussia, as increasingly radicalized French revolutionary leaders struggled to contend with enemies, both foreign and domestic. Seeking national unity, Maximilien Robespierre (1758–1794) and his allies pursued a comprehensive program of republican reforms, which they argued were necessary for the full expression of the general will. Anyone who was perceived as an obstacle to the implementation of that program was, by definition, an enemy of the French people. The Law of 22 Prairial, promulgated shortly before Robespierre's fall, concentrated power in the hands of Robespierre's select committees, at the same time that it removed the last vestiges of legal protection for those accused of political crimes. As you read it, think about how Robespierre and his allies might have justified the new law. Why might they have believed that the Law of 22 Prairial was necessary for the survival of the revolution?

1. In the Revolutionary Tribunal there shall be a president and four vice-presidents, one public prosecutor, four substitutes for the public prosecutor, and twelve judges.

2. The jurors shall be fifty in number.

3. The divers functions shall be performed by the citizens herein-after named; . . .

The Revolutionary Tribunal shall divide itself into sections, composed of twelve members, to wit: three judges and nine jurors, which jurors may not pass judgment unless they are seven in number.

From John Hall Stewart, ed., *A Documentary History of the French Revolution* (New York: Macmillan, 1951), pp. 528–531.

4. The Revolutionary Tribunal is instituted to punish the enemies of the people.

5. The enemies of the people are those who seek to destroy public liberty, either by force or by cunning.

6. The following are deemed enemies of the people: those who have instigated the re-establishment of monarchy, or have sought to disparage or dissolve the National Convention and the revolutionary and republican government of which it is the center;

Those who have betrayed the Republic in the command of places and armies, or in any other military function, carried on correspondence with the enemies of the Republic, labored to disrupt the provisioning or the service of the armies;

Those who have sought to impede the provisioning of Paris, or to create scarcity within the Republic;

Those who have supported the designs of the enemies of France, either by countenancing the sheltering and the impunity of conspirators and aristocracy, by persecuting and calumniating patriotism, by corrupting the mandataries of the people, or by abusing the principles of the Revolution or the laws or measures of the government by false and perfidious applications;

Those who have deceived the people or the representatives of the people, in order to lead them into undertakings contrary to the interests of liberty;

Those who have sought to inspire discouragement, in order to favor the enterprises of the tyrants leagued against the Republic;

Those who have disseminated false news in order to divide or disturb the people;

Those who have sought to mislead opinion and to prevent the instruction of the people, to deprave morals and to corrupt the public conscience, to impair the energy and the purity of revolutionary and republican principles, or to impede the progress thereof, either by counter-revolutionary or insidious writings, or by any other machination;

Contractors of bad faith who compromise the safety of the Republic, and squanderers of the public fortune, other than those included in the provisions of the law of 7 Frimaire;

Those who, charged with public office, take advantage of it in order to serve the enemies of the Revolution, to harass patriots, or to oppress the people;

Finally, all who are designated in previous laws relative to the punishment of conspirators and counter-revolutionaries, and who, by whatever means or by whatever appearances they assume, have made an attempt against the liberty, unity, and security of the Republic, or labored to prevent the strengthening thereof.

7. The penalty provided for all offences under the jurisdiction of the Revolutionary Tribunal is death.

8. The proof necessary to convict enemies of the people comprises every kind of evidence, whether material or moral, oral or written, which can naturally secure the approval of every just and reasonable mind; the rule of judgments

is the conscience of the jurors, enlightened by love of the *Patrie*; their aim, the triumph of the Republic and the ruin of its enemies; the procedure, the simple means which good sense dictates in order to arrive at a knowledge of the truth, in the forms determined by law.

It is confined to the following points.

9. Every citizen has the right to seize conspirators and counter-revolutionaries, and to arraign them before the magistrates. He is required to denounce them as soon as he knows of them.

10. Nobody may arraign anyone before the Revolutionary Tribunal except the National Convention, the Committee of Public Safety, the Committee of General Security, the representatives of the people who are commissioners of the Convention, and the public prosecutor at the Revolutionary Tribunal.

11. The constituted authorities in general may not exercise such right without having notified the Committee of Public Safety and the Committee of General Security and obtained their authorization.

12. The accused shall be examined publicly in the courtroom: the formality of the preceding secret examination is suppressed as superfluous; it shall take place only under special circumstances in which it is deemed useful for a knowledge of the truth.

13. If either material or moral proofs exist, apart from the attested proof, there shall be no further hearing of witnesses, unless such formality appears necessary, either to discover accomplices or for other important considerations of public interest.

14. In case there is occasion for such proof, the public prosecutor shall cause to be summoned those witnesses, whether for or against, who may enlighten justice.

15. All proceedings shall be conducted in public, and no written deposition shall be received, unless witnesses are so situated that they cannot come before the Tribunal; and in such case an express authorization of the Committees of Public Safety and General Security shall be necessary.

16. The law provides sworn patriots as counsel for calumniated patriots; it does not grant them to conspirators.

17. The pleadings completed, the jurors shall formulate their verdicts, and the judges shall pronounce the penalty in the manner determined by law.

The president shall propound the question with lucidity, precision, and simplicity. If it is presented in an equivocal or inexact fashion, the jury may ask that it be propounded in another manner.

18. The public prosecutor may not, on his own authority, discharge an accused person sent to the Tribunal, or one whom he himself has caused to be arraigned before it; in case there is no ground for accusation before the Tribunal, he shall make a written and motivated report thereon to the chamber of the council, which shall decide. But no accused person may be discharged from trial before the decision of the chamber has been communicated to the Committees of Public Safety and General Security, who shall examine it.

19. A duplicate register shall be kept of the persons arraigned before the Revolutionary Tribunal, one for the public prosecutor and the other for the Tribunal, and all accused persons shall be enrolled thereon as they are arraigned.

20. The Convention modifies all those provisions of previous laws which are at variance with the present law, and it does not intend that laws concerning the organization of the ordinary courts should apply to the crimes of counter-revolution or to the functioning of the Revolutionary Tribunal.

21. The report of the Committee shall be appended to the present decree as an instruction.

READING QUESTIONS

1. What groups and individuals are defined as "enemies of the people"?

2. What powers did the law give the state to identify and punish such people?

3. How might the law's authors have justified the lack of legal protections for those accused?

4. In your opinion, does the law constitute a betrayal of the revolution? Why or why not?

19-5 | NAPOLEON BONAPARTE, *The Napoleonic Code* (1804)

Napoleon Bonaparte (1769–1821) first gained fame as a general in France's revolutionary army, but his military achievements proved less lasting than his civil ones. When he took power in 1799, Napoleon ordered a new law code written for France, incorporating many of the National Assembly's 1789 reforms. Finished in 1804, the new civil code was easily read and understood by the average citizen. While it enshrined greater legal equality for men than had prevailed prior to 1789, it was, nonetheless, a socially conservative document. Nowhere is this more apparent than in the code's treatment of women. As had been the case under the monarchy, the new law code was predicated on a vision of politics and society centered on the authority of fathers and husbands. As you read this excerpt from the code, pay particular attention to the way it differentiates between the legal status of men and women.

Preliminary Title: Of the Publication, Effect, and Application of the Laws in General

1. The laws are executory throughout the whole French territory, by virtue of the promulgation thereof made by the First Consul. They shall be executed in every part of the Republic, from the moment at which their promulgation can have been known. The promulgation made by the First Consul shall be

From E. A. Arnold, ed. and trans., *A Documentary Survey of Napoleonic France* (Lanham, Md.: University Press of America, 1993), pp. 151–164, quoted in Laura Mason and Tracey Rizzo, eds., *The French Revolution: A Document Collection* (New York: Houghton Mifflin, 1999), pp. 340–347.

taken to be known in the department which shall be the seat of government, one day after the promulgation; and in each of the other departments, after the expiration of the same interval augmented by one day for every ten myriameters[1] (about twenty ancient leagues[2]) between the town in which the promulgation shall have been made, and the chief place of each department.

2. The law ordains for the future only; it has no retrospective operation.

3. The laws of police and public security bind all the inhabitants of the territory. Immovable property, although in the possession of foreigners, is governed by the French law. The laws relating to the condition and privileges of persons govern Frenchmen, although residing in a foreign country. . . .

6. Private agreements must not contravene the laws which concern public order and good morals.

Book I: Of Persons

Title I: Of the Enjoyment and Privation of Civil Rights

1. The exercise of civil rights is independent of the quality of citizen, which is only acquired and preserved conformably to the constitutional law. . . .

8. Every Frenchman shall enjoy civil rights.

Chapter VI: Of the Respective Rights and Duties of Married Persons

212. Married persons owe to each other fidelity, succor, assistance.

213. The husband owes protection to his wife, the wife obedience to her husband.

214. The wife is obliged to live with her husband, and to follow him to every place where he may judge it convenient to reside: the husband is obliged to receive her, and to furnish her with every necessity for the wants of life, according to his means and station.

215. The wife cannot plead in her own name, without the authority of her husband, even though she should be a public trader, or non-communicant, or separate in property.

216. The authority of the husband is not necessary when the wife is prosecuted in a criminal manner, or relating to police.

217. A wife, although noncommunicant or separate in property, cannot give, pledge, or acquire by free or chargeable title, without the concurrence of her husband in the act, or his consent in writing.

218. If the husband refuses to authorize his wife to plead in her own name, the judge may give her authority.

---

[1]**myriameters**: Ten thousand meters, or ten kilometers. One of the Revolution's accomplishments was to replace the many local systems of measurement in France with a unified, easy-to-use metric system.

[2]**leagues**: Roman leagues; about two kilometers. The Roman Empire's systems of measurement survived long after its political structure crumbled.

219. If the husband refuses to authorize his wife to pass an act, the wife may cause her husband to be cited directly before the court of the first instance, of the circle of their common domicil[e], which may give or refuse its authority, after the husband shall have been heard, or duly summoned before the chamber of council.

220. The wife, if she is a public trader, may, without the authority of her husband, bind herself for that which concerns her trade; and in the said case she binds also her husband, if there be a community between them. She is not reputed a public trader if she merely retails goods in her husband's trade, but only when she carries on a separate business.

221. When the husband is subjected to a condemnation, carrying with it an afflictive or infamous punishment, although it may have been pronounced merely for contumacy,[3] the wife, though of age, cannot, during the continuance of such punishment, plead in her own name or contract, until after authority given by the judge, who may in such case give his authority without hearing or summoning the husband. . . .

226. The wife may make a will without the authority of her husband. . . .

Title VI: Of Divorce

Section II: Of the Provisional Measures to Which the Petition for Cause Determinate May Give Rise

267. The provisional management of the children shall rest with the husband, petitioner, or defendant, in the suit for divorce, unless it be otherwise ordered for the greater advantage of the children, on petition of either the mother, or the family, or the government commissioner. . . .

271. Every obligation contracted by the husband at the expense of the community, every alienation made by him of immovable property dependent upon it, subsequent to the date of the order mentioned in article 238, shall be declared void, if proof be given, moreover, that it has been made or contracted in fraud of the rights of the wife. . . .

Title IX: Of Paternal Power

375. A father who shall have cause of grievous dissatisfaction at the conduct of a child, shall have the following means of correction.

376. If the child has not commenced his sixteenth year, the father may cause him to be confined for a period which shall not exceed one month; and to this effect the president of the court of the circle shall be bound, on his petition, to deliver an order of arrest.

377. From the age of sixteen years commenced to the majority or emancipation, the father is only empowered to require the confinement of his child during six months at the most; he shall apply to the president of the aforesaid court,

---

[3]**contumacy:** Refusal to obey legal authority.

who, after having conferred thereon with the commissioner of government, shall deliver an order of arrest or refuse the same, and may in the first case abridge the time of confinement required by the father. . . .

379. The father is always at liberty to abridge the duration of the confinement by him ordered or required. If the child after his liberation fall into new irregularities, his confinement may be ordered anew, according to the manner prescribed in the preceding articles. . . .

Book III: Modes of Acquiring Property

Title I: Of Successions

818. The husband may, without the concurrence of his wife, claim a distribution of objects movable or immovable fallen to her and which come into community; with respect to objects which do not come into community, the husband cannot claim the distribution thereof without the concurrence of his wife; he can only demand a provisional distribution in case he has a right to the enjoyment of her property. The co-heirs of the wife cannot claim final distribution without suing the husband and his wife. . . .

Title II: Donations and Wills

905. A married woman cannot make donation during life without the assistance or the special consent of her husband, or without being thereto authorized by the law, conformably to what is prescribed by articles 217 and 219, under the title "Of Marriage." She shall not need either the consent of her husband, or the authorization of the law, in order to dispose by will. . . .

Chapter IV: Of Donations During Life

Section II: Of the Administration of the Community, and of the Effect of the Acts of Either of the Married Parties Relating to the Conjugal Union

1421. The husband alone administers the property of the community. He may sell it, alienate and pledge it without the concurrence of his wife. . . .

1424. Fines incurred by the husband for a crime not importing civil death, may be sued for out of the property of the community, saving the compensation due to the wife; such as are incurred by the wife cannot be put in execution except out of her bare property in her personal goods, so long as the community continues. . . .

1427. The wife cannot bind herself nor engage the property of the community, even to free her husband from prison, or for the establishment of their children in case of her husband's absence, until she shall have been thereto authorized by the law.

1428. The husband has the management of all the personal property of the wife. He may prosecute alone all possessory actions and those relating to movables, which belong to his wife. He cannot alienate the personal immovables of his wife without her consent. He is responsible for all waste in the personal goods of his wife, occasioned by the neglect of conservatory acts.

READING QUESTIONS

1. What groups in French society would benefit most from these laws?
2. What about these laws seems radical, and what seems rooted in tradition?
3. What legal and economic rights do women enjoy under the code?
4. What similarities are there in the way the code treats women and children? What significance should we attach to these similarities?

19-6 | Challenging the Limits of Equality

MARY WOLLSTONECRAFT, *A Vindication of the Rights of Woman* (1792)

The French Constitution of 1791, drafted by the same National Assembly that passed the "Declaration of the Rights of Man," confined full citizenship to a limited number of property-holding men. While many Enlightenment ideals that underlay the Revolution had developed in salons overseen by upper-class women, prevailing thought held that women lacked the intellectual and emotional capacity to participate in politics. The English radical Mary Wollstonecraft disagreed. Her response was *A Vindication of the Rights of Woman*, written to French diplomat Charles Talleyrand, who had recently advocated a very limited and almost exclusively domestic education for women.

My own sex, I hope, will excuse me, if I treat them like rational creatures, instead of flattering their fascinating graces, and viewing them as if they were in a state of perpetual childhood, unable to stand alone. I earnestly wish to point out in what true dignity and human happiness consists—I wish to persuade women to endeavor to acquire strength, both of mind and body, and to convince them that the soft phrases, susceptibility of heart, delicacy of sentiment, and refinement of taste, are almost synonymous with epithets of weakness, and that those beings who are only the objects of pity will soon become objects of contempt.

Dismissing those soft pretty feminine phrases, which the men condescendingly use to soften our slavish dependence, and despising that weak elegancy of mind, exquisite sensibility, and sweet docility of manners, supposed to be the

From Mary Wollstonecraft, *A Vindication of the Rights of Woman* (1792), ed. Carol H. Poston (New York: W. W. Norton, 1975), pp. 9–10, 27, 31.

sexual characteristics of the weaker vessel, I wish to show that elegance is inferior to virtue, that the first object of laudable ambition is to obtain a character as a human being, regardless of the distinction of sex.

Youth is the season for love in both sexes; but in those days of thoughtless enjoyment provision should be made for the more important years of life, when reflection takes place of sensation. The woman who has only been taught to please will soon find that her charms are oblique sunbeams and that they cannot have much effect on her husband's heart when they are seen every day, when the summer is passed and gone. Will she then have sufficient native energy to look into herself for comfort, and cultivate her dormant faculties? or, is it not more rational to expect that she will try to please other men?

Why must the female mind be tainted by coquettish arts to gratify the sensualist and prevent love from subsiding into friendship, or compassionate tenderness, when there are not qualities on which friendship can be built? Let the honest heart show itself, and reason teach passion to submit to necessity; or, let the dignified pursuit of virtue and knowledge raise the mind above those emotions. . . .

If then women are not a swarm of ephemeron triflers, why should they be kept in ignorance under the specious name of innocence? . . . As to the argument respecting the subjection in which the sex has ever been held, it retorts on man. The many have always been enthralled by the few; and monsters, who scarcely have shown any discernment of human excellence, have tyrannized over thousands of their fellow-creatures. . . . China is not the only country where a living man has been made a God. Men have submitted to superior strength to enjoy with impunity the pleasure of the moment; women have only done the same, and therefore till it is proved that the courtier, who servilely resigns the birthright of a man, is not a moral agent, it cannot be demonstrated that woman is essentially inferior to man because she has always been subjugated.

READING QUESTIONS

1. How might a man and a woman read this document differently? Is it addressed to men or women?

2. In what ways does Wollstonecraft accept that women are inferior? Does this weaken or strengthen her argument?

3. Based on Wollstonecraft's argument, what can you discern about a stereotypical woman of the time? How does she behave? How do men respond to her?

4. What connection might Wollstonecraft have made between education and fitness for the exercise of political rights? How might her vision of female education have differed from that promoted by Talleyrand?

19-7 | The Revolution in the French Colonies

FRANÇOIS DOMINIQUE TOUSSAINT L'OUVERTURE, *A Black Revolutionary Leader in Haiti* (1797)

The impact of the French Revolution and the Napoleonic Wars was not limited to Europe. Societies across the Americas were shaken by events in France. In the United States, support or opposition to the revolution was a key line of division between emerging political parties. In South America, independence movements flared up in colony after colony. And, in the sugar islands of the Caribbean, oppressed slaves rose in revolt, determined to have their full share in the rights of men. In 1792, after French colonial rulers arrested the leader of a Caribbean slave delegation in Paris, freed slave Toussaint Breda (who later changed his name to "L'Ouverture," as he had "opened" the way to liberty) emerged as the leader of a massive revolt on the French island of Saint-Domingue (known since gaining its independence as Haiti). In the letter included here, L'Ouverture appealed to French leaders to reject calls by the colonial planter class for re-establishment of slavery in the French colonies and to support the cause of liberty.

The impolitic and incendiary discourse of Vaublanc[1] has not affected the blacks nearly so much as their certainty of the projects which the proprietors of San Domingo are planning: insidious declarations should not have any effect in the eyes of wise legislators who have decreed liberty for the nations. But the attempts on that liberty which the colonists propose are all the more to be feared because it is with the veil of patriotism that they cover their detestable plans. We know that they seek to impose some of them on you by illusory and specious promises, in order to see renewed in this colony its former scenes of horror. Already perfidious emissaries have stepped in among us to ferment the destructive leaven prepared by the hands of liberticides [i.e., murderers of liberty]. But they will not succeed. I swear it by all that liberty holds most sacred. My attachment to France, my knowledge of the blacks, make it my duty not to leave you ignorant either of the crimes which they meditate or the oath that we renew, to bury ourselves under the ruins of a country revived by liberty rather than suffer the return of slavery.

It is for you, Citizens Directors, to turn from over our heads the storm which the eternal enemies of our liberty are preparing in the shades of silence. It is for you to enlighten the legislature, it is for you to prevent the enemies of the present system from spreading themselves on our unfortunate shores to sully it with new crimes. Do not allow our brothers, our friends, to be sacrificed to men who wish to reign over the ruins of the human species. But no, your wisdom will enable you to avoid the dangerous snares which our common enemies hold out for you. . . .

From François Dominique Toussaint L'Ouverture, Letter, in *The Black Jacobins*, 2d ed., ed. C. L. R. James (New York: Vintage Books, 1963), pp. 195–197.

[1]**Vaublanc**: The count of Vaublanc was a royalist and proponent of freeing the slaves and giving them citizenship, in opposition to L'Ouverture's more moderate views.

I send you with this letter a declaration which will acquaint you with the unity that exists between the proprietors of San Domingo who are in France, those in the United States, and those who serve under the English banner. You will see there a resolution, unequivocal and carefully constructed, for the restoration of slavery; you will see there that their determination to succeed has led them to envelop themselves in the mantle of liberty in order to strike it more deadly blows. You will see that they are counting heavily on my complacency in lending myself to their perfidious views by my fear for my children. It is not astonishing that these men who sacrifice their country to their interests are unable to conceive how many sacrifices a true love of country can support in a better father than they, since I unhesitatingly base the happiness of my children on that of my country, which they and they alone wish to destroy.

I shall never hesitate between the safety of San Domingo and my personal happiness; but I have nothing to fear. It is to the solicitude of the French Government that I have confided my children. . . . I would tremble with horror if it was into the hands of the colonists that I had sent them as hostages; but even if it were so, let them know that in punishing them for the fidelity of their father, they would only add one degree more to their barbarism, without any hope of ever making me fail in my duty. . . . Blind as they are! They cannot see how this odious conduct on their part can become the signal of new disasters and irreparable misfortunes, and that far from making them regain what in their eyes liberty for all has made them lose, they expose themselves to a total ruin and the colony to its inevitable destruction. Do they think that men who have been able to enjoy the blessing of liberty will calmly see it snatched away? They supported their chains only so long as they did not know any condition of life more happy than that of slavery. But to-day when they have left it, if they had a thousand lives they would sacrifice them all rather than be forced into slavery again. But no, the same hand which has broken our chains will not enslave us anew. France will not revoke her principles, she will not withdraw from us the greatest of her benefits. She will protect us against all our enemies; she will not permit her sublime morality to be perverted, those principles which do her most honor to be destroyed, her most beautiful achievement to be degraded, and her Decree of 16 Pluviose[2] which so honors humanity to be revoked. But if, to re-establish slavery in San Domingo, this was done, then I declare to you it would be to attempt the impossible: we have known how to face dangers to obtain our liberty, we shall know how to brave death to maintain it.

This, Citizens Directors, is the morale of the people of San Domingo, those are the principles that they transmit to you by me.

---

[2]**Decree of 16 Pluviose**: In 1793, French revolutionaries reorganized their calendar to remove the Christian elements; the event marking year one moved from the birth of Jesus to the adoption of the French constitution in 1792. The fifth month, roughly corresponding to April, known for its rains, became Pluviose, which loosely translates as "rainy." The specific decree to which L'Ouverture refers abolished slavery in French colonies in April 1794.

My own you know. It is sufficient to renew, my hand in yours, the oath that I have made, to cease to live before gratitude dies in my heart, before I cease to be faithful to France and to my duty, before the god of liberty is profaned and sullied by the liberticides, before they can snatch from my hands that sword, those arms, which France confided to me for the defense of its rights and those of humanity, for the triumph of liberty and equality.

READING QUESTIONS

1. Who is the intended audience of this document? What is L'Ouverture trying to convince them to do?

2. What reasons might persuade the French to reimpose slavery in Haiti, and what reasons might they have for defending its abolition?

3. In what way is L'Ouverture seeking to find common ground with the French? Why?

■ COMPARATIVE AND DISCUSSION QUESTIONS ■

1. How would you explain the difference in tone between the "Notebooks of Grievances" and Abbé Sieyès's "What Is the Third Estate"? What changed between the summer and fall of 1789?

2. In what ways did the points expressed in the "Notebooks of Grievances" find their way into the "Declaration of the Rights of Man"? Were any points left out of the declaration? If so, why do you suppose they were excluded?

3. Compare and contrast the "Declaration of the Rights of Man and of the Citizen," the "Law of 22 Prairial," and the Napoleonic Code. What light do they shed on the evolution of French politics between 1789 and 1804?

4. What similarities exist between the arguments of Mary Wollstonecraft and Toussaint L'Ouverture for their groups' inclusion in the new political order? What differences can you discern?

5. Based on the "Declaration of the Rights of Man," Mary Wollstonecraft's argument, and Toussaint L'Ouverture's letter, what were the limits of liberty and equality promised by the Revolution?

20

The Revolution in Energy and Industry

ca. 1780–1850

The term "Industrial Revolution" was coined almost 150 years ago to describe the technological, economic, and social transformations that took place first in Great Britain and then elsewhere in Europe and the United States. Between 1780 and 1850, traditional English society, in which the overwhelming majority of the population worked in agriculture, gave way to an industrial society wherein the majority lived in urban settings and worked in the manufacturing or service sectors. These changes gave rise to similarly momentous alterations in patterns of work, social hierarchies, material culture, and the regional and global balance of power. In the short run, working and living conditions for ordinary Europeans worsened. In the long run, industrialization led to a vast expansion in the economy, providing jobs and goods for a rapidly growing population, and fueling the West's global pre-eminence in the nineteenth and twentieth centuries. Historians still debate whether "revolution" is an apt description for changes that took place over many decades, but there is little doubt that the consequences of those changes were profound.

20-1 | Predicting a Population Catastrophe

THOMAS MALTHUS, *An Essay on the Principle of Population* (1798)

Thomas Malthus (1766–1834) was an Anglican clergyman by training but was deeply interested in demography, or the study of human population. His 1798 book *An Essay on the Principle of Population* is widely regarded as the foundational text on the subject, and his

From Thomas Malthus, *An Essay on the Principle of Population* (London: J. Johnson, 1798), pp. 18–38.

argument—that, unchecked by birth control, human populations increase faster than their food supplies—remains relevant today, as manufacturers, farmers, politicians, and scientists alike debate the earth's ability to sustain its population indefinitely.

I said that population, when unchecked, increased in a geometrical ratio, and subsistence for man in an arithmetical ratio.

Let us examine whether this position be just. I think it will be allowed, that no state has hitherto existed (at least that we have any account of) where the manners were so pure and simple, and the means of subsistence so abundant, that no check whatever has existed to early marriages, among the lower classes, from a fear of not providing well for their families, or among the higher classes, from a fear of lowering their condition in life. Consequently in no state that we have yet known has the power of population been left to exert itself with perfect freedom.

Whether the law of marriage be instituted or not, the dictate of nature and virtue seems to be an early attachment to one woman. Supposing a liberty of changing in the case of an unfortunate choice, this liberty would not affect population till it arose to a height greatly vicious; and we are now supposing the existence of a society where vice is scarcely known. In a state therefore of great equality and virtue, where pure and simple manners prevailed, and where the means of subsistence were so abundant that no part of the society could have any fears about providing amply for a family, the power of population being left to exert itself unchecked, the increase of the human species would evidently be much greater than any increase that has been hitherto known.

In the United States of America, where the means of subsistence have been more ample, the manners of the people more pure, and consequently the checks to early marriages fewer, than in any of the modern states of Europe, the population has been found to double itself in twenty-five years. This ratio of increase, though short of the utmost power of population, yet as the result of actual experience, we will take as our rule, and say, that population, when unchecked, goes on doubling itself every twenty-five years or increases in a geometrical ratio.

Let us now take any spot of earth, this Island for instance, and see in what ratio the subsistence it affords can be supposed to increase. We will begin with it under its present state of cultivation. If I allow that by the best possible policy, by breaking up more land and by great encouragements to agriculture, the produce of this Island may be doubled in the first twenty-five years, I think it will be allowing as much as any person can well demand.

In the next twenty-five years, it is impossible to suppose that the produce could be quadrupled. It would be contrary to all our knowledge of the qualities of land. The very utmost that we can conceive, is, that the increase in the second twenty-five years might equal the present produce. Let us then take this for our rule, though certainly far beyond the truth, and allow that, by great exertion, the whole produce of the Island might be increased every twenty-five years, by a quantity of subsistence equal to what it at present produces. The most enthusiastic speculator cannot suppose a greater increase than this. In a few centuries it would make every acre of land in the Island like a garden.

Yet this ratio of increase is evidently arithmetical. It may be fairly said, therefore, that the means of subsistence increase in an arithmetical ratio.

Let us now bring the effects of these two ratios together. The population of the Island is computed to be about seven millions, and we will suppose the present produce equal to the support of such a number. In the first twenty-five years the population would be fourteen millions, and the food being also doubled, the means of subsistence would be equal to this increase. In the next twenty-five years the population would be twenty-eight millions, and the means of subsistence only equal to the support of twenty-one millions. In the next period, the population would be fifty-six millions, and the means of subsistence just sufficient for half that number. And at the conclusion of the first century the population would be one hundred and twelve millions and the means of subsistence only equal to the support of thirty-five millions, which would leave a population of seventy-seven millions totally unprovided for.

A great emigration necessarily implies unhappiness of some kind or other in the country that is deserted. For few persons will leave their families, connections, friends, and native land, to seek a settlement in untried foreign climes, without some strong subsisting causes of uneasiness where they are, or the hope of some great advantages in the place to which they are going. But to make the argument more general and less interrupted by the partial views of emigration, let us take the whole earth, instead of one spot, and suppose that the restraints to population were universally removed. If the subsistence for man that the earth affords was to be increased every twenty-five years by a quantity equal to what the whole world at present produces, this would allow the power of production in the earth to be absolutely unlimited, and its ratio of increase much greater than we can conceive that any possible exertions of mankind could make it.

Taking the population of the world at any number, a thousand millions, for instance, the human species would increase in the ratio of — 1, 2, 4, 8, 16, 32, 64, 128, 256, 512, etc. and subsistence as — 1, 2, 3, 4, 5, 6, 7, 8, 9, 10, etc. In two centuries and a quarter, the population would be to the means of subsistence as 512 to 10: in three centuries as 4096 to 13, and in two thousand years the difference would be almost incalculable, though the produce in that time would have increased to an immense extent.

No limits whatever are placed to the productions of the earth; they may increase for ever and be greater than any assignable quantity. Yet still the power of population being a power of a superior order, the increase of the human species can only be kept commensurate to the increase of the means of subsistence by the constant operation of the strong law of necessity acting as a check upon the greater power. The effects of this check remain now to be considered.

Among plants and animals the view of the subject is simple. They are all impelled by a powerful instinct to the increase of their species, and this instinct is interrupted by no reasoning or doubts about providing for their offspring.

Wherever therefore there is liberty, the power of increase is exerted, and the superabundant effects are repressed afterwards by want of room and nourishment, which is common to animals and plants, and among animals by becoming the prey of others.

The effects of this check on man are more complicated. Impelled to the increase of his species by an equally powerful instinct, reason interrupts his career and asks him whether he may not bring beings into the world for whom he cannot provide the means of subsistence. In a state of equality, this would be the simple question. In the present state of society, other considerations occur. Will he not lower his rank in life? Will he not subject himself to greater difficulties than he at present feels? Will he not be obliged to labor harder? And if he has a large family, will his utmost exertions enable him to support them? May he not see his offspring in rags and misery, and clamoring for bread that he cannot give them? And may he not be reduced to the grating necessity of forfeiting his independence, and of being obliged to the sparing hand of charity for support?

These considerations are calculated to prevent, and certainly do prevent, a very great number in all civilized nations from pursuing the dictate of nature in an early attachment to one woman. And this restraint almost necessarily, though not absolutely so, produces vice. Yet in all societies, even those that are most vicious, the tendency to a virtuous attachment is so strong that there is a constant effort towards an increase of population. This constant effort as constantly tends to subject the lower classes of the society to distress and to prevent any great permanent amelioration of their condition.

The way in which these effects are produced seems to be this. We will suppose the means of subsistence in any country just equal to the easy support of its inhabitants. The constant effort towards population, which is found to act even in the most vicious societies, increases the number of people before the means of subsistence are increased. The food therefore which before supported seven millions must now be divided among seven millions and a half or eight millions. The poor consequently must live much worse, and many of them be reduced to severe distress. The number of laborers also being above the proportion of the work in the market, the price of labor must tend toward a decrease, while the price of provisions would at the same time tend to rise. The laborer therefore must work harder to earn the same as he did before. During this season of distress, the discouragements to marriage, and the difficulty of rearing a family are so great that population is at a stand. In the mean time the cheapness of labor, the plenty of laborers, and the necessity of an increased industry amongst them, encourage cultivators to employ more labor upon their land, to turn up fresh soil, and to manure and improve more completely what is already in tillage, till ultimately the means of subsistence become in the same proportion to the population as at the period from which we set out. The situation of the laborer being then again tolerably comfortable, the restraints to population are in some degree loosened, and the same retrograde and progressive movements with respect to happiness are repeated. . . .

Many reasons occur why this oscillation has been less obvious, and less decidedly confirmed by experience, than might naturally be expected. One principal reason is that the histories of mankind that we possess are histories only of the higher classes. We have but few accounts that can be depended upon of the manners and customs of that part of mankind where these retrograde and progressive movements chiefly take place. A satisfactory history of this kind, on one people, and of one period, would require the constant and minute attention of an observing mind during a long life. Some of the objects of inquiry would be, in what proportion to the number of adults was the number of marriages, to what extent vicious customs prevailed in consequence of the restraints upon matrimony, what was the comparative mortality among the children of the most distressed part of the community and those who lived rather more at their ease, what were the variations in the real price of labor, and what were the observable differences in the state of the lower classes of society with respect to ease and happiness, at different times during a certain period.

Such a history would tend greatly to elucidate the manner in which the constant check upon population acts and would probably prove the existence of the retrograde and progressive movements that have been mentioned, though the times of their vibrations must necessarily be rendered irregular from the operation of many interrupting causes, such as the introduction or failure of certain manufactures, a greater or less prevalent spirit of agricultural enterprise, years of plenty, or years of scarcity, wars and pestilence, poor laws, the invention of processes for shortening labor without the proportional extension of the market for the commodity, and, particularly, the difference between the nominal and real price of labor, a circumstance which has perhaps more than any other contributed to conceal this oscillation from common view. . . .

But the want of freedom in the market of labor, which occurs more or less in all communities, either from parish laws, or the more general cause of the facility of combination among the rich, and its difficulty among the poor, operates to prevent the price of labor from rising at the natural period, and keeps it down some time longer; perhaps till a year of scarcity, when the clamor is too loud and the necessity too apparent to be resisted. The true cause of the advance in the price of labor is thus concealed, and the rich affect to grant it as an act of compassion and favor to the poor, in consideration of a year of scarcity, and, when plenty returns, indulge themselves in the most unreasonable of all complaints, that the price does not again fall, when a little rejection would show them that it must have risen long before but from an unjust conspiracy of their own. But though the rich by unfair combinations contribute frequently to prolong a season of distress among the poor, yet no possible form of society could prevent the almost constant action of misery upon a great part of mankind, if in a state of inequality, and upon all, if all were equal.

The theory on which the truth of this position depends appears to me so extremely clear that I feel at a loss to conjecture what part of it can be denied. That population cannot increase without the means of subsistence is a proposition so evident that it needs no illustration. That population does invariably increase where there are the means of subsistence, the history of every people that have ever existed will abundantly prove. And that the superior power of population cannot be checked without producing misery or vice, the ample portion of these too bitter ingredients in the cup of human life and the continuance of the physical causes that seem to have produced them bear too convincing a testimony.

READING QUESTIONS

1. How, according to Malthus, do wages and the availability of work influence population growth?

2. What do Malthus's arguments, especially those on the means of limiting human population growth voluntarily, suggest about views on gender relations? What does he mean in arguing that the considerations that lead men not to marry at an early age "almost necessarily, though not absolutely so, [produce] vice"?

3. Why did Malthus's predictions fail to come true in Europe and the United States? What factors did he fail to take into account?

SOURCES IN CONVERSATION

Life as an Industrial Worker at Mid-Century

By the mid-nineteenth century, industrialization had taken a firm hold in Britain, the northern United States, and much of northern Europe. Britain was still the most industrialized nation on earth, but Germany and the United States were rapidly gaining ground. As workers and their families poured into industrial centers in search of work, conditions in industrial cities grew grim. Unplanned and unregulated growth combined with industrial pollution to produce crowded and unhealthy working-class neighborhoods. For individuals who were new to factory work, almost as challenging as the industrial urban environment was the adjustment to industrial labor itself. Men, women, and children who were accustomed to the informality and relative slow pace of the rural economy and the artisanal shop found them themselves subjected to rigid industrial discipline. In time, urban conditions would improve and industrial workers would fight for, and win, greater control of their working lives. In the 1830s and 1840s, however, such gains were far in the future.

20-2 | FRIEDRICH ENGELS, *The Condition of the Working Class in England in 1844* (1844)

Friedrich Engels (1820–1895) is best known today as Karl Marx's collaborator and coauthor of *The Communist Manifesto* (1848). He was also a social scientist in his own right, and *The Condition of the Working Class in England in 1844* was a pioneering sociological study. His account of conditions in Manchester's working-class neighborhoods was based on extensive firsthand experience acquired while overseeing his family's cotton textile interests in the city.

Manchester lies at the foot of the southern slope of a range of hills, which stretch hither from Oldham . . . and contains about four hundred thousand inhabitants, rather more than less. The town itself is peculiarly built, so that a person may live in it for years, and go in and out daily without coming into contact with a working-people's quarter or even with workers, that is, so long as he confines himself to his business or to pleasure walks. This arises chiefly from the fact, that by unconscious tacit agreement, as well as with outspoken conscious determination, the working-people's quarters are sharply separated from the sections of the city reserved for the middle-class. . . .

I may mention just here that the mills almost all adjoin the rivers or the different canals that ramify throughout the city, before I proceed at once to describe the laboring quarters. First of all, there is the old town of Manchester, which lies between the northern boundary of the commercial district and the Irk. Here the streets, even the better ones, are narrow and winding, as Todd Street, Long Millgate, Withy Grove, and Shude Hill, the houses dirty, old, and tumble-down, and the construction of the side streets utterly horrible. Going from the Old Church to Long Millgate, the stroller has at once a row of old-fashioned houses at the right, of which not one has kept its original level; these are remnants of the old pre-manufacturing Manchester, whose former inhabitants have removed with their descendants into better built districts, and have left the houses, which were not good enough for them, to a population strongly mixed with Irish blood. Here one is in an almost undisguised working-men's quarter, for even the shops and beer houses hardly take the trouble to exhibit a trifling degree of cleanliness. But all this is nothing in comparison with the courts and lanes which lie behind, to which access can be gained only through covered passages, in which no two human beings can pass at the same time. Of the irregular cramming together of dwellings in ways which defy all rational plan, of the tangle in which they are crowded literally one upon the other, it is impossible to convey an idea. And it is not the buildings surviving from the old times of Manchester which are to blame for this; the confusion has only recently reached its height when every scrap of

From Friedrich Engels, *The Condition of the Working-Class in England in 1844* (London: Swan Sonnenschein & Co., 1892), pp. 45, 48–53.

space left by the old way of building has been filled up and patched over until not a foot of land is left to be further occupied.

The south bank of the Irk is here very steep and between fifteen and thirty feet high. On this declivitous hillside there are planted three rows of houses, of which the lowest rise directly out of the river, while the front walls of the highest stand on the crest of the hill in Long Millgate. Among them are mills on the river, in short, the method of construction is as crowded and disorderly here as in the lower part of Long Millgate. Right and left a multitude of covered passages lead from the main street into numerous courts, and he who turns in thither gets into a filth and disgusting grime, the equal of which is not to be found—especially in the courts which lead down to the Irk, and which contain unqualifiedly the most horrible dwellings which I have yet beheld. In one of these courts there stands directly at the entrance, at the end of the covered passage, a privy without a door, so dirty that the inhabitants can pass into and out of the court only by passing through foul pools of stagnant urine and excrement. This is the first court on the Irk above Ducie Bridge—in case any one should care to look into it. Below it on the river there are several tanneries which fill the whole neighborhood with the stench of animal putrefaction [i.e., rotting carcasses]. Below Ducie Bridge the only entrance to most of the houses is by means of narrow, dirty stairs and over heaps of refuse and filth. The first court below Ducie Bridge, known as Allen's Court, was in such a state at the time of the cholera[1] that the sanitary police ordered it evacuated, swept, and disinfected with chloride of lime. Dr. Kay[2] gives a terrible description of the state of this court at that time. Since then, it seems to have been partially torn away and rebuilt; at least looking down from Ducie Bridge, the passer-by sees several ruined walls and heaps of debris with some newer houses. The view from this bridge, mercifully concealed from mortals of small stature by a parapet as high as a man, is characteristic for the whole district. At the bottom flows, or rather stagnates, the Irk, a narrow, coal-black, foul-smelling stream, full of debris and refuse, which it deposits on the shallower right bank.

In dry weather, a long string of the most disgusting, blackish-green, slime pools are left standing on this bank, from the depths of which bubbles of miasmatic gas constantly arise and give forth a stench unendurable even on the bridge forty or fifty feet above the surface of the stream. But besides this, the stream itself is checked every few paces by high weirs, behind which slime and refuse accumulate and rot in thick masses. Above the bridge are tanneries, bone mills, and gasworks, from which all drains and refuse find their way into the Irk, which receives further the contents of all the neighboring sewers and privies. It may

---

[1]**at the time of the cholera**: Cholera, a disease caused by the contamination of water supplies with human excrement, first appeared in Britain in 1831.

[2]**Dr. Kay**: Dr. James Kay, later Sir James Kay-Shuttlesworth (1804–1877), author of *The Moral and Physical Condition of the Working-Class Employed in the Cotton Manufacture in Manchester* (1832).

be easily imagined, therefore, what sort of residue the stream deposits. Below the bridge you look upon the piles of debris, the refuse, filth, and offal from the courts on the steep left bank; here each house is packed close behind its neighbor and a piece of each is visible, all black, smoky, crumbling, ancient, with broken panes and window frames. The background is furnished by old barrack-like factory buildings. On the lower right bank stands a long row of houses and mills; the second house being a ruin without a roof, piled with debris; the third stands so low that the lowest floor is uninhabitable, and therefore without windows or doors. Here the background embraces the pauper burial-ground, the station of the Liverpool and Leeds railway, and, in the rear of this, the Workhouse, the "Poor-Law Bastille"[3] of Manchester, which, like a citadel, looks threateningly down from behind its high walls and parapets on the hilltop, upon the working-people's quarter below.

Above Ducie Bridge, the left bank grows more flat and the right bank steeper, but the condition of the dwellings on both banks grows worse rather than better. He who turns to the left here from the main street, Long Millgate, is lost; he wanders from one court to another, turns countless corners, passes nothing but narrow, filthy nooks and alleys, until after a few minutes he has lost all clue, and knows not whither to turn. Everywhere half or wholly ruined buildings, some of them actually uninhabited, which means a great deal here; rarely a wooden or stone floor to be seen in the houses, almost uniformly broken, ill-fitting windows and doors, and a state of filth! Everywhere heaps of debris, refuse, and offal; standing pools for gutters, and a stench which alone would make it impossible for a human being in any degree civilized to live in such a district. The newly-built extension of the Leeds railway, which crosses the Irk here, has swept away some of these courts and lanes, laying others completely open to view. Immediately under the railway bridge there stands a court, the filth and horrors of which surpass all the others by far, just because it was hitherto so shut off, so secluded that the way to it could not be found without a good deal of trouble. I should never have discovered it myself, without the breaks made by the railway, though I thought I knew this whole region thoroughly. Passing along a rough bank, among stakes and washing-lines, one penetrates into this chaos of small one-storied, one-roomed huts, in most of which there is no artificial floor; kitchen, living and sleeping-room all in one. In such a hole, scarcely five feet long by six broad, I found two beds—and such bedsteads and beds!—which, with a staircase and chimney-place, exactly filled the room. In several others I found absolutely nothing, while the door stood open, and the inhabitants leaned against it. Everywhere before the doors refuse and offal; that any sort of pavement lay underneath could not be seen but only felt, here and there, with the feet. This whole collection of cattle-sheds for human beings was surrounded on two sides by houses and a factory, and on the

---

[3]**Poor-Law Bastille:** The Poor Law legislation passed in 1834 mandated that all able-bodied recipients of public charity forfeit any property they possessed and live and labor in workhouses.

third by the river, and besides the narrow stair up the bank, a narrow door-way alone led out into another almost equally ill-built, ill-kept labyrinth of dwellings. . . .

If we leave the Irk and penetrate once more on the opposite side from Long Millgate into the midst of the working-men's dwellings, we shall come into a somewhat newer quarter, which stretches from St. Michael's Church to Withy Grove and Shude Hill. Here there is somewhat better order. In place of the chaos of buildings, we find at least long straight lanes and alleys or courts, built according to a plan and usually square. But if, in the former case, every house was built according to caprice, here each lane and court is so built, without reference to the situation of the adjoining ones. . . .

Here, as in most of the working-men's quarters of Manchester, the pork-raisers rent the courts and build pig-pens in them. In almost every court one or even several such pens may be found, into which the inhabitants of the court throw all refuse and offal, whence the swine grow fat; and the atmosphere, confined on all four sides, is utterly corrupted by putrefying animal and vegetable substances. . . .

Such is the Old Town of Manchester, and on re-reading my description, I am forced to admit that instead of being exaggerated, it is far from black enough to convey a true impression of the filth, ruin, and uninhabitableness, the defiance of all considerations of cleanliness, ventilation, and health which characterize the construction of this single district, containing at least twenty to thirty thousand inhabitants. And such a district exists in the heart of the second city of England, the first manufacturing city of the world. If any one wishes to see in how little space a human being can move, how little air—and *such* air!—he can breathe, how little of civilization he may share and yet live, it is only necessary to travel hither. True, this is the *Old* Town, and the people of Manchester emphasize the fact whenever any one mentions to them the frightful condition of this Hell upon Earth; but what does that prove? Everything which here arouses horror and indignation is of recent origin, belongs to the *industrial epoch.*

READING QUESTIONS

1. How was it possible, as Engels claimed, that middle-class residents of Manchester's suburbs could pass through the working-class districts closer to the city center on their way to and from work, "without coming into contact with a working-people's quarter or even with workers"? What does this claim suggest about economic segregation in the city?

2. "Of the irregular cramming together of dwellings in ways which defy all rational plan, of the tangle in which they are crowded literally one upon the other, it is impossible to convey an idea," Engels remarked of one district. Why might Manchester have developed in this way?

3. What might his remark about the Long Millgate district containing a "population strongly mixed with Irish blood" suggest about Engels's racial attitudes?

20-3 | *Factory Rules in Berlin* (1844)

The rigid rules and regulations of the factory floor offered a stark contrast to the chaos and squalor of working-class neighborhoods in industrial cities. Determined to maximize efficiency, and with it profits, factory owners imposed strict rules on their workers. This 1844 set of rules for a Berlin factory provides an example of industrial discipline. As you read the rules, ask yourself why factory owners might have thought them to be necessary. What light do they shed on the power of owners over workers in mid-nineteenth-century Europe?

In every large works, and in the co-ordination of any large number of workmen, good order and harmony must be looked upon as the fundamentals of success, and therefore the following rules shall be strictly observed.

Every man employed in the concern named below shall receive a copy of these rules, so that no one can plead ignorance. Its acceptance shall be deemed to mean consent to submit to its regulations.

(1) The normal working day begins at all seasons at 6 a.m. precisely and ends, after the usual break of half an hour for breakfast, an hour for dinner and half an hour for tea, at 7 p.m., and it shall be strictly observed.

Five minutes before the beginning of the stated hours of work until their actual commencement, a bell shall ring and indicate that every worker employed in the concern has to proceed to his place of work, in order to start as soon as the bell stops.

The doorkeeper shall lock the door punctually at 6 a.m., 8.30 a.m., 1 p.m. and 4.30 p.m.

Workers arriving 2 minutes late shall lose half an hour's wages; whoever is more than 2 minutes late may not start work until after the next break, or at least shall lose his wages until then. Any disputes about the correct time shall be settled by the clock mounted above the gatekeeper's lodge.

These rules are valid both for time- and for piece-workers, and in cases of breaches of these rules, workmen shall be fined in proportion to their earnings. The deductions from the wage shall be entered in the wage-book of the gatekeeper whose duty they are; they shall be unconditionally accepted as it will not be possible to enter into any discussions about them.

(2) When the bell is rung to denote the end of the working day, every workman, both on piece- and on day-wage, shall leave his workshop and the yard, but is not allowed to make preparations for his departure before the bell rings. Every breach of this rule shall lead to a fine of five silver groschen to the sick fund. Only those who have obtained special permission by the overseer may stay on in the workshop in order to work. — If a workman has worked beyond the closing bell, he must give his name to the gatekeeper on leaving, on pain of losing his payment for the overtime.

From S. Pollard and C. Holmes, ed., *Documents of European Economic History*, vol. 1 (London: Edward Arnold Ltd., 1968), pp. 534–536.

(3) No workman, whether employed by time or piece, may leave before the end of the working day, without having first received permission from the overseer and having given his name to the gatekeeper. Omission of these two actions shall lead to a fine of ten silver groschen payable to the sick fund.

(4) Repeated irregular arrival at work shall lead to dismissal. This shall also apply to those who are found idling by an official or overseer, and refuse to obey their order to resume work.

(5) Entry to the firm's property by any but the designated gateway, and exit by any prohibited route, e.g. by climbing fences or walls, or by crossing the Spree, shall be punished by a fine of fifteen silver groschen to the sick fund for the first offences, and dismissal for the second.

(6) No worker may leave his place of work otherwise than for reasons connected with his work.

(7) All conversation with fellow-workers is prohibited; if any worker requires information about his work, he must turn to the overseer, or to the particular fellow-worker designated for the purpose.

(8) Smoking in the workshops or in the yard is prohibited during working hours; anyone caught smoking shall be fined five silver groschen for the sick fund for every such offence.

(9) Every worker is responsible for cleaning up his space in the workshop, and if in doubt, he is to turn to his overseer. — All tools must always be kept in good condition, and must be cleaned after use. This applies particularly to the turner, regarding his lathe.

(10) Natural functions must be performed at the appropriate places, and whoever is found soiling walls, fences, squares, etc., and similarly, whoever is found washing his face and hands in the workshop and not in the places assigned for the purpose, shall be fined five silver groschen for the sick fund.

(11) On completion of his piece of work, every workman must hand it over at once to his foreman or superior, in order to receive a fresh piece of work. Pattern makers must on no account hand over their patterns to the foundry without express order of their supervisors. No workman may take over work from his fellow-workman without instruction to that effect by the foreman.

(12) It goes without saying that all overseers and officials of the firm shall be obeyed without question, and shall be treated with due deference. Disobedience will be punished by dismissal.

(13) Immediate dismissal shall also be the fate of anyone found drunk in any of the workshops.

(14) Untrue allegations against superiors or officials of the concern shall lead to stern reprimand, and may lead to dismissal. The same punishment shall be meted out to those who knowingly allow errors to slip through when supervising or stocktaking.

(15) Every workman is obliged to report to his superiors any acts of dishonesty or embezzlement on the part of his fellow workmen. If he omits to do so, and it is shown after subsequent discovery of a misdemeanour that he knew about it at the time, he shall be liable to be taken to court as an accessory after

the fact and the wage due to him shall be retained as punishment. Conversely, anyone denouncing a theft in such a way as to allow conviction of the thief shall receive a reward of two Thaler, and, if necessary, his name shall be kept confidential. — Further, the gatekeeper and the watchman, as well as every official, are entitled to search the baskets, parcels, aprons etc. of the women and children who are taking the dinners into the works, on their departure, as well as search any worker suspected of stealing any article whatever. . . .

(18) Advances shall be granted only to the older workers, and even to them only in exceptional circumstances. As long as he is working by the piece, the workman is entitled merely to his fixed weekly wage as subsistence pay; the extra earnings shall be paid out only on completion of the whole piece contract. If a workman leaves before his piece contract is completed, either of his own free will, or on being dismissed as punishment, or because of illness, the partly completed work shall be valued by the general manager with the help of two overseers, and he will be paid accordingly. There is no appeal against the decision of these experts.

(19) A free copy of these rules is handed to every workman, but whoever loses it and requires a new one, or cannot produce it on leaving, shall be fined 2½ silver groschen, payable to the sick fund.

Moabit, August, 1844.

READING QUESTIONS

1. How did the author of the rules explain their necessity? How might the workers' view of the rules have differed from that of the factory owner?

2. What aspects of worker behavior seem to be of most concern to the factory owner?

3. What do the rules suggest about differences between industrial and rural notions of time?

20-4 | NED LUDD, *Yorkshire Textile Workers Threaten a Factory Owner* (ca. 1811–1812)

In the early nineteenth century, the new mechanization of textile manufacturing endangered the livelihoods of the handworkers engaged in manual textile production. During the years 1811–1816, many English hosiery weavers found themselves replaced by stocking frames. Croppers, whose task was to finish woven cloth by cropping (shearing) it, were threatened by the introduction of the shearing frame. The workers retaliated by smashing the "detestable" machines that had claimed their jobs. They adopted the name "Luddites" after a likely

From G. D. H. Cole and A. W. Filson, eds., *British Working Class Documents: Selected Documents 1789–1875* (London: Macmillan, 1951), pp. 113–115.

apocryphal Edward "Ned" Ludd, lauded as the first to destroy a shearing frame. Hostile missives, like that which follows, were often sent to the owners of stocking or shearing frames, and made frequent reference to "King Ludd," a protector of the downtrodden.

Sir,

Information has just been given in, that you are a holder [owner] of those detestable Shearing Frames, and I was desired by my men to write to you, and give you fair warning to pull them down, and for that purpose I desire that you will understand I am now writing to you, you will take notice that if they are not taken down by the end of next week, I shall detach one of my lieutenants with at least 300 men to destroy them, and further more take notice that if you give us the trouble of coming thus far, we will increase your misfortunes by burning your buildings down to ashes. . . . We hope for assistance from the French Emperor[1] in shaking off the Yoke of the Rottenest, wickedest, and most Tyrannical Government that ever existed. . . . We will never lay down our arms till the House of Commons passes an act to put down all the machinery hurtfull [sic] to the Commonality and repeal that[2] to the Frame Breakers. . . .

Signed by the General of the Army of Redressers,
Ned Ludd, Clerk

READING QUESTIONS

1. Why do you think the Luddites resorted to threats and violence rather than peacefully seeking redress through the political process?

2. Why, in a threat to an individual factory owner, do you think the anonymous author of this letter denounced Britain's government as "the Rottenest, wickedest, and most Tyrannical . . . that ever existed"?

3. Why might the Luddites have expected the French emperor Napoleon to be their savior?

---

[1]**assistance from the French Emperor**: Great Britain was engaged in a lengthy war against the French emperor, Napoleon Bonaparte.

[2]**repeal that**: In response to the wave of machine breaking, Parliament made such crimes capital offenses.

20-5 | Creating an Industrial Utopia

ROBERT OWEN, *A New View of Society* (1813)

Robert Owen (1771–1858) first gained prominence as a successful textile manufacturer who treated his employees generously and beneficently. He later became a tireless promoter of educational reform, and was an early "utopian" socialist and trade-union advocate, providing the inspiration for the founding of the Grand National Consolidated Trades Union in 1834. None of Owen's schemes for socialist communities succeeded, nor did the early trade unions, but his theories about educating children were very influential during his own lifetime and remain current today.

According to the last returns under the Population Act, the poor and working classes of Great Britain and Ireland have been found to exceed twelve millions of persons, or nearly three-fourths of the population of the British Islands.

The characters of these persons are now permitted to be very generally formed without proper guidance or direction, and, in many cases, under circumstances which *must* train them to the extreme of vice and misery; and of course render them the worst and most dangerous subjects in the empire; while the far greater part of the remainder of the community are educated upon the most mistaken principles of human nature, such, indeed, as cannot fail to produce a general conduct throughout society, totally unworthy of the character of rational beings.

The first thus unhappily situated are the poor and the uneducated profligate among the working classes, who are now trained to commit crimes, which they are afterwards *punished* for committing.

The second is the remaining mass of the population, who are now *instructed* to *believe*, or at least to acknowledge, that certain principles are *unerringly true*, and to *act* as though they were *grossly false*; thus filling the world with *folly* and *inconsistency*, and making society, throughout all its ramifications, a scene of insincerity.

This state of matters has continued for a long period, its evils have been and are continually increasing, until they now cry aloud for efficient corrective measures, or general disorder must ensue. . . .

Did these circumstances not exist to an extent almost incredible, could it be necessary *now* to contend for a principle regarding Man, which scarcely requires more than to be fairly stated to make it self-evident? This principle is, "THAT ANY CHARACTER, FROM THE BEST TO THE WORST, FROM THE MOST IGNORANT TO THE MOST ENLIGHTENED, MAY BE GIVEN TO ANY COMMUNITY, EVEN TO THE WORLD AT LARGE, BY APPLYING CERTAIN MEANS WHICH ARE TO A GREAT EXTENT AT THE COMMAND AND

From Robert Owen, *A New View of Society, or Essays on the Principle of the Formation of Human Character and the Application of the Principle to Practice* (London: Richard Taylor and Co., 1813), pp. 5–6, 9, 26–28, 35–36, 38–41, 49–51.

UNDER THE CONTROL, OR EASILY MADE SO, OF THOSE WHO POSSESS THE GOVERNMENT OF NATIONS."

The principle as now stated is a broad one, and, if it should be found to be true, cannot fail to give a new character to legislative proceedings, and *such* a character as will be most favorable to the well-being of society. . . .

Children are without exception passive agents, or wonderfully contrived compounds, which by due preparation and accurate attention, founded on a correct knowledge of the subject, may be formed collectively into any Human character. And although these original compounds like all the other works of the Great Directing Power of the Universe, possess endless varieties, yet they all partake of that plastic nature or quality, which, by perseverance under judicious management, may be ultimately molded into the very image of rational wishes and desires.

And in the next place, these principles cannot fail soon to create those feelings, which without force, or the production of any counteracting motive, will irresistibly lead those who possess them to make due allowance for the difference of sentiments and manners not only among their friends and countrymen, but also among the inhabitants of every region on the earth, even including their enemies. For, with this insight into the formation of character, where is there any conceivable foundation for private displeasure or public enmity? Say, if it be within the sphere of possibility that children can be trained to acquire *that* knowledge and *these* feelings? The child of eight years growth, who from infancy has been rationally trained in these principles, will readily discover and trace from whence the opinions and habits of his associates have arisen, and why they possess them. And at the same age he will have acquired reasons sufficiently powerful to exhibit to him in strong colors the irrationality of being angry with an individual for possessing qualities which, as an unavoidable passive agent during the formation of those qualities, he had not the means of preventing. Such must be the impressions which these principles will make on the mind of every such child; and in lieu of generating anger or displeasure, they will produce commiseration and pity for those individuals, who possess either habits or sentiments which appear to him to be destructive of their own comfort, pleasure, or happiness, and will promote in him a desire to remove those causes of distress, that his own feelings of commiseration and pity may be also removed. And the pleasure which he cannot avoid experiencing by this mode of conduct, will likewise stimulate him to the most active endeavors to withdraw all those circumstances which surround any part of mankind with causes of misery, and to replace them with others which have a tendency to increase their happiness. He must then also strongly entertain the desire to "do good to *all* men," and even to "love his enemies."

In the year 1784 the late Mr. Dale[1] of Glasgow founded a spinning and weaving manufactory near the falls of the Clyde, in the county of Lanark in Scotland;

---

[1] **the late Mr. Dale**: Robert Owen's father-in-law.

and about that period cotton mills were first introduced into the northern part of the kingdom.

It was the power which could be obtained from the falls of water which induced Mr. Dale to erect his mills in this situation, for in other respects it was not well chosen: the country around was uncultivated; the inhabitants were poor, and few in number; and the roads in the neighborhood were so bad, that the falls of Clyde now so celebrated were then unknown to strangers.

It was therefore necessary to collect a new population to supply the infant establishment with laborers. This however was no light task; for all the regularly trained Scotch peasantry disdained the idea of working from early till late, day after day, within cotton mills. Two modes only to obtain these laborers occurred: the one, to procure children from the various public charities in the country; and the other, to induce families to settle around the works.

To accommodate the first, a large house was erected, which ultimately contained about five hundred children, who were procured chiefly from workhouses and charities in Edinburgh.

These children were to be fed, clothed, and educated; and these duties Mr. Dale performed with the benevolence which he was known to possess. . . .

The benevolent proprietor spared no expense which could give comfort to the poor children which it contained. The rooms provided for them were spacious, always clean, and well ventilated; the food was of the best quality, and most abundant; the clothes were neat and useful; a surgeon was kept in constant pay to direct how to prevent as well as cure disease; and the best instructors which the country afforded were appointed to teach such branches of education as were deemed likely to be useful to children in their situation; and kind, well disposed persons were appointed to superintend all their proceedings. Nothing, in short, at first sight seemed wanting to render it a most complete charity.

But to defray the expense of these well devised arrangements, and support the establishment generally, it was absolutely necessary that the children should be employed within the mills from six o'clock in the morning to seven in the evening summer and winter; and after these hours their education commenced. The directors of the public charities from mistaken economy, would not consent to send the children under their care to cotton mills, unless the children were received by the proprietors at the ages of six, seven, and eight. And Mr. Dale was under the necessity of accepting them at those ages, or stopping the manufactory which he had commenced.

It is not to be supposed that children so young could remain, with the interval of meals only, from six in the morning until seven in the evening, in constant employment on their feet within cotton mills, and afterwards acquire much proficiency in education. And so it proved; for the greater part of them became dwarfs in body and mind, and many of them deformed. Their labor through the day, and their education at night, became so irksome, that numbers of them continually ran away, and almost all looked forward with impatience and anxiety to the expiration of their apprenticeship of seven, eight, and nine years, which generally expired when they were from thirteen to fifteen years old. At this period of life, unaccustomed to provide for themselves, and unacquainted with the world, they usually went to Edinburgh or Glasgow, where boys and girls were soon assailed by the innumerable temptations which all large towns present; and many of them fell sacrifices to those temptations.

Thus were Mr. Dale's arrangements and kind solicitude for the comfort and happiness of these children rendered in their ultimate effect almost nugatory. They were sent to be employed, and without their labor he could not support them; but, while under his care, he did all that any individual circumstanced as he was could do for his fellow-creatures.

The error proceeded from the children being sent from the workhouses at an age far too young for employment; they ought to have been detained four years longer, and educated; and then all the evils which followed would have been prevented.

And if such be a true picture not overcharged of parish apprentices to our manufacturing system under the best and most humane regulations, in what colors must it be exhibited under the worst? . . .

[Once Owen himself was put in charge of the factory,] the system of receiving apprentices from public charities was abolished; permanent settlers with large families were encouraged, and comfortable houses were built for their accommodation.

The practice of employing children in the mills, of six, seven, and eight years of age, was discontinued, and their parents advised to allow them to acquire health and education until they were ten years old. (It may be remarked, that even this age is too early to keep them at constant employment in manufactories, from six in the morning to seven in the evening. Far better would it be for the children, their parents, and for society, that the first should not commence employment until they attain the age of twelve, when their education might be finished, and their bodies would be more competent to undergo the fatigue and exertions required of them. When parents can be trained to afford this additional time to their children without inconvenience, they will, of course, adopt the practice now recommended.)

The children were taught reading, writing, and arithmetic, during five years, that is, from five to ten, in the village school, without expense to their parents; and all the modern improvements in education have been adopted, or are in process of adoption: some facilities in teaching arithmetic have been also introduced, which were peculiar to this school, and found very advantageous. They may therefore be taught and well trained before they engage in any regular employment. Another important consideration is, that all their instruction is rendered a pleasure and delight to them; they are much more anxious for the hour of school time to arrive, than end: they therefore make a rapid progress; and it may be safely asserted, that if they shall not be trained to form such characters as may be the most wished and desired, not one particle of the fault will proceed from the children; but the cause will rest in the want of a true knowledge of human nature, in those who have the management of them and their parents.

READING QUESTIONS

1. Why was Owen opposed to child labor?

2. What does Owen believe regarding human nature and behavior, especially as they pertain to the poor, criminal, or undereducated?

3. According to Owen, what purposes did education serve for the children of the working class?

20-6 | Child Labor in an Industrial Age
The Child of the Factory (1842)

Child labor was neither a novelty nor a product of the Industrial Revolution; children in traditional agricultural societies were (and are) put to work as soon as they were capable of contributing to the family economy. Yet the circumstances associated with industrialization, in particular the factory system of labor organization, focused public attention on the phenomenon as never before—first in Britain and then, as the illustration suggests, in continental Europe. The consequence, again beginning in Britain, was a humanitarian outcry leading to legislation limiting and eventually prohibiting child labor in factories. This illustration accompanied an article written about children in the cotton textile industry in France.

From *Les Français Peints par Eux-Mêmes: Encyclopédie Morale du Dix-Neuvième Siècle*, vol. 1 (Paris: L. Curmer, 1841), p. 257. Bibliothèque des Arts Decoratifs, Paris, France/Archives Charmet/The Bridgeman Art Library.

READING QUESTIONS

1. On what grounds might contemporaries, including many members of the working class, have defended child labor?

2. Are all of the children depicted in the illustration actually working? If not, then why might they be in the factory?

■ COMPARATIVE AND DISCUSSION QUESTIONS ■

1. What similarities do you see between Malthus's arguments and those of Adam Smith (Document 17-3) regarding the "wages of labor"? What differences?

2. How might Malthus have reacted to the conditions in Manchester described by Engels, and why might he have reacted that way?

3. What do you think Malthus would say about Owen's views on human nature? Why? What do you think John Locke (Document 15-6) would say about them, and why?

4. What do you think Owen thought of the Luddites? Why?

5. What might Owen have thought about the Berlin factory rules? What kinds of rules would you expect him to devise for his own workers?

21

Ideologies and Upheavals
1815–1850

The rapid social changes brought about by the Industrial Revolution combined with the political and intellectual legacy of the French Revolution to give rise to a number of competing ideologies, each offering a different response to the social and economic challenges of the early nineteenth century. Conservatives were committed to protecting the social status quo, pre-revolutionary political norms, and what they saw as traditional values. Liberals, by contrast, sought an end to government controls over the economy, and called for the establishment of representative political institutions grounded in written constitutions. Communists offered yet another solution—the seizure of the means and ownership of production by the working class—while Chartists sought the enfranchisement of all adult males. For all the hardships wrought by industrialization, the population of England rose dramatically in the nineteenth century. At the same time, the population of Ireland shrank from about eight million to scarcely six million during the 1840s as people fled the devastating conditions of the potato famine.

21-1 | Arguing Against Higher Wages for Workers
DAVID RICARDO, *On Wages* (1817)

After Adam Smith, David Ricardo (1772–1823) is almost certainly the most famous classical liberal economist. A prolific writer on "political economy," Ricardo penned the 1817 treatise *On the Principles of Political Economy and Taxation*, from which the following excerpt is drawn. Unlike Smith, who advocated the "liberal reward of labor" because "it increases the industry of the common people," Ricardo argued that laws of supply and demand should apply to wages as well as to products. Given a surplus of labor like that in nineteenth-century England, wages would inevitably sink. In the wake of Ricardo's highly influential writings, economics became widely known as "the dismal science."

From *The Works of David Ricardo*, ed. J. R. McCulloch (London: John Murray, 1881), pp. 31, 50–58.

Money, from its being a commodity obtained from a foreign country, from its being the general medium of exchange between all civilized countries, and from its being also distributed among those countries in proportions which are ever changing with every improvement in commerce and machinery, and with every increasing difficulty of obtaining food and necessaries for an increasing population, is subject to incessant variations. In stating the principles which regulate exchangeable value and price, we should carefully distinguish between those variations which belong to the commodity itself, and those which are occasioned by a variation in the medium in which value is estimated, or price expressed.

A rise in wages, from an alteration in the value of money, produces a general effect [i.e., inflation] on price, and for that reason it produces no real effect whatever on profits. On the contrary, a rise of wages, from the circumstance of the laborer being more liberally rewarded, or from a difficulty of procuring the necessaries on which wages are expended, does not, except in some instances, produce the effect of raising price, but has a great effect in lowering profits. In the one case, no greater proportion of the annual labor of the country is devoted to the support of the laborers; in the other case, a larger portion is so devoted.

Labor, like all other things which are purchased and sold, and which may be increased or diminished in quantity, has its natural and its market price. The natural price of labor is that price which is necessary to enable the laborers, one with another, to subsist and to perpetuate their race, without either increase or diminution.

The power of the laborer to support himself, and the family which may be necessary to keep up the number of laborers, does not depend on the quantity of money which he may receive for wages, but on the quantity of food, necessaries, and conveniences become essential to him from habit, which that money will purchase.[1] The natural price of labor, therefore, depends on the price of the food, necessaries, and conveniences required for the support of the laborer and his family. With a rise in the price of food and necessaries, the natural price of labor will rise; with the fall in their price, the natural price of labor will fall.

With the progress of society the natural price of labor has always a tendency to rise, because one of the principal commodities by which its natural price is regulated [food], has a tendency to become dearer, from the greater difficulty of producing it. As, however, the improvements in agriculture, the discovery of new markets, whence provisions may be imported, may for a time counteract the tendency to a rise in the price of necessaries, and may even occasion their natural price to fall, so will the same causes produce the correspondent effects on the natural price of labor.

The natural price of all commodities, excepting raw produce and labor, has a tendency to fall, in the progress of wealth and population; for though, on one

---

[1] **The quantity of food . . . purchase**: The concept of "real wages" or "purchasing power." It is not the wage itself that matters, but what that wage can buy.

hand, they are enhanced in real value, from the rise in the natural price of the raw material of which they are made, this is more than counterbalanced by the improvements in machinery, by the better division and distribution of labor, and by the increasing skill, both in science and art, of the producers.

The market price of labor is the price which is really paid for it, from the natural operation of the proportion of the supply to the demand; labor is dear when it is scarce, and cheap when it is plentiful. However much the market price of labor may deviate from its natural price, it has, like commodities, a tendency to conform to it.

It is when the market price of labor exceeds its natural price, that the condition of the laborer is flourishing and happy, that he has it in his power to command a greater proportion of the necessaries and enjoyments of life, and therefore to rear a healthy and numerous family.

When, however, by the encouragement which high wages give to the increase of population, the number of laborers is increased, wages again fall to their natural price, and indeed from a reaction sometimes fall below it.

When the market price of labor is below its natural price, the condition of the laborers is most wretched: then poverty deprives them of those comforts which custom renders absolute necessaries. It is only after their privations have reduced their number, or the demand for labor has increased, that the market price of labor will rise to its natural price, and that the laborer will have the moderate comforts which the natural rate of wages will afford.

Notwithstanding the tendency of wages to conform to their natural rate, their market rate may, in an improving society, for an indefinite period, be constantly above it; for no sooner may the impulse, which an increased capital gives to a new demand for labor, be obeyed, than another increase of capital may produce the same effect; and thus, if the increase of capital be gradual and constant, the demand for labor may give a continued stimulus to an increase of people. . . .

Thus, then, with every improvement of society, with every increase in its capital, the market wages of labor will rise; but the permanence of their rise will depend on the question, whether the natural price of labor has also risen; and this again will depend on the rise in the natural price of those necessaries on which the wages of labor are expended. . . .

As population increases, these necessaries will be constantly rising in price, because more labor will be necessary to produce them. If, then, the money wages of labor should fall, whilst every commodity on which the wages of labor were expended rose, the laborer would be doubly affected, and would be soon totally deprived of subsistence. Instead, therefore, of the money wages of labor falling, they would rise; but they would not rise sufficiently to enable the laborer to purchase as many comforts and necessaries as he did before the rise in the price of those commodities. . . .

These, then, are the laws by which wages are regulated, and by which the happiness of far the greatest part of every community is governed. Like all other contracts, wages should be left to the fair and free competition of the market, and should never be controlled by the interference of the legislature.

The clear and direct tendency of the poor laws[2] is in direct opposition to these obvious principles: it is not, as the legislature benevolently intended, to amend the condition of the poor, but to deteriorate the condition of both poor and rich; instead of making the poor rich, they are calculated to make the rich poor; and whilst the present laws are in force, it is quite in the natural order of things that the fund for the maintenance of the poor should progressively increase till it has absorbed all the net revenue of the country, or at least so much of it as the state shall leave to us, after satisfying its own never-failing demands for the public expenditure.

This pernicious tendency of these laws is no longer a mystery, since it has been fully developed by the able hand of Mr. Malthus;[3] and every friend to the poor must ardently wish for their abolition.

READING QUESTIONS

1. Explain the difference between *natural price* and *market price*.

2. Given a free market (that is to say no minimum wage laws or other government interference) for labor and a surplus of laborers, what would, according to Ricardo, happen to wages?

3. Why do you think Ricardo argues that the Poor Law, which was intended "to amend the condition of the poor," conversely "deteriorate[s] the condition of both poor and rich; instead of making the poor rich, [it is] calculated to make the rich poor"?

4. To what extent did the mechanization of manufacturing and the replacement of skilled handicraft workers by semiskilled "machine tenders" reinforce Ricardo's argument?

SOURCES IN CONVERSATION

Conservatism, Liberalism, and Socialism

The differences between conservatism, liberalism, and socialism were not ones of emphasis or degree. They were, instead, rooted in fundamental disagreements about human nature, the relationship between society and the individual, and the possibility and desirability of social, economic, and

---

[2]**poor laws**: The English Poor Law (1601) enabled local authorities to levy taxes (the "poor rates") for the assistance and relief of the deserving poor. As such, they amounted to a rudimentary social safety net.

[3]**Mr. Malthus**: Thomas Malthus, whose *Essay on the Principle of Population* (see Document 20-1) was a major influence on Ricardo's thought.

political change. Conservatives, liberals, and socialists had different views of Europe's past and different visions of Europe's future. In significant ways, the political upheavals of the nineteenth century were battles over these competing outlooks. As you read these excerpts from the writings of Metternich, Mill, Marx, and Engels, concentrate on identifying the core assumptions that inform each author's work. How did each author's assumptions shape the solutions they proposed to the challenges facing nineteenth-century Europe?

21-2 | KLEMENS VON METTERNICH, *Political Confession of Faith* (1820)

Prince Klemens von Metternich (1773–1859) was Austria's foreign secretary from 1809 until driven into exile during the revolution of 1848. As the key figure at the Congress of Vienna, he was widely credited as principal architect of the peace settlement that ended the Napoleonic wars and ushered in the "long peace" of the nineteenth century. As a member of the landed aristocracy and a staunch upholder of the established social hierarchy, Metternich was a fervent foe of liberalism and nationalism, both of which he regarded as dangerous revolutionary doctrines.

The Source of the Evil

Man's nature is immutable. The first needs of society are and remain the same, and the differences which they seem to offer find their explanation in the diversity of influences, acting on the different races by natural causes, such as the diversity of climate, barrenness or richness of soil, insular or continental position, &c. &c. These local differences no doubt produce effects which extend far beyond purely physical necessities; they create and determine particular needs in a more elevated sphere; finally, they determine the laws, and exercise an influence even on religions.

It is, on the other hand, with institutions as with everything else. Vague in their origin, they pass through periods of development and perfection, to arrive in time at their decadence; and, conforming to the laws of man's nature, they have, like him, their infancy, their youth, their age of strength and reason, and their age of decay.

Two elements alone remain in all their strength, and never cease to exercise their indestructible influence with equal power. These are the precepts of morality, religious as well as social, and the necessities created by locality. From

From Klemens von Metternich, *Memoirs of Prince Metternich, 1815–1829*, vol. 3, ed. Richard von Metternich (New York: Charles Scribner and Sons, 1881), pp. 456–458, 461–463, 469–471, 473–476.

the time that men attempt to swerve from these bases, to become rebels against these sovereign arbiters of their destinies, society suffers from a *malaise* which sooner or later will lead to a state of convulsion. The history of every country, in relating the consequences of such errors, contains many pages stained with blood, but we dare to say, without fear of contradiction, one seeks in vain for an epoch when an evil of this nature has extended its ravages over such a vast area as it has done at the present time. . . .

The progress of the human mind has been extremely rapid in the course of the last three centuries. This progress having been accelerated more rapidly than the growth of wisdom (the only counterpoise to passions and to error); a revolution prepared by the false systems, the fatal errors into which many of the most illustrious sovereigns of the last half of the eighteenth century fell, has at last broken out in a country advanced in knowledge [i.e., France], and enervated by pleasure, in a country inhabited by a people whom one can only regard as frivolous, from the facility with which they comprehend and the difficulty they experience in judging calmly. . . .

France had the misfortune to produce the greatest number of these men. It is in her midst that religion and all that she holds sacred, that morality and authority, and all connected with them, have been attacked with a steady and systematic animosity, and it is there that the weapon of ridicule has been used with the most ease and success.

Drag through the mud the name of God and the powers instituted by His divine decrees, and the revolution will be prepared! Speak of a social contract, and the revolution is accomplished! The revolution was already completed in the palaces of Kings, in the drawing-rooms and boudoirs of certain cities, while among the great mass of the people it was still only in a state of preparation. . . .

The scenes of horror which accompanied the first phases of the French Revolution prevented the rapid propagation of its subversive principles beyond the frontiers of France, and the wars of conquest which succeeded them gave to the public mind a direction little favorable to revolutionary principles. Thus the Jacobin propaganda failed entirely to realize criminal hopes.

Nevertheless the revolutionary seed had penetrated into every country and spread more or less. It was greatly developed under the *régime* of the military despotism of Bonaparte. His conquests displaced a number of laws, institutions, and customs; broke through bonds sacred among all nations, strong enough to resist time itself; which is more than can be said of certain benefits conferred by these innovators. From these perturbations it followed that the revolutionary spirit could in Germany, Italy, and later on in Spain, easily hide itself under the veil of patriotism. . . .

We are convinced that society can no longer be saved without strong and vigorous resolutions on the part of the Governments still free in their opinions and actions.

We are also convinced that this may yet be, if the Governments face the truth, if they free themselves from all illusion, if they join their ranks and take their stand on a line of correct, unambiguous, and frankly announced principles.

By this course the monarchs will fulfill the duties imposed upon them by Him who, by entrusting them with power, has charged them to watch over the maintenance of justice, and the rights of all, to avoid the paths of error, and tread firmly in the way of truth. Placed beyond the passions which agitate society, it is in days of trial chiefly that they are called upon to despoil realities of their false appearances, and to show themselves as they are, fathers invested with the authority belonging by right to the heads of families, to prove that, in days of mourning, they know how to be just, wise, and therefore strong, and that they will not abandon the people whom they ought to govern to be the sport of factions, to error and its consequences, which must involve the loss of society. The moment in which we are putting our thoughts on paper is one of these critical moments. The crisis is great; it will be decisive according to the part we take or do not take. . . .

Union between the monarchs is the basis of the policy which must now be followed to save society from total ruin. . . .

The first principle to be followed by the monarchs, united as they are by the coincidence of their desires and opinions, should be that of maintaining the stability of political institutions against the disorganized excitement which has taken possession of men's minds—the immutability of principles against the madness of their interpretation; and respect for laws actually in force against a desire for their destruction. . . .

Let [the governments] in these troublous times be more than usually cautious in attempting real ameliorations, not imperatively claimed by the needs of the moment, to the end that good itself may not turn against them—which is the case whenever a Government measure seems to be inspired by fear.

Let them not confound concessions made to parties with the good they ought to do for their people, in modifying, according to their recognized needs, such branches of the administration as require it.

Let them give minute attention to the financial state of their kingdoms, so that their people may enjoy, by the reduction of public burdens, the real, not imaginary, benefits of a state of peace.

Let them be just, but strong; beneficent, but strict.

Let them maintain religious principles in all their purity, and not allow the faith to be attacked and morality interpreted according to the *social contract* or the visions of foolish sectarians.

Let them suppress Secret Societies, that gangrene of society.

In short, let the great monarchs strengthen their union, and prove to the world that if it exists, it is beneficent, and ensures the political peace of Europe: that it is powerful only for the maintenance of tranquility at a time when so many attacks are directed against it; that the principles which they profess are paternal and protective, menacing only the disturbers of public tranquility. . . .

To every great State determined to survive the storm there still remain many chances of salvation, and a strong union between the States on the principles we have announced will overcome the storm itself.

READING QUESTIONS

1. According to Metternich, what aspects of human society are changeable? Which are not?

2. From Metternich's point of view, why was the French Revolution a great evil? What steps did he suggest must be taken to prevent a similar revolutionary outbreak in the future?

3. What is Metternich's attitude toward organized religion? What connection did he make between religion, morality, and the stability of society and the state?

4. Why does Metternich place such emphasis on monarchical power?

21-3 | JOHN STUART MILL, *On Liberty* (1859)

The English philosopher John Stuart Mill (1806–1873) was, perhaps, the most important liberal theorist of the nineteenth century. His numerous works explored the relationship between the individual, society, and the state, in an effort to identify and define the rights and interests of each. For Mill, the freedom of the individual was paramount, and any state that placed unjust or unwarranted limitations on individual liberty was, by definition, tyrannical. Thus, in Mill's work we see a clear connection between liberty and the term "liberalism." In this excerpt from *On Liberty*, Mill identified the central principles that guided his political philosophy.

The object of this Essay is to assert one very simple principle, as entitled to govern absolutely the dealings of society with the individual in the way of compulsion and control, whether the means used be physical force in the form of legal penalties, or the moral coercion of public opinion. That principle is, that the sole end for which mankind are warranted, individually or collectively, in interfering with the liberty of action of any of their number, is self-protection. That the only purpose for which power can be rightfully exercised over any member of a civilized community, against his will, is to prevent harm to others. His own good, either physical or moral, is not a sufficient warrant. He cannot rightfully be compelled to do or forbear because it will be better for him to do so, because it will make him happier, because, in the opinions of others, to do so would be wise, or even right. These are good reasons for remonstrating with him, or reasoning with him, or persuading him, or entreating him, but not for compelling him, or visiting him with any evil in case he do otherwise. To justify that, the conduct from which it is desired to deter him, must be calculated to produce evil to some one else. The only part of the conduct of any one, for which he is amenable to society, is that which concerns others. In the part which merely concerns himself, his independence is, of right, absolute. Over himself, over his own body and mind, the individual is sovereign. . . .

From John Stuart Mill, *On Liberty* (London: John W. Parker and Son, West Strand, 1859), pp. 21–22, 26–27.

This, then, is the appropriate region of human liberty. It comprises, first, the inward domain of consciousness; demanding liberty of conscience, in the most comprehensive sense; liberty of thought and feeling; absolute freedom of opinion and sentiment on all subjects, practical or speculative, scientific, moral, or theological. The liberty of expressing and publishing opinions may seem to fall under a different principle, since it belongs to that part of the conduct of an individual which concerns other people; but, being almost of as much importance as the liberty of thought itself, and resting in great part on the same reasons, is practically inseparable from it. Secondly, the principle requires liberty of tastes and pursuits; of framing the plan of our life to suit our own character; of doing as we like, subject to such consequences as may follow: without impediment from our fellow-creatures, so long as what we do does not harm them, even though they should think our conduct foolish, perverse, or wrong. Thirdly, from this liberty of each individual, follows the liberty, within the same limits, of combination among individuals; freedom to unite, for any purpose not involving harm to others: the persons combining being supposed to be of full age, and not forced or deceived.

No society in which these liberties are not, on the whole, respected, is free, whatever may be its form of government; and none is completely free in which they do not exist absolute and unqualified. The only freedom which deserves the name, is that of pursuing our own good in our own way, so long as we do not attempt to deprive others of theirs, or impede their efforts to obtain it. Each is the proper guardian of his own health, whether bodily, or mental and spiritual. Mankind are greater gainers by suffering each other to live as seems good to themselves, than by compelling each to live as seems good to the rest.

READING QUESTIONS

1. According to Mill, what single principle should govern the dealings of society with the individual?

2. What individual rights did Mill identify? Why did he think they were so important?

3. What role did individual conscience play in Mill's philosophy? What does this suggest about his attitude toward state-sponsored religion?

21-4 | KARL MARX AND FRIEDRICH ENGELS, *The Communist Manifesto* (1848)

Karl Marx (1818–1883) and Friedrich Engels (1820–1895) are credited as the founders of communism. In formulating their theories, Marx and Engels drew on the work of earlier economists,

From Karl Marx and Friedrich Engels, *Selected Works*, vol. 1 (Moscow: Progress Publishers, 1969), pp. 2–12, 32, www.marxists.org/archive/marx/works/download/manifest.pdf.

particularly Adam Smith and David Ricardo, and on Thomas Malthus's demographic theories, as well as their familiarity with living and working conditions in England's industrial centers. Their *Communist Manifesto*, first published in London as a pamphlet (written in German), opens with the proclamation that "the history of all hitherto existing society is the history of class struggles." The authors predicted the eventual triumph of the working class (proletariat) over the middle class (bourgeoisie) and the establishment of a classless society in which wealth would be equally distributed.

[Preamble]

A specter is haunting Europe—the specter of communism. All the powers of old Europe have entered into a holy alliance to exorcise this specter: Pope and Tsar, Metternich and Guizot,[1] French Radicals and German police-spies.

Where is the party in opposition that has not been decried as communistic by its opponents in power? Where is the opposition that has not hurled back the branding reproach of communism, against the more advanced opposition parties, as well as against its reactionary adversaries?

Two things result from this fact:

I. Communism is already acknowledged by all European powers to be itself a power.

II. It is high time that Communists should openly, in the face of the whole world, publish their views, their aims, their tendencies, and meet this nursery tale of the Specter of Communism with a manifesto of the party itself.

To this end, Communists of various nationalities have assembled in London and sketched the following manifesto, to be published in the English, French, German, Italian, Flemish, and Danish languages.

Chapter 1: Bourgeois and Proletarians

The history of all hitherto existing society is the history of class struggles.

Freeman and slave, patrician and plebeian, lord and serf, guild-master and journeyman, in a word, oppressor and oppressed, stood in constant opposition to one another, carried on an uninterrupted, now hidden, now open fight, a fight that each time ended, either in a revolutionary reconstitution of society at large, or in the common ruin of the contending classes.

In the earlier epochs of history, we find almost everywhere a complicated arrangement of society into various orders, a manifold gradation of social rank. In ancient Rome we have patricians, knights, plebeians, slaves; in the Middle Ages, feudal lords, vassals, guild-masters, journeymen, apprentices, serfs; in almost all of these classes, again, subordinate gradations.

---

[1]**Guizot**: François Pierre Guillaume Guizot (1787–1874), French politician and prime minister (1847–1848).

The modern bourgeois society that has sprouted from the ruins of feudal society has not done away with class antagonisms. It has but established
new classes, new conditions of oppression, new forms of struggle in place of the
old ones.

Our epoch, the epoch of the bourgeoisie, possesses, however, this distinct
feature: it has simplified class antagonisms. Society as a whole is more and more
splitting up into two great hostile camps, into two great classes directly facing
each other—Bourgeoisie and Proletariat.

From the serfs of the Middle Ages sprang the chartered burghers of the earliest towns. From these burgesses the first elements of the bourgeoisie were
developed.

The discovery of America, the rounding of the Cape, opened up fresh ground
for the rising bourgeoisie. . . .

The feudal system of industry, in which industrial production was monopo-
lized by closed guilds, now no longer sufficed for the growing wants of the new
markets. The manufacturing system took its place. The guild-masters were
pushed on one side by the manufacturing middle class; division of labor between
the different corporate guilds vanished in the face of division of labor in each
single workshop.

Meantime the markets kept ever growing, the demand ever rising. Even
manufacturer no longer sufficed. Thereupon, steam and machinery revolution-
ized industrial production. The place of manufacture was taken by the giant,
Modern Industry; the place of the industrial middle class by industrial million-
aires, the leaders of the whole industrial armies. . . . The modern bourgeoisie is
itself the product of a long course of development, of a series of revolutions in the
modes of production and of exchange.

Each step in the development of the bourgeoisie was accompanied by a corresponding political advance of that class. An oppressed class under the sway of
the feudal nobility, an armed and self-governing association in the medieval
commune: here independent urban republic (as in Italy and Germany); there tax-
able "third estate" of the monarchy (as in France); afterwards, in the period of
manufacturing proper, serving either the semi-feudal or the absolute monarchy
as a counterpoise against the nobility, and, in fact, cornerstone of the great monarchies in general, the bourgeoisie has at last, since the establishment of Modern
Industry and of the world market, conquered for itself, in the modern representative State, exclusive political sway. The executive of the modern state is but a
committee for managing the common affairs of the whole bourgeoisie.

The bourgeoisie, historically, has played a most revolutionary part.

The bourgeoisie, wherever it has got the upper hand, has put an end to all
feudal, patriarchal, idyllic relations . . . [and] has substituted naked, shameless,
direct, brutal exploitation.

The bourgeoisie has stripped of its halo every occupation hitherto honored
and looked up to with reverent awe. It has converted the physician, the lawyer,
the priest, the poet, the man of science, into its paid wage laborers.

The bourgeoisie has torn away from the family its sentimental veil, and has reduced the family relation to a mere money relation. . . .

The bourgeoisie cannot exist without constantly revolutionizing the instruments of production, and thereby the relations of production, and with them the whole relations of society. Conservation of the old modes of production in unaltered form, was, on the contrary, the first condition of existence for all earlier industrial classes. Constant revolutionizing of production, uninterrupted disturbance of all social conditions, everlasting uncertainty and agitation distinguish the bourgeois epoch from all earlier ones. . . .

The need of a constantly expanding market for its products chases the bourgeoisie over the entire surface of the globe. It must nestle everywhere, settle everywhere, establish connections everywhere.

The bourgeoisie has through its exploitation of the world market given a cosmopolitan character to production and consumption in every country. To the great chagrin of Reactionists, it has drawn from under the feet of industry the national ground on which it stood. All old-established national industries have been destroyed or are daily being destroyed. They are dislodged by new industries, whose introduction becomes a life and death question for all civilized nations, by industries that no longer work up indigenous raw material, but raw material drawn from the remotest zones; industries whose products are consumed, not only at home, but in every quarter of the globe. . . .

The bourgeoisie, by the rapid improvement of all instruments of production, by the immensely facilitated means of communication, draws all, even the most barbarian, nations into civilization. The cheap prices of commodities are the heavy artillery with which it batters down all Chinese walls, with which it forces the barbarians' intensely obstinate hatred of foreigners to capitulate. It compels all nations, on pain of extinction, to adopt the bourgeois mode of production; it compels them to introduce what it calls civilization into their midst, i.e., to become bourgeois themselves. In one word, it creates a world after its own image.

The bourgeoisie has subjected the country to the rule of the towns. It has created enormous cities, has greatly increased the urban population as compared with the rural, and has thus rescued a considerable part of the population from the idiocy of rural life. Just as it has made the country dependent on the towns, so it has made barbarian and semi-barbarian countries dependent on the civilized ones, nations of peasants on nations of bourgeois, the East on the West.

The bourgeoisie keeps more and more doing away with the scattered state of the population, of the means of production, and of property. . . .

We see then: the means of production and of exchange, on whose foundation the bourgeoisie built itself up, were generated in feudal society. At a certain stage in the development of these means of production and of exchange, the conditions under which feudal society produced and exchanged, the feudal organization of agriculture and manufacturing industry, in one word, the feudal relations of property became no longer compatible with the already developed productive forces; they became so many fetters. They had to be burst asunder; they were burst asunder.

Into their place stepped free competition, accompanied by a social and political constitution adapted in it, and the economic and political sway of the bourgeois class.

A similar movement is going on before our own eyes. . . . It is enough to mention the commercial crises that by their periodical return put the existence of the entire bourgeois society on its trial, each time more threateningly. In these crises, a great part not only of the existing products, but also of the previously created productive forces, are periodically destroyed. In these crises, there breaks out an epidemic that, in all earlier epochs, would have seemed an absurdity — the epidemic of over-production. Society suddenly finds itself put back into a state of momentary barbarism; it appears as if a famine, a universal war of devastation, had cut off the supply of every means of subsistence; industry and commerce seem to be destroyed; and why? Because there is too much civilization, too much means of subsistence, too much industry, too much commerce. The productive forces at the disposal of society no longer tend to further the development of the conditions of bourgeois property; on the contrary, they have become too powerful for these conditions, by which they are fettered, and so soon as they overcome these fetters, they bring disorder into the whole of bourgeois society, endanger the existence of bourgeois property. The conditions of bourgeois society are too narrow to comprise the wealth created by them. And how does the bourgeoisie get over these crises? On the one hand by enforced destruction of a mass of productive forces; on the other, by the conquest of new markets, and by the more thorough exploitation of the old ones. That is to say, by paving the way for more extensive and more destructive crises, and by diminishing the means whereby crises are prevented.

The weapons with which the bourgeoisie felled feudalism to the ground are now turned against the bourgeoisie itself.

But not only has the bourgeoisie forged the weapons that bring death to itself; it has also called into existence the men who are to wield those weapons — the modern working class — the proletarians.

In proportion as the bourgeoisie, i.e., capital, is developed, in the same proportion is the proletariat, the modern working class, developed — a class of laborers, who live only so long as they find work, and who find work only so long as their labor increases capital. These laborers, who must sell themselves piecemeal, are a commodity, like every other article of commerce, and are consequently exposed to all the vicissitudes of competition, to all the fluctuations of the market.

Owing to the extensive use of machinery, and to the division of labor, the work of the proletarians has lost all individual character, and, consequently, all charm for the workman. He becomes an appendage of the machine, and it is only the most simple, most monotonous, and most easily acquired knack, that is required of him. Hence, the cost of production of a workman is restricted, almost entirely, to the means of subsistence that he requires for maintenance, and for the propagation of his race. But the price of a commodity, and therefore also of labor, is equal to its cost of production. In proportion, therefore, as the repulsiveness of the work increases, the wage decreases. Nay more, in proportion as the use of machinery and division of labor increases, in the same proportion the burden of toil also increases, whether by prolongation of the working hours, by the increase of the work exacted in a given time or by increased speed of machinery, etc.

Modern Industry has converted the little workshop of the patriarchal master into the great factory of the industrial capitalist. Masses of laborers, crowded into the factory, are organized like soldiers. As privates of the industrial army they are placed under the command of a perfect hierarchy of officers and sergeants. Not only are they slaves of the bourgeois class, and of the bourgeois State; they are daily and hourly enslaved by the machine, by the overlooker, and, above all, by the individual bourgeois manufacturer himself. The more openly this despotism proclaims gain to be its end and aim, the more petty, the more hateful and the more embittering it is.

The less the skill and exertion of strength implied in manual labor, in other words, the more modern industry becomes developed, the more is the labor of men superseded by that of women. Differences of age and sex have no longer any distinctive social validity for the working class. All are instruments of labor, more or less expensive to use, according to their age and sex.

No sooner is the exploitation of the laborer by the manufacturer, so far, at an end, that he receives his wages in cash, than he is set upon by the other portions of the bourgeoisie, the landlord, the shopkeeper, the pawnbroker, etc.

The lower strata of the middle class—the small tradespeople, shopkeepers, and retired tradesmen generally, the handicraftsmen and peasants—all these sink gradually into the proletariat, partly because their diminutive capital does not suffice for the scale on which Modern Industry is carried on, and is swamped in the competition with the large capitalists, partly because their specialized skill is rendered worthless by new methods of production. Thus the proletariat is recruited from all classes of the population.

The proletariat goes through various stages of development. With its birth begins its struggle with the bourgeoisie. At first the contest is carried on by individual laborers, then by the workpeople of a factory, then by the operative of one trade, in one locality, against the individual bourgeois who directly exploits them. They direct their attacks not against the bourgeois conditions of production, but against the instruments of production themselves; they destroy imported wares that compete with their labor, they smash to pieces machinery, they set factories ablaze, they seek to restore by force the vanished status of the workman of the Middle Ages.

At this stage, the laborers still form an incoherent mass scattered over the whole country, and broken up by their mutual competition. If anywhere they unite to form more compact bodies, this is not yet the consequence of their own active union, but of the union of the bourgeoisie, which class, in order to attain its own political ends, is compelled to set the whole proletariat in motion, and is moreover yet, for a time, able to do so. At this stage, therefore, the proletarians do not fight their enemies, but the enemies of their enemies, the remnants of absolute monarchy, the landowners, the non-industrial bourgeois, the petty bourgeois. Thus, the whole historical movement is concentrated in the hands of the bourgeoisie; every victory so obtained is a victory for the bourgeoisie.

But with the development of industry, the proletariat not only increases in number; it becomes concentrated in greater masses, its strength grows, and it feels that strength more. The various interests and conditions of life within the ranks of the proletariat are more and more equalized, in proportion as machinery obliterates all distinctions of labor, and nearly everywhere reduces wages to the same low level. The growing competition among the bourgeois, and the resulting commercial crises, make the wages of the workers ever more fluctuating. The increasing improvement of machinery, ever more rapidly developing, makes their livelihood more and more precarious; the collisions between individual workmen and individual bourgeois take more and more the character of collisions between two classes. Thereupon, the workers begin to form combinations (Trades Unions) against the bourgeois; they club together in order to keep up the rate of wages; they found permanent associations in order to make provision beforehand for these occasional revolts. Here and there, the contest breaks out into riots.

Now and then the workers are victorious, but only for a time. The real fruit of their battles lies, not in the immediate result, but in the ever expanding union of the workers. This union is helped on by the improved means of communication that are created by modern industry, and that place the workers of different localities in contact with one another. It was just this contact that was needed to centralize the numerous local struggles, all of the same character, into one national struggle between classes. But every class struggle is a political struggle. And that union, to attain which the burghers of the Middle Ages, with their miserable highways, required centuries, the modern proletarian, thanks to railways, achieve in a few years.

This organization of the proletarians into a class, and, consequently into a political party, is continually being upset again by the competition between the workers themselves. But it ever rises up again, stronger, firmer, mightier. It compels legislative recognition of particular interests of the workers, by taking advantage of the divisions among the bourgeoisie itself. Thus, the ten-hours' bill in England was carried.

Altogether collisions between the classes of the old society further, in many ways, the course of development of the proletariat. The bourgeoisie finds itself involved in a constant battle. At first with the aristocracy; later on, with those portions of the bourgeoisie itself, whose interests have become antagonistic to the progress of industry; at all time with the bourgeoisie of foreign countries. In all these battles, it sees itself compelled to appeal to the proletariat, to ask for help, and thus, to drag it into the political arena. The bourgeoisie itself, therefore, supplies the proletariat with its own elements of political and general education, in other words, it furnishes the proletariat with weapons for fighting the bourgeoisie. . . .

Of all the classes that stand face to face with the bourgeoisie today, the proletariat alone is a really revolutionary class. The other classes decay and finally disappear in the face of Modern Industry; the proletariat is its special and essential product.

The lower middle class, the small manufacturer, the shopkeeper, the artisan, the peasant, all these fight against the bourgeoisie, to save from extinction their existence as fractions of the middle class. They are therefore not revolutionary, but conservative. Nay more, they are reactionary, for they try to roll back the wheel of history. If by chance, they are revolutionary, they are only so in view of their impending transfer into the proletariat; they thus defend not their present, but their future interests, they desert their own standpoint to place themselves at that of the proletariat.

The "dangerous class," [*lumpenproletariat*] the social scum, that passively rotting mass thrown off by the lowest layers of the old society, may, here and there, be swept into the movement by a proletarian revolution; its conditions of life, however, prepare it far more for the part of a bribed tool of reactionary intrigue.

In the condition of the proletariat, those of old society at large are already virtually swamped. . . .

All the preceding classes that got the upper hand sought to fortify their already acquired status by subjecting society at large to their conditions of appropriation. The proletarians cannot become masters of the productive forces of society, except by abolishing their own previous mode of appropriation, and thereby also every other previous mode of appropriation. They have nothing of their own to secure and to fortify; their mission is to destroy all previous securities for, and insurances of, individual property.

All previous historical movements were movements of minorities, or in the interest of minorities. The proletarian movement is the self-conscious, independent movement of the immense majority, in the interest of the immense majority. The proletariat, the lowest stratum of our present society, cannot stir, cannot raise itself up, without the whole superincumbent strata of official society being sprung into the air. Though not in substance, yet in form, the struggle of the proletariat with the bourgeoisie is at first a national struggle. The proletariat of each country must, of course, first of all settle matters with its own bourgeoisie.

In depicting the most general phases of the development of the proletariat, we traced the more or less veiled civil war, raging within existing society, up to the point where that war breaks out into open revolution, and where the violent overthrow of the bourgeoisie lays the foundation for the sway of the proletariat.

Hitherto, every form of society has been based, as we have already seen, on the antagonism of oppressing and oppressed classes. But in order to oppress a class, certain conditions must be assured to it under which it can, at least, continue its slavish existence. . . . The essential conditions for the existence and for the sway of the bourgeois class is the formation and augmentation of capital; the condition for capital is wage-labor. Wage-labor rests exclusively on competition between the laborers. The advance of industry, whose involuntary promoter is the bourgeoisie, replaces the isolation of the laborers, due to competition, by the revolutionary combination, due to association. The development of Modern Industry, therefore, cuts from under its feet the very foundation on which the bourgeoisie produces and appropriates products. What the bourgeoisie therefore produces, above all, are its own grave-diggers. Its fall and the victory of the proletariat are equally inevitable. . . .

Chapter 4: Position of the Communists in Relation to the Various Existing Opposition Parties

The Communists disdain to conceal their views and aims. They openly declare that their ends can be attained only by the forcible overthrow of all existing social conditions. Let the ruling classes tremble at a Communistic revolution. The proletarians have nothing to lose but their chains. They have a world to win.

WORKERS OF ALL COUNTRIES, UNITE!

READING QUESTIONS

1. How do Marx and Engels describe the power relationship between the bourgeoisie and the proletariat? How is it changing?

2. In Marx and Engels's view, what is the fundamental source of historical change?

3. Why, according to Marx and Engels, is a working-class revolution against the capitalist middle class inevitable? What do they suggest workers do to hasten the arrival of the revolution?

21-5 | Following Mademoiselle Liberté
EUGÈNE DELACROIX, *Liberty Leading the People* (1830)

Marianne, a female figure representing liberty and reason, became a central element in French political iconography during the French Revolution. From that point forward, French artists have used Marianne to connect the political events of their day to France's revolutionary legacy, drawing on this powerful symbol of the promise of the revolution to give meaning to their own struggles. The work of French artist Eugène Delacroix (1798–1863) provides an example of this phenomenon. In 1830, with France once again convulsed by revolutionary upheaval, Delacroix placed Marianne in the thick of the Parisian street fighting, leading a crowd of revolutionaries forward over their fallen comrades, pointing the way toward the realization of France's national destiny.

"28 July 1830," Delacroix, Ferdinand Victor Eugene (1798–1863) / Louvre, Paris, France / The Bridgeman Art Library.

READING QUESTIONS

1. What social classes are represented in the painting? What do they suggest about the political alliances that shaped the revolution of 1830?

2. How might we interpret the fact that liberty is portrayed as a young woman? How might we react to the fact that her dress is torn to reveal her breasts?

3. What does Delacroix's painting suggest about the place of the French Revolution in French national identity in the early nineteenth century?

21-6 | Workers Demand the Vote
The People's Charter (1838)

In 1832 a major reform of Britain's Parliament took place. Although working-class agitation was a significant factor in pressuring the government to act, the newly created uniform borough (town) voting franchise excluded almost the entire working class from the electorate. One response to this outcome was Chartism, an explicitly working-class political movement

London Working Men's Association, "Six Points of the People's Charter," www.chartists.net/The-six-points.htm, accessed March 11, 2013.

based on "The People's Charter," a list of demands embodied in a petition to Parliament. The charter was drawn up by six members of Parliament—Daniel O'Connell, John Arthur Roebuck, John Temple Leader, Charles Hindley, Thomas Perronet Thompson, and William Sharman Crawford—and six working-class radicals—Henry Hetherington, John Cleave, James Watson, Richard Moore, William Lovett, and Henry Vincent. Although overwhelmingly rejected when it was presented to Parliament in 1839, 1842, and 1848, five of the charter's six demands (annual Parliamentary elections being the exception) became law by 1918.

1. **A vote** for every man twenty-one years of age, of sound mind, and not undergoing punishment for crime.
2. **The ballot**[1]—To protect the elector in the exercise of his vote.
3. **No property qualification** for Members of Parliament[2]—thus enabling the constituencies to return the man of their choice, be he rich or poor.
4. **Payment of members,** thus enabling an honest tradesman, working man, or other person, to serve a constituency, when taken from his business to attend to the interests of the Country.
5. **Equal constituencies** securing the same amount of representation for the same number of electors, instead of allowing small constituencies to swamp the votes of large ones.
6. **Annual Parliaments,** thus presenting the most effectual check to bribery and intimidation, since though a constituency might be bought once in seven years (even with the ballot), no purse could buy a constituency (under a system of universal suffrage) in each ensuing twelve-month; and since members, when elected for a year only, would not be able to defy and betray their constituents as now.

READING QUESTIONS

1. Given that roughly 80 percent of Great Britain's population was working class, what would have been the political consequences of the first point of the Charter's enactment?

2. The Charter calls for an end to property qualifications for members of Parliament and also for payment of MPs. What do these two demands suggest about the nature of Parliamentary representation in early- and mid-nineteenth-century Britain? Who was running the country?

---

[1]**The ballot:** Secret ballot. At the time voting took place *viva voce*, out loud and in public, which many argued led to intimidation of voters.

[2]**No property qualification . . . Parliament:** At the time candidates for Parliament had to possess at least £300 in property. Since a skilled working man might earn £75 a year, the property qualification amounted to four years' wages.

21-7 | The Misery of the Potato Famine

WILLIAM STEUART TRENCH, *Realities of Irish Life* (1847)

As an Irish land agent, William Steuart Trench (1808–1872) was a firsthand witness to the ravages of the potato famine. A fungus, the potato blight, attacked the crop repeatedly during the years 1845–1848. The British government's limited efforts to provide help for the Irish were wholly inadequate. The Irish poor, whose diets consisted of little other than potatoes, were the victims of a Malthusian demographic disaster; between 1841 and 1851 Ireland's population fell between 20 and 25 percent. Estimates of the death toll range from around 750,000 to double that figure. Hundreds of thousands of the more fortunate Irish emigrated.

I did not see a child playing in the streets or on the roads; no children are to be seen outside the doors but a few sick and dying children. . . . In the districts which are now being depopulated by starvation, coffins are only used for the more wealthy. The majority were taken to the grave without any coffin, and buried in their rags: in some instances even the rags are taken from the corpse to cover some still living body. . . .

I then proceeded to Cappagh, which is a coast-guard station, in the midst of a starving population, which had been collected round mines which are not now worked. . . . On the evening before, I had heard of a boy living on the road to Cappagh, who had seen a dog tearing the head, and neck, and ribs of a man. I wished to learn the truth of this from the boy himself. He told me that the fact was so, and that his little brother had on another occasion seen another dog tearing the head of a man. The younger boy remarked that he had seen the remains of the head the day before in an adjoining field. I asked him to lead me to the spot, which he did, and I there found a part of the human head and under-jaw, gnawed, but marked with blood. I placed it under ground. . . .

On arriving at Cappagh, in the first house I saw a dead child lying in a corner of the house, and two children, pale as death, with their heads hanging down upon their breasts sitting by a small fire. The father had died on the road coming home from work. One of the children, a lad seventeen years of age, had been found, in the absence of his mother, who was looking for food, lying dead, with his legs held out of the fire by the little child which I then saw lying dead. Two other children had also died. The mother and the two children still alive had lived on one dish of barley for the last four days. On entering another house the doctor said, "Look there, Sir, you can't tell whether they are boys or girls." Taking up a skeleton child, he said, "Here is the way it is with them all; their legs swing and rock like the legs of a doll, they have the smell of mice."

From William Steuart Trench, *Realities of Irish Life* (London: Longmans, Green, 1868), pp. 394–398.

READING QUESTIONS

1. Why do you think the British government failed to take effectual action to alleviate the famine?

2. The blight, which affected potato harvests throughout northern Europe, did not produce a similar catastrophe in Britain. Why might Britain have been spared?

■ COMPARATIVE AND DISCUSSION QUESTIONS ■

1. In what ways did Thomas Malthus's theories in his *Essay on the Principle of Population* (Document 20-1) affect Ricardo's views about the supply and demand of labor?

2. Compare and contrast the vision of human nature articulated by Metternich, Mill, and Marx and Engels. How did the authors' ideas about the individual shape their views of society and social change?

3. What do you think Marx and Engels derived from Ricardo's essay "On Wages" in formulating their theory of class struggle?

4. Why do you think Marx and Engels specifically named Metternich as one of communism's foes in the preamble to the *Communist Manifesto*? Was their emphasis warranted? What would Metternich think of his detractors, and why?

5. How do you think Marx and Engels regarded the Chartist movement, and why?

6. How might Metternich have responded to Delacroix's *Liberty Leading the People*? What alternative description of the legacy of the French Revolution might he have offered?

7. Describe the connections between the conditions of the Irish potato famine detailed in Trench's account and the economic philosophy outlined by Ricardo.

22

Life in the Emerging Urban Society
1840–1914

In the second half of the nineteenth century, Germany, France, and the United States followed Britain's lead and became industrialized nations. All witnessed the growth of the middle and working classes—and experienced the deplorable sanitary conditions that accompanied rapid urbanization. By the 1860s, however, significant advances in public health and medical science had increased the life expectancy of the urban poor. Politically, the expansion of the electorate in Britain, Germany, and France meant that, by 1884, the working class was the largest voting bloc in all three nations, although throughout Europe, women of all classes still lacked the vote. In the intellectual realm, literary realists challenged the romanticism of the first half of the century, basing their work on observation instead of emotion and rejecting pastoral scenes for gritty depictions of urban working-class life, while the theory of evolution and its outgrowth, Social Darwinism, seemed to directly defy the religious revival cultivated during the Romantic movement. The following documents reflect the facts that Britain set the mold for urbanization and industrialization—modernity—and that British thinkers were at the forefront of public health, scientific, and pseudo-scientific trends.

22-1 | Sanitation and Public Health

EDWIN CHADWICK, *Inquiry into the Sanitary Conditions of the Poor* (1842)

Sir Edwin Chadwick (1800–1880), a disciple of the radical philosopher Jeremy Bentham, spent his life in pursuit of social and sanitary reform. Bentham, Chadwick, and other radicals known as utilitarians shared many views with nineteenth-century liberals. Both liberals and utilitarians believed in human rationality and the concept of human progress, and both believed that poverty was chiefly the consequence of individual moral failings. The two groups parted ways sharply, however, over the role of government. Nineteenth-century liberals argued that government intervention was an impediment to social and economic progress. Utilitarians, in contrast, believed that the only measure of a policy's worth was its utility—that is, the degree to which it improved society as a whole. If, in particular situations, such as public health, government intervention could be shown to have a positive effect, the utilitarians had no ideological objection to such intervention.

After as careful an examination of the evidence collected as I have been enabled to make, I beg leave to recapitulate the chief conclusions which that evidence appears to me to establish.

First, as to the extent and operation of the evils which are the subject of this inquiry:—

That the various forms of epidemic, endemic, and other disease[1] caused, or aggravated, or propagated chiefly amongst the laboring classes by atmospheric impurities produced by decomposing animal and vegetable substances, by damp and filth, and close and overcrowded dwellings prevail amongst the population in every part of the kingdom, whether dwelling in separate houses, in rural villages, in small towns, in the larger towns—as they have been found to prevail in the lowest districts of the metropolis.

That such disease, wherever its attacks are frequent, is always found in connection with the physical circumstances above specified, and that where those circumstances are removed by drainage, proper cleansing, better ventilation, and other means of diminishing atmospheric impurity, the frequency and intensity of such disease is abated; and where the removal of the noxious agencies appears to be complete, such disease almost entirely disappears.

From Edwin Chadwick, *Report . . . from the Poor Law Commissioners on an Inquiry into the Sanitary Conditions of the Labouring Population of Great Britain* (London: W. Clowes and Sons, 1842), pp. 369–372.

[1]**epidemic, endemic, and other disease**: The laboring classes were plagued by cholera, typhus, typhoid fever, tuberculosis (known then as "consumption"), and numerous respiratory ailments primarily caused by air pollution and occupational hazards such as cotton dust ("Brown Lung").

The high prosperity in respect to employment and wages, and various and abundant food, have afforded to the laboring classes no exemptions from attacks of epidemic disease, which have been as frequent and as fatal in periods of commercial and manufacturing prosperity as in any others.

That the formation of all habits of cleanliness is obstructed by defective supplies of water.

That the annual loss of life from filth and bad ventilation are greater than the loss from death or wounds in any wars in which the country has been engaged in modern times.

That of the 43,000 cases of widowhood, and 112,000 cases of destitute orphanage relieved from the poor's rates in England and Wales alone, it appears that the greatest proportion of deaths of the heads of families occurred from the above specified and other removable causes; that their ages were under 45 years; that is to say, 13 years below the natural probabilities of life as shown by the experience of the whole population of Sweden. . . .

That, measuring the loss of working ability amongst large classes by the instances of gain, even from incomplete arrangements for the removal of noxious influences from places of work or from abodes, that this loss cannot be less than eight or ten years.

That the ravages of epidemics and other diseases do not diminish but tend to increase the pressure of population.

That in the districts where the mortality is greatest the births are not only sufficient to replace the numbers removed by death, but to add to the population.

That the younger population, bred up under noxious physical agencies, is inferior in physical organization and general health to a population preserved from the presence of such agencies.

That the population so exposed is less susceptible of moral influences, and the effects of education are more transient than with a healthy population.

That these adverse circumstances tend to produce an adult population short-lived, improvident, reckless, and intemperate, and with habitual avidity for sensual gratifications.

That these habits lead to the abandonment of all the conveniences and decencies of life, and especially lead to the overcrowding of their homes, which is destructive to the morality as well as the health of large classes of both sexes.

That defective town cleansing fosters habits of the most abject degradation and tends to the demoralization of large numbers of human beings, who subsist by means of what they find amidst the noxious filth accumulated in neglected streets and bye-places.

That the expenses of local public works are in general unequally and unfairly assessed, oppressively and uneconomically collected, by separate collections, wastefully expended in separate and inefficient operations by unskilled and practically irresponsible officers.

That the existing law for the protection of the public health and the constitutional machinery for reclaiming its execution, such as the Courts Leet,[2] have fallen into desuetude, and are in the state indicated by the prevalence of the evils they were intended to prevent.

Secondly. As to the means by which the present sanitary condition of the laboring classes may be improved: —

The primary and most important measures, and at the same time the most practicable, and within the recognized province of public administration, are drainage, the removal of all refuse of habitations, streets, and roads, and the improvement of the supplies of water.

That the chief obstacles to the immediate removal of decomposing refuse of towns and habitations have been the expense and annoyance of the hand labor and cartage requisite for the purpose.

That this expense may be reduced to one-twentieth or to one-thirtieth, or rendered inconsiderable, by the use of water and self-acting means of removal by improved and cheaper sewers and drains. . . .

That appropriate scientific arrangements for public drainage would afford important facilities for private land-drainage, which is important for the health as well as sustenance of the laboring classes.

That the expense of public drainage, of supplies of water laid on in houses, and of means of improved cleansing would be a pecuniary [monetary] gain, by diminishing the existing charges attendant on sickness and premature mortality.

That for the protection of the laboring classes and of the ratepayers against inefficiency and waste in all new structural arrangements for the protection of the public health, and to ensure public confidence that the expenditure will be beneficial, securities should be taken that all new local public works are devised and conducted by responsible officers qualified by the possession of the science and skill of civil engineers. . . .

That for the prevention of the disease occasioned by defective ventilation and other causes of impurity in places of work and other places where large numbers are assembled, and for the general promotion of the means necessary to prevent disease, that it would be good economy to appoint a district medical officer independent of private practice, and with the securities of special qualifications and responsibilities to initiate sanitary measures and reclaim the execution of the law.

That by the combinations of all these arrangements, it is probable that the full ensurable period of life indicated by the Swedish tables; that is, an increase of 13 years at least, may be extended to the whole of the laboring classes.

---

[2]**Courts Leet**: Law courts dating back to medieval times, when the administration of justice was overseen by individual noblemen. Many early industrial towns, Manchester among them, lacked comprehensive municipal governments until the 1830s and afterward, and thus such antiquated institutions like Courts Leet confronted situations which their creators had never envisioned and for which they were, as Chadwick suggests, wholly inadequate.

That the attainment of these and the other collateral advantages of reducing existing charges and expenditure are within the power of the legislature, and are dependent mainly on the securities taken for the application of practical science, skill, and economy in the direction of local public works.

And that the removal of noxious physical circumstances, and the promotion of civic, household, and personal cleanliness, are necessary to the improvement of the moral condition of the population; for that sound morality and refinement in manners and health are not long found coexistent with filthy habits amongst any class of the community.

READING QUESTIONS

1. What, according to Chadwick, was the chief source of disease? Why does he say this?

2. What sorts of solutions does he offer to improve public health? What role did he believe government should play?

3. According to Chadwick, what is the relationship between sanitation and morality? Do you agree with his assessment? Why or why not?

22-2 | Life in London's East End
JACK LONDON, *The People of the Abyss* (1902)

Although known chiefly for works of fiction like *The Call of the Wild*, American author (and socialist) Jack London (1876–1916) also published nonfiction works. *The People of the Abyss* was based on his firsthand experience of living in the slums of London's East End for several months, where he pretended to be a stranded American sailor in order to observe the realities of working-class life. London's project reflects the larger trend towards realism in nineteenth- and early-twentieth-century art and literature. In both Europe and the United States, artists, writers, and reformers sought to document social reality as a first step toward advancing the cause of social justice.

Chapter XLX: The Ghetto

The City of Dreadful Monotony the East End is often called, especially by well-fed, optimistic sightseers, who look over the surface of things and are merely shocked by the intolerable sameness and meanness of it all. If the East End is worthy of no worse title than The City of Dreadful Monotony, and if working people are unworthy of variety and beauty and surprise, it would not be such a bad place in which to live. But the East End does merit a worse title. It should be called The City of Degradation.

From Jack London, *The People of the Abyss* (New York: Macmillan, 1903), pp. 210–218, 276–277, 314–317.

While it is not a city of slums, as some people imagine, it may well be said to be one gigantic slum. From the standpoint of simple decency and clean manhood and womanhood, any mean street, of all its mean streets, is a slum. Where sights and sounds abound which neither you nor I would care to have our children see and hear is a place where no man's children should live, and see and hear. Where you and I would not care to have our wives pass their lives is a place where no other man's wife should have to pass her life. For here, in the East End, the obscenities and brute vulgarities of life are rampant. There is no privacy. The bad corrupts the good, and all fester together. Innocent childhood is sweet and beautiful; but in East London innocence is a fleeting thing, and you must catch them before they crawl out of the cradle, or you will find the very babes as unholily wise as you.

The application of the Golden Rule determines that East London is an unfit place in which to live. Where you would not have your own babe live, and develop, and gather to itself knowledge of life and the things of life, is not a fit place for the babes of other men to live. . . . Political economy and the survival of the fittest can go hang if they say otherwise. What is not good enough for you is not good enough for other men, and there's no more to be said. . . .

The mean streets merely look mean from the outside, but inside the walls are to be found squalor, misery, and tragedy. While the following tragedy may be revolting to read, it must not be forgotten that the existence of it is far more revolting. In Devonshire Place, Lisson Grove, a short while back died an old woman of seventy-five years of age. At the inquest the coroner's officer stated that "all he found in the room was a lot of old rags covered with vermin. He had got himself smothered with the vermin. The room was in a shocking condition, and he had never seen anything like it. Everything was absolutely covered with vermin."

The doctor said: "He found deceased lying across the fender on her back. She had one garment and her stockings on. The body was quite alive with vermin, and all the clothes in the room were absolutely gray with insects. Deceased was very badly nourished and was very emaciated. She had extensive sores on her legs, and her stockings were adherent to those sores. The sores were the result of vermin."

A man present at the inquest wrote: "I had the evil fortune to see the body of the unfortunate woman as it lay in the mortuary; and even now the memory of that grewsome [sic] sight makes me shudder. There she lay in the mortuary shell, so starved and emaciated that she was a mere bundle of skin and bones. Her hair, which was matted with filth, was simply a nest of vermin. Over her bony chest leaped and rolled hundreds, thousands, myriads of vermin."

If it is not good for your mother and my mother so to die, then it is not good for this woman, whosoever's mother she might be, so to die. . . .

In such conditions, the outlook for children is hopeless. They die like flies, and those that survive, survive because they possess excessive vitality and a capacity of adaptation to the degradation with which they are surrounded. They have no home life. In the dens and lairs in which they live they are exposed to all that is obscene and indecent. And as their minds are made rotten, so are their bodies made rotten by bad sanitation, overcrowding, and underfeeding. When a father and mother live with three or four children in a room where the children take turn about in sitting up to drive the rats away from the sleepers, when those children never have enough to eat and are preyed upon and made miserable and weak by swarming vermin, the sort of men and women the survivors will make can readily be imagined. . . .

Five men can produce bread for a thousand. One man can produce cotton cloth for 250 people, woolens for 300, and boots and shoes for 1000. Yet it has been shown throughout the pages of this book that English folk by the millions do not receive enough food, clothes, and boots. Then arises the third and inexorable question: *If Civilization has increased the producing power of the average man, why has it not bettered the lot of the average man?*

There can be one answer only—MISMANAGEMENT. Civilization has made possible all manner of creature comforts and heart's delights. In these the average Englishman does not participate. If he shall be forever unable to participate, then Civilization falls. There is no reason for the continued existence of an artifice so avowed a failure. But it is impossible that men should have reared this tremendous artifice in vain. It stuns the intellect. To acknowledge so crushing a defeat is to give the death-blow to striving and progress.

One other alternative, and one other only, presents itself. *Civilization must be compelled to better the lot of the average man.* This accepted, it becomes at once a question of business management. Things profitable must be continued; things unprofitable must be eliminated. Either the Empire is a profit to England or it is a loss. If it is a loss, it must be done away with. If it is a profit, it must be managed so that the average man comes in for a share of the profit.

If the struggle for commercial supremacy is profitable, continue it. If it is not, if it hurts the worker and makes his lot worse than the lot of a savage, then fling foreign markets and industrial empire overboard. For it is a patent fact that if 40,000,000 people, aided by Civilization, possess a greater individual producing power than the Inuit,[1] then those 40,000,000 people should enjoy more creature comforts and heart's delights than the Inuits enjoy. . . .

In short, society must be reorganized, and a capable management put at the head. That the present management is incapable, there can be no discussion. . . . Blood empire is greater than political empire, and the English of the New World and the Antipodes are strong and vigorous as ever. But the political empire under which they are nominally assembled is perishing. The political machine known as the British Empire is running down. In the hands of its management it is losing momentum every day.

It is inevitable that this management, which has grossly and criminally mismanaged, shall be swept away. Not only has it been wasteful and inefficient, but it has misappropriated the funds. Every worn-out, pasty-faced pauper, every

---

[1]**Inuit**: Aboriginal peoples of the arctic regions of Russia, North America, and Greenland.

blind man, every prison babe, every man, woman, and child whose belly is gnawing with hunger pangs, is hungry because the funds have been misappropriated by the management.

Nor can one member of this managing class plead not guilty before the judgment bar of Man. "The living in their houses, and in their graves the dead," are challenged by every babe that dies of innutrition, by every girl that flees the sweater's den to the nightly promenade of Piccadilly,[2] by every worked-out toiler that plunges into the canal. The food this managing class eats, the wine it drinks, the shows it makes, and the fine clothes it wears, are challenged by eight million mouths which have never had enough to fill them, and by twice eight million bodies which have never been sufficiently clothed and housed.

There can be no mistake. Civilization has increased man's producing power an hundred fold, and through mismanagement the men of Civilization live worse than the beasts, and have less to eat and wear and protect them from the elements than the savage Inuit in a frigid climate who lives to-day as he lived in the stone age ten thousand years ago.

READING QUESTIONS

1. To what causes does Jack London attribute the widespread poverty and misery among metropolitan London's poor?

2. Who might he have hoped to influence with his work? What strategies did he employ in his effort to persuade his readers to take action?

3. What connections did London make between conditions in the East End and the condition of the British Empire? What were the political implications of the connections he made?

SOURCES IN CONVERSATION

Separate Spheres

The nineteenth-century societal ideal of separate spheres for men and women was predicated on the assumption that men and women had very different natures. Men were seen as both physically and mentally suited to the rough-and-tumble world of economic competition. It was men, therefore, that would provide the income that made the middle-class lifestyle possible, doing battle on behalf of their families in the office and the

---

[2]**that flees the sweater's den . . . Piccadilly:** That leaves work in a sweatshop to engage in prostitution.

marketplace. Women, in contrast, were soft and yielding. Providers of comfort and care by nature, their job was to create a home that was a refuge for their husbands from the rigors of the outside world. It was the wife's role to remind her husband through her behavior, appearance, and the home she made of the values that made the struggle for advancement worthwhile. Thus, in theory, men and women formed a partnership, with each making a contribution to their joint achievement of the middle-class ideal.

22-3 | ISABELLA BEETON, *Mrs. Beeton's Book of Household Management* (1861)

Isabella Beeton (1836–1865) was a British journalist whose earliest articles appeared in the *English Woman's Domestic Magazine*, one of the first magazines targeted specifically at middle-class women. *Mrs. Beeton's Book of Household Management*, first published in 1861, contained more than 2,700 entries of recipes and practical instructions, from how to keep moths from attacking clothes to how to care for horses. A bestseller that was continually reprinted, it was almost certainly the most widely consulted book on the subject in the decades following its appearance. The excerpts included here focus on the responsibilities of servants. For middle-class and elite women, management of servants was one of their most important tasks. Such women were not expected to cook and clean, but they were responsible for making sure that their households were the well-ordered havens of cleanliness and tranquility demanded by promoters of the late-nineteenth-century cult of domesticity.

Masters and Mistresses.—It has been said that good masters and mistresses make good servants, and this to a great extent is true. There are certainly some men and women in the wide field of servitude whom it would be impossible to train into good servants, but the conduct of both master and mistress is seldom without its effect upon these dependents. They are not mere machines, and no one has a right to consider them in that light. The sensible master and the kind mistress know, that if servants depend on them for their means of living, in their turn they are dependent on their servants for very many of the comforts of life; and that, with a proper amount of care in choosing servants, and treating them like reasonable beings, and making slight excuses for the shortcomings of human nature, they will, save in some exceptional case, be tolerably well served, and, in most instances, surround themselves with attached domestics. . . .

The Lady's-Maid.—The qualifications a lady's maid should possess are a thorough knowledge of hair dressing, dressmaking and repairing and restoring clothes. She should be able to pack well, and her taste, being often called into requisition in matters of dress, should be good. It is also essential that she be well spoken, quiet in manner and quick; that she should be clean and honest goes

From Isabella Beeton, *Mrs. Beeton's Book of Household Management* (London: Ward, Lock and Co., 1888), pp. 1454, 1471, 1473, 1478–1479, 1481–1482.

without saying. A lady's maid having so much more intercourse with her mistress than any other servant should not only possess, but learn, discretion from day to day. To know when to speak and when to be silent, and to be willing to bear with patience any little caprices of taste and temper with which she may have to contend.

Her first duty in the morning, after having performed her own toilet, is to prepare the bath and everything for dressing for her mistress, taking her an early cup of tea if she requires one. She then examines the clothes put off by her mistress the evening before, either to put them away, or to see that they are all in order to put on again. During the winter and in wet weather, the dresses should be carefully examined, and the mud removed. Dresses of tweed, and other woolen materials may be laid out on a table and brushed all over; but in general, even in woolen fabrics, the lightness of the tissues renders brushing unsuitable to dresses, and it is better to remove the dust from the folds by beating them lightly with a handkerchief or thin cloth. Silk dresses should never be brushed, but rubbed with a piece of merino, or other soft material, of a similar color, kept for the purpose. Summer dresses . . . simply require shaking; but if the muslin be tumbled, it must be ironed afterwards. If the dresses require slight repair, it should be done at once: "a stitch in time saves nine." . . .

A waiting-maid who wishes to make herself useful will study the fashion-books with attention, so as to be able to aid her mistress's judgment in dressing, according to the prevailing fashion, with such modifications as her style and figure require. She will also, if she has her mistress's interest at heart, employ her spare time in repairing and making up dresses which have served one purpose, to serve another also; or turning many things, unfitted for her mistress, to use for the younger branches of the family. The lady's-maid may thus render herself invaluable to her mistress, and increase her own happiness in so doing. The exigencies of fashion and luxury are such, that all ladies, except those of the very highest rank, will consider themselves fortunate in having about them a thoughtful person, capable of diverting their finery to a useful purpose. . . .

Duties of the Housemaid.—"Cleanliness is next to godliness," saith the proverb, and "order" is in the next degree; the housemaid, then, may be said to be the handmaiden to two of the most prominent virtues. Her duties are very numerous, and many of the comforts of the family depend on their performance; but they are simple and easy to a person naturally clean and orderly, and desirous of giving satisfaction. . . .

The first duty of the housemaid in winter is to open the shutters of all the lower rooms in the house, and take up the hearthrugs of those rooms which she is going to "do" before breakfast. In some families, where there is only a cook and housemaid kept, and where the drawing-rooms are large, the cook has the care of the dining-room, and the housemaid that of the breakfast-room, library, and drawing-rooms. After the shutters are all opened, she sweeps the breakfast-room, sweeping the dust towards the fire-place, of course previously removing the fender. She should then lay a cloth (generally made of coarse wrappering) over the carpet in front of the stove, and on this should place her housemaid's box, containing black-lead brushes, leathers, emery-paper, cloth, black lead, and all utensils necessary for cleaning a grate, with the cinder-pail on the other side. She now sweeps up the ashes, and deposits them in her cinder-pail, which is a japanned tin pail, with a wire-sifter inside, and a closely-fitting top. In this pail the cinders are sifted, and reserved for use in the kitchen or under the copper, the ashes only being thrown away. The cinders disposed of, she proceeds to black-lead the grate, producing the black lead, the soft brush for laying it on, her blacking and polishing brushes, from the box which contains her tools. This housemaid's box should be kept well stocked. Having blackened, brushed, and polished every part, and made all clean and bright, she now proceeds to lay the fire. . . .

Bright grates require unceasing attention to keep them in perfect order. A day should never pass without the housemaid rubbing with a dry leather the polished parts of a grate, as also the fender and fire-irons. A careful and attentive housemaid should have no occasion ever to use emery-paper for any part but the bars, which, of course, become blackened by the fire. (Some mistresses, to save labor, have a double set of bars, one set bright for the summer, and another black set to use when fires are in requisition.) . . .

The several fires lighted, the housemaid proceeds with her dusting, and polishing the several pieces of furniture in the breakfast-parlor, leaving no corner unvisited. Before sweeping the carpet, it is a good practice to sprinkle it all over with tea-leaves, which not only lay all dust, but give a slightly fragrant smell to the room. It is now in order for the reception of the family; and where there is neither footman nor parlor-maid, she now proceeds to the dressing-room, and lights her mistress's fire, if she is in the habit of having one to dress by. Her mistress is called, hot water placed in the dressing-room for her use, her clothes — as far as they are under the house-maid's charge — put before the fire to air, hanging a fire-guard on the bars where there is one, while she proceeds to prepare the breakfast. . . .

READING QUESTIONS

1. What do Beeton's instructions about the management and duties of household servants tell us about how life in modern urban societies has altered over the past century and a half?

2. What does Beeton infer are some of the most typical problems that exist between masters and servants?

3. What does this excerpt tell us about class divisions, and about Beeton's attitudes toward the "lower orders," from which servants came?

4. What do the daily chores described here reveal about nineteenth-century attitudes toward work and the use of time?

5. Britain's aristocracy had been managing servants for centuries at the time this guide was published. To whom do you think Beeton was imparting her instructions, regardless of the grandeur of the households she describes?

22-4 | *Dressing the Respectable Woman* (ca. 1890)

The clothes worn by late-nineteenth-century middle-class and elite women concerned with respectability were form-fitting, multilayered, cumbersome, and uncomfortable. In order to achieve what was seen as the ideal female silhouette, women began by putting on a set of rigid undergarments, including whale-bone corsets, an operation that required the assistance of a servant. Once dressed, the fashionable woman remained dependent on her servants, since her attire restricted her movement and made physical labor all but impossible.

Cregmile, Kate R. (1891–1923) / Cincinnati Art Museum, Ohio, USA / The Bridgeman Art Library.

READING QUESTIONS

1. What details about the dress catch your attention? Why?

2. Do you think it likely that nineteenth-century women had waists as narrow as this dress suggests? What would have been required for a typical woman to fit into this dress?

3. What does the dress tell you about late-nineteenth-century ideas about the "perfect" female body?

4. What connections can you make between this dress and nineteenth-century ideas about the social and economic roles of elite and middle-class women?

22-5 | Women and the Industrial World

CLARA ZETKIN, *Women's Work and the Trade Unions* (1887)

German socialist and feminist Clara Zetkin (1857–1933) was an influential politician and women's suffragist from 1878 until her forced exile by the Nazi regime shortly before her death. A friend of many prominent German radicals including Wilhelm Liebknecht, one of the founders of the German Social Democratic (i.e., Socialist) Party, Zetkin was part of the first generation of modern European feminists. Like their British, French, and American counterparts, late-nineteenth-century German feminists—most of them, like Zetkin, from middle-class backgrounds—devoted the bulk of their energies to obtaining the vote. Zetkin founded the German social democratic women's movement and, for more than twenty-five years, edited the Social Democratic Party's women's newspaper *Die Gleichheit* (*Equality*).

It is not just the women workers who suffer because of the miserable payment of their labor. The male workers, too, suffer because of it. As a consequence of their low wages, the women are transformed from mere competitors into unfair competitors who push down the wages of men. Cheap women's labor eliminates the work of men and if the men want to continue to earn their daily bread, they must put up with low wages. Thus women's work is not only a cheap form of labor, it also cheapens the work of men and for that reason it is doubly appreciated by the capitalist, who craves profits. The economic advantages of the industrial activity of proletarian women only aid the tiny minority of the sacrosanct guild of coupon clippers and extortionists of profit.

From Clara Zetkin, "Women's Work and the Trade Unions" in *Clara Zetkin, Selected Writings*, ed. Philip S. Foner (New York: International Publishers, 1984), pp. 54–56.

Given the fact that many thousands of female workers are active in industry, it is vital for the trade unions to incorporate them into their movement. In individual industries where female labor plays an important role, any movement advocating better wages, shorter working hours, etc., would be doomed from the start because of the attitude of those women workers who are not organized. Battles which began propitiously enough, ended up in failure because the employers were able to play off non-union female workers against those that are organized in unions. These non-union workers continued to work (or took up work) under any conditions, which transformed them from competitors in dirty work to scabs [nonunion strikebreakers].

Certainly one of the reasons for these poor wages for women is the circumstances that female workers are practically unorganized. They lack the strength which comes with unity. They lack the courage, the feeling of power, the spirit of resistance, and the ability to resist which is produced by the strength of an organization in which the individual fights for everybody and everybody fights for the individual. Furthermore, they lack the enlightenment and the training which an organization provides.

READING QUESTIONS

1. Why, according to Zetkin, do women and men compete for jobs? What is the consequence of that competition? What is Zetkin's solution to such competition?

2. Why might Zetkin have advocated the peaceful organization of women into trade unions rather than striving for a communist revolution?

3. What do the author's arguments suggest about the nature and extent of working-class political power in late-nineteenth-century Germany?

22-6 | A New Creation Story

CHARLES DARWIN, *The Descent of Man* (1871)

Charles Darwin (1809–1882) was the most prominent scientist in nineteenth-century Britain. His major works, *On the Origin of Species by Means of Natural Selection* (1859) and *The Descent of Man* (1871) put forward the theory of natural selection, and argued that humans were closely related to the great apes, respectively. They are the foundational texts for modern evolutionary science, although they were immensely controversial on publication, and are still objects of heated contention.

The main conclusion here arrived at, and now held by many naturalists who are well competent to form a sound judgment, is that man is descended from some

From Charles Darwin, *The Descent of Man and Selection in Relation to Sex* (New York: Appleton and Co., 1883), pp. 620–621, 623–624, 626–629, 633–634.

less highly organized form. . . . He who is not content to look, like a savage, at the phenomena of nature as disconnected, cannot any longer believe that man is the work of a separate act of creation. He will be forced to admit that the close resemblance of the embryo of man to that, for instance, of a dog—the construction of his skull, limbs, and whole frame on the same plan with that of other mammals, independently of the uses to which the parts may be put—the occasional reappearance of various structures, for instance of several muscles, which man does not normally possess, but which are common to the Quadrumana[1]—and a crowd of analogous facts—all point in the plainest manner to the conclusion that man is the co-descendant with other mammals of a common progenitor.

We have seen that man incessantly presents individual differences in all parts of his body and in his mental faculties. These differences or variations seem to be induced by the same general causes, and to obey the same laws as with the lower animals. In both cases similar laws of inheritance prevail. Man tends to increase at a greater rate than his means of subsistence; consequently he is occasionally subjected to a severe struggle for existence, and natural selection will have effected whatever lies within its scope. A succession of strongly-marked variations of a similar nature is by no means requisite; slight fluctuating differences in the individual suffice for the work of natural selection; not that we have any reason to suppose that in the same species, all parts of the organization tend to vary to the same degree. . . .

By considering the embryological structure of man,—the homologies which he presents with the lower animals,—the rudiments which he retains,—and the reversions to which he is liable, we can partly recall in imagination the former condition of our early progenitors; and can approximately place them in their proper place in the zoological series. We thus learn that man is descended from a hairy, tailed quadruped, probably arboreal in its habits, and an inhabitant of the Old World. This creature, if its whole structure had been examined by a naturalist, would have been classed amongst the Quadrumana, as surely as the still more ancient progenitor of the Old and New World monkeys. The Quadrumana and all the higher mammals are probably derived from an ancient marsupial animal, and this through a long line of diversified forms, from some amphibian-like creature, and this again from some fish-like animal. In the dim obscurity of the past we can see that the early progenitor of all the Vertebrata must have been an aquatic animal, provided with branchiæ,[2] with the two sexes united in the same individual, and with the most important organs of the body (such as the brain and heart) imperfectly or not at all developed. This animal seems to have been more like the larvæ of the existing marine Ascidians[3] than any other known form.

---

[1]**Quadrumana**: Term once used to describe primates with opposable digits (thumbs) on all four feet.
[2]**branchiæ**: Gills.
[3]**Ascidians**: Genus of mollusks.

The high standard of our intellectual powers and moral disposition is the greatest difficulty which presents itself, after we have been driven to this conclusion on the origin of man. But every one who admits the principle of evolution, must see that the mental powers of the higher animals, which are the same in kind with those of man, though so different in degree, are capable of advancement. . . .

The moral nature of man has reached its present standard, partly through the advancement of his reasoning powers and consequently of a just public opinion, but especially from his sympathies having been rendered more tender and widely diffused through the effects of habit, example, instruction, and reflection. It is not improbable that after long practice virtuous tendencies may be inherited. With the more civilized races, the conviction of the existence of an all-seeing Deity has had a potent influence on the advance of morality. Ultimately man does not accept the praise or blame of his fellows as his sole guide though few escape this influence, but his habitual convictions, controlled by reason, afford him the safest rule. His conscience then becomes the supreme judge and monitor. Nevertheless the first foundation or origin of the moral sense lies in the social instincts, including sympathy; and these instincts no doubt were primarily gained, as in the case of the lower animals, through natural selection.

The belief in God has often been advanced as not only the greatest but the most complete of all the distinctions between man and the lower animals. It is however impossible, as we have seen, to maintain that this belief is innate or instinctive in man. On the other hand a belief in all-pervading spiritual agencies seems to be universal, and apparently follows from a considerable advance in man's reason, and from a still greater advance in his faculties of imagination, curiosity, and wonder. I am aware that the assumed instinctive belief in God has been used by many persons as an argument for His existence. But this is a rash argument, as we should thus be compelled to believe in the existence of many cruel and malignant spirits, only a little more powerful than man; for the belief in them is far more general than in a beneficent Deity. The idea of a universal and beneficent Creator does not seem to arise in the mind of man, until he has been elevated by long-continued culture. . . .

I am aware that the conclusions arrived at in this work will be denounced by some as highly irreligious; but he who denounces them is bound to show why it is more irreligious to explain the origin of man as a distinct species by descent from some lower form, through the laws of variation and natural selection, than to explain the birth of the individual through the laws of ordinary reproduction. The birth both of the species and of the individual are equally parts of that grand sequence of events, which our minds refuse to accept as the result of blind chance. The understanding revolts at such a conclusion, whether or not we are able to believe that every slight variation of structure, — the union of each pair in marriage, — the dissemination of each seed, — and other such events, have all been ordained for some special purpose.

Sexual selection has been treated at great length in this work, for, as I have attempted to show, it has played an important part in the history of the organic world. I am aware that much remains doubtful, but I have endeavored to give a fair view of the whole case. In the lower divisions of the animal kingdom, sexual selection seems to have done nothing. . . . When, however, we come to the Arthropoda and Vertebrata,[4] even to the lowest classes in these two great Sub-Kingdoms, sexual selection has effected much. . . .

Sexual selection depends on the success of certain individuals over others of the same sex, in relation to the propagation of the species; while natural selection depends on the success of both sexes, at all ages, in relation to the general conditions of life. The sexual struggle is of two kinds; in the one it is between the individuals of the same sex, generally the males, in order to drive away or kill their rivals, the females remaining passive; while in the other, the struggle is likewise between the individuals of the same sex, in order to excite or charm those of the opposite sex, generally the females, which no longer remain passive, but select the more agreeable partners. . . .

The main conclusion arrived at in this work, namely that man is descended from some lowly organized form, will, I regret to think, be highly distasteful to many. But there can hardly be a doubt that we are descended from barbarians. The astonishment which I felt on first seeing a party of Fuegians[5] on a wild and broken shore will never be forgotten by me, for the reflection at once rushed into my mind—such were our ancestors. These men were absolutely naked and bedaubed with paint, their long hair was tangled, their mouths frothed with excitement, and their expression was wild, startled, and distrustful. They possessed hardly any arts, and like wild animals lived on what they could catch; they had no government, and were merciless to every one not of their own small tribe. He who has seen a savage in his native land will not feel much shame, if forced to acknowledge that the blood of some more humble creature flows in his veins. For my own part I would as soon be descended from that heroic little monkey, who braved his dreaded enemy in order to save the life of his keeper, or from that old baboon, who descending from the mountains, carried away in triumph his young comrade from a crowd of astonished dogs—as from a savage who delights to torture his enemies, offers up bloody sacrifices, practices infanticide without remorse, treats his wives like slaves, knows no decency, and is haunted by the grossest superstitions.

Man may be excused for feeling some pride at having risen, though not through his own exertions, to the very summit of the organic scale; and the fact of his having thus risen, instead of having been aboriginally placed there, may give him hope for a still higher destiny in the distant future. But we are not here concerned with hopes or fears, only with the truth as far as our reason permits us to discover it; and I have given the evidence to the best of my ability. We must, however, acknowledge, as it seems to me, that man with all his noble qualities,

---

[4]**Arthropoda and Vertebrata**: Insects and vertebrates (animals with spinal columns), respectively.

[5]**Fuegians**: Inhabitants of Tierra del Fuego, at the tip of South America; Patagonians.

with sympathy which feels for the most debased, with benevolence which extends not only to other men but to the humblest living creature, with his god-like intellect which has penetrated into the movements and constitution of the solar system—with all these exalted powers—Man still bears in his bodily frame the indelible stamp of his lowly origin.

READING QUESTIONS

1. On what grounds does Darwin base his argument that "man is descended from some less highly organized form"? Are they compelling? Why or why not?

2. Why does Darwin maintain that the "assumed instinctive belief in God [that] has been used by many persons as an argument for His existence," is "a rash argument"?

3. What assumptions about human civilization and progress are hinted at in this work?

22-7 | Weeding Out the Weak

HERBERT SPENCER, *Social Statics: Survival of the Fittest Applied to Humankind* (1851)

Like Darwin, Herbert Spencer (1820–1903) was an English intellectual, although his work concerned philosophy and social theory rather than science. Spencer was one of the earliest champions of what would later be called "Social Darwinism"—the use of the concept of evolution to justify social inequality and to "demonstrate" the racial superiority of people of northern European ancestry. The following excerpt comes from his first major work, *Social Statics* (1851), which attracted relatively little attention on publication, but contains many of the ideas that would make Spencer one of the most well-known and influential British intellectuals during the 1870s and 1880s.

In common with its other assumptions of secondary offices, the assumption by a government of the office of Reliever-general to the poor, is necessarily forbidden by the principle that a government cannot rightly do anything more than protect. In demanding from a citizen contributions for the mitigation of distress—contributions not needed for the due administration of men's rights—the state is, as we have seen, reversing its function, and diminishing that liberty to exercise the faculties which it was instituted to maintain. Possibly . . . some will assert that by satisfying the wants of the pauper, a government is in reality extending his liberty to exercise his faculties. . . . But this statement of the case implies a confounding of two widely different things. To enforce the fundamental law—to take care that every man has freedom to do all that he wills, provided

From Herbert Spencer, "Social Statics," in *Liberalism: Its Meaning and History*, ed. J. Salwyn Schapiro (New York: Van Nostrand Reinhold, 1958), pp. 136–137.

he infringes not the equal freedom of any other man—this is the special purpose for which the civil power exists. Now insuring to each the right to pursue within the specified limits the objects of his desires without let or hindrance, is quite a separate thing from insuring him satisfaction. . . .

Pervading all nature we may see at work a stern discipline, which is a little cruel that it may be very kind. That state of universal warfare maintained throughout the lower creation, to the great perplexity of many worthy people, is at bottom the most merciful provision which the circumstances admit of. . . . The poverty of the incapable, the distresses that come upon the imprudent, the starvation of the idle, and those shoulderings aside of the weak by the strong, which leave so many "in shallows and in miseries," are the decrees of a large, farseeing benevolence. It seems hard that an unskillfulness which with all its efforts he cannot overcome, should entail hunger upon the artisan. It seems hard that a laborer incapacitated by sickness from competing with his stronger fellows, should have to bear the resulting privations. It seems hard that widows and orphans should be left to struggle for life or death. Nevertheless, when regarded not separately, but in connection with the interests of universal humanity, these harsh fatalities are seen to be full of the highest beneficence—the same beneficence which brings to early graves the children of diseased parents, and singles out the low-spirited, the intemperate, and the debilitated as the victims of an epidemic.

READING QUESTIONS

1. What, according to Spencer, is the "fundamental law"? Do you agree with it? Why or why not? Where else have you seen this "fundamental law"?

2. On what grounds could Spencer argue that the death of "the children of diseased parents" was in the "interests of universal humanity" and "full of the highest beneficence" for mankind?

3. What might explain the appeal of Spencer's ideas? In what ways did he provide "scientific" support for prevailing social, cultural, and racial assumptions?

■ COMPARATIVE AND DISCUSSION QUESTIONS ■

1. In what ways does Beeton's *Book of Household Management* reflect the new nineteenth-century awareness of sanitation's relationship to health, made explicit in Chadwick's report?

2. Contrast Beeton's depiction of a middle-class home with London's description of the housing of the working-class poor. What does this suggest about the distribution of wealth in industrial Britain?

3. How might Spencer respond to the condition of the British poor as described by Chadwick and London? What might Chadwick and London say to Spencer?

4. What would Robert Owen (Document 20-5) propose as a solution to the problems described by London and Chadwick?

5. How would Locke (Document 18-3) and Metternich (Document 21-2) respond to Darwin's contention that "the moral nature of man has reached its present standard, partly through the advancement of his reasoning powers and consequently of a just public opinion, but especially from his sympathies having been rendered more tender and widely diffused through the effects of habit, example, instruction, and reflection"?

6. Compare and contrast Darwin's and Spencer's views on civilization and human survival. How might Darwin have responded to the pseudo-Darwinian arguments put forward by late-nineteenth and early-twentieth-century proponents of white racial supremacy?

7. What do you think Darwin and Spencer would say in response to Zetkin's arguments about women and labor competition? Why?

23

The Age of Nationalism
1850–1914

Before 1848, nationalism was a revolutionary ideology, often concerned with rebelling against autocratic forms of government or against external rule. Romantics saw in the shared history and culture of particular peoples an argument for the overthrow of imperial domination. Liberals linked nationalism to economic progress and the protection of individual liberty, convinced that both could be achieved only if the will of the people was expressed through representative government. In the second half of the nineteenth century, however, conservative leaders such as Germany's Otto von Bismarck harnessed the power of nationalism to garner support for conservative, even reactionary, governments and policies. While nationalism served as a catalyst for political unification in Italy and Germany, just as often it led to division and conflict. The United States fought a bloody and bitter civil war between 1861 and 1865 over the power of the federal government to stop the expansion of slavery. France went from the Second Republic to the Second Empire, and then faced the secession of Paris from France in 1871. Conflicting nationalisms undermined the strength and stability of the Austro-Hungarian Empire. Toward the end of the century, the adoption of nationalism as the basis for personal identity led to horrifying violence against perceived outsiders, particularly Europe's Jewish population. The Dreyfus affair in France (1894–1906) spurred a Jewish nationalist movement—Zionism—as some members of Europe's Jewish community became convinced that lasting peace and security for Jews could be achieved only through the foundation of a Jewish nation-state.

23-1 | Romantic Nationalism in Italy

The First Meeting Between Mazzini and Garibaldi (1833)

The decades-long struggle for Italian unification brought together a number of different strands of nineteenth-century nationalism. While Cavour's vision of constitutional monarchy and economic liberalism would eventually win out, the radical republicanism of Giuseppe Mazzini and Giuseppe Garibaldi, steeped in romantic nationalism, played a crucial role in the process. Mazzini and Garibaldi fired the public imagination with the idea of Italian cultural unity, of the unique role the Italian people could play in world events if they put aside their differences and concentrated on their shared history, culture, and traditions. In this image, created after unification had been achieved, we see Mazzini (at right) and Garibaldi (at left) meeting for the very first time in Marseille, France, in 1833. As you examine the image, focus on the details. What is Mazzini pointing at? What should we make of the crumpled papers on the floor?

De Agostini Picture Library / G. Dagli Orti / The Bridgeman Art Library.

READING QUESTIONS

1. What does the image suggest about the relationship between Mazzini and Garibaldi?

2. What importance should we attach to the group of men clustered around a table in the background?

3. What symbolic importance should we attach to the papers on the floor and the bust on the wall? What do they suggest about Mazzini's role in the process of Italian unification?

Nationalism and the Conservative Order

In the early nineteenth century, nationalism was strongly associated with revolution, with a desire to overthrow the existing political order. Thus, in the decades following the defeat of Napoleon, conservatives were generally united in their hatred of nationalism. Over time, however, many conservatives came to see nationalism as a powerful weapon for defeating their ideological rivals and reinforcing the political and social status quo. By co-opting the nationalist program of their ideological rivals, conservatives could claim to represent the interests of "the people," even as they maintained the power of traditional elites. The documents included below represent two very different perspectives on this development.

23-2 | GIORGIO ASPRONI, *Reflections on the Death of Cavour* (1860)

Count Camillo Benso di Cavour (1810–1861), the architect of Italian unification, was no friend of revolution. While committed to liberal economic policies, secularization of public life, and civil liberties, Cavour was also determined that Italy should be a constitutional monarchy. For Cavour, monarchy was the "strength and glory" Italy, and his paramount goal as he pushed for Italian unification was that his king, Victor Emmanuel II of Piedmont, should lead the new nation. Given this, it is not surprising that more radical Italian nationalists tended to see Cavour as a traitor to their cause. In this diary entry, a Sardinian official, Giorgio Asproni, reacted to what would prove to be a false rumor that Cavour had died. As you read it, think about the sources of Asproni's antipathy to Cavour. How did Cavour's Italy differ from the one Asproni had hoped to see created?

From Martin Clark, ed., *The Italian Risorgimento*, 2d ed. (Harlow, U.K.: Pearson Education Limited, 2009), pp. 122–123.

It is cowardice to rejoice at the fate that awaits all mortals, and for my part I am indifferent to the loss of this statesman. His death, however, is providential for Italy. It will be extremely difficult, I should say impossible, for the moderate party to find anyone with the same combination of qualities to succeed him. He was from an aristocratic family, very rich, versatile, full of imagination, cunning and practised in the affairs of this world, quite unscrupulous, with no moral restraint, relaxed and courteous in his manner, but greedy and insatiable when it came to money or power. Wide-ranging in ideas, incomparable in intrigue, quick to grasp the point, blindly stubborn in his anger, he was determined to take any step, however dangerous, to defeat his opponents and maintain himself in office. He was lavish with banquets, jobs, decorations, handshakes, kind words, and secret service funds; he corrupted the electorate and the press, deceived public opinion and for ten years was complete master of the country. He has died now that his star looked like waning, and quite certainly he would have fallen in less than a year; but God knows what new evils he would have brought about in that period of omnipotence. He was small in stature, with a round face rather like Napoleon's, and reddish-white in complexion; fair hair, almost red, turning half-white in recent years; very large head, wide forehead, lively blue eyes, firm regular nose; his hair was becoming thinner and he was becoming half-bald. When he was still hoping to win me over politically, he was friendly and promised all kinds of good things for Sardinia. Once he found that I was firm in my principles, that I could neither be bought nor threatened and that my needs were few, he opposed me obstinately. He treated Sardinia as badly as he possibly could, and made a secret commitment to Louis Napoleon to cede it to France. Now he is no more; but the consequences of his stubborn war against revolution, which alone can bring independence, greatness and liberty to Italy, live on. The priests will say that he was struck down by the hand of God: perhaps they poisoned him. I say that he was a fortunate man both in life and in death, for a sudden end to life is a truly enviable stroke of good luck.

READING QUESTIONS

1. What crimes and abuses did Asproni claim Cavour committed?

2. How did he characterize his own relationship with Cavour? What does his characterization suggest about the nature of Italian government under Cavour?

3. In your opinion, is Asproni's description of Cavour fair? Why or why not?

23-3 | OTTO VON BISMARCK, *Speech Before the Reichstag: On the Law for Workers' Compensation* (1884)

Otto von Bismarck, the chancellor of Germany from 1871 to 1890, combined two ideas that were considered opposites in the first half of the century: nationalism and conservatism. The nineteenth-century liberal focus on individualism stripped the upper classes of their obligation to the lower, creating an opportunity for conservatives like Bismarck. By offering support to the working classes, Bismarck undermined the claim made by liberals that their policies expressed the will of the people. At the same time, he made the revolutionary platforms put forward by socialists and communists less appealing to working people. One of the places this struggle played out was in the protections afforded to workers, which liberals saw as interfering with the property rights of factory owners. Below, Bismarck lays out his vision of the proper relationship between the state and its citizens. As you read it, ask yourself what obligations Bismarck believed the state had to the people. What obligations did the people owe the state in return?

Deputy von Vollmar has expressed his astonishment that . . . we are making new and different proposals. Gentlemen, that is not our fault. Yesterday Deputy Bamberger[1] compared the business of government with that of a cobbler who measures shoes, which he thereupon examines as to whether they are suitable for him or not and accordingly accepts or rejects them. I am by no means dissatisfied with this humble comparison, by which you place the united governments in the perspective of a shoemaker taking measurements for Herr Bamberger. The profession of government in the sense of Frederick the Great is to serve the people, and may it be also as a cobbler; the opposite is to dominate the people. We want to serve the people. But I make the demand on Herr Bamberger that he act as my co-shoemaker in order to make sure that no member of the public goes barefoot, and to create a suitable shoe for the people in this crucial area.

Deputy von Vollmar[2] then proceeded to the connection that he imputes between our proposal and the Socialist Law.[3] It is not correct, as he conceives it, that we made the proposal in order to win more support for the Socialist Law. There is, indeed, a connection between the two, but it is quite different. At the time of the submission of the Socialist Law the government, and particularly His Majesty the Emperor and, if I am not in error, also the majority of the Reichstag,

From Jan Goldstein and John W. Boyer, eds., *University of Chicago, Readings in Western Civilization*, vol. 8, *Nineteenth-Century Europe: Liberalism and Its Critics*, trans. John W. Boyer (Chicago: University of Chicago Press, 1988), pp. 419–425.

[1]**Deputy Bamberger**: Ludwig Bamberger (1823–1899) was an economist and founder of the German Liberal Party, one of Bismarck's sometimes reluctant allies.

[2]**Deputy von Vollmar**: Georg Heinrich von Vollmar (1850–1922) was a Socialist politician and thus one of Bismarck's opponents in this debate.

[3]**the Socialist Law**: Passed in 1878, it made illegal the meetings and publications of the German Social Democratic Party, though members could (and did) still run for office.

underwrote certain promissory notes for the future and gave assurances that as a corollary to this Socialist Law a serious effort for the betterment of the fate of the workers should go hand in hand. In my opinion that is the complement to the Socialist Law; if you have persistently decided not to improve the situation of the workers, then I understand that you reject the Socialist Law. For it is an injustice on the one hand to hinder the self-defense of a large class of our fellow citizens and on the other hand not to offer them aid for the redress of that which causes the dissatisfaction. That the Social Democratic leaders wish no advantage for this law, that I understand; dissatisfied workers are just what they need. Their mission is to lead, to rule, and the necessary prerequisite for that is numerous dissatisfied classes. They must naturally oppose any attempt of the government, however well intentioned it may be, to remedy this situation, if they do not wish to lose control over the masses they mislead. Therefore, I place no value on the objections that come from the leaders of the Social Democrats; I would place a very high value on the objections that come from the workers in general. Our workers, thank God, are not all Social Democrats and are not to such a degree unresponsive to the efforts of the confederated governments to help them, perhaps also not to the difficulties that these efforts meet in the parliamentary arena. . . . I in no way support an absolutist government. . . .

[The real question] is whether the state—by state I always mean the empire—whether the state has the right to abandon to chance the performance of a responsibility of the state, namely, to protect the worker from accidents and need when he is injured or becomes old, so that private companies form that charge premiums from the workers and the employers at whatever rates the market will bear. . . . As soon as the state concerns itself with these matters at all, however—and I believe that it is the state's duty to concern itself—it must strive for the least expensive form and must take no advantage from it, and above all not lose sight of the benefit for the poor and the needy. Otherwise one could indeed relinquish the fulfillment of certain state duties, such as among other things the care of the poor, in the widest sense of the word, as well as schools and national defense to private stock companies. . . . In the same way one can continue to believe that the whole of the state's responsibility must in the end be left to the voluntary formation of private stock companies. The whole problem is rooted in the question: does the state have the responsibility to care for its helpless fellow citizens, or does it not? I maintain that it does have this duty, and to be sure, not simply the Christian state, as I once permitted myself to allude to with the words "practical Christianity," but rather every state by its very nature. It would be madness for a corporate body or a collectivity to take charge of those objectives that the individual can accomplish; those goals that the community can fulfill with justice and profit should be relinquished to the community. There are objectives that only the state in its totality can fulfill. . . . Among the last mentioned objectives [of the state] belong national defense [and] the general system of transportation. . . . To these belong also the help of persons in distress and the prevention of such justified complaints as in fact provide excellent material for exploitation by the Social Democrats. That is the responsibility of the state from which the state will not be able to withdraw in the long run.

If one argues against my position that this is socialism, then I do not fear that at all. The question is, where do the justifiable limits of state socialism lie? Without such a boundary we could not manage our affairs. Each law for poor relief is socialism. . . .

There scarcely exists nowadays a word with which more abuse is committed than the word *free*. . . . According to my experience, everyone understands by *freedom* only the freedom for oneself and not for others, as well as the responsibility of others to refrain absolutely from any limitation of one's own freedom. In short, by *freedom* they actually mean *domination*; by *freedom of speech* they understand the domination of the speaker; by *freedom of the press* the predominant and preponderant influence of editorial offices and of newspapers. Indeed gentlemen, and I am not speaking here in confessional terms, in all confessions, by *freedom of the church* the domination of the priests is very frequently understood. . . . I have no desire to speak of human weakness, but rather of the human custom which establishes the importance of the individual person, the dominance of individual persons and their influence over the general public, precisely on the pretext that freedom demands it. That is indeed more strikingly realized in our own history than in any other. In the centuries of the decay of the German Empire, German freedom was always sharply accentuated. What did this mean? The freedom of the princes from the emperor, and the power of the nobles over the serfs! They wanted for their part to be free; that means, *to be free* was for them and also for others identical with the concept *to dominate*. They did not feel themselves to be free unless they dominated. Therefore, whenever I read the word *free* before another adjective, I become very suspicious. . . . Deputy Bamberger expressed subsequently his regret concerning the "socialist fad." It is, however, a harsh expression when one characterizes as a "socialist fad" the careful decision of the allied governments in Germany, weighed for three years, which they again, for the third time, propose to you in the hope finally to obtain your approval. Perhaps the whole institution of the state is a socialist fad. If everyone could live on his own, perhaps everyone would be much more free, but also much less protected and guarded. If the Deputy calls the proposal a socialist whim, I reply simply that it is untrue, and my assertion is as justified as his. He uses further the expression that the old age and disability care "were chimerical plans." . . . There is nothing about our proposal that is chimerical. Our proposals are completely genuine; they are the result of an existing need. . . . The fulfillment of a state responsibility is never a chimera, and as such I recognize it as a legislative responsibility. It is in fact not a pleasant occupation to devote these public cobbler services to a customer like Deputy Bamberger, who treats us with scorn and ingratitude in the face of real exertions, and who characterizes as a "fad" and a "chimera" the proposal that was worked out in order to make it acceptable to you. I would like to suggest in general that we might be somewhat milder in the expressions with which we mutually characterize our efforts.

READING QUESTIONS

1. What is Bismarck's conception of "freedom," and what role does he see for it in the German Empire over which he presides?

2. What, according to Bismarck, makes his proposals different from those of the socialists he opposes?

3. What areas did Bismarck think fit for private for-profit activity? What areas did he reserve for the state? Why?

23-4 | A Revolution in Paris

JOHN LEIGHTON, *Paris Under the Commune* (1871)

The triumph of the centralized nation-state was not predestined, and there were periodic outbursts of resistance to the centralization of political power and identity it represented. One such uprising came in Paris in the spring of 1871, sparked by the defeat of France in the Franco-Prussian War and the election of a large majority of conservatives and monarchists to the National Assembly. Convinced that the forces of conservatism were responsible for France's military humiliation and that the incoming National Assembly would betray the principles of the French Revolution, the people of Paris rose in revolt and declared their independence from the national government. For a few months, the Paris Commune promoted a decentralized, bottom-up approach to government, before it was brutally suppressed by the armed forces of the newly formed Third Republic in attacks that left twenty thousand Parisians dead. Here an Englishman, John Leighton, gives his (often hostile) impressions of the Commune. In this excerpt from his description of life under the Commune, Leighton focused his attention on a decree that annulled the payment of rents for the last quarter of 1871.

"Citizens," says the *Official Journal* this morning, "your Commune is constituted." Then follows decree upon decree. White posters are being stuck up everywhere. Why are they at the Hôtel de Ville, if not to publish decrees? The conscription is abolished. We shall see no more poor young fellows marching through the town with their numbers in their caps, and fired with that noble patriotism which is imbibed in the cabarets at so much a glass. We shall have no more soldiers, but to make up for that we shall all be National Guards. As to the landlords, their vexation is extreme; even the tenants do not seem so satisfied as they ought to be. Not to have to pay any rent is very delightful, certainly, but they scarcely dare believe in such good fortune. Thus when Orpheus, trying to rescue Eurydice from "the infernal regions," interrupts with "his

From John Leighton, *Paris Under the Commune, or, The Seventy-three Days of the Second Siege* (London: Bradbury, Evans, and Co., 1871), pp. 79–82.

harmonious strains" the tortures of eternal punishment, Prometheus did not doubtless show as much delight as he ought to have done, on discovering that the beak of the vulture was no longer gnawing at his vitals, "scarcely daring to believe in such good fortune." Orpheus is the Commune; Eurydice, Liberty; "the infernal regions," the Government of the 4th September; "the harmonious strains," the decrees of the Commune; Prometheus, the tenant; and the vulture, the landlord![1]

In plain terms, however—forgive me for joking on such a subject—the decree which annuls the payment of the rents for the quarters ending October 1870, January 1871, and April 1871, does not appear to me at all extravagant, and really I do not see what there is to object to in the following lines which accompany it: —

> In consideration of the expenses of the war having been chiefly sustained by the industrial, commercial, and working portion of the population, it is but just that the proprietors of houses and land should also bear their part of the burthen. . . .

Let us talk it over together, Mr. Landlord. You have a house and I live in it. It is true that the chimneys smoke, and that you most energetically refuse to have them repaired. However, the house is yours, and you possess most decidedly the right of making a profit by it. Understand, once for all, that I never contest your right. As for me, I depend upon my wit, I do not possess much, but I have a tool—it may be either a pen, or a pencil, or a hammer—which enables me, in the ordinary course of things, to live and to pay with more or less regularity my quarter's rent. If I had not possessed this tool, you would have taken good care not to let me inhabit your house or any part or portion thereof, because you would have considered me in no position to pay you your rent. Now, during the war my tool has unquestionably rendered me but poor service. It has remained ignobly idle in the inkstand, in the folio, or on the bench. Not only have I been unable to use it, but I have also in some sort lost the knack of handling it; I must have some time to get myself into working order again. While I was working but little, and eating less, what were you doing? Oh! I do not mean to say that you were as flourishing as in the triumphant days of the Empire, but still I have not heard of any considerable number of landlords being found begging at the corners of the streets, and I do not fancy you made yourselves conspicuous by your assiduous attendance at the Municipal Cantines. I have even heard that you or many of your brother-landlords took pretty good care not to

---

[1]**Orpheus . . . the landlord**: In Greek mythology, Orpheus, who charmed the king and queen of the underworld with the music from his lyre, was allowed to bring his dead wife Eurydice back to earth as long as he did not look behind him. When he turned around too soon, Eurydice had to return to the underworld forever. Prometheus stole fire from the god Zeus and gave it to humans; as punishment, Zeus chained him to a rock, where every day a vulture came to eat his liver, and every day it grew back, so that he had to endure the torment over again.

be in Paris during the Prussian siege, and that you contented yourselves with forming the most ardent wishes, for the final triumph of French arms, from beneath the wide-spreading oaks of your châteaux in Touraine and Beauce, or from the safe haven of a Normandy fishing village; while we, accompanied it is true by your most fervent prayers, took our turn at mounting guard, on the fortifications during the bitter cold nights, or knee-deep in the mud of the trenches. However, I do not blame those who sought safety in flight; each person is free to do as he pleases; what I object to is your coming back and saying, "During seven or eight months you have done no work, you have been obliged to pawn your furniture to buy bread for your wife and children; I pity you from the bottom of my heart—be so kind as to hand me over my three quarters' rent." No, a thousand times no; such a demand is absurd, wicked, ridiculous; and I declare that if there is no possible compromise between the strict execution of the law and his decree of the Commune, I prefer, without the least hesitation, to abide by the latter; I prefer to see a little poverty replace for a time the long course of prosperity that has been enjoyed by this very small class of individuals, than to see the last articles of furniture of five hundred thousand suffering wretches, put up to auction and knocked down for one-twentieth part of their value. There must, however, be some way of conciliating the interests of both landlords and tenants. Would it be sufficient to accord delays to the latter, and force the former to wait a certain time for their money? I think not; if I were allowed three years to pay off my three quarters' rent, I should still be embarrassed. The tool of the artisan is not like the peasant's plot of ground, which is more productive after having lain fallow. During the last few sad months, when I had no work to do, I was obliged to draw upon the future, a future heavily mortgaged; when I shall perhaps scarcely be able to meet the expenses of each day, will there be any possibility of acquitting the debts of the past? You may sell my furniture if the law gives you the right to do so, but I shall not pay!

The only possible solution, believe me, is that in favor of the tenants, only it ought not to be applied in so wholesale a fashion. Inquiries should be instituted, and to those tenants from whom the war has taken away all possibility of payment an unconditional receipt should be delivered: to those who have suffered less, a proportionate reduction should be allowed; but those whom the invasion has not ruined or seriously impoverished—and the number is large, among provision merchants, café keepers, and private residents—let those pay directly. In this way the landlords will lose less than one may imagine, because it will be the lowest rents that will be forfeited. The decree of the Commune is based on a right principle, but too generally applied.

The new Government—for it is a Government—does not confine itself to decrees. It has to install itself in its new quarters and make arrangements.

In a few hours it has organized more than ten committees—the executive, the financial, the public-service, the educational, the military, the legal, and the committee of public safety. No end of committees and committeemen: it is to be hoped that the business will be promptly dispatched!

READING QUESTIONS

1. Who, based on Leighton's discussion, makes up the nation? How does it affect your reading of this passage to know that Leighton spent much of his book mocking and denouncing the Paris Commune?

2. What is Leighton's complaint with this specific decree of the commune? Does he seem reasonable? What groups in French society might have agreed with him? What groups might have disagreed with him?

23-5 | An Indictment of France's Military Elite
ÉMILE ZOLA, *"J'Accuse" the French Army* (1898)

In 1898 and 1899 the case of Alfred Dreyfus, a Jewish captain in the French army who was falsely accused and convicted of treason on the basis of falsified evidence, split France apart. On one side was the army, joined by anti-Semites and most of the Catholic establishment. On the other side stood civil libertarians and most of the more radical republicans. The support offered to Dreyfus by prominent republicans and intellectuals, including novelist Émile Zola, proved critical to securing the reopening of his case and his eventual exoneration. In this excerpt from Zola's famous letter entitled "J'Accuse," Zola accused the French military high command of conspiracy to subvert justice, an action that opened Zola up to a retaliatory prosecution for libel.

Dreyfus knows several languages: a crime. No compromising papers were found in his possession: a crime. He sometimes visited his native country:[1] a crime. He is industrious and likes to find out about everything: a crime. He is calm: a crime. He is worried: a crime. . . .

I accuse Lieutenant-Colonel du Paty de Clam[2] of having been the diabolical, but I would fain believe the unwitting, artisan of the miscarriage of justice, and thereafter of having defended his unhallowed work for three years by the most clumsy and culpable machinations.

I accuse General Mercier[3] of having become, at all events through weakness, an accomplice in one of the greatest iniquities of the age.

From Émile Zola, "J'Accuse" in Armand Charpentier, *The Dreyfus Case*, trans. Lewis May (London: Geoffrey Bles, 1935), pp. 142–144.

[1]**his native country**: Dreyfus was from Alsace (Alsatia in German), a French province at the time of his birth, but taken by Germany in 1871. For Dreyfus to visit his childhood home, he had to cross the new national border.

[2]**Lieutenant-Colonel du Paty de Clam**: Armand Mercier Paty de Clam was the French counterintelligence officer who conducted the first accusation against Dreyfus, and who remained convinced of Dreyfus's guilt long after the actual author of the document that began the case was revealed.

[3]**General Mercier**: Mercier was the war minister who originated the case against Dreyfus and continued it to avoid political embarrassment after making public pronouncements of his certainty of Dreyfus's guilt.

I accuse General Billot[4] of having had in his hands sure proofs of the innocence of Dreyfus and of having hushed them up, of having incurred the guilt of
crimes against humanity and justice, for political ends and to save the face of the
General Staff.

I accuse General de Boisdeffre and General Gonse[5] of having been participa-
tors in the same crime, actuated, the one no doubt by clerical partisanship, the
other, it may be, by that esprit de corps which would make the Army and the
War Office the sacred Ark of the Covenant.

I accuse General de Pellieux and Major Ravary[6] of conducting a disgraceful
inquiry, by which I mean an inquiry characterized by the most monstrous par-
tiality, of which we have, in the report of the latter of these two men, an imperish-
able monument of stupid audacity.

I accuse the three handwriting experts, MM. Belhomme, Varinard, and
Couard, of drawing up misleading and lying reports, unless, indeed, a medical
examination should reveal them to be suffering from some pathological abnor-
mality of sight and judgment.

I accuse the War Office of conducting an abominable campaign in the Press,
and particularly in the newspapers l'Eclair and l'Echo de Paris, in order to mislead
public opinion and to conceal their own misdeeds.

I accuse the first Court-Martial of acting contrary to law by condemning an
accused man on the strength of a secret document; and I accuse the second Court-
Martial of having, in obedience to orders, concealed that illegality, and of committing in its turn the crime of knowingly acquitting a guilty man.

In bringing these charges, I am not unaware that I render myself liable to
prosecution under Clauses 30 and 31 of the Act of the 29th of July, which deals
with defamation of character in the public Press. But I do so of my own free will
and with my eyes open.

As for those whom I accuse, I do not know them, I have never seen them. I
entertain for them neither hatred nor ill-will. They are so far as I am concerned
mere entities, spirits of social maleficence, and the action to which I have here
committed myself is but a revolutionary means of hastening the explosion of
Truth and Justice.

I have but one passion, and that is for light, and I plead in the name of that
humanity which has so greatly suffered and has a right to happiness. My fiery

---

[4]**General Billot**: Jean-Baptiste Billot was a French general and war minister during the later
stages of the Dreyfus affair, 1896–1898.

[5]**General de Boisdeffre and General Gonse**: Boisdeffre was the chief of staff of the French
Army—its highest-ranking soldier—at the time of the initial accusation, and according to Zola,
a strong supporter of the Catholic clergy in France. General Gonse was the general to whom the
counterintelligence division (called for secrecy purposes the Statistical Section) reported.

[6]**General de Pellieux and Major Ravary**: Pellieux was the general who investigated the
accusations against Esterhazy—the man later proved to have committed the crime of which
Dreyfus was accused—and found him innocent. Ravary oversaw the handwriting analysts, and
reported on their findings, which turned out to be inaccurate.

protest is but the outcry of my soul. Let them drag me, then, into a Court of Justice and let the matter be thrashed out in broad daylight. I am ready.

READING QUESTIONS

1. What risks did Zola take by publishing this letter? What might explain his willingness to take those risks?

2. Based on this document, what was the relationship between the needs of the accused and the needs of the state in nineteenth-century France? How did Zola oppose this conception of justice?

3. Although the actions of the court that convicted Dreyfus were popular, were they compatible with the idea of government by the consent of the governed, which the French Third Republic claimed to embody?

■ COMPARATIVE AND DISCUSSION QUESTIONS ■

1. How might Asproni interpret the image of Mazzini and Garibaldi's first meeting?

2. What connections can you make between nationalism and the resurgence of conservatism in the second half of the nineteenth century? What light do the documents by Asproni, Leighton, and Bismarck shed on this question?

3. What picture of French politics in the decades following the defeat of France in the Franco-Prussian War is painted in the documents by Leighton and Zola? What connections can you make between the suppression of the Paris Commune and the Dreyfus affair?

24

The West and the World
1815–1914

Industrialization played a central role in nineteenth-century European imperialism. At the same time that industrialization created skyrocketing demand in Europe for raw materials and new markets, it provided Europeans with the wealth and technology that made global domination possible. While Europeans often cast imperialism in economic terms, they also justified expansion and colonization in other ways. Some believed that Europeans had a responsibility to spread their "superior" Western culture and religion to less fortunate regions of the world. Others, drawing on distorted interpretations of Darwin's theory of evolution, claimed a biological right of conquest, arguing that human progress depended on the subjugation of the weak by the strong. The results of European imperialism were mixed. The fortunes made from the extraction of raw materials and the exploitation of colonial labor were offset by limited success in establishing new markets and the costs associated with conquest and colonial rule. Moreover, the penetration of European culture into colonized societies was often shallow, and European missionaries and educators were dismayed to discover that many non-Europeans were quite content with their own culture and religion. Finally, while industrial innovation catapulted Europe into a position of global dominance, native resistance never fully faded, and an undercurrent of fear persisted among the uninvited occupiers.

SOURCES IN CONVERSATION

Economic Imperialism and Military Expansion

While cultural and religious considerations played a prominent role in creating public support for imperialism, the decisions of policymakers were most often driven by economic and military concerns. From the point of view of governments and commercial interests, competition for overseas colonies was an extension of the internal competition between European nations for dominance. Economic and military considerations often went hand in hand, and, in the end, the control of colonial empires depended on military force. The effective deployment of such force required the acquisition of new naval ports and military outposts. Thus, the need to defend colonial possessions justified further imperial expansion, which, in turn, required ever larger, more advanced armies and navies.

24-1 | COMMISSIONER LIN ZEXU, *Letter to Queen Victoria* (1839)

China, the most populous country on earth in the nineteenth century, was an irresistible target for Europeans interested in finding new markets for their products. Unfortunately for such would-be traders, the Chinese showed little interest in aiding Western economic expansion. The Chinese imperial government's reluctance to allow Western access, combined with poverty and general disinterest in Western goods, restricted trade until the British discovered they had a product that would sell in China—opium. Lin Zexu, the imperial commissioner for the southern province of Guangdong, attempted to suppress the opium trade, and published this open letter to the British queen in 1839. The British were, evidently, unimpressed with Lin Zexu's appeal. That same year, the British started the First Opium War (1839–1842) to ensure their continued right to sell opium in China.

We have heard that in your own country opium is prohibited with the utmost strictness and severity: this is a strong proof that you know full well how hurtful it is to mankind. Since then you do not permit it to injure your own country, you ought not to have the injurious drug transferred to another country, and above all others, how much less to the Inner Land! Of the products which China exports to your foreign countries, there is not one which is not beneficial to mankind in some shape or other. There are those which serve for food, those which are

From William H. McNeil and Mitsuko Iriye, eds., *Readings in World History*, vol. 9, *Modern Asia and Africa* (New York: Oxford University Press, 1971), pp. 111–118.

useful, and those which are calculated for re-sale; but all are beneficial. Has China (we should like to ask) ever yet sent forth a noxious article from its soil? Not to speak of our tea and rhubarb, things which your foreign countries could not exist a single day without, if we of the Central Land were to grudge you what is beneficial, and not to compassionate your wants, then wherewithal could you foreigners manage to exist? And further, as regards your woolens, camlets [goat or camel hair cloth], and longells [cloth of a specific weave], were it not that you get supplied with our native raw silk, you could not get these manufactured! If China were to grudge you those things which yield a profit, how could you foreigners scheme after any profit at all? Our other articles of food, such as sugar, ginger, cinnamon, &c., and our other articles for use, such as silk piece-goods, chinaware, &c., are all so many necessaries of life to you; how can we reckon up their number! On the other hand, the things that come from your foreign countries are only calculated to make presents of, or serve for mere amusement. It is quite the same to us if we have them, or if we have them not. If then these are of no material consequence to us of the Inner Land, what difficulty would there be in prohibiting and shutting our market against them? It is only that our heavenly dynasty most freely permits you to take off her tea, silk, and other commodities, and convey them for consumption everywhere, without the slightest stint or grudge, for no other reason, but that where a profit exists, we wish that it be diffused abroad for the benefit of all the earth!

Your honorable nation takes away the products of our Central Land, and not only do you thereby obtain food and support for yourselves, but moreover, by re-selling these products to other countries you reap a threefold profit. Now if you would only not sell opium, this threefold profit would be secured to you: how can you possibly consent to forgo it for a drug that is hurtful to men, and an unbridled craving after gain that seems to know no bounds! Let us suppose that foreigners came from another country, and brought opium into England, and seduced the people of your country to smoke it, would not you, the sovereign of the said country, look upon such a procedure with anger, and in your just indignation endeavor to get rid of it? . . .

We have heard that in London the metropolis where you dwell, as also in Scotland, Ireland, and other such places, no opium whatever is produced. It is only in sundry parts of your colonial kingdom of Hindostan,[1] such as Bengal, Madras, Bombay, Patna, Malwa, Benares, Malacca, and other places where the very hills are covered with the opium plant, where tanks are made for the preparing of the drug; month by month, and year by year, the volume of the poison increases, its unclean stench ascends upwards, until heaven itself grows angry, and the very gods thereat get indignant! You, the queen of the said honorable nation, ought immediately to have the plant in those parts plucked up by the very root! Cause the land there to be hoed up afresh, sow in its stead the five

---

[1]**Hindostan**: British India, particularly the northwestern section, in today's India and Pakistan.

grains, and if any man dare again to plant in these grounds a single poppy, visit his crime with the most severe punishment. . . .

Suppose the subject of another country were to come to England to trade, he would certainly be required to comply with the laws of England, then how much more does this apply to us of the celestial empire! Now it is a fixed statute of this empire, that any native Chinese who sells opium is punishable with death, and even he who merely smokes it, must not less die.

READING QUESTIONS

1. What tone did Lin assume in his letter to the English queen? In what ways did he appeal to Victoria's sense of fairness and morality?

2. How did Lin characterize the commercial relationship between China and Britain? What light does this shed on Chinese resistance to British imports?

3. How might a British imperialist have justified the export of opium into China in defiance of the wishes of the Chinese government?

4. What does the fact that the British government was willing to go to war over opium exports tell you about the motives behind British imperialism?

24-2 | JULES FERRY, *Speech Before the French Chamber of Deputies* (1884)

Over the course of the nineteenth century, European imperialism gained momentum. As one region after another came under European control, many European leaders became convinced that they were engaged in a fight for national survival. If they failed to secure new colonies, and do so as quickly as possible, others would, and the inevitable result would be a decline in relative power and influence. In this 1884 speech before the Chamber of Deputies, French prime minister Jules Ferry exhorted his compatriots to commit themselves to conquest and colonization. As you read it, pay particular attention to the arguments Ferry advanced in support of his position. In Ferry's view, why was it vital for France to compete for overseas colonies?

The policy of colonial expansion is a political and economic system . . . that can be connected to three sets of ideas: economic ideas; the most far-reaching ideas of civilization; and ideas of a political and patriotic sort.

In the area of economics, I am placing before you, with the support of some statistics, the considerations that justify the policy of colonial expansion, as seen from the perspective of a need, felt more and more urgently by the industrialized

From Jules François Camille Ferry, "Speech Before the French Chamber of Deputies, March 28, 1884," *Discours et Opinions de Jules Ferry*, ed. Paul Robiquet (Paris: Armand Colin & Cie., 1897), 1. 5, pp. 199–201, 210–211, 215–218. Translated by Ruth Kleinman in *Brooklyn College Core Four Sourcebook*.

population of Europe and especially the people of our rich and hardworking country of France: the need for outlets [that is, for exports]. Is this a fantasy? Is this a concern [that can wait] for the future? Or is this not a pressing need, one may say a crying need, of our industrial population? I merely express in a general way what each one of you can see for himself in the various parts of France. Yes, what our major industries [textiles, etc.], irrevocably steered by the treaties of 1860–1861[1] into exports, lack more and more are outlets. Why? Because next door Germany is setting up trade barriers; because across the ocean the United States of America have become protectionists, and extreme protectionists at that; because not only are these great markets . . . shrinking, becoming more and more difficult of access, but these great states are beginning to pour into our own markets products not seen there before. This is true not only for our agriculture, which has been so sorely tried . . . and for which competition is no longer limited to the circle of large European states. . . . Today, as you know, competition, the law of supply and demand, freedom of trade, the effects of speculation, all radiate in a circle that reaches to the ends of the earth. . . . That is a great complication, a great economic difficulty; . . . an extremely serious problem. It is so serious, gentlemen, so acute, that the least informed persons must already glimpse, foresee, and take precautions against the time when the great South American market that has, in a manner of speaking, belonged to us forever will be disputed and perhaps taken away from us by North American products. Nothing is more serious; there can be no graver social problem; and these matters are linked intimately to colonial policy.

Gentlemen, we must speak more loudly and more honestly! We must say openly that indeed the higher races have a right over the lower races. . . .

I repeat, that the superior races have a right because they have a duty. They have the duty to civilize the inferior races. . . . In the history of earlier centuries these duties, gentlemen, have often been misunderstood; and certainly when the Spanish soldiers and explorers introduced slavery into Central America, they did not fulfill their duty as men of a higher race. . . . But, in our time, I maintain that European nations acquit themselves with generosity, with grandeur, and with sincerity of this superior civilizing duty.

I say that French colonial policy, the policy of colonial expansion, the policy that has taken us under the Empire [the Second Empire, of Napoleon III, 1852–1871], to Saigon, to Indochina [Vietnam], that has led us to Tunisia, to Madagascar—I say that this policy of colonial expansion was inspired by . . . the fact that a navy such as ours cannot do without safe harbors, defenses, supply centers on the high seas. . . . Are you unaware of this? Look at a map of the world.

Gentlemen, these are considerations that merit the full attention of patriots. The conditions of naval warfare have greatly changed. . . . At present, as you know, a warship, however perfect its design, cannot carry more than two weeks' supply of coal; and a vessel without coal is a wreck on the high seas, abandoned

---

[1] **the treaties of 1860–1861**: Negotiations between the British and French governments that resulted in lower trade barriers, particularly in lower tariffs on French wines.

to the first occupier. Hence the need to have places of supply, shelters, ports for defense and provisioning. . . . And that is why we needed Tunisia; that is why we needed Saigon and Indochina; that is why we need Madagascar . . . and why we shall never leave them! . . . Gentlemen, in Europe such as it is today, in this competition of the many rivals we see rising up around us, some by military or naval improvements, others by the prodigious development of a constantly growing population; in a Europe, or rather in a universe thus constituted, a policy of withdrawal or abstention is simply the high road to decadence! In our time nations are great only through the activity they deploy; it is not by spreading the peaceable light of their institutions . . . that they are great, in the present day.

Spreading light without acting, without taking part in the affairs of the world, keeping out of all European alliances and seeing as a trap, an adventure, all expansion into Africa or the Orient—for a great nation to live this way, believe me, is to abdicate and, in less time than you may think, to sink from the first rank to the third and fourth.

READING QUESTIONS

1. Why did Ferry argue that French survival depended on the acquisition of an empire?

2. What might Ferry have meant when he said that there was no more urgent social question than imperialism?

3. What moral arguments did Ferry put forward in favor of imperialism? Given the emphasis in his speech on economic and military issues, why do you think Ferry felt compelled to include such arguments?

24-3 | British Conquests in Africa
The Rhodes Colossus (1892)

There were no limits to the British fortune hunter Cecil Rhodes's (1853–1902) ambitions or to the steps he was willing to take to achieve his ends. Rhodes saw in the British imperialist expansion in Africa an opportunity both to amass a fabulous personal fortune and to add to Britain's global power and prestige. A committed Social Darwinist, Rhodes had no moral qualms about the conquest and economic exploitation of native peoples. In his view, human progress was achieved through racial competition, a competition Rhodes was certain would end in British domination of the globe. In this 1892 cartoon first published in the British magazine *Punch*, Rhodes is depicted as the embodiment of Britain's African empire.

From *Punch*, 10 December 1892, English School (19th century) / Private Collection / The Bridgeman Art Library.

PUNCH, OR THE LONDON CHARIVARI. [DECEMBER 10, 1892.

THE RHODES COLOSSUS
STRIDING FROM CAPE TOWN TO CAIRO.

READING QUESTIONS

1. How might the majority of British readers have responded to this cartoon? What is your personal reaction to the cartoon?

2. What does the cartoon suggest about British ambitions in Africa? What obstacles stood in the way of the achievement of those ambitions?

24-4 | A White Explorer in Black Africa

HENRY MORTON STANLEY, *Autobiography* (1909)

In 1871, while working as a journalist for the *New York Herald*, Sir Henry Morton Stanley (1841–1904) led an expedition to locate Dr. David Livingstone, a popular explorer and missionary who had gone missing in central Africa. Upon reading about Stanley's exploration of the Congo basin, Leopold II, king of the Belgians, became interested in acquiring an empire in Africa and hired Stanley to carry out a series of expeditions on his behalf. In time, Leopold would establish a personal empire in the Congo that was notorious, even among Europeans, for the unspeakably brutal exploitation of the native population. Stanley's autobiography, however, paints a very different picture of the interactions between whites and blacks in central Africa. As you read this excerpt, pay particular attention to Stanley's assumptions about white racial superiority. How did racial thinking shape his understanding of his experiences in the Congo?

Ngalyema, chief of Stanley Pool district, had demanded and received four thousand five hundred dollars' worth of cotton, silk, and velvet goods for granting me the privilege of establishing a station in a wilderness of a place at the commencement of up-river navigation. Owing to this, I had advanced with my wagons to within ten miles of the Pool. I had toiled at this work the best part of two years, and whenever I cast a retrospective glance at what the task had cost me, I felt that it was no joke, and such that no money would bribe me to do over again. Such a long time had elapsed since Ngalyema had received his supplies, that he affected to forget that he had received any; and, as I still continued to advance towards him after the warnings of his messengers, he collected a band of doughty warriors, painted their bodies with diagonal stripes of ochre, soot, chalk, and yellow, and issued fiercely to meet me.

Meantime, the true owners of the soil had enlightened me respecting Ngalyema's antecedents. He was only an enterprising native trader in ivory and slaves, who had fled from the north bank; but, though he had obtained so much money from me by pretences, I was not so indignant at this as at the audacity with which he chose to forget the transaction, and the impudent demand for another supply which underlay this. Ngalyema, having failed to draw any

From Henry Morton Stanley, *Autobiography*, ed. Dorothy Stanley (New York: Houghton Mifflin, 1909), pp. 339–344, 384–385.

promise by sending messengers, thought he could extort it by appearing with a warlike company. Meantime, duly warned, I had prepared a surprise for him.

I had hung a great Chinese Gong conspicuously near the principal tent. Ngalyema's curiosity would be roused. All my men were hidden, some in the steamboat on top of the wagon, and in its shadow was a cool place where the warriors would gladly rest after a ten-mile march; other of my men lay still as death under tarpaulins, under bundles of grass, and in the bush round about the camp. By the time the drum-taps and horns announced Ngalyema's arrival, the camp seemed abandoned except by myself and a few small boys. I was indolently seated in a chair, reading a book, and appeared too lazy to notice anyone; but suddenly looking up and seeing my 'brother Ngalyema' and his warriors scowlingly regarding me, I sprang up, and seized his hands, and affectionately bade him welcome, in the name of sacred fraternity, and offered him my own chair.

He was strangely cold, and apparently disgruntled, and said: —

"Has not my brother forgotten his road? What does he mean by coming to this country?"

"Nay, it is Ngalyema who has forgotten the blood-bond which exists between us. It is Ngalyema who has forgotten the mountains of goods which I paid him. What words are these of my brother?"

"Be warned, Rock-Breaker. Go back before it is too late. My elders and people all cry out against allowing the white man to come into our country. Therefore, go back before it be too late. Go back, I say, the way you came."

Speech and counter-speech followed. Ngalyema had exhausted his arguments; but it was not easy to break faith and be uncivil, without plausible excuse. His eyes were reaching round seeking to discover an excuse to fight, when they rested on the round, burnished face of the Chinese gong.

"What is that?" he said.

"Ah, that—that is a fetish."

"A fetish! A fetish for what?"

"It is a war-fetish, Ngalyema. The slightest sound of that would fill this empty camp with hundreds of angry warriors; they would drop from above, they would spring up from the ground, from the forest about, from everywhere."

"Sho! Tell that story to the old women, and not to a chief like Ngalyema. My boy tells me it is a kind of a bell. Strike it and let me hear it."

"Oh, Ngalyema, my brother, the consequences would be too dreadful! Do not think of such a thing!"

"Strike it, I say."

"Well, to oblige my dear brother Ngalyema, I will."

And I struck hard and fast, and the clangorous roll rang out like thunder in the stillness. Only for a few seconds, however, for a tempest of human voices was heard bursting into frightful discords, and from above, right upon the heads of the astonished warriors, leaped yelling men; and from the tents, the huts, the forest round about, they came by sixes, dozens, and scores, yelling like madmen, and seemingly animated with uncontrollable rage. The painted warriors became panic-stricken; they flung their guns and powder-kegs away, forgot their chief, and all thoughts of loyalty, and fled on the instant, fear lifting their heels high in the air; or, tugging at their eyeballs and kneading the senses confusedly, they saw, heard, and suspected nothing, save that the limbo of fetishes had broken loose!

But Ngalyema and his son did not fly. They caught the tails of my coat, and we began to dance from side to side, a loving triplet, myself being the foremost, to ward off the blow savagely aimed at my "brothers," and cheerfully crying out, "Hold fast to me, my brothers. I will defend you to the last drop of my blood. Come one, come all," etc.

Presently the order was given, "Fall in!" and quickly the leaping forms became rigid, and the men stood in two long lines in beautiful order, with eyes front, as though "at attention." Then Ngalyema relaxed his hold of my coat-tails, and crept from behind, breathing more freely; and, lifting his hand to his mouth, exclaimed, in genuine surprise "Eh, Mamma! Where did all these people come from?"

"Ah, Ngalyema, did I not tell you that thing was a powerful fetish? Let me strike it again, and show you what else it can do."

"No! No! No!" he shrieked. "I have seen enough!"

The day ended peacefully. I was invited to hasten on to Stanley Pool. The natives engaged themselves by the score to assist me in hauling the wagons. My progress was thenceforward steady and uninterrupted, and in due time the wagons and goods-columns arrived at their destination. . . .

Some of you may, perhaps, wonder at the quiet inoffensiveness of the natives, who, on a former expedition, had worried my soul by their ferocity and wanton attacks, night and day; but a very simple explanation of it may be found in Livingstone's Last Journals, dated 28th October, 1870. He says: "Muini Mukata, who has travelled further than most Arabs, said to me, 'If a man goes with a good-natured, civil tongue, he may pass through the worst people in Africa unharmed.' This is true, but time also is required; one must not run through a country, but give the people time to become acquainted with you, and let their worst fears subside."

Now on the expedition across Africa I had no time to give, either to myself or to them. The river bore my heavy canoes downward; my goods would never have endured the dawdling requirement by the system of teaching every tribe I met who I was. To save myself and my men from certain starvation, I had to rush on and on, right through. But on this expedition, the very necessity of making roads to haul my enormous six-ton wagons gave time for my reputation to travel ahead of me. My name, purpose, and liberal rewards for native help, naturally exaggerated, prepared a welcome for me, and transformed my enemies of the old time into workmen, friendly allies, strong porters, and firm friends. I was greatly forbearing also; but, when a fight was inevitable, through open violence, it was sharp and decisive. Consequently, the natives rapidly learned that though everything was to be gained by friendship with me, wars brought nothing but ruin. . . .

The dark faces light up with friendly gleams, and a budding of good will may perhaps date from this trivial scene. To such an impressionable being as an African native, the self-involved European, with his frigid, imperious manner, pallid white face, and dead, lustreless eyes, is a sealed book.

We had sown seeds of good-will at every place we had touched, and each tribe would spread diffusively the report of the value and beauty of our labors. Pure benevolence contains within itself grateful virtues. Over natural people nothing has greater charm or such expansible power; its influence grows without effort; its subtlety exercises itself on all who come within hearing of it. Coming in such innocent guise, it offends not; there is naught in it to provoke resentment. Provided patience and good temper guides the chief of Stanley Falls station, by the period of the return of the steamers, the influence of the seedling just planted there will have been extended from tribe to tribe far inland, and amid the persecuted fugitives from the slave-traders. . . .

When a young white officer quits England for the first time, to lead blacks, he has got to learn to unlearn a great deal. . . . We must have white men in Africa; but the raw white is a great nuisance there during the first year. In the second year, he begins to mend; during the third year, if his nature permits it, he has developed into a superior man, whose intelligence may be of transcendent utility for directing masses of inferior men.

My officers were possessed with the notion that my manner was "hard," because I had not many compliments for them. That is the kind of pap which we may offer women and boys. Besides, I thought they were superior natures, and required none of that encouragement, which the more childish blacks almost daily received.

READING QUESTIONS

1. In what ways did Stanley seek to present himself as a "great" explorer? What factors did he see as decisive in his success?

2. What attitudes did Stanley display toward the natives he encountered? In his view, how did the blacks benefit from his "friendship"?

3. How did Stanley seem to view the Europeans with whom he works? What does the final paragraph reveal about nineteenth-century attitudes toward masculinity?

4. In what ways does the excerpt hint at the violence that would characterize Belgian rule in the years to come?

24-5 | An Anti-Imperialist Pamphlet

MARK TWAIN, *King Leopold's Soliloquy* (1905)

Belgium led the way in colonizing sub-Saharan Africa, under the flag of the Congo Free State, a benevolent organization that claimed to bring the benefits of European civilization to Africa. In fact, it produced massive profits for Leopold II, at tremendous human cost to the Congo natives. Despite tight Belgian control over travel to the Congo, reports filtered out of forced labor and horrific punishments for workers who failed to meet rubber production quotas. In 1905 Mark Twain published an anti-imperialist pamphlet written from Leopold's perspective, interspersed with images like the ones included here.

It is all the same old thing—tedious repetitions and duplications of shop-worn episodes; mutilations, murders, massacres, and so on, and so on, till one gets drowsy over it. Mr. Morel[1] intrudes at this point, and contributes a comment which he could just as well have kept to himself—and throws in some italics, of course; these people can never get along without italics:

"It is one heartrending story of human misery from beginning to end, and *it is all recent.*"

Meaning 1904 and 1905. I do not see how a person can act so. This Morel is a king's subject, and reverence for monarchy should have restrained him from reflecting upon me with that exposure. This Morel is a reformer; a Congo reformer. That sizes *him* up. He publishes a sheet in Liverpool called *The West African Mail*, which is supported by the voluntary contributions of the sap-headed and the soft-hearted; and every week it steams and reeks and festers with up-to-date "Congo atrocities" of the sort detailed in this pile of pamphlets here. I will suppress it. I suppressed a Congo atrocity book there, after it was actually in print; it should not be difficult for me to suppress a newspaper.

[Studies some photographs of mutilated negroes—throws them down. Sighs.]

The kodak has been a sore calamity to us. The most powerful enemy that has confronted us, indeed. In the early years we had no trouble in getting the press to "expose" the tales of the mutilations as slanders, lies, inventions of busy-body American missionaries and exasperated foreigners who found the "open door" of the Berlin-Congo charter closed against them when they innocently went out there to trade; and by the press's help we got the Christian nations everywhere to turn an irritated and unbelieving ear to those tales and say hard things about the

---

From Mark Twain, *King Leopold's Soliloquy: A Defense of His Congo Rule* (Boston: The P. R. Warren Co., 1905), pp. 38–40.

[1]**Mr. Morel**: E. D. Morel (1873–1924); British author and socialist politician who wrote important exposés of Leopold's brutality in the Congo.

tellers of them. Yes, all things went harmoniously and pleasantly in those good days, and I was looked up to as the benefactor of a down-trodden and friendless people. Then all of a sudden came the crash! That is to say, the incorruptible *kodak*—and all the harmony went to hell! The only witness I have encountered in my long experience that I couldn't bribe. Every Yankee missionary and every interrupted trader sent home and got one; and now—oh, well, the pictures get sneaked around everywhere, in spite of all we can do to ferret them out and suppress them. Ten thousand pulpits and ten thousand presses are saying the good word for me all the time and placidly and convincingly denying the mutilations. Then that trivial little kodak, that a child can carry in its pocket, gets up, uttering never a word, and knocks them dumb!

READING QUESTIONS

1. What does this pamphlet suggest about the role of public opinion in nineteenth- and early-twentieth-century imperialism?

2. In Twain's opinion, how did the invention of the handheld camera change the debate over imperialism? What similarities do you see between the dynamic Twain described and the role of new information technology in shaping current global political debates?

24-6 | Questioning the Economics of Imperialism

J. A. HOBSON, *Imperialism* (1902)

Not all Europeans were imperialists, although anti-imperialists were typically in the minority. One of the underlying assumptions of empire was that colonies would trade exclusively with their mother countries, a theory at odds with Adam Smith's eighteenth-century vision of free trade. In 1902, John Atkinson Hobson, an English economist, published a critique of the prevailing link between colonies, economies, and national security, questioning the benefits of imperialism for the colonizing countries. His work influenced the communist leader Lenin's later critique of imperialism.

Although the new Imperialism has been bad business for the nation, it has been good business for certain classes and certain trades within the nation. The vast expenditure on armaments, the costly wars, the grave risks and embarrassments of foreign policy, the stoppage of political and social reforms within Great Britain, though fraught with great injury to the nation, have served well the present business interests of certain industries and professions.

It is idle to meddle with politics unless we clearly recognize this central fact and understand what these sectional interests are which are the enemies of national safety and the commonwealth. We must put aside the merely sentimental diagnosis which explains wars or other national blunders by outbursts of patriotic animosity or errors of statecraft. Doubtless at every outbreak of war not only the man in the street but the man at the helm is often duped by the cunning with which aggressive motives and greedy purposes dress themselves in defensive clothing. There is, it may be safely asserted, no war within memory, however nakedly aggressive it may seem to the dispassionate historian, which has not been presented to the people who were called upon to fight as a necessary defensive policy, in which the honor, perhaps the very existence, of the State was involved. . . .

What is the direct economic outcome of Imperialism? A great expenditure of public money upon ships, guns, military and naval equipment and stores, growing and productive of enormous profits when a war, or an alarm of war, occurs; new public loans and important fluctuations in the home and foreign Bourses

From Louis L. Snyder, ed., *The Imperialism Reader: Documents and Readings on Modern Expansionism* (Princeton, N.J.: Van Nostrand, 1962), pp. 322–323.

[essentially a stock market]; more posts for soldiers and sailors and in the diplomatic and consular services; improvement of foreign investments by the substitution of the British flag for a foreign flag; acquisition of markets for certain classes of exports, and some protection and assistance for trades representing British houses in these manufactures; employment for engineers, missionaries, speculative miners, ranchers, and other emigrants.

Certain definite business and professional interests feeding upon imperialistic expenditure, or upon the results of that expenditure, are thus set up in opposition to the common good, and, instinctively feeling their way to one another, are found united in strong sympathy to support every new imperialist exploit. . . .

With them stand the great manufacturers for export trade, who gain a living by supplying the real or artificial wants of the new countries we annex or open up. . . . The proportion which such trade bears to the total industry of Great Britain is very small, but some of it is extremely influential and able to make a definite impression upon politics, through chambers of commerce, Parliamentary representatives, and semi-political, semi-commercial bodies like the Imperial South African Association or the China League.

The shipping trade has a very definite interest which makes for Imperialism. This is well illustrated by the policy of State subsidies now claimed by shipping firms as a retainer, and in order to encourage British shipping for purposes of imperial safety and defense.

The services are, of course, imperialist by conviction and by professional interest, and every increase of the army and navy enhances their numerical strength and the political power they exert. . . .

What is true of Great Britain is true likewise of France, Germany, the United States, and of all countries in which modern capitalism has placed large surplus savings in the hands of a plutocracy or of a thrifty middle class. A well-recognized distinction is drawn between creditor and debtor countries. Great Britain has been for some time by far the largest creditor country, and the policy by which the investing classes use the instrument of the State for private business purposes is most richly illustrated in the recent history of her wars and annexations.[1] But France, Germany, and the United States are advancing fast along the same path. . . .

Investors who have put their money in foreign lands, upon terms which take full account of risks connected with the political conditions of the country, desire to use the resources of their Government to minimize these risks, and so to enhance the capital value and the interest of their private investments. The

---

[1]**recent history of . . . wars and annexations**: One such example was the British government's decision to buy the khedive of Egypt's stock shares in the Suez Canal Company in 1875, about 40 percent of the company. This led to British control of the canal, and of Egypt when the khedive was unable to pay his debts. The most recent example would have been the expansion of the British Cape colony into the Boers' (European farmers of Dutch descent) Transvaal territories, resulting in the 1899–1902 Boer War. British companies gained access to gold and diamond mining as a result of the war.

investing and speculative classes in general also desire that Great Britain should take other foreign areas under her flag in order to secure new areas for profitable investment and speculation.

READING QUESTIONS

1. Based on this selection, what groups does Hobson see benefiting from imperialism? In what ways are the interests of these groups the same as or different from the interests of the nation as a whole?

2. What negative outcomes does Hobson believe result from imperial competition?

3. What is Hobson's attitude toward war, particularly regarding the relationship between the government and the citizens of the nation in wartime?

▪ COMPARATIVE AND DISCUSSION QUESTIONS ▪

1. Based on the documents included in this chapter, how would you characterize the motives behind the new imperialism?

2. Compare the documents produced by the Westerners, Stanley, Twain, and Hobson. Where do they seem to differ, and what similarities can you see? What differences in perspective might account for their different ideas on colonization?

3. Based on their documents, would Commissioner Lin agree with Hobson's views on the dangers of imperial trade?

4. Compare and contrast the Twain pamphlet and the Cecil Rhodes cartoon. How did each try to shape public opinion about imperialism? How might Rhodes have responded to accusations similar to those leveled by Twain against Leopold II?

5. How might Ferry respond to Hobson's argument? What critique would Hobson offer of Ferry's position?

25

War and Revolution
1914–1919

The outbreak of World War I was greeted with widespread European enthusiasm. For decades, Europe's Great Powers had been divided into alliance blocs in anticipation of a conflict. The currents of extreme nationalism, competition for overseas colonies, and Social Darwinism that characterized the prewar era convinced many that war was not only inevitable, but desirable—a brief, decisive test of "survival of the fittest." In reality, the conflict was a long, brutal contest in which the combatants had to mobilize all of their resources—people, raw materials, transportation infrastructure, and factories—in a "total war" that made little distinction between soldiers and civilians. In the trenches on the western front, the war stagnated into a contest of attrition. In the east, the collapse of the Russian Empire paved the way for the eventual Soviet state, but did not lead to a German victory. In the end, the human and economic costs of the war dwarfed all previous conflicts. Despite this, and despite the efforts of U.S. President Woodrow Wilson to use the subsequent peace negotiations to forge a new, more peaceful international order, the world emerged from global war in 1919 as divided and unstable as ever. Within two decades, a new round of conflict in Europe would spark a second world war, this one even more destructive than the first.

25-1 | Germany Gives Austria a Blank Check

CHANCELLOR THEOBALD VON BETHMANN-HOLLWEG, *Telegram to the German Ambassador at Vienna* (July 6, 1914)

The assassination of Archduke Franz Ferdinand, heir to the Austro-Hungarian throne, in June 1914 provided the Austrian government with an excuse to launch a punitive war against Serbia. Tensions between Austria and Serbia had already resulted in the one war, and the assassination seemed to many in Austria to present a perfect start to a second. There was, however, a problem. An Austrian attack on Serbia would almost certainly result in an attack on Austria by Serbia's ally Russia. This was a risk the Austrians were willing to take, but only if they could count on the assistance of Germany, with which Austria had a defensive alliance. With this in mind, Austrian diplomats looked to Berlin for guidance before they took any irreversible steps. This telegram, the famous "blank check," was Germany's response to those inquiries. Heartened by the support it offered, Austria went to war against Serbia, setting off a chain reaction that would quickly engulf all of Europe.

Confidential. For Your Excellency's personal information and guidance
The Austro-Hungarian Ambassador yesterday delivered to the Emperor[1] a confidential personal letter from the Emperor Francis Joseph,[2] which depicts the present situation from the Austro-Hungarian point of view, and describes the measures which Vienna has in view.[3] A copy is now being forwarded to Your Excellency.

I replied to Count Szagyeny[4] today on behalf of His Majesty that His Majesty sends his thanks to the Emperor Francis Joseph for his letter and would soon answer it personally. In the meantime His Majesty desires to say that he is not blind to the danger which threatens Austria-Hungary and thus the Triple Alliance[5] as a result of the Russian and Serbian Pan-Slavic[6] agitation. Even though His Majesty is known to feel no unqualified confidence in Bulgaria and her ruler, and naturally inclines more toward our old ally Rumania and her

---

From Louis L. Snyder ed., *Documents of German History* (New Brunswick, N.J.: Rutgers University Press, 1958), pp. 310–311.

[1]**Emperor**: German Emperor Wilhelm II (r. 1888–1918).
[2]**Emperor Francis Joseph**: Emperor of Austria-Hungary (r. 1848–1916).
[3]**the measures which Vienna has in view**: That is, a war against Serbia.
[4]**Count Szagyeny**: László Szőgyény-Marich (1841–1916), Austro-Hungarian ambassador to Berlin.
[5]**Triple Alliance**: Germany and Austria-Hungary signed what was known as the Dual Alliance in 1879; three years later Italy joined the pact, and it was thenceforth called the Triple Alliance.
[6]**Pan-Slavic agitation**: Russians and Serbs both spoke Slavic languages; Bethmann-Hollweg was alleging that Serbia, egged on by Russia, was trying to provoke a confrontation with Austria-Hungary.

Hohenzollern prince,[7] yet he quite understands that the Emperor Francis Joseph, in view of the attitude of Rumania and of the danger of a new Balkan alliance aimed directly at the Danube Monarchy,[8] is anxious to bring about an understanding between Bulgaria and the Triple alliance. . . . His Majesty will, further more, make an effort at Bucharest, according to the wishes of the Emperor Francis Joseph, to influence King Carol[9] to the fulfillment of the duties of his alliance, to the renunciation of Serbia, and to the suppression of the Rumanian agitations directed against Austria-Hungary.

Finally, as far as concerns Serbia, His Majesty, of course, cannot interfere in the dispute now going on between Austria-Hungary and that country, as it is a matter not within his competence. The Emperor Francis Joseph may, however, rest assured that His Majesty will faithfully stand by Austria-Hungary, as is required by the obligations of his alliance and of his ancient friendship.

READING QUESTIONS

1. What circumstances might have induced the German emperor to pledge to "faithfully stand by" Austria-Hungary and its emperor?

2. What about this message might have earned it the description "blank check," and why?

3. In what ways did both the German and Austrian governments misjudge the situation? What did they expect to happen as a result of their actions?

---

[7]**no unqualified confidence in Bulgaria . . . Rumania and her Hohenzollern prince**: Austria-Hungary was seeking Bulgarian support for its planned war against Serbia; Wilhelm II preferred an alliance with Romania, which was ruled by a member of the German royal family, the Hohenzollerns.

[8]**the attitude of Rumania and . . . a new Balkan alliance aimed . . . at the Danube Monarchy**: Wilhelm II appreciated Austria-Hungary's mistrust of Romania, and its fear of an alliance of Balkan states directed against the Dual Monarchy.

[9]**Bucharest . . . to influence King Carol**: Bucharest was Romania's capital and Carol its king.

World War I in the Trenches and in the Air

Trench warfare epitomized the anonymity of warfare in the industrial era. Each side rained down countless artillery shells on the enemy lines, bringing death to men the gunners would never see. Machine guns were not aimed at individuals, but at crowds of men. The victims of poison gas were selected by chance, as shifting winds pushed gas clouds in one direction or another. The exceptions, at least in the public imagination, to this faceless war were found in the air. Each side lionized its "aces," presenting them as knights from a bygone era who still lived by the code of chivalry. Their war was depicted as one made up of a series of aerial jousts, of single combat between two honorable individuals. As you examine the photographs included below, think about the contrasts they imply. How did Europeans respond to the anonymity of industrial warfare? Why was it important to celebrate the feats of men like Manfred von Richthofen, the "Red Baron"?

25-2 | *Klaxon Horn Used to Warn of Gas Attacks* (1917)

In this 1917 photograph, a French soldier wearing a gas mask mans a Klaxon horn used to warn his fellow soldiers of an impending gas attack. As you examine the photograph, focus on the details that reveal aspects of industrial warfare. What does this photograph tell you about the differences between World War I and earlier conflicts?

Illustration from *The Illustrated War News*, 24 January 1917, French photographer (20th century) / Private Collection / The Stapleton Collection / The Bridgeman Art Library.

READING QUESTIONS

1. What light does the photograph shed on the role of new military technology in World War I?

2. How does the photograph reflect the anonymity of modern warfare?

3. What does the photograph suggest to you about the experience of ordinary soldiers in World War I?

25-3 | *Baron Manfred von Richthofen* (1917)

Baron Manfred von Richthofen (1892–1918) was the most famous flying ace of World War I. Nicknamed the "Red Baron," he was credited with shooting down eighty enemy aircraft. In this official portrait, he wears the "Blue Max," Prussia's highest military award. By the time of his death in April 1918, Richthofen was a national hero in Germany. This was no accident. His accomplishments were heavily publicized by the German government, and photographs such as this one were widely published in German magazines and newspapers. Richthofen himself played a part in creating his public legend. In 1917, at the request and direction of military officials, Richthofen wrote a brief autobiography titled "The Red Battle Flyer." As you examine the photograph, think about the contrast it presents to the photograph of the French soldier (see Document 25-2). Why did both the German government and the German people find heroes like Richthofen necessary?

German photographer (20th century) / Private Collection / Peter Newark Military Pictures / The Bridgeman Art Library.

READING QUESTIONS

1. What made Richthofen such a good subject for government propaganda? What role might the fact that he was an aristocrat have played in this context?

2. What military values were associated with Richthofen and other flying aces? Why might governments on both sides have considered it important to find ways to link the fighting in World War I to those values?

25-4 | Women and the War

HELENA SWANWICK, *The War in Its Effect Upon Women* (1916)

The years immediately preceding World War I had witnessed a massive and sometimes violent campaign for women's suffrage in Britain. Helena Swanwick, a German-born academic and journalist, was one of the prominent participants in that campaign, editing the suffragist newspaper *Common Cause* from 1909 to 1914. When war broke out, Swanwick split with much of the suffragist leadership which supported Britain's participation. Throughout the conflict, she advocated a negotiated peace and the establishment of an international organization to maintain it. As a feminist and a socialist, she regarded the war as an opportunity for women to improve their social, economic, and political status.

How has the war affected women? How will it affect them? Women, as half the human race, are compelled to take their share of evil and good with men, the other half. The destruction of property, the increase of taxation, the rise of prices, the devastation of beautiful things in nature and art—these are felt by men as well as by women. Some losses doubtless appeal to one or the other sex with peculiar poignancy, but it would be difficult to say whose sufferings are the greater, though there can be no doubt at all that men get an exhilaration out of war which is denied to most women. When they see pictures of soldiers encamped in the ruins of what was once a home, amidst the dead bodies of gentle milch [*sic*] cows, most women would be thinking too insistently of the babies who must die for need of milk to entertain the exhilaration which no doubt may be felt at "the good work of our guns." When they read of miles upon miles of kindly earth made barren, the hearts of men may be wrung to think of wasted toil, but to women the thought suggests a simile full of an even deeper pathos; they will think of the millions of young lives destroyed, each one having cost the

---

From Helena Swanwick, "The War in Its Effect Upon Women," in *World War I and European Society*, ed. Marilyn Shevin-Coetzee and Frans Coetzee (Lexington, Mass.: D. C. Heath, 1995), pp. 160–164, 166.

travail and care of a mother, and of the millions of young bodies made barren by the premature death of those who should have been their mates. The millions of widowed maidens in the coming generation will have to turn their thoughts away from one particular joy and fulfillment of life. While men in war give what is, at the present stage of the world's development, the peculiar service of men, let them not forget that in rendering that very service they are depriving a corresponding number of women of the opportunity of rendering what must, at all stages of the world's development, be the peculiar service of women. After the war, men will go on doing what has been regarded as men's work; women, deprived of their own, will also have to do much of what has been regarded as men's work. These things are going to affect women profoundly, and one hopes that the reconstruction of society is going to be met by the whole people—men and women—with a sympathetic understanding of each other's circumstances. When what are known as men's questions are discussed, it is generally assumed that the settlement of them depends upon men only; when what are known as women's questions are discussed, there is never any suggestion that they can be settled by women independently of men. Of course they cannot. But, then, neither can "men's questions" be rightly settled so. In fact, life would be far more truly envisaged if we dropped the silly phrases "men's and women's questions"; for, indeed, there are no such matters, and all human questions affect all humanity.

Now, for the right consideration of human questions, it is necessary for humans to understand each other. This catastrophic war will do one good thing if it opens our eyes to real live women as they are, as we know them in workaday life, but as the politician and the journalist seem not to have known them. When war broke out, a Labour newspaper, in the midst of the news of men's activities, found space to say that women would feel the pinch, because their supply of attar of roses would be curtailed. It struck some women like a blow in the face. When a great naval engagement took place, the front page of a progressive daily was taken up with portraits of the officers and men who had won distinction, and the back page with portraits of simpering mannequins in extravagantly fashionable hats; not frank advertisement, mind you, but exploitation of women under the guise of news supposed to be peculiarly interesting to the feeble-minded creatures.

When a snapshot was published of the first women ticket collectors in England, the legend underneath the picture ran "Super-women"! It took the life and death of Edith Cavell[1] to open the eyes of the Prime Minister to the fact that there were thousands of women giving life and service to their country. "A year ago we did not know it," he said, in the House of Commons. Is that indeed so? Surely in our private capacities as ordinary citizens, we knew not only of the women whose portraits are in the picture papers (mostly pretty ladies of the

---

[1]**Edith Cavell**: British nurse working in Belgium, who was executed by the Germans for providing aid to Belgian insurgents.

music hall or of society), but also of the toiling millions upon whose courage and ability and endurance and goodness of heart the great human family rests. Only the politicians did not know, because their thoughts were too much engrossed with faction fights to think humanly; only the journalists would not write of them, because there was more money in writing the columns which are demanded by the advertisers of feminine luxuries. Anyone who has conducted a woman's paper knows the steady commercial pressure for that sort of "copy." . . .

The Need for Production

It is often forgotten that for full prosperity a country needs to be producing as much wealth as possible, consistently with the health, freedom, and happiness of its people. To arrive at this desired result, it is quite clear that as many people as possible should be employed productively, and it is one of the unhappy results of our economic anarchy that employers have found it profitable to have a large reserve class of unemployed and that wage-earners have been driven to try and diminish their own numbers and to restrict their own output. To keep women out of the "labor market" (by artificial restrictions, such as the refusal to work with them, or the refusal to allow them to be trained, or the refusal to adapt conditions to their health requirements) is in truth antisocial. But it is easy to see how such antisocial restrictions have been forced upon the workers, and it is futile to blame them. A way must be found out of industrial war before we can hope that industry will be carried on thriftily. Men and women must take counsel together and let the experience of the war teach them how to solve economic problems by co-operation rather than conflict. Women have been increasingly conscious of the satisfaction to be got from economic independence, of the sweetness of earned bread, of the dreary depression of subjection. They have felt the bitterness of being "kept out"; they are feeling the exhilaration of being "brought in." They are ripe for instruction and organization in working for the good of the whole. . . .

Readjustment of Employment

Most people were astonished in 1914 at the rapidity with which industry and social conditions adapted themselves to the state of war, and there are those who argue that, because the fears of very widespread and continued misery at the outbreak of the war were not justified, we need not have any anxiety about any widespread and continued misery at the establishment of peace. Certainly depression or panic are worse than useless, and a serene and cheerful heart will help to carry the nation beyond difficulties. But comfortable people must beware of seeming to bear the sorrows of others with cheerfulness, and a lack of preparation for easily foreseen contingencies will not be forgiven by those who suffer from carelessness or procrastination. We know quite well what some, at least, of our problems are going to be, and the fool's paradise would lead straight to revolution.

It would be wise to remember that the dislocation of industry at the outbreak of the war was easily met; first, because the people thrown out by the cessation of one sort of work were easily absorbed by the increase of another sort; second, because there was ample capital and credit in hand; third, because the State was prepared to shoulder many risks and to guarantee stability; fourth, because there was an untapped reservoir of women's labor to take the place of men's. The problems after the war will be different, greater, and more lasting. . . . Because it will obviously be impossible for all to find work quickly (not to speak of the right kind of work), there is almost certain to be an outcry for the restriction of work in various directions, and one of the first cries (if we may judge from the past) will be to women: "Back to the Home!" This cry will be raised whether the women have a home or not. . . . We must understand the unimpeachable right of the man who has lost his work and risked his life for his country, to find decent employment, decent wages and conditions, on his return to civil life. We must also understand the enlargement and enhancement of life which women feel when they are able to live by their own productive work, and we must realize that to deprive women of the right to live by their work is to send them back to a moral imprisonment (to say nothing of physical and intellectual starvation), of which they have become now for the first time fully conscious. And we must realize the exceeding danger that conscienceless employers may regard women's labor as preferable, owing to its cheapness and its docility, and that women, if unsympathetically treated by their male relatives and fellow workers, may be tempted to continue to be cheap and docile in the hands of those who have no desire except that of exploiting them and the community. The kind of man who likes "to keep women in their place" may find he has made slaves who will be used by his enemies against him. Men need have no fear of free women; it is the slaves and the parasites who are a deadly danger.

The demand for equal wage for equal work has been hotly pressed by men since the war began, and it is all to the good so far as it goes. But most men are still far from realizing the solidarity of their interests with those of women in all departments of life, and are still too placidly accepting the fact that women are sweated over work which is not the same as that of men. They don't realize yet that starved womanhood means starved manhood, and they don't enough appreciate the rousing and infectious character of a generous attitude on the part of men, who, in fighting the women's battles unselfishly and from a love of right, would stimulate the women to corresponding generosity. There are no comrades more staunch and loyal than women, where men have engaged their truth and courage. But men must treat them as comrades; they must no longer think only of how they can "eliminate female labor"; they must take the women into their trade unions and other organizations, and they must understand that the complexities of a woman's life are not of her invention or choosing, but are due to her function as mother of men. The sexual side of a woman's life gravely affects the economic side, and we can never afford to overlook this. As mothers and homemakers women are doing work of the highest national importance and economic value, but this value is one which returns to the nation as a whole and only in small and very uncertain part to the women themselves.... Unless men are prepared to socialize the responsibilities of parenthood, one does not see how women's labor is ever to be organized for the welfare of the whole, nor does one see how women are to perform their priceless functions of motherhood as well as possible if they are to be penalized for them in the future as they have been in the past. . . .

Enfranchisement and Emancipation

The course and conduct of the war, throwing upon women greater and greater responsibilities, bringing home to them how intimately their own lives and all they hold dear and sacred are affected by the government of the country, will tend greatly to strengthen and enlarge their claim for a share in the government. The growth of what was known as "militancy," in the last few years of the British suffrage movement, was the disastrous result of the long denial of justice, the acrid fruit of government which had become coercion, because it was no longer by consent.[2] Now that, for two years past, the women of Great Britain have made common cause with their men in this time of stress, the heat of the internal conflict has died down, and one hears on all sides that prominent anti-suffragists have become ardent suffragists, while others have declared their resolve at any rate never again to *oppose* the enfranchisement of women. The battle of argument was won long ago, but we are not, as a people, much given to theory; custom has a very strong hold over us. The shock of war has loosened that hold, and now almost every one who used to oppose, when asked whether women should be given votes, would reply: "Why not? They have earned them!" I cannot admit that representation is a thing that people should be called upon to "earn," nor that, if essential contribution to the nation is to count as "earning," the women have not earned the vote for just as long as the men. . . .

What the war has put in a fresh light, so that even the dullest can see, is that if the State may claim women's lives and those of their sons and husbands and lovers, if it may absorb all private and individual life, as at present, then indeed the condition of those who have no voice in the State is a condition of slavery, and Englishmen don't feel quite happy at the thought that their women are still slaves, while their Government is saying they are waging a war of liberation. Many women had long ago become acutely aware of their ignominious position, but the jolt of the war has made many more aware of it.

---

[2]**"militancy," in the last few years . . . consent**: During the years preceding the war's outbreak, "militant" suffragists, led by Emmeline Pankhurst, had conducted a campaign of domestic terrorism to publicize their cause.

READING QUESTIONS

1. Having studied Swanwick's essay, how would you answer the two questions she poses at its beginning? "How has the war affected women? How will it affect them?"

2. Swanwick noted that the war brought about a major increase in the number of women in the workforce. What did she foresee happening to those women when the war ended?

3. What connections can you make between the developments Swanwick described and the achievement of women's suffrage in countries across Europe in the decade following the war?

25-5 | Preparing for the Coming Revolution

VLADIMIR I. LENIN, *What Is to Be Done?* (1902)

Marx's vision of revolutionary change was developed with the industrialized countries of northern Europe in mind. It was the industrial working class that would create the revolution. Through workers' groups, trade unions, and political parties, the proletariat would organize themselves into an irresistible force that would crush the bourgeoisie. The expansion of male suffrage in Britain, France, Germany, and Italy facilitated this process by bringing working-class people into the electorate. Russian socialist revolutionaries were, therefore, faced with two key problems. First, Russia remained staunchly autocratic, and the formation of political opposition groups was illegal. Second, Russian industry was still in its infancy, and, thus, there was no sizable industrial working class to serve as the bulwark of the revolution. With these problems in mind, the Russian revolutionary Vladimir Lenin (1870–1924) outlined a revised socialist strategy in his pamphlet "What Is to Be Done?"

The history of all countries shows that the working class, exclusively by its own effort, is able to develop only trade union consciousness, *i.e.*, it may itself realize the necessity for combining in unions, for fighting against the employers and for striving to compel the government to pass necessary labor legislation, etc. The theory of socialism, however, grew out of the philosophic, historical, and economic theories that were elaborated by the educated representatives of the propertied classes, the intellectuals. According to their social status, the founders of modern scientific socialism, Marx and Engels, themselves belonged to the bourgeois intelligentsia. Similarly, in Russia, the theoretical doctrine of Social Democracy[1] arose quite independently of the spontaneous growth of the labor movement; it arose as a natural and inevitable outcome of the development of ideas among the revolutionary socialist intelligentsia. At the time of which we

From *Collected Works of Vladimir Ilyich Lenin*, vol. 5 (Moscow: Foreign Languages Publishing House, 1961). Marxists Internet Archive. Web. February 23, 2010.

[1]**Social Democracy**: Lenin is referring to revolutionary communism, rather than moderate, democratic socialist parties.

are speaking, *i.e.*, the middle of the nineties [1890s], this doctrine not only represented the completely formulated program of the Emancipation of Labor group,[2] but had already won the adherence of the majority of the revolutionary youth in Russia. . . .

It is only natural that a Social Democrat, who conceives the political struggle as being identical with the "economic struggle against the employers and the government," should conceive of an "organization of revolutionaries" as being more or less identical with an "organization of workers." And this, in fact, is what actually happens; so that when we talk about organization, we literally talk in different tongues. I recall a conversation I once had with a fairly consistent Economist, with whom I had not been previously acquainted. We were discussing the pamphlet *Who Will Make the Political Revolution?* and we were very soon agreed that the principal defect in that brochure was that it ignored the question of organization. We were beginning to think that we were in complete agreement with each other—but as the conversation proceeded, it became clear that we were talking of different things. My interlocutor accused the author of the brochure just mentioned of ignoring strike funds, mutual aid societies, etc.; whereas I had in mind an organization of revolutionaries as an essential factor in "making" the political revolution. After that became clear, I hardly remember a single question of importance upon which I was in agreement with that Economist!

What was the source of our disagreement? The fact that on questions of organization and politics the Economists are forever lapsing from Social Democracy into trade unionism. The political struggle carried on by the Social Democrats is far more extensive and complex than the economic struggle the workers carry on against the employers and the government. Similarly (and indeed for that reason), the organization of a revolutionary Social Democratic Party must inevitably *differ* from the organizations of the workers designed for the latter struggle. A workers' organization must in the first place be a trade organization; secondly, it must be as wide as possible; and thirdly, it must be as public as conditions will allow (here, and further on, of course, I have only autocratic Russia in mind). On the other hand, the organizations of revolutionaries must consist first and foremost of people whose profession is that of a revolutionary (that is why I speak of organizations of *revolutionaries*, meaning revolutionary Social Democrats). In view of this common feature of the members of such an organization, *all distinctions as between workers and intellectuals*, and certainly distinctions of trade and profession, must be obliterated. Such an organization must of necessity be not too extensive and as secret as possible. . . .

I assert:

1. that no movement can be durable without a stable organization of leaders to maintain continuity;

---

[2]**Emancipation of Labor group**: First Russian Marxist political organization, founded in 1883.

2. that the more widely the masses are spontaneously drawn into the struggle and form the basis of the movement and participate in it, the more necessary is it to have such an organization, and the more stable must it be (for it is much easier for demagogues to sidetrack the more backward sections of the masses);

3. that the organization must consist chiefly of persons engaged in revolutionary activities as a profession;

4. that in a country with an autocratic government, the more we *restrict* the membership of this organization to persons who are engaged in revolutionary activities as a profession and who have been professionally trained in the art of combating the political police, the more difficult will it be to catch the organization, and the *wider* will be the circle of men and women of the working class or of other classes of society able to join the movement and perform active work in it. . . .

The active and widespread participation of the masses will not suffer; on the contrary, it will benefit by the fact that a "dozen" experienced revolutionaries, no less professionally trained than the police, will centralize all the secret side of the work—prepare leaflets, work out approximate plans and appoint bodies of leaders for each urban district, for each factory district and to each educational institution, etc. (I know that exception will be taken to my "undemocratic" views, but I shall reply to this altogether unintelligent objection later on.) The centralization of the more secret functions in an organization of revolutionaries will not diminish, but rather increase the extent and the quality of the activity of a large number of other organizations intended for wide membership and which, therefore, can be as loose and as public as possible, for example, trade unions, workers' circles for self-education and the reading of illegal literature, and socialist and also democratic circles for *all other sections of the population*, etc., etc. We must have *as large a number as possible* of such organizations having the widest possible variety of functions, but it is absurd and dangerous to *confuse those with organizations of revolutionaries*, to erase the line of demarcation between them, to dim still more the masses already incredibly hazy appreciation of the fact that in order to "serve" the mass movement we must have people who will devote themselves exclusively to Social Democratic activities, and that such people must *train* themselves patiently and steadfastly to be professional revolutionaries.

Aye, this appreciation has become incredibly dim. The most grievous sin we have committed in regard to organization is that *by our primitiveness we have lowered the prestige of revolutionaries in Russia.* A man who is weak and vacillating on theoretical questions, who has a narrow outlook, who makes excuses for his own slackness on the ground that the masses are awakening spontaneously; who resembles a trade union secretary more than a people's tribune, who is unable to conceive of a broad and bold plan, who is incapable of inspiring even his opponents with respect for himself, and who is inexperienced and clumsy in his own professional art—the art of combating the political police—such a man is not a revolutionary but a wretched amateur!

Let no active worker take offense at these frank remarks, for as far as insufficient training is concerned, I apply them first and foremost to myself. I used to work in a circle that set itself great and all-embracing tasks; and every member of that circle suffered to the point of torture from the realization that we were proving ourselves to be amateurs at a moment in history when we might have been able to say, paraphrasing a well-known epigram: "Give us an organization of revolutionaries, and we shall overturn the whole of Russia!"

READING QUESTIONS

1. Judging by his remarks, what sort of attitude did Lenin have toward the working class?

2. Why, if Lenin advocated establishing *"as large a number as possible"* of traditional trade unions and similar organizations, did he also maintain that there was urgent need for secret organization of "professional revolutionaries"?

3. What connections can you make between the positions Lenin outlined in this pamphlet and the future development of Communist government under the Bolsheviks?

25-6 | Making the World Safe for Democracy
WOODROW WILSON, *The Fourteen Points* (1918)

When war broke out in 1914, the overwhelming majority of Americans were opposed to U.S. involvement, seeing the war as an "Old World" conflict that had little to do with America's national interests. President Woodrow Wilson (1856–1924) matched his policies to public opinion, running for re-election in 1916 on the slogan "He kept us out of war." As the war dragged on, however, it became increasingly difficult for the United States to remain neutral, and by the spring of 1917 Wilson was ready to ask Congress for a declaration of war against Germany. In his message to Congress, Wilson justified his request by linking the war to essential American political values. Those values were further elaborated in his "Fourteen Points," Wilson's plan for a postwar international order that would keep the peace and pave the way for the spread of democracy around the world.

1. Open covenants of peace, openly arrived at. Diplomacy shall proceed always frankly and in the public view.
2. Absolute freedom of navigation upon the seas, outside territorial waters.
3. The removal, so far as possible, of all economic barriers and the establishment of an equality of trade conditions.
4. Adequate guarantees given and taken that national armaments will be reduced.

Woodrow Wilson, "The Fourteen Points," in *The Great Events of the Great War*, ed. Charles F. Horne (New York: National Alumni, 1920), 6:3–6.

5. A free, open-minded, and absolutely impartial adjustment of all colonial claims. In determining all such questions of sovereignty the interests of the populations concerned must have equal weight with the equitable claims of the Government whose title is to be determined.
6. The evacuation of all Russian territory.
7. Belgium must be evacuated and restored. Without this healing act the whole structure and validity of international law is forever impaired.
8. All French territory should be freed and the invaded portions restored; and the wrong done to France by Prussia in 1871 in the matter of Alsace-Lorraine[1] should be righted.
9. A readjustment of the frontiers of Italy should be effected along clearly recognizable lines of nationality.
10. The peoples of Austria-Hungary, whose place among the nations we wish to see safeguarded and assured, should be accorded the freest opportunity of autonomous development.
11. Rumania, Serbia, and Montenegro should be evacuated; occupied territories restored; Serbia accorded free and secure access to the sea; and international guarantees of the political and economic independence and territorial integrity of the several Balkan states should be entered into.
12. Nationalities which are now under Turkish rule should be assured an unmolested opportunity of autonomous development, and the Dardanelles should be permanently opened as a free passage to the ships and commerce of all nations.
13. An independent Polish state should be erected which should be assured a free and secure access to the sea.
14. A general association of nations must be formed, for the purpose of affording mutual guarantees of political independence and territorial integrity to great and small states alike.

READING QUESTIONS

1. How did Wilson want to treat Germany?
2. On what underlying principles did Wilson base points six through thirteen?
3. What do you think prompted Wilson's demand for "absolute freedom of the seas"?
4. In your opinion, was Wilson's plan practical and realistic? Why or why not?

---

[1]**the wrong done to ... Alsace-Lorraine**: The German states, headed by Prussia, defeated France in the Franco-German War (1870–1871), and annexed all of Alsace and about two-thirds of Lorraine, both of them French provinces prior to the war.

25-7 | The Bitter Taste of Defeat

A Defeated Germany Contemplates the Peace Treaty (1919)

Unlike the Congress of Vienna (1814–1815), in which defeated France participated, the Treaty of Versailles was written without German input. Indeed, the German government was only presented with the completed treaty and told that it faced the choice of signing it or having the Allied armies resume their advance. By June 1919, the German army had been entirely demobilized. Moreover, the Allied naval blockade, which contributed to approximately 750,000 civilian deaths by starvation and disease during its duration, remained in place until Germany signed the treaty on June 28, 1919. The following document captures the reaction of Germany's most important legislative body, the National Assembly of the Germany Republic, to the treaty.

Bauer,[1] [Social Democratic Party, acting chancellor]: Ladies and gentlemen!

The Reich president has entrusted me with the formation of a new cabinet, to replace the Scheidemann[2] government which has resigned. . . . The resignation of the cabinet resulted from its inability to reach an undivided position regarding the peace treaty that has been presented to us. . . . For each of us who were members of the former government it was a bitterly difficult matter to take a position between feelings of indignation and cold rage. And not less difficult was the decision to join this new government whose first and most pressing task it is to conclude this unjust peace. . . . We are here because of our sense of responsibility, aware that it is our damnable duty to try to salvage what can be salvaged. . . .

No matter how each one of us feels about the question of acceptance or rejection, we are all united about one thing: in strong criticism of this peace treaty (*"Very true!"*) to which we are being forced to affix our signatures! When this draft was first presented to us, it was greeted with a unanimous protest of indignation and rejection from our people. We defied disappointment and hoped for the indignation of the entire world. . . .

Rejection did not mean averting the treaty. (*"Very true!" from the Social Democrats.*) A no vote would only have meant a short delay of the yes vote. (*"Very true!"*) Our ability to resist has been broken; we do not have the capability to avert [signing]. . . . In the name of the national government, ladies and gentlemen, I ask you in view of the circumstances and pending ratification by the National Assembly,[3] to sign the peace treaty laid before you! . . .

From "Deutsche Parlamentsdebatten" in *The Making of Modern Germany*, ed. and trans. Benjamin Sax and Dieter Kuntz (Lexington, Mass.: D. C. Heath, 1992), pp. 45–47.

[1]**Bauer**: Gustav Adolf Bauer (1870–1944); German chancellor, August 1919–March 1920.

[2]**Scheidemann**: German journalist and politician Philipp Scheidemann (1865–1939), who led a short-lived government from February to June of 1919.

[3]**pending ratification . . . Assembly**: It was a vote by individual delegates, and, as the socialists were in a majority, the treaty was accepted even though, as Bauer states, they hated it too. The vote was 237 to 138 for *conditional* acceptance.

The government of the German Republic pledges to fulfill the imposed conditions of the peace. The government, however, wishes during this solemn occasion to express its views quite clearly. . . . The imposed conditions exceed the limits of Germany's ability to comply. . . .

Moreover, we emphatically declare that we cannot accept Article 231 of the peace treaty, which demands that Germany accept responsibility for singly initiating the war. (*Applause.*)

Gröber,[4] *delegate of the Center Party:* Honored Assembly! The Center Party delegation of the National Assembly wishes to acknowledge the government's declaration. We accept this program and will support this government and accept [cabinet] participation. . . . We say we are prepared to accept the responsibility of fulfilling its terms as far as is humanly possible, but we do not recognize a responsibility for carrying out conditions that are impossible or intolerable. However, although these are oppressive and hardly fulfillable conditions and will have a detrimental effect on the German people, we must also take other facts into account.

First, the peace will shortly bring hundreds of thousands of prisoners back to German families. . . . Second, the peace will end starvation. . . . Third, only the peace will give us the possibility of economically rebuilding Germany. . . . Fourth, the peace also allows us to maintain our German unity. . . .

Schiffer,[5] *delegate of the DDP* [German Democratic Party]: Contrary to the first two speakers, I wish to declare to this esteemed assembly, that the great majority of my political friends have decided to withhold their approval of the peace treaty laid before us. . . .

Count von Posadowsky,[6] *delegate of the DNVP* [German National People's Party]: Our Fatherland finds itself in the most difficult hour of its history. The enemy stands before our gates, and in the country there are disconcerting signs of internal breakup. . . . We in our party are aware of the ramifications for our people which a rejection of the peace treaty will entail. (*"Very true!" from the right.*) The resultant harm, however, will only be temporary, but if we accept this treaty we will abandon countless generations of our people to misery. . . . For us, acceptance of the treaty is impossible for many reasons. . . . In addition to making Germany defenseless, there is also the matter of theft of our territory. . . .

Haase,[7] *delegate of the USPD* [Independent Social Democratic Party]: We know that the peace treaty will bring incredible burdens for our people. . . . Nonetheless, we have no choice but to accept the treaty. Not only will rejection increase the harm, it will moreover mean sure ruin. (*Agreement from the Independent Social*

---

[4]**Gröber**: Conrad Gröber (1872–1948); Catholic archbishop and politician.

[5]**Schiffer**: Eugen Schiffer (1860–1954); German politician.

[6]**Count von Posadowsky**: Arthur Adolf Graf von Posadowsky-Wehner (1845–1932); German politician.

[7]**Haase**: Hugo Haase (1863–1919); German jurist, politician, and pacifist.

Democrats.) Our people are in this desperate situation only because of the wicked warmongers and war extenders. . . .

Kahl,[8] *delegate of the DVP* [German People's Party]: Gentlemen! The German People's Party unanimously rejects this peace. . . . We reject it because to accept it would mean the destruction of the German state. . . . We reject because we cannot justify the separation of precious segments of German earth, such as the eastern provinces, from the Motherland. . . . Yes, if only we had swords in our hands! (*Laughter from the Social Democrats.*) Then we would easily find a response! (*"Very true" from the right.*)

READING QUESTIONS

1. Why were all of the speakers unhappy with the Treaty of Versailles?
2. On what grounds did Bauer, Gröber, and Haase advocate accepting the treaty?
3. On what grounds did Schiffer, Posadowsky, and Kahl advocate its rejection?
4. In your opinion, does this document help support the charge, later leveled by right-wing Germans, that by accepting the treaty the left had "stabbed Germany in the back"? Why or why not?

■ COMPARATIVE AND DISCUSSION QUESTIONS ■

1. Compare and contrast the photograph of a French soldier wearing a gas mask and the portrait of Baron von Richthofen. How might images like the former have made images like the latter necessary?
2. Compare and contrast Swanwick's views regarding women's place in the workforce during World War I with those of Clara Zetkin (Document 22-5) regarding prewar industrial society. What had changed? How?
3. What do Swanwick's and Lenin's differing views about the route to social and economic progress (women's emancipation in Swanwick's case, workers' emancipation in Lenin's) suggest about the political environments in which each lived?
4. How might Woodrow Wilson have responded to the German debate over the peace treaty? With what aspects of the German position might he have sympathized?

---

[8]**Kahl**: Wilhelm Kahl (1849–1932); German academic and politician.

The Age of Anxiety
1880–1940

The Enlightenment faith in the power of reason and the inevitability of human progress increasingly came under attack in the late nineteenth century. Scientific advances, technological innovation, and increased productive capacity had not led to dramatic social progress. In the view of critics of Enlightenment rationalism like Friedrich Nietzsche and Sigmund Freud, the fact that the march of civilization had not, apparently, civilized human beings, pointed toward the need for new models of human behavior, models that gave more weight to instincts, emotions, and irrationality. While the beginnings of twentieth-century cultural and intellectual trends can be found in the late nineteenth century, the true turning point was World War I. The unprecedented death and destruction of the Great War shook Europeans' confidence in rationality and progress to the core. For many, after the events of 1914–1919, the world would never be the same. This feeling of fundamental disruption was heightened by the continuing tensions between the combatants over the terms of the peace. It was against this backdrop of uncertainty and disorientation, that the world was plunged into depression in the 1930s. When the Great Depression (1929–1939) hit the United States, the subsequent worldwide financial crisis forced many Europeans to reconsider their most basic beliefs about economic, political, and social relationships.

26-1 | Discovering the Self
SIGMUND FREUD, *The Interpretation of Dreams* (1900)

Sigmund Freud (1856–1939), a Viennese psychoanalyst, stunned the European intellectual world when he published *The Interpretation of Dreams* in 1900, in which he argued that human behavior was largely irrational, driven by instincts and memories that were buried

From James Strachey, trans. and ed., *The Interpretation of Dreams* (New York: Basic Books, 1955), pp. 613–621.

deep within the unconscious mind. Thus, Freud offered a direct challenge to the intellectual and moral certainties of the previous century. In this excerpt from *The Interpretation of Dreams*, Freud explained the value of his study of dreams, describing them as vital evidence for uncovering the true relationship between the conscious and unconscious mind.

The unconscious is the true psychical reality; in its innermost nature it is as much unknown to us as the reality of the external world, and it is as incompletely presented by the data of consciousness as is the external world by the communications of our sense organs.

Now that the old antithesis between conscious life and dream-life has been reduced to its proper proportions by the establishment of unconscious psychical reality, a number of dream-problems with which earlier writers were deeply concerned have lost their significance. Thus some of the activities whose successful performance in dreams excited astonishment are no longer to be attributed to dreams but to unconscious thinking, which is active during the day no less than at night. If, as Scherner[1] has said, dreams appear to engage in making symbolic representations of the body, we now know that those representations are the product of certain unconscious fantasies (deriving, probably, from sexual impulses) which find expression not only in dreams but also in hysterical phobias and other symptoms. If a dream carries on the activities of the day and completes them and even brings valuable fresh ideas to light, all we need do is strip it of the dream disguise, which is the product of dream-work and the mark of assistance rendered by obscure forces from the depths of the mind . . . the intellectual achievement is due to the same mental forces which produce every similar result during the daytime. We are probably inclined greatly to over-estimate the conscious character of intellectual and artistic production as well. Accounts given us by some of the most highly productive men, such as Goethe[2] and Helmholtz,[3] show rather that what is essential and new in their creations came to them without premeditation and as an almost ready-made whole. There is nothing strange if in other cases, where a concentration of every intellectual faculty was needed, conscious activity also contributed its share. But it is the much-abused privilege of conscious activity, wherever it plays a part, to conceal every other activity from our eyes.

It would scarcely repay the trouble if we were to treat the historical significance of dreams as a separate topic. A dream may have impelled some chieftain to embark upon a bold enterprise the success of which has changed history. But this only raises a fresh problem so long as a dream is regarded as an alien power in contrast to the other more familiar forces of the mind; no such problem remains

---

[1]**Scherner**: Karl Albert Scherner; psychologist who published an 1861 work on dream theory, *The Life of Dreams*.

[2]**Goethe**: Johann Wolfgang von Goethe (1749–1832); German author of the classical and romantic schools, most famous for his dramatic retelling of Faust's deal with the devil.

[3]**Helmholtz**: Hermann Ludwig Ferdinand von Helmholtz (1821–1894); German doctor who wrote extensively on perception and theory of science.

if a dream is recognized as a *form of expression* of impulses which are under the pressure of resistance during the day but which have been able to find reinforcement during the night from deep-lying sources of excitation. The respect paid to dreams in antiquity is, however, based upon correct psychological insight and is the homage paid to the uncontrolled and indestructible forces in the human mind, to the "demonic" power which produces the dream-wish and which we find at work in our unconscious. . . .

What role is now left, in our representation of things, to the phenomenon of consciousness, once so all-powerful and over-shadowing all else? None other than that of a sense-organ for the perception of psychic qualities. . . .

The whole multiplicity of the problems of consciousness can only be grasped by an analysis of the thought processes in hysteria. These give one the impression that the transition from a preconscious to a conscious cathexis[4] is marked by a censorship similar to that between the *Ucs.* [unconscious] and the *Pcs.* [preconscious]. This censorship, too, only comes into force above a certain quantitative limit, so that thought-structures of low intensity escape it. Examples of every possible variety of how a thought can be withheld from consciousness or can force its way into consciousness under certain limitations are to be found included within the framework of psychoneurotic phenomena; and they all point to the intimate and reciprocal relations between censorship and consciousness. I will bring these psychological reflections to an end with a report. . . .

I was called in to a consultation last year to examine an intelligent and unembarrassed-looking girl. She was most surprisingly dressed. For though as a rule a woman's clothes are carefully considered down to the last detail, she was wearing one of her stockings hanging down and two of the buttons on her blouse were undone. She complained of having pains in her leg and, without being asked, exposed her calf. But what she principally complained of was, to use her own words, that she had a feeling in her body as though there was something "stuck into it" which was "moving backwards and forwards" and was "shaking" her through and through: sometimes it made her whole body feel "stiff." My medical colleague, who was present at the examination, looked at me; he found no difficulty in understanding the meaning of her complaint. But what struck both of us as extraordinary was the fact that it meant nothing to the patient's mother — though she must often have found herself in the situation which her child was describing. The girl herself had no notion of the bearing of her remarks; for if she had, she would never have given voice to them. In this case it had been possible to hoodwink the censorship into allowing a fantasy which would normally have been kept in the preconscious to emerge into consciousness under the innocent disguise of making a complaint. . . .

Thus I would look for the *theoretical* value of the study of dreams in the contributions it makes to psychological knowledge and in the preliminary light it

---

[4]**cathexis:** For Freud, this term represented the libido's energy, the driving force in most human behavior.

throws on the problems of psychoneuroses. Who can guess the importance of the results which might be obtained from a thorough understanding of the structure and functions of the mental apparatus, since even the present state of our knowledge allows us to exert a favorable therapeutic influence on the curable forms of psychoneurosis? But what of the *practical* value of this study—I hear the question raised—as a means towards an understanding of the mind, towards a revelation of the hidden characteristics of individual men? Have not the unconscious impulses brought out by dreams the importance of real forces in mental life? Is the ethical significance of suppressed wishes to be made light of—wishes which, just as they lead to dreams, may some day lead to other things?

I do not feel justified in answering these questions. I have not considered this side of the problem of dreams further. I think, however, that the Roman emperor was in the wrong when he had one of his subjects executed because he had dreamt of murdering the emperor. He should have begun by trying to find out what the dream meant; most probably its meaning was not what it appeared to be. And even if a dream with another content had had this act of *lèse majesté*[5] as its meaning, would it not be right to bear in mind Plato's dictum that the virtuous man is content to *dream* what a wicked man really *does*? I think it is best, therefore, to acquit dreams. Whether we are to attribute *reality* to unconscious wishes, I cannot say. It must be denied, of course, to any transitional or intermediate thoughts. If we look at unconscious wishes reduced to their most fundamental and truest shape, we shall have to conclude, no doubt, that *psychical* reality is a particular form of existence not to be confused with *material* reality. Thus there seems to be no justification for people's reluctance in accepting responsibility for the immorality of their dreams. When the mode of functioning of the mental apparatus is rightly appreciated and the relation between the conscious and the unconscious understood, the greater part of what is ethically objectionable in our dream and fantasy lives will be found to disappear. In the words of Hanns Sachs:[6] "If we look in our consciousness at something that has been told us by a dream about a contemporary (real) situation, we ought not to be surprised to find that the monster which we saw under the magnifying glass of analysis turns out to be a tiny infusorian."[7]

Actions and consciously expressed opinions are as a rule enough for practical purposes in judging men's characters. Actions deserve to be considered first and foremost; for many impulses which force their way through to consciousness are even then brought to nothing by the real forces of mental life before they can mature into deeds. In fact, some impulses often meet with no psychical obstacles to their progress, for the very reason that the unconscious is certain that they will be stopped at some other stage. It is in any case instructive to get to

---

[5]*lèse majesté*: Insulting the monarch; an act of treason.

[6]**H. Sachs**: Hanns Sachs (1881–1947); Viennese psychologist and student of Freud's who later wrote an admiring biography of his teacher.

[7]**infusorian**: Single-celled organism.

know the much trampled soil from which our virtues proudly spring. Very rarely does the complexity of a human character, driven hither and thither by dynamic forces, submit to a choice between simple alternatives, as our antiquated morality would have us believe.

And the value of dreams for giving us knowledge of the future? There is of course no question of that. It would be truer to say instead that they give us knowledge of the past. For dreams are derived from the past in every sense. Nevertheless the ancient belief that dreams foretell the future is not wholly devoid of truth. By picturing our wishes as fulfilled, dreams are after all leading us into the future. But this future, which the dreamer pictures as the present, has been molded by his indestructible wish into a perfect likeness of the past.

READING QUESTIONS

1. According to Freud, what forms the basis of human behavior? What does he present as evidence of this pathway to expression?

2. What role did Freud assign the conscious mind in directing and controlling human behavior?

3. How might someone who believed in the absolute responsibility of individuals for their actions, particularly their moral actions, respond to Freud's theories?

26-2 | A Female Impressionist's Perspective

MARY CASSATT, *Reading Le Figaro* (1878)

The American painter Mary Cassatt (1844–1926) spent most of her adult life in France, where she became close friends with Edgar Degas and an important participant in the Impressionist movement. As much as the Impressionists were committed to innovation, they were aware of and connected to the artistic traditions of the past. Cassatt's *Reading Le Figaro* provides an example of this mix of old and new. There is a long tradition in European painting of depictions of women reading. Such paintings include scenes of women reading prayer books in the sixteenth century, letters in the seventeenth century, and novels in the eighteenth century. In many ways, Cassatt's work fits squarely within this tradition, except for the fact that her subject is shown reading a national political newspaper. As you examine the painting, think about the implications of this choice.

READING QUESTIONS

1. How would you characterize the subject of Cassatt's painting? What kind of a person is she? What are we, as viewers, meant to think about her?

2. What importance should we attach to Cassatt's choice of reading material for her subject? How does the choice of reading material challenge the viewer to take a fresh look at the reader?

26-3 | An Analysis of the Versailles Treaty

JOHN MAYNARD KEYNES, *The Economic Consequences of the Peace* (1920)

Of all the observers at Versailles, British economist John Maynard Keynes was one of the most prescient. Upset that negotiators had given insufficient thought to the economic consequences of the treaty, Keynes warned Europe's leaders that their actions would lead to economic disaster, a prediction that seemed to come true in 1923, with the German economic collapse, and again in 1929 with the U.S. stock market crash and ensuing Great Depression. As you read Keynes's criticism of the treaty, pay particular attention to the connections he makes between economic policy and political stability.

The Treaty includes no provisions for the economic rehabilitation of Europe,— nothing to make the defeated Central Empires[1] into good neighbors, nothing to stabilize the new States of Europe,[2] nothing to reclaim Russia; nor does it promote in any way a compact of economic solidarity amongst the Allies themselves; no agreement was reached at Paris for restoring the disordered finances of France and Italy, or to adjust the systems of the Old World and the New.

The Council of Four[3] paid no attention to these issues, being preoccupied with others,—Clemenceau to crush the economic life of his enemy, Lloyd George to do a deal and bring home something which would pass muster for a week, the President to do nothing that was not just and right. It is an extraordinary fact that the fundamental economic problems of a Europe starving and disintegrating before their eyes, was the one question in which it was impossible to arouse the interest of the Four. Reparation was their main excursion into the economic field, and they settled it as a problem of theology, of politics, of electoral chicane, from every point of view except that of the economic future of the States whose destiny they were handling. . . .

For the immediate future events are taking charge, and the near destiny of Europe is no longer in the hands of any man. The events of the coming year will not be shaped by the deliberate acts of statesmen, but by the hidden currents, flowing continually beneath the surface of political history, of which no one can predict the outcome. In one way only can we influence these hidden currents,—by setting in motion those forces of instruction and imagination which

---

From John Maynard Keynes, *The Economic Consequences of the Peace* (New York: Harcourt, Brace and Howe, 1920), pp. 226–227, 296–297.

[1]**Central Empires**: Germany, Austria-Hungary, and the Ottoman Empire—the losing alliance in the Great War.

[2]**new States of Europe**: The Treaty of Versailles dismembered the Austro-Hungarian and German Empires in the process creating newly independent states, including Czechoslovakia, Hungary, Yugoslavia, Lithuania, Latvia, and Estonia.

[3]**Council of Four**: The leaders of the Allied nations at Versailles: Woodrow Wilson of the United States, Georges Clemenceau of France, David Lloyd George of Great Britain, and Vittorio Orlando of Italy.

change opinion. The assertion of truth, the unveiling of illusion, the dissipation of hate, the enlargement and instruction of men's hearts and minds, must be the means.

In this autumn of 1919, in which I write, we are at the dead season of our fortunes. The reaction from the exertions, the fears, and the sufferings of the past five years is at its height. Our power of feeling or caring beyond the immediate questions of our own material well-being is temporarily eclipsed. The greatest events outside our own direct experience and the most dreadful anticipations cannot move us.

We have been moved already beyond endurance, and need rest. Never in the lifetime of men now living has the universal element in the soul of man burnt so dimly.

READING QUESTIONS

1. What motivations does Keynes believe shaped the treaty that emerged from the Versailles negotiations? Whose motivations were they? What does he think should have influenced the treaty instead?

2. In what ways does Keynes think Europeans have lost control of their lives? What, if any, ideas does he seem to offer to help them recover that control?

3. What about Keynes's document suggests that reason is not the driving force in international relations?

4. As Keynes portrays them, how have the citizens of the warring countries responded to the peace?

26-4 | Postwar Economic Crisis in Germany
Hyperinflation in Germany (1923)

The French occupation of the Ruhr in 1923 set off a chain of events that had cataclysmic consequences for the German economy. In response to the occupation, the German government ordered the people of the Ruhr to stop working. As the cost of supporting the striking workers and their employers mounted, the government began printing money to meet its obligations. The result was runaway inflation that obliterated the value of the German mark. This German cartoon from 1923 dramatized the impact of inflation on German families. In it, a mother holds up her starving child above a rising sea of bank notes, crying out for bread as she struggles to keep herself from being drowned in the accumulating piles of worthless money.

Universal History Archive / UIG / The Bridgeman Art Library.

READING QUESTIONS

1. What does the cartoon suggest about the consequences of hyperinflation for ordinary Germans? What might explain the artist's choice to use the metaphor of drowning to illustrate those consequences?

2. How might the experience of hyperinflation have challenged the values and expectations of middle-class Germans?

3. What connections can you make between hyperinflation and political developments in Germany in the 1920s and 1930s?

The Great Depression in Great Britain and Germany

As the Great Depression took hold, and unemployment and economic insecurity grew, European governments struggled to respond to the crisis. Although the impact of the depression was uneven, with some countries experiencing a longer and deeper downturn than others, all European governments found their legitimacy challenged by their inability, or unwillingness, to ameliorate the suffering of millions of their citizens. The sources included below explore the economic and political impact of the depression in Great Britain and Germany. As you examine them, think about what they tell you about the differences in the conditions in each country. What common problems did the two countries face? Why were the political and economic consequences of the depression so much greater in Germany than in Great Britain?

26-5 | SIR PERCY MALCOLM STEWART, *Parliament Addresses the Great Depression in Britain* (1934)

Great Britain's response to the depression was dictated by classical economic theory: when tax revenues drop, government spending should drop as well. Thus, throughout the 1930s, Great Britain matched declines in government revenue with cuts in spending, and did little to intervene in the economy on behalf of the unemployed. This approach seemed to be borne out by the relatively speedy recovery of the British economy. This recovery was, however, uneven. Government policies contributed to the growth of new industries in the south. In the industrial north, in contrast, long-term decline only deepened. In 1934, under mounting public pressure, Parliament commissioned a study of the depressed regions of the country. This excerpt from the resulting report summarizes some of the key findings.

From "First and Second Reports of the Commissioner for the Special Areas [England and Wales]," in *Documents and Readings in the History of Europe Since 1918*, rev. and enlarged ed., ed. W. C. Langsam (Philadelphia: Lippincott, 1951), pp. 303–304, 306.

25. The Special Areas[1] are in their present unfortunate position owing to the decline of the main industries, coal mining, ship building and iron and steel, which attracted such large numbers of workers to them during the nineteenth century under more prosperous conditions. It seems unlikely that these industries will again employ the numbers engaged in them even up to ten years ago. During the period of prosperity large communities with full equipment of railways, roads, houses, schools, and other municipal and social services were created. Many millions of pounds were spent in building up these services. A large proportion of the inhabitants have been associated with the Areas for several generations; they are bound to the Areas by ties of home and family and religion, by local patriotism and, especially in Wales, by a fervent national spirit and, sometimes, a distinctive language. It is natural, therefore, that wherever one goes in these Areas one should be met by the demand that something should be done to attract fresh industries to the Area. This is the general request, and I regard it as at once the most important and the most difficult of my duties to try to satisfy it. I have given more time and personal attention to this side of my work than to any other, but it must be frankly admitted that up to the present the results have been negligible. Many of the negotiations I have initiated with this end in view were necessarily confidential, and it would only prejudice the present slender chances of success if I were to give a full account of them. The following paragraphs will, however, indicate the main lines on which I have been working.

26. In the first place I approached a number of the larger and more prosperous firms in the country in the hope that I might persuade them to open new branches of their industry in one or other of the Special Areas. Without exception they were sympathetic to my representations, but except in one case they had good reasons which made it impossible for them to accede to my request. . . .

29. Some hundreds of new factories have been established in recent years in the Midlands and South, but very few in the Special Areas. Why is this so? The main reasons appear to fall in the following categories: —

(1) Inaccessibility to markets. This applies particularly to Cumberland.[2] . . .

(2) High rates.[3] These probably have a deterrent effect on employers out of proportion to their real significance. . . .

(3) Fear of industrial unrest. This fear is very general and is bred from past disputes mainly in the coal-mining industry. It prevails particularly with regard to South Wales, but the facts scarcely warrant the attitude

---

[1]**The Special Areas**: Specifically, the areas in South Wales supported by coal mining and areas such as Sheffield and Lancashire in northern England that were formerly centers of manufacturing and industry.

[2]**Cumberland**: One of the two English counties that border Scotland—the other is Northumberland—and one of the industrial areas hardest hit by unemployment in Great Britain.

[3]**High rates**: Shipping rates, meaning that freight was more expensive to ship.

adopted. Statistics apart from those of coal-mining do not justify the fear which undoubtedly exists in the minds of many employers. . . .

(4) The fact that the areas are, and for some years have been, suffering from industrial depression. This factor, coupled with the common application to them of the term "depressed" or "distressed" areas, has itself a deterrent effect. While it is true that "trade brings trade," the converse unfortunately is equally true. Unemployment undermines business confidence and reduces purchasing power. A vicious circle is thus set up. . . .

(5) Difficulty in obtaining finance to start new industries. . . .

255. . . . Probably the most serious human problem of the Special Areas is that presented by unemployment among young men between 18 and 21. . . .

256. Many of these young persons have done practically no work; they have been brought up in a home where the father has been continuously out of work, and they have little or no conception that a man's ordinary occupation should be such as will provide the means of subsistence for himself and for his family. They have seen their own families and their friends kept for years by the State, and they have come to accept this as a normal condition of life. It is hardly surprising in the circumstances that young persons with this background and upbringing should be ready victims of all manner of demoralizing influences. In short, these young persons present in my view the most tragic aspect of the problem of the Special Areas and one fraught with great danger to the State.

READING QUESTIONS

1. What factors made the Special Areas particularly unsuited for new business?

2. In what ways was the report concerned with workers, and in what ways with employers?

3. Why did the authors of the report think action in the Special Areas was necessary? What social and political dangers did they associate with industrial decline?

26-6 | HEINRICH HAUSER, *With the Unemployed in Germany* (1933)

The Great Depression struck Germany with greater force than any other country, with unemployment soaring to nearly 40 percent. Still suffering from the hardships created by wartime destruction, reparations payments, and hyperinflation, the German people were faced with the second economic catastrophe in less than a decade. These excerpts from the writings of German journalist Heinrich Hauser capture something of the suffering and despair of Germany's unemployed.

From Heinrich Hauser, "With Germany's Unemployed," *The Living Age* 344 (Mar. 1933), pp. 27–38.

An almost unbroken chain of homeless men extends the whole length of the great Hamburg-Berlin highway.

There are so many of them moving in both directions, impelled by the wind or making their way against it, that they could shout a message from Hamburg to Berlin by word of mouth.

It is the same scene for the entire two hundred miles, and the same scene repeats itself. . . . All the highways in Germany over which I traveled this year presented the same aspect. . . .

Most of the hikers paid no attention to me. They walked separately or in small groups, with their eyes on the ground. And they had the queer, stumbling gait of barefooted people, for their shoes were slung over their shoulders. Some of them were guild members—carpenters with embroidered wallets, knee breeches, and broad felt hats; milkmen with striped red shirts, and bricklayers with tall black hats,—but they were in a minority. Far more numerous were those whom one could assign to no special profession or craft—unskilled young people, for the most part, who had been unable to find a place for themselves in any city or town in Germany, and who had never had a job and never expected to have one. There was something else that had never been seen before—whole families that had piled all their goods into baby carriages and wheelbarrows that they were pushing along as they plodded forward in dumb despair. It was a whole nation on the march.

I saw them—and this was the strongest impression that the year 1932 left with me—I saw them, gathered into groups of fifty or a hundred men, attacking fields of potatoes. I saw them digging up the potatoes and throwing them into sacks while the farmer who owned the field watched them in despair and the local policeman looked on gloomily from the distance. I saw them staggering toward the lights of the city as night fell, with their sacks on their backs. What did it remind me of? Of the War, of the worst periods of starvation in 1917 and 1918, but even then people paid for the potatoes. . . .

I saw that the individual can know what is happening only by personal experience. I know what it is to be a tramp. I know what cold and hunger are. I know what it is to spend the night outdoors or behind the thin walls of a shack through which the wind whistles. I have slept in holes such as hunters hide in, in hayricks, under bridges, against the warm walls of boiler houses, under cattle shelters in pastures, on a heap of fir-tree boughs in the forest. But there are two things that I have only recently experienced—begging and spending the night in a municipal lodging house.

I entered the huge Berlin municipal lodging house in a northern quarter of the city. . . .

There was an entrance arched by a brick vaulting, and a watchman sat in a little wooden sentry box. His white coat made him look like a doctor. We stood waiting in the corridor. Heavy steam rose from the men's clothes. Some of them sat down on the floor, pulled off their shoes, and unwound the rags that were bound around their feet. More people were constantly pouring in the door, and we stood closely packed together. Then another door opened. The crowd pushed forward, and people began forcing their way almost eagerly through this door, for it was warm in there. Without knowing it I had already caught the rhythm of the municipal lodging house. It means waiting, waiting, standing around, and then suddenly jumping up. . . .

We now stand in a long hall, down the length of which runs a bar dividing the hall into a narrow and a wide space. All the light is on the narrow side. There under yellow lamps that hang from the ceiling on long wires sit men in white smocks. We arrange ourselves in long lines, each leading up to one of these men, and the mill begins to grind. . . .

As the line passes in single file the official does not look up at each new person to appear. He only looks at the paper that is handed to him. These papers are for the most part invalid cards or unemployment certificates. The very fact that the official does not look up robs the homeless applicant of self-respect, although he may look too beaten down to feel any. . . .

Now it is my turn and the questions and answers flow as smoothly as if I were an old hand. But finally I am asked, "Have you ever been here before?"

"No."

"No?" The question reverberates through the whole room. The clerk refuses to believe me and looks through his card catalogue. But no, my name is not there. The clerk thinks this strange, for he cannot have made a mistake, and the terrible thing that one notices in all these clerks is that they expect you to lie. They do not believe what you say. They do not regard you as a human being but as an infection, something foul that one keeps at a distance. He goes on. "How did you come here from Hamburg?"

"By truck."

"Where have you spent the last three nights?"

I lie coolly.

"Have you begged?"

I feel a warm blush spreading over my face. It is welling up from the bourgeois world that I have come from. "No."

A coarse peal of laughter rises from the line, and a loud, piercing voice grips me as if someone had seized me by the throat: "Never mind. The day will come, comrade, when there's nothing else to do." And the line breaks into laughter again, the bitterest laughter I have ever heard, the laughter of damnation and despair. . . .

Again the crowd pushes back in the kind of rhythm that is so typical of a lodging house, and we are all herded into the undressing room. . . . I cling to the man who spoke to me. He is a Saxon with a friendly manner and he has noticed that I am a stranger here. A certain sensitiveness, an almost perverse, spiritual alertness makes me like him very much.

Out of a big iron chest each of us takes a coat hanger that would serve admirably to hit somebody over the head with. As we undress the room becomes filled with the heavy breath of poverty. We are so close together that we brush against each other every time we move. Anyone who has been a soldier, anyone who has been to a public bath is perfectly accustomed to the look of naked bodies. But I have never seen anything quite so repulsive as all these hundreds of withered human frames. For in the homeless army the majority are men who have already been defeated in the struggle of life, the crippled, old, and sick. There is no repulsive disease of which traces are not to be seen here. There is no form of mutilation or degeneracy that is not represented, and the naked bodies of the old men are in a disgusting state of decline. . . .

It is superfluous to describe what follows. Towels are handed out . . . then nightgowns—long, sacklike affairs made of plain unbleached cotton but freshly washed. Then slippers. . . .

Distribution of spoons, distribution of enameled-ware bowls with the words "Property of the City of Berlin" written on their sides. Then the meal itself. A big kettle is carried in. Men with yellow smocks have brought it and men with yellow smocks ladle out the food. These men, too, are homeless and they have been expressly picked by the establishment and given free food and lodging and a little pocket money in exchange for their work about the house.

Where have I seen this kind of food distribution before? In a prison that I once helped to guard in the winter of 1919 during the German civil war. There was the same hunger then, the same trembling, anxious expectation of rations. Now the men are standing in a long row, dressed in their plain nightshirts that reach to the ground, and the noise of their shuffling feet is like the noise of big wild animals walking up and down the stone floor of their cages before feeding time. . . .

My next recollection is sitting at table in another room on a crowded bench that is like a seat in a fourth-class railway carriage. Hundreds of hungry mouths make an enormous noise eating their food. The men sit bent over their food like animals who feel that someone is going to take it away from them. They hold their bowl with their left arm part way around it, so that nobody can take it away, and they also protect it with their other elbow and with their head and mouth, while they move the spoon as fast as they can between their mouth and the bowl. . . .

We shuffle into the sleeping room, where each bed has a number painted in big letters on the wall over it. You must find the number that you have around your neck, and there is your bed, your home for one night. It stands in a row with fifty others and across the room there are fifty more in a row. . . .

Only a few people, very few, move around at all. The others lie awake and still, staring at their blankets, wrapped up in themselves but not sleeping. Only an almost soldierly sense of comradeship, an inner self-control engendered by the presence of so many people, prevents the despair that is written on all these faces from expressing itself. The few who are moving about do so with the tormenting consciousness of men who merely want to kill time. They do not believe in what they are doing.

Going to sleep means passing into the unconscious, eliminating the intelligence. And one can read deeply into a man's life by watching the way he goes to sleep. For we have not always slept in municipal lodgings. There are men among us who still move as if they were in a bourgeois bedchamber. . . .

The air is poisoned with the breath of men who have stuffed too much food into empty stomachs. There is also a sickening smell of lysol. It seems completely terrible to me. . . . Animals die, plants wither, but men always go on living.

READING QUESTIONS

1. To what other period in Germany's history did Hauser compare the depression? How might that have influenced his perception of the current situation?

2. In this account, what was the attitude of the people with power toward those without it, and how did that affect the job and relief seekers?

3. According to Hauser, what impact did the depression have on perceptions of social and economic class?

26-7 | German Communist Party Poster (1932)

Economic turmoil in Germany increased the appeal of radical political parties, as Germans from across the social spectrum grew convinced that mainstream parties were incapable of solving the country's problems. Seeking to take advantage of this favorable economic climate, Nazis and communists alike promised to address the fundamental needs of the German people. The slogan on this 1932 Communist Party election poster captures the desperate mood of the early 1930s: "If you want work, freedom, and food, vote red!" The document in the background is a worker's unemployment card.

Courtesy of CCI / The Art Archive at Art Resource, N.Y.

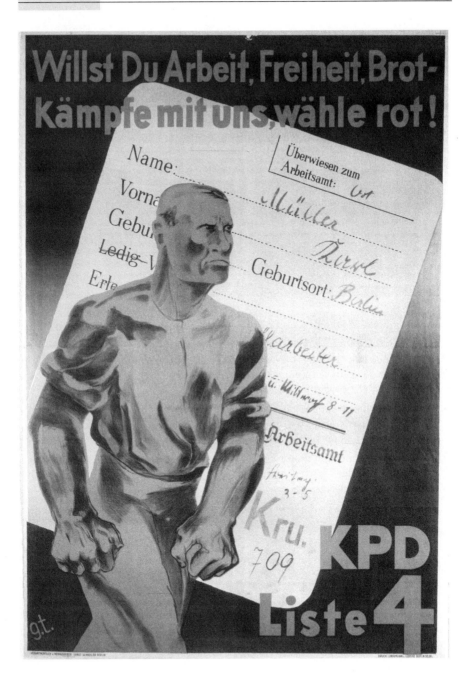

READING QUESTIONS

1. What does the poster's slogan suggest about the focus of political debate in early 1930s Germany?

2. At what groups in German society might this poster have been aimed? What clues does the poster provide about its intended target audience?

■ COMPARATIVE AND DISCUSSION QUESTIONS ■

1. What aspects of Keynes's critique of the Treaty of Versailles are confirmed by the cartoon depicting the impact of hyperinflation and the German Communist Party poster?

2. What policies might Keynes have suggested in response to the problems outlined in the report on the Special Areas?

3. If the nineteenth century's science was defined by certainty, in what ways do these documents undermine that certainty? Do any of these authors see this loss of certainty as a good thing? Why or why not?

4. How might the Social Darwinists, particularly Herbert Spencer (Document 22-7) respond to the report of the commissioner for the Special Areas? In what ways might the depression support or undercut Spencer's ideology?

5. Compare the report on the Special Areas with Hauser's narrative. How do their perspectives differ? What differences might that lead to in their approach to the problems of the depression?

27

Dictatorships and the Second World War

1919–1945

The period of anxiety and depression that followed the Great War led many to question whether democracy and capitalism could meet the challenges of modern society. In this context, radical political parties gained new prominence in every European nation. In Italy, Benito Mussolini and the Fascists seized power in the early 1920s, providing a model and an ideology for the right-wing dictatorships of the 1930s. In the Soviet Union after 1928, Joseph Stalin led his nation through a brutal and repressive "second revolution" that used the tools of totalitarianism to establish Stalin's absolute power and to force the rapid industrialization of the Soviet Union. In 1933, Germany's new chancellor and Nazi Party leader, Adolf Hitler, began plans to create a German Nazi empire based on the ideology of Aryan supremacy. Hampered by their own worries, other nations, including Great Britain, seemed powerless to stop Germany's remilitarization or to check Hitler's aggressive expansion. The invasion of Poland in 1939 by Germany and the Soviet Union demonstrated beyond the shadow of a doubt that negotiation with Hitler was futile, and France and Great Britain declared war, marking the start of World War II. Even as the Germans carried out their plans for the conquest and domination of Europe, they pursued another of Hitler's key objectives, the extermination of all European Jews.

27-1 | An American Admirer of Fascism

RICHARD WASHBURN CHILD, *Foreword to the Autobiography of Benito Mussolini* (1928)

Fascism's appeal was not limited to Germany, Italy, and Spain, or even to Europe. Observers around the world, including the United States, saw in fascism a way to counter the perceived threat of Communist influence and expansion and to put an end to the social and economic conflicts that plagued postwar Europe. Richard Washburn Child was the United States Ambassador to Italy from 1921 to 1924. An ardent supporter of Benito Mussolini, Child was among those who urged Mussolini to march on Rome in 1922 and to topple Italy's democratic government. After he returned to the United States, Child became editor of the *Saturday Evening Post*, a position he used to spread Mussolini's message and promote his policies. In this excerpt from Child's foreword to Mussolini's 1928 autobiography, which was published in serial form in the *Post*, Child expressed his unbridled admiration for "Il Duce."

Perhaps when approval or disapproval, theories and isms, pros and cons, are all put aside the only true measure of a man's greatness from a wholly unpartisan view-point may be found in the answer to this question:

"How deep and lasting has been the effect of a man upon the largest number of human beings—their hearts, their thoughts, their material welfare, their relation to the universe?"

In our time it may be shrewdly forecast that no man will exhibit dimensions of permanent greatness equal to those of Mussolini.

Admire him or not, approve his philosophies or not, concede the permanence of his success or not, consider him superman or not, as you may, he has put to a working test, on great and growing numbers of mankind, programmes, unknown before, in applied spirituality, in applied plans, in applied leadership, in applied doctrines, in the applied principle that contents are more important than labels on bottles. He has not only been able to secure and hold an almost universal following; he has built a new state upon a new concept of a state. He has not only been able to change the lives of human beings but he has changed their minds, their hearts, their spirits. He has not merely ruled a house; he has built a new house.

He has not merely put it on paper or into orations; he has laid the bricks.

It is one thing to administer a state. The one who does this well is called statesman. It is quite another thing to make a state. Mussolini has made a state. That is superstatesmanship.

I knew him before the world at large, outside of Italy, had ever heard of him; I knew him before and after the moment he leaped into the saddle and in the days when he, almost single-handed, was clearing away chaos' own junk pile from Italy. . . .

Benito Mussolini, *My Autobiography* (New York: Charles Scribner and Sons, 1928), pp. x–xi, xvi–xvii.

The first time I ever saw him he came to my residence sometime before the march on Rome and I asked him what would be his programme for Italy. His answer was immediate: "Work and discipline."

I remember I thought at that time that the phrase sounded a little evangelical, a phrase of exhortation. But a mere demagogue would never choose it. Wilson's slogans of Rights and Peace and Freedom[1] are much more popular and gain easier currency than sterner phrases. It is easier even for a sincere preacher, to offer soft nests to one's followers; it is more difficult to excite enthusiasm for stand-up doctrines. Any analysis and weighing of Mussolini's greatness must include recognition that he has made popular throughout a race of people, and perhaps for others, a standard of obligation of the individual not only exacting but one which in the end will be accepted voluntarily. Not only is it accepted voluntarily but with an almost spiritual ecstasy which has held up miraculously in Italy during years, when all the so-called liberals in the world were hovering over it like vultures, croaking that if it were not dead it was about to die.

It is difficult to lead men at all. It is still more difficult to lead them away from self-indulgence. It is still more difficult to lead them so that a new generation, so that youth itself, appears as if born with a new spirit, a new virility bred in the bones. It is difficult to govern a state and difficult to deal cleanly and strongly with a static programme applied to a static world; but it is more difficult to build a new state and deal cleanly and strongly with a dynamic programme applied to a dynamic world.

This man, who looks up at me with that peculiar nodding of his head and raising of the eyebrows, has done it. There are few in the world's history who have. I had considered the phrase "Work and discipline" as a worthy slogan, as a good label for an empty bottle. Within six years this man, with a professional opposition which first barked like Pomeranians at his heels and then ran away to bark abroad, has made the label good, has filled the bottle, has turned concept into reality.

READING QUESTIONS

1. What qualities did Child admire in Mussolini?

2. How did Child characterize the essence of Mussolini's fascist program? In Child's view, how did the fascist state differ from the liberal state?

3. How might an American audience have responded to Child's foreword? What groups in American society might have found Mussolini, as described by Child, most appealing?

---

[1]**Wilson's slogans of Rights and Peace and Freedom**: Child, a Republican, was a fierce opponent of President Woodrow Wilson and the program he put forward for a new international order at the end of World War I.

27-2 | A Culture of Paranoia and Coercion
VLADIMIR TCHERNAVIN, *I Speak for the Silent* (1930)

To maintain his power and Communist rule in the Soviet Union, Joseph Stalin instituted a massive security apparatus that pervaded most aspects of Soviet life. Vladimir Tchernavin was a scientist in the northwestern port city of Murmansk, working to transform the Soviet Union from an agrarian to an industrial state. Such an ambitious project was bound to have its share of failures, but in the climate of paranoia that pervaded Stalinist society, such failures were attributed to sabotage, and sabotage was brutally punished.

It was my second day in prison—my second cross-examination. I was called before the tea ration was given out and had only time to eat an apple.

"How do you do?" the examining officer asked, scanning me attentively to see if I showed signs of a sleepless night.

"All right."

"It isn't so good in your cell. You are in 22?"

"A cell like any other."

"Well, did you do any thinking? Are you going to tell the truth today?"

"Yesterday I told only the truth."

He laughed. "What will it be today—not the truth?"

Then he returned to the subject of the cell.

"I tried to choose a better cell for you, but we are so crowded. I hope we will come to an understanding and that I will not be forced to change the regime I have ordered for you. The third category is the mildest: exercise in the yard, permission to receive food parcels from outside, a newspaper and books. The first two categories are much stricter. Remember, however, that it depends entirely on me; any minute you may be deprived of everything and transferred to solitary confinement. Or rather, this depends not on me but on your own behavior, your sincerity. The more frank your testimony, the better will be the conditions of your imprisonment. . . ."

He spoke slowly, looking me straight in the eye, emphasizing his words with evident pleasure and relish, watching for their effect.

"Did you know Scherbakoff? He was a strong man, but I broke him and forced him to confess."

With great difficulty I controlled myself before replying.

"I don't doubt for a minute that you use torture, and if you believe that this assists in discovering the truth and speeding up the investigation, and since Soviet laws permit its use, I would suggest that you don't give up medieval methods: a little fire is a wonderful measure. Try it! I am not afraid of you. Even with that you can't get anything out of me."

"Well, we will see about that later. Now let's get down to business. Let's talk

From Vladimir Tchernavin, *I Speak for the Silent* (Newton Centre, Mass.: Charles T. Branford, 1935), pp. 116–120.

about your acquaintances. Did you know V. K. Tolstoy, the wrecker, executed in connection with the case of the '48'?"[1]

"Yes, I knew him. How could I not know him when he was the director of the fishing industry in the north?" I replied in frank astonishment. "We both worked in it for more than twenty years."

"And did you (know) him well?"

"Very well."

"How long did you know him?"

"From childhood."

His manner changed completely; he hurriedly picked up a statement sheet and placed it in front of me. "Write down your confession."

"What confession?"

"That you knew Tolstoy, that you were in friendly relation with him from such and such a time. I see that we will come to an understanding with you; your frankness will be appreciated. Write."

He evidently was in a hurry, did not quite know what he was saying, afraid that I might reverse my statements.

I took the sheet and wrote down what I had said.

"Excellent. Let's continue."

Then followed a barrage of questions about Tolstoy, about Scherbakoff and other people that I had known. He did not find me quite so tractable and we launched into a battle of wits that kept up hour after hour. He questioned me with insistence and in great detail, trying without success to make me give dates.

"You'll not succeed in outwitting me," he snapped sharply. "I advise you not to try. I am going home to dinner now and you will stay here till evening. This examination will continue—not for a day or two, but for months and, if necessary, for years. Your strength is not equal to mine. I will force you to tell us what we need."

After threatening me still further he handed me some sheets of paper.

"You are going to state in writing your opinion regarding the building of a fertilization factory in Murmansk, its equipment and work in the future. I'll soon be back; when I return, your comments on these questions must be completed."

He put on his overcoat and left. His assistant took his place, and I busied myself with my writing. It was three or four hours before he returned, already evening.

Although I had eaten almost nothing for three days, I was still in good fighting form. He questioned me about the buying of a ship from abroad, trying to make me say that here was "wrecking," because the price had been exorbitant and the ship itself had proved unsatisfactory. It was most confusing and his questions far-fetched. We talked and we argued, but I would not give the answers he wanted.

He began on another tack. . . .

---

[1] **the case of the '48'**: Tchernavin refers to the accusation and subsequent execution of forty-eight prominent Russian scientists accused of sabotaging the food supply in 1930.

"All right," he said. "And what is your attitude regarding the subject of the fish supply in the Sea of Barents in connection with the construction of trawlers as provided for by the Five-Year Plan?"

Now he had broached a subject with which I could have a direct connection. The evening was already changing into night, but I was still sitting in the same chair. I was becoming unconscious of time: was it my second day in prison or my tenth? In spite of the depressing weariness, mental and physical, which was taking hold of me, I told him that I thought the fresh fish supply should be minutely and thoroughly investigated. I tried to make him see the hazards of the fishing industry in Murmansk and the enormous equipment that would be necessary to meet the proposals of the Five-Year Plan.

"And thus you confess that you doubted the practicability of the Five-Year Plan?" he said with a smile of smug satisfaction.

What could one say? I believed, as did everybody, that the plan was absurd, that it could not be fulfilled. For exactly such statements—no, for only a suspicion of having such thoughts—forty-eight men had been shot.

READING QUESTIONS

1. From the perspective of the state, what purposes would be served by arresting and torturing Vladimir Tchernavin?

2. What incentives could Tchernavin have for resisting, and what might convince him to comply with the interrogator?

3. Based on your reading of this account, what relationship did truth and guilt have in the Stalinist justice system?

SOURCES IN CONVERSATION

Propaganda and the Totalitarian State

Totalitarian governments may have dismissed liberal democracy as a failed system of government whose time had passed, but that did not mean that totalitarian leaders could ignore the power of public opinion, or that they did not need to communicate with their people. If such leaders were to remake their societies, defeat their enemies, and "change history," they would need the cooperation of the masses, and one of the most important tools for acquiring that cooperation was propaganda. In the first document included below, Adolf Hitler explained the essential elements of effective propaganda. In the second, two Soviet posters from the early days of World War II illustrate the way Soviet propagandists adjusted their messages to mesh with the values and beliefs of their intended audience.

27-3 | ADOLF HITLER, *Mein Kampf: The Art of Propaganda* (1924)

While in prison for a failed 1923 coup attempt, Hitler dictated his autobiography, *Mein Kampf* (*My Struggle*), detailing his views on politics and society. Based on his interpretation of the end of the Great War, Hitler argued that Germany had been defeated not by Allied armies, but by the failure of German propaganda to effectively counter Allied propaganda, something he proposed to change when he came to power. At the time of its publication, *Mein Kampf* was not popular, but it proved prophetic: one of Hitler's first acts as chancellor was to establish the Ministry for Enlightenment and Propaganda in March 1933.

The psyche of the great masses is not receptive to anything that is halfhearted and weak. . . .

To whom should propaganda be addressed? To the scientifically trained intelligentsia or to the less educated masses?

It must be addressed always and exclusively to the masses. . . .

All propaganda must be popular and its intellectual level must be adjusted to the most limited intelligence among those it is addressed to. Consequently, the greater the mass it is intended to reach, the lower its purely intellectual level will have to be. . . .

The art of propaganda lies in understanding the emotional ideas of the great masses and finding, through a psychologically correct form, the way to the attention and thence to the heart of the broad masses. The fact that our bright boys do not understand this merely shows how mentally lazy and conceited they are.

Once we understand how necessary it is for propaganda to be adjusted to the broad mass, the following rule results:

It is a mistake to make propaganda many-sided, like scientific instruction, for instance. The receptivity of the great masses is very limited, their intelligence is small, but their power of forgetting is enormous. In consequence of these facts, all effective propaganda must be limited to a very few points and must harp on these in slogans until the last member of the public understands what you want him to understand by your slogan. As soon as you sacrifice this slogan and try to be many-sided, the effect will piddle away, for the crowd can neither digest nor retain the material offered. In this way, the result is weakened and in the end entirely cancelled out. . . .

The broad mass of a nation does not consist of diplomats, or even professors of political law, or even individuals capable of forming a rational opinion; it consists of plain mortals, wavering and inclined to doubt and uncertainty. As soon as our own propaganda admits so much as a glimmer of right on the other side, the foundation for doubt in our own right has been laid. . . .

From Adolf Hitler, *Mein Kampf,* trans. Ralph Mannheim (Boston: Houghton Mifflin, 1943), pp. 42, 179–185.

The people in their overwhelming majority are so feminine by nature and attitude that sober reasoning determines their thoughts and actions far less than emotion and feeling. . . . But the most brilliant propagandist technique will yield no success unless one fundamental principle is borne in mind constantly and with unflagging attention. It must confine itself to a few points and repeat them over and over. Here, as so often in this world, persistence is the first and most important requirement for success. . . .

The purpose of propaganda is not to provide interesting distraction for blasé young gentlemen, but to convince, and what I mean is to convince the masses. But the masses are slow-moving, and they always require a certain time before they are ready even to notice a thing, and only after the simplest ideas are repeated thousands of times will the masses finally remember them. . . .

[During World War I] at first the claims of the [enemy] propaganda were so impudent that people thought it insane; later, it got on people's nerves; and in the end, it was believed.

READING QUESTIONS

1. What are Hitler's main suggestions for the propagandist who wants to be successful?

2. In Hitler's view, what role did rational, factual argument play in propaganda? What about emotions and feelings?

3. What does Hitler's conception of who matters in society reveal about his attitudes toward both the powerful and the powerless members of his society?

27-4 | *Soviet Propaganda Posters* (1941 and 1945)

In the initial days of the German invasion of 1941, Soviet propaganda was of a piece with the messages of the 1920s and 1930s, emphasizing revolutionary and Leninist themes. Later efforts, however, reveal a dramatic shift in tactics. Instead of presenting the clash between the Soviet Union and Germany in ideological terms, Soviet propaganda focused on the essential emotional response of Soviet citizens to invasion, emphasizing nationalism and the defense of the motherland, and reviving Great Russian historical figures, even some from the tsarist era, as examples of heroic resistance to would-be conquerors. The poster featuring a massed Soviet army marching to victory under the banner of Lenin epitomizes the early approach to wartime propaganda. The poster below it, linking the fates of Hitler and Napoleon, illustrates the later approach.

[*top*] akg-images/RIA Novosti. Attributed to A. P. Voloshin. [*bottom*] Snark Archives © Photo 12/The Image Works.

READING QUESTIONS

1. What are the different ways in which Soviet soldiers are portrayed in the two images? How might this reflect a changing appreciation of the nature of the war?

2. How could the use of aristocratic generals from the nineteenth century be reconciled with the official Soviet emphasis on breaking with that tradition?

3. Why might Soviet citizens have found the later poster more inspiring than the earlier one?

27-5 | Freedom's Last Line of Defense

WINSTON CHURCHILL, *Speech Before the House of Commons* (June 18, 1940)

Once World War II began in 1939, much of central and western Europe quickly fell to the German *blitzkrieg* strategy. After sending troops to aid the French against the Germans in 1940, the British army lost most of its tanks, trucks, and other heavy equipment while evacuating from Dunkirk following a decisive Nazi victory. Germany held the deep-water ports along the English Channel crucial for an invasion, and had the most feared air force in Europe. Facing these grim prospects, Churchill addressed the House of Commons to rally a nation unenthusiastic about another war.

The military events which have happened during the past fortnight have not come to me with any sense of surprise. Indeed, I indicated a fortnight ago as clearly as I could to the House that the worst possibilities were open, and I made it perfectly clear then that whatever happened in France would make no difference to the resolve of Britain and the British Empire to fight on, "if necessary for years, if necessary alone." During the last few days we have successfully brought off the great majority of the troops we had on the lines of communication in France—a very large number, scores of thousands—and seven-eighths of the troops we have sent to France since the beginning of the war, that is to say, about 350,000 out of 400,000 men, are safely back in this country. Others are still fighting with the French, and fighting with considerable success in their local encounters with the enemy. We have also brought back a great mass of stores, rifles, and munitions of all kinds which had been accumulated in France during the last nine months.

From Winston Churchill, "June 18, 1940, Speech Before House of Commons," in *The Past Speaks*, 2d ed., ed. Walter Arnstein (Lexington, Mass.: D. C. Heath, 1993), 2:376–378.

We have, therefore, in this island to-day a very large and powerful military force. . . . This brings me, naturally, to the great question of invasion from the air and of the impending struggle between the British and German air forces. It seems quite clear that no invasion on a scale beyond the capacity of our land forces to crush speedily is likely to take place from the air until our air force has been definitely overpowered. In the meantime, there may be raids by parachute troops and attempted descents of airborne soldiers. We should be able to give those gentry a warm reception both in the air and if they reach the ground in any condition to continue the dispute. But the great question is, can we break Hitler's air weapon? Now, of course, it is a very great pity that we have not got an air force at least equal to that of the most powerful enemy within striking distance of these shores. But we have a very powerful air force which has proved itself far superior in quality, both in men and in many types of machine, to what we have met so far in the numerous fierce air battles which have been fought. In France, where we were at a considerable disadvantage and lost many machines on the ground, we were accustomed to inflict losses of as much as two to two and a half to one. In the fighting over Dunkirk, which was a sort of no man's land, we undoubtedly beat the German air force, and this gave us the mastery locally in the air, and we inflicted losses of three or four to one. . . .

There remains the danger of bombing attacks, which will certainly be made very soon upon us by the bomber forces of the enemy. It is true that the German bomber force is superior in numbers to ours, but we have a very large bomber force also which we shall use to strike at military targets in Germany without intermission. I do not at all underrate the severity of the ordeal which lies before us, but I believe our countrymen will show themselves capable of standing up to it. . . .

What General Weygand[1] called the "Battle of France" is over. I expect that the battle of Britain is about to begin. Upon this battle depends the survival of Christian civilization. Upon it depends our own British life and the long continuity of our institutions and our empire. The whole fury and might of the enemy must very soon be turned on us. Hitler knows that he will have to break us in this island or lose the war. If we can stand up to him all Europe may be free, and the life of the world may move forward into broad, sunlit uplands, but if we fail then the whole world, including the United States, and all that we have known and cared for, will sink into the abyss of a new dark age made more sinister, and perhaps more prolonged, by the lights of a perverted science. Let us therefore brace ourselves to our duty and so bear ourselves that if the British Commonwealth and Empire lasts for a thousand years men will still say, "This was their finest hour."

---

[1]**General Weygand**: General Maxime Weygand took command of all French forces on May 17, 1940, and held that post until the French surrender, after which he collaborated with the German occupation.

READING QUESTIONS

1. What reasons would Churchill have for mentioning the United States specifically in the last paragraph? For what audiences might this speech have been intended?

2. What could this speech reveal about Churchill's attitude toward the British citizenry and the concept of democratic rule in general?

3. How did Churchill characterize the situation facing the British people? Do you find his assessment convincing? Why or why not?

27-6 | Legislating Racial Purity

The Nuremberg Laws: The Centerpiece of Nazi Racial Legislation (1935)

Anti-Semitism was never a mere aspect of Hitler's political ideology; it was central to his vision of a new Germany. In Hitler's view, the achievement of Germany's national potential, its historical destiny, depended on the exclusion of the Jews from German life. The Jews were responsible for all of Germany's past miseries and, if left to their own devices, would do everything in their power to sabotage and undermine the construction of the glorious National Socialist future. The 1935 Nuremburg Laws, excerpted here, were the first formal steps toward Hitler's goal of a "Jew-free" Germany.

Article 5

1. A Jew is anyone who descended from at least three grandparents who were racially full Jews. Article 2, par. 2, second sentence will apply.

2. A Jew is also one who descended from two full Jewish parents, if: (a) he belonged to the Jewish religious community at the time this law was issued, or who joined the community later; (b) he was married to a Jewish person, at the time the law was issued, or married one subsequently; (c) he is the offspring from a marriage with a Jew, in the sense of Section 1, which was contracted after the Law for the Protection of German Blood and German Honor became effective. . . . (d) he is the offspring of an extramarital relationship, with a Jew, according to Section 1, and will be born out of wedlock after July 31, 1936. . . .

From U.S. Chief of Counsel for the Prosecution of Axis Criminality, *Nazi Conspiracy and Aggression* (Washington, D.C.: U.S. Government Printing Office, 1946), vol. 4, doc. no. 1417-PS, pp. 8–10; vol. 4, doc. no. 2000-PS, pp. 636–638.

Law for the Protection of German Blood and German Honor of 15 September 1935

Thoroughly convinced by the knowledge that the purity of German blood is essential for the further existence of the German people and animated by the inflexible will to safe-guard the German nation for the entire future, the Reichstag[1] has resolved upon the following law unanimously, which is promulgated herewith:

Section 1

1. Marriages between Jews and nationals of German or kindred blood are forbidden. Marriages concluded in defiance of this law are void, even if, for the purpose of evading this law, they are concluded abroad. . . .

Section 2

Relation[s] outside marriage between Jews and nationals of German or kindred blood are forbidden.

Section 3

Jews will not be permitted to employ female nationals of German or kindred blood in their household.

Section 4

1. Jews are forbidden to hoist the Reich and national flag and to present the colors of the Reich. . . .

Section 5

1. A person who acts contrary to the prohibition of section 1 will be punished with hard labor.
2. A person who acts contrary to the prohibition of section 2 will be punished with imprisonment or with hard labor.
3. A person who acts contrary to the provisions of sections 3 or 4 will be punished with imprisonment up to a year and with a fine or with one of these penalties.

---

[1]**Reichstag**: German legislative assembly; a holdover from Bismarck's Second Empire (1871–1919) that had little real power after it granted Hitler "temporary" dictatorial powers in March 1933.

READING QUESTIONS

1. According to the law, what made someone a Jew? Why is it important to the Nazis to establish a legal definition of Jewish status?

2. What do the laws tell you about the importance of biological "purity" in Nazi ideology?

3. Why might Jews have been forbidden to raise the national and Reich flags? What does this provision of the law suggest about the Nazi vision of the relationship of German Jews to the German nation as a whole?

27-7 | The First Steps Toward a "Final Solution"

ALFRED ROSENBERG, *The Jewish Question as a World Problem* (1941)

German military conquests in the early years of World War II allowed the Nazis to expand the scope of their anti-Jewish policies. What began as an effort to create a "Jew-free" Germany became a global crusade to resolve, once and for all, the "Jewish question." The Nazi propagandist and party official Alfred Rosenberg gave this speech on the "world Jewish problem" in a radio address in March of 1941. A few months later, he was appointed Reich Minister for the Occupied Eastern Territories. In the speech, Rosenberg rejected the idea of a Jewish state, outlined Germany's plans for Europe's Jews, and argued that world peace would be possible only when these plans had been brought to fruition.

The war which is being waged today by the German armed forces under the highest command of Adolf Hitler, is therefore a war of an immense reform. It does not only overcome the world of ideas of the French revolution, but it also exterminates directly all those racially infecting germs of Jewry and its bastards, which now since over a hundred years could develop without check among the European nations. The Jew question which for 2000 years was a problem for the European nations which was not solved, will now find its solution through the national socialistic revolution for Germany and whole Europe.

And if one asks, in which form, then we have to say the following to this: During these decades a lot has been talked about a Jewish state as solution, and Zionism appears to some harmless people perhaps even today as an honest attempt to contribute on the part of the Jews also something toward the solution of the Jewish question.

In reality there never was nor will there ever be a Jewish State.

Contrary to the other nations on this globe, Judaism is no vertical organization which comprises all professions, but has been always a horizontal class

Office of the U.S. Chief of Counsel for Prosecution of Axis Criminality, *Nazi Conspiracy and Aggression*, Vol. V (Washington, D.C.: U.S. Government Printing Office, 1946), pp. 554–557 [Doc. 2889-PS].

among the different nations, that class which carried on material and spiritual intermediate trade. Secondly, the space being considered in Palestine is in no way suitable for any Jewish state. It is too small to absorb what was formerly 10 and is now 15 million Jews; in other words, therefore impractical for solving the Jewish question. The purpose of Zionism, in reality, was not to solve the Jewish question in the sense of the coordination of the whole Jewish people, but lay in an entirely different direction.

It was intended to build in Palestine a purely Jewish center, a real legitimate Jewish state in order to be able, at first, to be represented at all diplomatic conferences with full rights as national Jew.

Secondly it was intended to make Palestine into a huge, economic staging area against the entire Near East. Thirdly, this Jewish state should have been an asylum for all those Jewish adventurers in the world who were evicted from the countries in which they acted. And, finally, nobody was even thinking of limiting even in the slightest, the so-called state civil rights of the Jews in Germany, England, America, and also France. The Jews therefore, would have maintained the rights of the Germans, Englishmen, Frenchmen etc., and the spaceless Jewish world state would have come constantly closer toward its realization, that is, an all-Jewish center without any interference of non-Jews and the Jewish high finance at the state rudder in all other countries of the world.

This dream is now finished. Now, just the reverse, we have to think of how and where to put the Jews. This can, as mentioned, not be done in a Jewish state, but only in a way which I shall call the Jewish reservation.

It is to be hoped that future statesmen will get together in order to gradually institute a settlement of Jews who, under experienced police supervision, now should do such useful work as they wanted to see done until now by non-Jews.

From an almost unlimited Jewish rule in all European countries to such a radical reverse, to an evacuation of this same Jewish race after 2,000 years of parasitism on the European continent, then only can one conceive through this an idea what an enormous philosophical and political revolution is in the making in Europe today.

Today the Jewish question is somewhat clear before our eyes. It is the problem of a simple national purity. It means the necessity for defense of inherent national tradition for all nations which still value culture and future. It is still a problem of economy for all those who cannot solve the social questions under the Jewish financial dictatorship. It is a political problem of power, because in many states the will has not yet been found to break this financial dictatorship of the Jewry. And, lastly, it is a historically ideological problem, given to the Europeans since the days when the first Jews immigrated to Rome. The totality of this as national socialist, have but one clear answer for all these questions:

For Germany the Jewish Question is only then solved, when the Last Jew has left the Greater German space.

Since Germany with its blood and its nationalism has now broken for always this Jewish dictatorship for all Europe, and has seen to it that Europe as a whole will become free from the Jewish parasitism once more, we may, I believe, also say for all Europeans: For Europe the Jewish question is only then solved, when the last Jew has left the European continent.

At that, it does not matter whether such a program can be realized in five, ten or twenty years. The transportation facilities in our time, if all nations join, would be strong enough to institute and to execute such a resettlement to a great extent. But the problem must and will one day be solved as we have visualized it from the first day of our fight—then accused utopists—and now proclaim it as strict realistic politicians. All nations are interested in the solution of this question, and we must declare here with all passion:

In this cleaning-up even Mr. Roosevelt with his Baruchs and his trophy film Jews will not be able to hamper us, but wholly to the contrary, just this proclamation that the Jewish parasitical spirit shall represent today the freedom of the world, will especially awaken all resistance of the German character, and the strongest military instrument which history has seen, the German Armed forces of Adolf Hitler, will take care of it that this last furious attempt to let the white race once more march against Europe for the benefit of the Jewish financial dominion, will find an end for all times.

We are of the opinion that this great war constitutes also a cleansing biological world revolution and that also those nations which are still opposed to us, will recognize at the end of the war, that Germany's business is today the business of the whole European continent, the business of the whole Jewish race, but also the business of all other cultured races on this globe who fight for a safe national cultural and state life. Thus we hope that one day, in a reasonable distribution of the great living spaces of this globe the nations will find that peace, that work and that prosperity which for decades have been harrassed by never-tiring parasitical activity. Thus, we consider today the Jewish question as one of the most important problems among the total politics of Europe, as a problem which must be solved and will be solved, and we hope, yes, we know already today, that all nations of Europe will march behind this cleansing at the end.

READING QUESTIONS

1. Why did Rosenberg reject the idea of a Jewish state in Palestine?

2. What solution did Rosenberg put forward for the "Jewish question"? Does it seem practical to you? Why or why not?

3. How did Rosenberg justify the expulsion of Europe's Jews and their confinement in a Jewish "reservation"?

4. In what ways did Rosenberg's speech foreshadow the Nazis eventual efforts to exterminate Europe's Jews? In your opinion, were schemes such as the one Rosenberg outlined ever truly entertained, or did Nazi leaders have extermination in mind from the beginning?

■ COMPARATIVE AND DISCUSSION QUESTIONS ■

1. What similarities can you see between German and Soviet attitudes toward their citizens, and how might this contrast with the British attitude expressed by Churchill?

2. Apply Hitler's definition of effective propaganda to Churchill's speech. Where does it seem Churchill agrees with Hitler's principles, and where does it seem he departs from them?

3. What connections can you make between the Nuremburg Laws and Rosenberg's speech on the "Jewish question"? In what ways was Rosenberg's plan a logical extension of the laws?

4. How might Child have responded to Churchill's speech? How might he have characterized the coming war?

28

Cold War Conflict and Consensus

1945–1965

Even before the war ended, tensions had emerged between the Allies, as the United States, the Soviet Union, and Great Britain each looked ahead to a postwar world that would be very different from the world of the 1920s and 1930s. Within five years, the Soviet Union and the United States had organized competing alliances, each aimed at thwarting the other's perceived efforts at expansion and global domination. The development of nuclear weapons brought a terrifying new dimension to Cold War conflict. Ironically, despite the ever-present threat of nuclear war between 1949 and 1991, these years were among the most peaceful of Europe's long history. American aid gave the Western European economies the means to recover, and the means to develop a consumer-oriented society, where the good life was measured in access to modern conveniences for everyday life. Meanwhile, those excluded in Western society, from women to the colonized, began to press, sometimes violently, for cultural and economic equality.

28-1 | The United States Rebuilds Europe

GEORGE C. MARSHAL, *An American Plan to Rebuild a Shattered Europe* (June 5, 1947)

At the conclusion of World War II, American policymakers were determined to avoid the mistake of withdrawing into neutrality as they had in 1919. George Marshall was the highest-ranking American officer in World War II and served as secretary of state for the Truman administration. When communist parties began to win elections in France and Italy, Marshall used a speech to Harvard University's graduating class to propose spending billions to rebuild

---

"The Address of Secretary Marshall at Harvard," *The New York Times*, June 6, 1947.

Europe, an initiative he believed would curtail the appeal of communist parties, reduce tensions within European societies, and advance American interests by creating strong allies and viable trade partners.

I need not tell you, gentlemen, that the world situation is very serious. That must be apparent to all intelligent people. I think one difficulty is that the problem is one of such enormous complexity that the very mass of facts presented to the public by press and radio make it exceedingly difficult for the man in the street to reach a clear appraisement of the situation. Furthermore, the people of this country are distant from the troubled areas of the earth and it is hard for them to comprehend the plight and consequent reactions of the long-suffering peoples, and the effect of those reactions on their governments in connection with our efforts to promote peace in the world.

In considering the requirements for the rehabilitation of Europe the physical loss of life, the visible destruction of cities, factories, mines, and railroads was correctly estimated, but it has become obvious during recent months that this visible destruction was probably less serious than the dislocation of the entire fabric of European economy. For the past ten years conditions have been highly abnormal.

The feverish preparation for war and the more feverish maintenance of the war effort engulfed all aspects of national economies. Machinery has fallen into disrepair or is entirely obsolete. Under the arbitrary and destructive Nazi rule, virtually every possible enterprise was geared into the German war machine. Long-standing commercial ties, private institutions, banks, insurance companies, and shipping companies disappeared, through loss of capital, absorption through nationalization, or by simple destruction.

In many countries, confidence in the local currency has been severely shaken. The breakdown of the business structure of Europe during the war was complete. Recovery has been seriously retarded by the fact that two years after the close of hostilities a peace settlement with Germany and Austria has not been agreed upon. But even given a more prompt solution of these difficult problems, the rehabilitation of the economic structure of Europe quite evidently will require a much longer time and greater effort than had been foreseen.

There is a phase of this matter which is both interesting and serious. The farmer has always produced the foodstuffs to exchange with the city dweller for the other necessities of life. This division of labor is the basis of modern civilization. At the present time it is threatened with breakdown. The town and city industries are not producing adequate goods to exchange with the food-producing farmer. Raw materials and fuel are in short supply. Machinery is lacking or worn out.

The farmer or the peasant cannot find the goods for sale which he desires to purchase. So the sale of his farm produce for money which he cannot use seems to him an unprofitable transaction. He, therefore, has withdrawn many fields from crop cultivation and is using them for grazing. He feeds more grain to stock and finds for himself and his family an ample supply of food, however short he may be on clothing and the other ordinary gadgets of civilization. Meanwhile, people in the cities are short of food and fuel. So the governments are forced to use their foreign money and credits to procure these necessities abroad. This process exhausts funds which are urgently needed for reconstruction. Thus a very serious situation is rapidly developing which bodes no good for the world. The modern system of the division of labor upon which the exchange of products is based is in danger of breaking down.

The truth of the matter is that Europe's requirements for the next three or four years of foreign food and other essential products—principally from America—are so much greater than her present ability to pay that she must have substantial additional help, or face economic, social, and political deterioration of a very grave character.

The remedy lies in breaking the vicious circle and restoring the confidence of the European people in the economic future of their own countries and of Europe as a whole. The manufacturer and the farmer throughout wide areas must be able and willing to exchange their products for currencies, the continuing value of which is not open to question.

Aside from the demoralizing effect on the world at large and the possibilities of disturbances arising as a result of the desperation of the people concerned, the consequences to the economy of the United States should be apparent to all. It is logical that the United States should do whatever it is able to do to assist in the return of normal economic health in the world, without which there can be no political stability and no assured peace.

Our policy is directed not against any country or doctrine but against hunger, poverty, desperation, and chaos. Its purpose should be the revival of a working economy in the world so as to permit the emergence of political and social conditions in which free institutions can exist. Such assistance, I am convinced, must not be on a piecemeal basis as various crises develop. Any assistance that this Government may render in the future should provide a cure rather than a mere palliative.

Any government that is willing to assist in the task of recovery will find full cooperation, I am sure, on the part of the United States Government. Any government which maneuvers to block the recovery of other countries cannot expect help from us. Furthermore, governments, political parties, or groups which seek to perpetuate human misery in order to profit therefrom politically or otherwise will encounter the opposition of the United States.

It is already evident that, before the United States Government can proceed much further in its efforts to alleviate the situation and help start the European world on its way to recovery, there must be some agreement among the countries of Europe as to the requirements of the situation and the part those countries themselves will take in order to give proper effect to whatever action might be undertaken by this Government. It would be neither fitting nor efficacious for this Government to undertake to draw up unilaterally a program designed to place Europe on its feet economically. This is the business of the Europeans. The initiative, I think, must come from Europe. The role of this country should consist of friendly aid in the drafting of a European program and of later support of such a program so far as it may be practical for us to do so. The program should be a joint one, agreed to by a number of, if not all, European nations.

An essential part of any successful action on the part of the United States is an understanding on the part of the people of America of the character of the problem and the remedies to be applied. Political passion and prejudice should have no part. With foresight, and a willingness on the part of our people to face up to the vast responsibility which history has clearly placed upon our country, the difficulties I have outlined can and will be overcome.

READING QUESTIONS

1. According to Marshall, what problems did Europe face after World War II? What solutions does he propose?

2. What light does the speech shed on the changed place of both Europe and the United States in the global economy?

3. In what ways does Marshall's speech hint at the growing tensions between the United States and the Soviet Union?

4. How did the Marshall Plan serve American national interests? What might explain the fact that the Soviets saw the plan as a hostile action?

28-2 | The Stalinist Gulag

ALEXANDER SOLZHENITSYN, *One Day in the Life of Ivan Denisovich* (1962)

After Joseph Stalin died in 1953, the Soviet Union backed away from many of his policies. The next Soviet leader, Nikita Khrushchev (r. 1953–1964), denounced the gulag—the terror and labor camps Stalin had created—and considerably relaxed censorship. In this new period of increased critical freedom, Alexander Solzhenitsyn was permitted to publish an account of his life in the camps, to which he had been sentenced in 1945 for criticizing Stalin's conduct of the war. His continued criticism of the Soviet regime led to his deportation to the West in 1974. Once in exile, Solzhenitsyn condemned both the repression of the Soviets and the materialism of the capitalist world.

At five o'clock that morning reveille was sounded, as usual, by the blows of a hammer on a length of rail hanging up near the staff quarters. The intermittent sounds barely penetrated the windowpanes on which the frost lay two fingers thick, and they ended almost as soon as they'd begun. It was cold outside, and campguard was reluctant to go on beating out the reveille for long.

From Alexander Solzhenitsyn, *One Day in the Life of Ivan Denisovich*, trans. Ralph Parker (New York: E. P. Dutton & Co., 1963), pp. 17–25.

The clanging ceased, but everything outside still looked like the middle of the night when Ivan Denisovich Shukhov got up to go to the bucket. It was pitch dark except for the yellow light cast on the window by three lamps—two in the outer zone, one inside the camp itself.

And no one came to unbolt the barracks door; there was no sound of the barrack orderlies pushing a pole into place to lift the barrel of excrement and carry it out.

Shukhov never overslept reveille. He always got up at once, for the next ninety minutes, until they assembled for work, belonged to him, not to the authorities, and any old-timer could always earn a bit—by sewing a pair of mittens for someone out of his old sleeve lining; or bringing some rich loafer in the squad his dry valenki[1]—right up to his bunk, so that he wouldn't have to stumble barefoot round the heap of boots looking for his own pair; or going the rounds to the warehouses, offering to be of service, sweeping up this or fetching that; or going to the mess hall to collect bowls from the tables and bring them stacked to the dishwashers—you're sure to be given something to eat there, though there were plenty of others at that game, more than plenty—and, what's worse, if you found a bowl with something left in it you could hardly resist licking it out. But Shukhov had never forgotten the words of his first squad leader, Kuziomin—a hard-bitten prisoner who had already been in for twelve years by 1943—who told the newcomers, just in from the front, as they sat beside a fire in a desolate cutting in the forest:

"Here, men, we live by the law of the taiga.[2] But even here people manage to live. The ones that don't make it are those who lick other men's leftovers, those who count on the doctors to pull them through, and those that squeal on their buddies."

As for squealers, he was wrong there. Those people were sure to get through the camp alright. Only, they were saving their own skin at the expense of other people's blood.

Shukhov always arose at reveille. But this day he didn't. He had felt strange the evening before, feverish, with pains all over his body. He hadn't been able to get warm all through the night. Even in his sleep he had felt at one moment that he was getting seriously ill, at another that he was getting better. He had wished morning would never come.

But morning came as usual.

Anyway, where would you get warm in a place like this, with the windows iced over and the white cobwebs of frost all along the huge barracks where the walls joined the ceiling!

He didn't get up. He lay there in his bunk on the top tier, his head buried in a blanket and a coat, both feet stuffed into one tucked-up sleeve of his wadded jacket.

---

[1]**valenki:** Knee-high felt boots worn in winter.
[2]**taiga:** Cold, coniferous forestland. The taiga comprises a large portion of Siberia, where the camps were located.

He couldn't see, but his ears told him everything going on in the barrack room and especially in the corner his squad occupied. He heard the heavy tread of the orderlies carrying one of the big barrels of excrement along the passage outside. A light job, that was considered, a job for the infirm, but just you try and carry out the muck without spilling any. He heard some of the 75th slamming bunches of boots onto the floor from the drying shed. Now their own men were doing it (it was their own squad's turn, too, to dry valenki). Tiurin, the squad leader, and his deputy Pavlo put on their valenki without a word but he heard their bunks creaking. Now Pavlo would be going off to the bread-storage and Tiurin to the staff quarters to see the P.P.D.[3]

Ah, but not simply to report as usual to the authorities for the daily assignment. Shukhov remembered that this morning his fate hung in the balance: they wanted to shift the 104th from the building shops to a new site, the "Socialist Way of Life" settlement. It lay in open country covered with snowdrifts, and before anything else could be done there they would have to dig holes and put up posts and attach barbed wire to them. Wire themselves in, so that they wouldn't run away. Only then would they start building.

There wouldn't be a warm corner for a whole month. Not even a doghouse. And fires were out of the question. There was nothing to build them with. Let your work warm you up, that was your only salvation.

No wonder the squad leader looked so worried, that was his job — to elbow some other squad, some bunch of suckers, into the assignment of the 104th. Of course with empty hands you got nowhere. He'd have to take a pound of salt pork to the senior official there, if not a couple of pounds.

There's never any harm in trying, so why not have a go at the dispensary and get a few days off if you can? After all, he did feel as though every limb was out of joint.

Then Shukhov wondered which of the campguards was on duty that morning. It was "One-and-a-half" Ivan's turn, he recalled. Ivan was a thin, weedy, dark-eyed sergeant. At first sight he looked like a real bastard, but when you got to know him he turned out to be the most good-natured of the guards on duty; he didn't put you in the guardhouse, he didn't haul you off before the authorities. So Shukhov decided he could lie in his bunk a little longer, at least while Barracks 9 was at the mess hall.

The whole four-bunk frame began to shake and sway. Two of its occupants were getting up at the same time: Shukhov's top-tier neighbor, Alyosha the Baptist, and Buinovsky, the ex-naval captain down below.

The orderlies, after removing both barrels of excrement, began to quarrel about which of them should go for hot water. They quarreled naggingly, like old women.

"Hey you, cackling like a couple of hens!" bellowed the electric welder in the 20th squad. "Get going." He flung a boot at them.

---

[3]**P.P.D.**: Production Planning Department.

The boot thudded against a post. The squabbling stopped.

In the next squad the deputy squad leader growled quietly: "Vasily Fyodorovich, they've cheated us again at the supply depot, the dirty rats. They should have given us four twenty-five ounce loaves and I've only got three. Who's going to go short?"

He kept his voice down, but of course everyone in the squad heard him and waited fearfully to learn who would be losing a slice of bread that evening.

Shukhov went on lying on his sawdust mattress, as hard as a board from long wear. If only it could be one thing or the other—let him fall into a real fever or let his aching joints ease up.

Meanwhile Alyosha was murmuring his prayers and Buinovsky had returned from the latrines, announcing to no one in particular but with a sort of malicious glee: "Well, sailors, grit your teeth. It's twenty below, for sure."

Shukhov decided to report sick.

At that very moment his blanket and jacket were imperiously jerked off him. He flung his coat away from his face and sat up. Looking up at him, his head level with the top bunk, was the lean figure of The Tartar.

So the fellow was on duty out of turn and had stolen up.

"S 854," The Tartar read from the white strip that had been stitched to the back of his black jacket. "Three days' penalty with work."

The moment they heard that peculiar choking voice of his, everyone who wasn't up yet in the whole dimly lit barracks, where two hundred men slept in bug-ridden bunks, stirred to life and began dressing in a hurry.

"What for, citizen chief?" asked Shukhov with more chagrin than he felt in his voice.

With work—that wasn't half so bad. They gave you hot food and you had no time to start thinking. Real jail was when you were kept back from work.

"Failing to get up at reveille. Follow me to the camp commandant's office," said The Tartar lazily.

His crumpled, hairless face was imperturbable. He turned, looking around for another victim, but now everybody, in dim corners and under the lights, in upper bunks and in lower, had thrust their legs into their black wadded trousers or, already dressed, had wrapped their coats around themselves and hurried to the door to get out of the way until The Tartar had left.

Had Shukhov been punished for something he deserved he wouldn't have felt so resentful. What hurt him was that he was always one of the first to be up. But he knew he couldn't plead with The Tartar. And, protesting merely for the sake of form, he hitched up his trousers (a bedraggled scrap of cloth had been sewn on them, just above the left knee, with a faded black number), slipped on his jacket (here the same digits appeared twice—on the chest and on the back), fished his valenki from the heap on the floor, put his hat on (with his number on a patch of cloth at the front), and followed The Tartar out of the barrack room.

The whole 104th saw him go, but no one said a word—what was the use, and anyway what could they say? The squad leader might have tried to do something, but he wasn't there. And Shukhov said nothing to anyone. He didn't want to irritate The Tartar. Anyway he could rely on the others in his squad to keep his breakfast for him.

The two men left the barracks. The cold made Shukhov gasp.

Two powerful searchlights swept the camp from the farthest watchtowers. The border lights, as well as those inside the camp, were on. There were so many of them that they outshone the stars.

With the snow creaking under their boots, the prisoners hurried away, each on his own business, some to the parcels office, some to hand in cereals to be cooked in the "individual" kitchen. All kept their heads down, buried in their buttoned-up coats, and all were chilled to the bone, not so much from the actual cold as from the prospect of having to spend the whole day in it. But The Tartar in his old army coat with the greasy blue tabs walked at a steady pace, as though the cold meant nothing to him.

They walked past the high wooden fence around the guardhouse, the only brick building in the camp; past the barbed wire that protected the camp bakery from the prisoners; past the corner of the staff quarters where the length of frosted rail hung on thick strands of wire; past another pole with a thermometer hanging on it (in a sheltered spot, so that the registered temperature shouldn't drop too low). Shukhov looked hopefully out of the corner of an eye at the milk-white tube — if it had shown –41° they ought not to be sent out to work. But today it was nowhere near –41°.

They walked into the staff quarters and The Tartar led him straight to the guardroom; and Shukhov realized, as he had guessed on the way there, that he wasn't being sent to the guardhouse at all — it was simply that the guardroom floor needed scrubbing. The Tartar told him he was going to let him off, and ordered him to scrub the floor.

Scrubbing the guardroom floor had been the job of a special prisoner who wasn't sent to work outside the camp — a staff orderly. The fellow had long ago made himself at home in the staff quarters; he had access to the offices of the camp commandant, the man in charge of discipline, and the security officer (the Father Confessor, they called him). When working for them he sometimes heard things that even the guards didn't know, and after a time he got a big head and came to consider scrubbing the floor for rank-and-file campguards a bit beneath him. Having sent for him once or twice, the guards discovered what was in the wind and began to pick on other prisoners for floor-scrubbing.

In the guardroom the stove was throwing out a fierce heat. Two guards in grubby tunics were playing checkers, and a third, who had not bothered to remove his sheepskin and valenki, lay snoring on a narrow bench. In one corner of the room stood an empty pail with a rag inside.

Shukhov was delighted. He thanked The Tartar for letting him off and said: "From now on I'll never get up late again."

The rule in this place was a simple one: when you'd finished you left. And now that he'd been given work to do, Shukhov's aches and pains seemed to have gone. He picked up the pail and, bare-handed — in his hurry he'd forgotten to take his mittens from under his pillow — went to the well.

Several of the squad leaders who were on their way to the P.P.D. had gathered near the pole with the thermometer, and one of the younger ones, a former Hero of the Soviet Union, shinnied up it and wiped off the instrument.

The others shouted advice from below:

"See you don't breathe on it. It'll push up the temperature."

"Push it up? Not fucking likely. *My* breath won't have any effect."

Tiurin of the 104th—Shukhov's squad—was not among them. Shukhov put down the pail, tucked his hands into his sleeves, and watched with interest.

The man up the pole shouted hoarsely: "Seventeen and a half. Not a damn bit more."

And, taking another look for sure, slid down.

"Oh, it's cockeyed. It always lies," someone said. "Do you think they'd ever hang one up that gave the true temperature?"

The squad leaders scattered. Shukhov ran to the well. The frost was trying to nip his ears under his earflaps, which he had lowered but not tied.

The top of the well was so thickly coated with ice that he only just managed to slip the bucket into the hole. The rope hung stiff as a ramrod.

With numb hands he carried the dripping bucket back to the guardroom and plunged his hands into the water. It felt warm.

The Tartar was no longer there. The guards—there were four now—stood in a group. They'd given up their checkers and their nap and were arguing about how much cereal they were going to get in January (food was in short supply at the settlement, and although rationing had long since come to an end, certain articles were sold to them, at a discount, which were not available to the civilian inhabitants).

"Shut that door, you scum. There's a draft," said one of the guards.

No sense in getting your boots wet in the morning. Even if Shukhov had dashed back to his barracks he wouldn't have found another pair to change into. During eight years' imprisonment he had known various systems for allocating footwear: there'd been times when he'd gone through the winter without valenki at all, or leather boots either, and had had to make shift with rope sandals or a sort of galoshes made of scraps of motor tires—"Chetezes" they called them, after the Cheliabinsk tractor works. Now the footwear situation seemed better; in October Shukhov had received (thanks to Pavlo, whom he trailed to the warehouse) a pair of ordinary, hard-wearing leather boots, big enough for a double thickness of rags inside. For a week he went about as though he'd been given a birthday present, kicking his new heels. Then in December the valenki arrived, and, oh, wasn't life wonderful?

But some devil in the bookkeeper's office had whispered in the commandant's ear that valenki should be issued only to those who surrendered their boots. It was against the rules for a prisoner to possess two pairs of footwear at the same time. So Shukhov had to choose. Either he'd have to wear leather throughout the winter, or surrender the boots and wear valenki even in the thaw. He'd taken such good care of his new boots, softening the leather with grease! Ah, nothing had been so hard to part with in all his eight years in camps as that pair of boots! They were tossed into a common heap. Not a hope of finding your own pair in the spring.

READING QUESTIONS

1. What motivations does Solzhenitsyn ascribe to the inhabitants of the gulags? Do they seem particularly criminal to you? Why or why not?

2. In what ways could this passage contradict the official Soviet image of the U.S.S.R. as a "worker's paradise"?

3. What motivations might the Soviet leadership have had for allowing this publication?

28-3 | Stalin Denounces Churchill

JOSEPH STALIN, *Interview Regarding Winston Churchill's Iron Curtain Speech* (March 14, 1946)

On March 5, 1946, Winston Churchill delivered his famous "iron curtain" speech to an audience in Fulton, Missouri. In it, Churchill described the division of Europe into rival camps, one free and democratic, the other bound by the shackles of Soviet totalitarianism. In Churchill's view, democratic values were the joint heritage of Great Britain and the United States, and it was their duty to protect and promote those values around the world. Days later, Joseph Stalin responded to Churchill's speech in an interview with the Soviet newspaper *Pravda*. As you read the interview, ask yourself who Stalin's intended audience might have been. Who did he want to influence, and how did he go about doing so?

Q. How do you assess the last speech of Mr. Churchill which was made in the United States? . . . Can one consider that the speech of Mr. Churchill is damaging to the cause of peace and security?

A. [Stalin says] Undoubtedly, yes. In substance, Mr. Churchill now stands in the position of a firebrand of war. And Mr. Churchill is not alone here. He has friends not only in England but also in the United States of America.

In this respect, one is reminded remarkably of Hitler and his friends. Hitler began to set war loose by announcing his racial theory, declaring that only people speaking the German language represent a fully valuable nation. Mr. Churchill begins to set war loose also by a racial theory, maintaining that only nations speaking the English language are fully valuable nations, called upon to decide the destinies of the entire world. . . .

In substance, Mr. Churchill and his friends in England and the United States present nations not speaking the English language with something like an

"Stalin's Reply to Churchill" (interview with *Pravda*), *New York Times*, March 14, 1946, p. 4.

ultimatum: "Recognize our lordship voluntarily and then all will be well. In the contrary case, war is inevitable." . . . There is no doubt that the setup of Mr. Churchill is a setup for war, a call to war with the Soviet Union. . . .

Q. How do you assess that part of Mr. Churchill's speech in which he attacks the democratic regime of the European countries which are our neighbors and in which he criticizes the good neighborly relations established between these countries and the Soviet Union?

A. [Stalin says] . . . Mr. Churchill maintains that Warsaw, Berlin, Prague, Vienna, Budapest, Belgrade, Bucharest and Sofia, all these famous cities and the populations of those areas, are within the Soviet sphere and are all subjected to Soviet influence and to the increasing control of Moscow. . . . To begin with, it is quite absurd to speak of the exclusive control of the USSR in Vienna and Berlin, where there are Allied control councils with representatives of four states, where the USSR has only one-fourth of the voices.

Secondly, one cannot forget the following fact: the Germans carried out an invasion of the USSR through Finland, Poland, Rumania, Bulgaria and Hungary. The Germans were able to carry out the invasion through these countries by reason of the fact that these countries had governments inimical to the Soviet Union.

As a result of the German invasion, the Soviet Union has irrevocably lost in battles with the Germans, and also during the German occupation and through the expulsion of Soviet citizens to German slave labor camps, about seven million people. In other words, the Soviet Union has lost in men several times more than Britain and the United States together.

READING QUESTIONS

1. What aspects of the interview might have been seen as most provocative in the West? Why?

2. How does Stalin justify Soviet intervention in eastern Europe? Do you find his position convincing? Why or why not?

3. How might this interview have been received outside of Europe? How might readers in Asia and Africa have responded to Stalin's characterization of American and British policy?

Challenging the Prewar Social and Political Order

For countless people around the world, World War II was a transformative experience. The Allies had claimed to fight for democracy, egalitarianism, and individual liberty, values that seemed to many in colonized Asia and Africa to be incompatible with the continuance of European imperial rule. Colonial troops had fought and died in the war, and colonial peoples had provided labor and resources. With the war over, and much of Europe in ruins, in colony after colony independence movements sprang up to claim the autonomy that many felt they had earned. The war also changed the lives and outlook of women in Europe and the United States. During the war, millions of women had entered the workforce, often taking jobs in industries that had previously been reserved for men. The experience was a key factor in the emergence of a resurgent women's rights movement in the decades after the war, a movement whose participants saw the right to vote as only one small step toward true equality. As you read these excerpts from the writings of Frantz Fanon and Simone de Beauvoir, ask yourself how the war might have shaped their perspectives. What role did the war play in sparking movements for greater equality and social justice in the decades following 1945?

28-4 | FRANTZ FANON, *The Wretched of the Earth* (1961)

A number of factors contributed to accelerating decolonization in the decades after 1945. Perhaps most important, World War II had bankrupted the European imperial powers and left their industrial infrastructure in ruins. Beyond this, the values for which the war had been fought were seen by many as inconsistent with colonialism, and emerging science undermined the rhetoric of white supremacy that had for so long been used to justify European global expansion. Finally, the Soviet Union played an active role in promoting "Wars of National Liberation," both as a way to gain new allies around the world and to strike a blow against the power and prestige of the West. Key to the process of decolonization was the realization on the part of the colonized that they possessed their own culture and worth. In the excerpt included here from *The Wretched of the Earth*, European-trained Algerian psychiatrist Frantz Fanon encouraged his countrymen to turn their backs on Europe and take up the task of building their own future.

From Frantz Fanon, *The Wretched of the Earth*, trans. Constance Farrington (New York: Grove Press, 1963), pp. 311–316. Marxists Internet Archive, http://marxists.org/subject/africa/fanon/conclusion.htm, accessed March 1, 2010.

Come, then, comrades; it would be as well to decide at once to change our ways. We must shake off the heavy darkness in which we were plunged, and leave it behind. The new day which is already at hand must find us firm, prudent, and resolute.

We must leave our dreams and abandon our old beliefs and friendships of the time before life began. Let us waste no time in sterile litanies and nauseating mimicry. Leave this Europe where they are never done talking of Man, yet murder men everywhere they find them, at the corner of every one of their own streets, in all the corners of the globe. For centuries they have stifled almost the whole of humanity in the name of a so-called spiritual experience. Look at them today swaying between atomic and spiritual disintegration.

And yet it may be said that Europe has been successful in as much as everything that she has attempted has succeeded.

Europe undertook the leadership of the world with ardor, cynicism, and violence. Look at how the shadow of her palaces stretches out ever farther! Every one of her movements has burst the bounds of space and thought. Europe has declined all humility and all modesty; but she has also set her face against all solicitude and all tenderness.

She has only shown herself parsimonious and niggardly where men are concerned; it is only men that she has killed and devoured.

So, my brothers, how is it that we do not understand that we have better things to do than to follow that same Europe?

That same Europe where they were never done talking of Man, and where they never stopped proclaiming that they were only anxious for the welfare of Man: today we know with what sufferings humanity has paid for every one of their triumphs of the mind.

Come, then, comrades, the European game has finally ended; we must find something different. We today can do everything, so long as we do not imitate Europe, so long as we are not obsessed by the desire to catch up with Europe.

Europe now lives at such a mad, reckless pace that she has shaken off all guidance and all reason, and she is running headlong into the abyss; we would do well to avoid it with all possible speed.

Yet it is very true that we need a model, and that we want blueprints and examples. For many among us the European model is the most inspiring. We have therefore seen in the preceding pages to what mortifying setbacks such an imitation has led us. European achievements, European techniques, and the European style ought no longer to tempt us and to throw us off our balance.

When I search for Man in the technique and the style of Europe, I see only a succession of negations of man, and an avalanche of murders.

The human condition, plans for mankind, and collaboration between men in those tasks which increase the sum total of humanity are new problems, which demand true inventions.

Let us decide not to imitate Europe; let us combine our muscles and our brains in a new direction. Let us try to create the whole man, whom Europe has been incapable of bringing to triumphant birth.

Two centuries ago, a former European colony decided to catch up with Europe. It succeeded so well that the United States of America became a monster, in which the taints, the sickness, and the inhumanity of Europe have grown to appalling dimensions.

Comrades, have we not other work to do than to create a third Europe? The West saw itself as a spiritual adventure. It is in the name of the spirit, in the name of the spirit of Europe, that Europe has made her encroachments, that she has justified her crimes and legitimized the slavery in which she holds four-fifths of humanity.

Yes, the European spirit has strange roots. All European thought has unfolded in places which were increasingly more deserted and more encircled by precipices; and thus it was that the custom grew up in those places of very seldom meeting man.

A permanent dialogue with oneself and an increasingly obscene narcissism never ceased to prepare the way for a half delirious state, where intellectual work became suffering and the reality was not at all that of a living man, working and creating himself, but rather words, different combinations of words, and the tensions springing from the meanings contained in words. Yet some Europeans were found to urge the European workers to shatter this narcissism and to break with this unreality.

But in general the workers of Europe have not replied to these calls; for the workers believe, too, that they are part of the prodigious adventure of the European spirit.

All the elements of a solution to the great problems of humanity have, at different times, existed in European thought. But Europeans have not carried out in practice the mission which fell to them, which consisted of bringing their whole weight to bear violently upon these elements, of modifying their arrangement and their nature, of changing them and, finally, of bringing the problem of mankind to an infinitely higher plane.

Today, we are present at the stasis of Europe. Comrades, let us flee from this motionless movement where gradually dialectic is changing into the logic of equilibrium. Let us reconsider the question of mankind. Let us reconsider the question of cerebral reality and of the cerebral mass of all humanity, whose connections must be increased, whose channels must be diversified and whose messages must be re-humanized.

Come, brothers, we have far too much work to do for us to play the game of rearguard. Europe has done what she set out to do and on the whole she has done it well; let us stop blaming her, but let us say to her firmly that she should not make such a song and dance about it. We have no more to fear; so let us stop envying her.

The Third World today faces Europe like a colossal mass whose aim should be to try to resolve the problems to which Europe has not been able to find the answers.

But let us be clear: what matters is to stop talking about output, and intensification, and the rhythm of work.

No, there is no question of a return to Nature. It is simply a very concrete question of not dragging men towards mutilation, of not imposing upon the brain rhythms which very quickly obliterate it and wreck it. The pretext of catching up must not be used to push man around, to tear him away from himself or from his privacy, to break and kill him.

No, we do not want to catch up with anyone. What we want to do is to go forward all the time, night and day, in the company of Man, in the company of all men. The caravan should not be stretched out, for in that case each line will hardly see those who precede it; and men who no longer recognize each other meet less and less together, and talk to each other less and less.

It is a question of the Third World starting a new history of Man, a history which will have regard to the sometimes prodigious theses which Europe has put forward, but which will also not forget Europe's crimes, of which the most horrible was committed in the heart of man, and consisted of the pathological tearing apart of his functions and the crumbling away of his unity. And in the framework of the collectivity there were the differentiations, the stratification and the bloodthirsty tensions fed by classes; and finally, on the immense scale of humanity, there were racial hatreds, slavery, exploitation, and above all the bloodless genocide which consisted in the setting aside of fifteen thousand millions of men.

So, comrades, let us not pay tribute to Europe by creating states, institutions, and societies which draw their inspiration from her.

Humanity is waiting for something other from us than such an imitation, which would be almost an obscene caricature.

If we want to turn Africa into a new Europe, and America into a new Europe, then let us leave the destiny of our countries to Europeans. They will know how to do it better than the most gifted among us.

But if we want humanity to advance a step farther, if we want to bring it up to a different level than that which Europe has shown it, then we must invent and we must make discoveries.

If we wish to live up to our peoples' expectations, we must seek the response elsewhere than in Europe.

Moreover, if we wish to reply to the expectations of the people of Europe, it is no good sending them back a reflection, even an ideal reflection, of their society and their thought with which from time to time they feel immeasurably sickened.

For Europe, for ourselves and for humanity, comrades, we must turn over a new leaf, we must work out new concepts, and try to set afoot a new man.

READING QUESTIONS

1. What is Fanon's fundamental critique of Western society? What evidence does he use to support these claims?

2. How does Fanon's training as a psychiatrist show through in his discussion of the flaws of the West?

3. Why might Fanon argue that a "return to nature" is neither possible nor desirable? Does this mean that he still accepts part of the European worldview?

28-5 | SIMONE DE BEAUVOIR, *The Second Sex* (1949)

In twentieth-century Europe, women achieved many goals of the nineteenth century's feminists, notably the rights to vote and to own property. Simone de Beauvoir (1908–1986)—a French writer and companion of the existentialist philosopher Jean-Paul Sartre—was part of the generation of women who wanted full inclusion in society, but realized that suffrage and property rights did not always translate to social equality. De Beauvoir's writing took up the complex issues of attitudes and values, and was particularly concerned with the persistence of traditional attitudes long after the circumstances that had created them no longer existed.

French law no longer includes obedience among a wife's duties, and every woman citizen has become a voter; these civic liberties remain abstract if there is no corresponding economic autonomy; the kept woman—wife or mistress—is not freed from the male just because she has a ballot paper in her hands; while today's customs impose fewer constraints on her than in the past, such negative licenses have not fundamentally changed her situation; she remains a vassal, imprisoned in her condition. It is through work that woman has been able, to a large extent, to close the gap separating her from the male; work alone can guarantee her concrete freedom. The system based on her dependence collapses as soon as she ceases to be a parasite; there is no longer need for a masculine mediator between her and the universe. The curse on the woman vassal is that she is not allowed to do anything; so she stubbornly pursues the impossible quest for being through narcissism, love, or religion. . . . It is also understandable that a shopgirl, an office worker, or a secretary should not want to give up the advantages of having a male to lean on. I have already said that it is an almost irresistible temptation for a young woman to be part of a privileged caste when she can do so simply by surrendering her body; she is doomed to have love affairs because her wages are minimal for the very high standard of living society demands of her; if she settles for what she earns, she will be no more than a pariah: without decent living accommodations or clothes, all amusement and even love will be refused her. Virtuous people preach asceticism to her; in fact, her diet is often as austere as a Carmelite's; but not everyone can have God as a lover: she needs to please men to succeed in her life as a woman. So she will accept help: her employer cynically counts on this when he pays her a pittance. Sometimes this help will enable her to improve her situation and achieve real independence; but sometimes she will give up her job to become a kept woman. She often does both: she frees herself from her lover through work, and she escapes work thanks to her lover; but then she experiences the double servitude

From Simone de Beauvoir, *The Second Sex*, trans. Constance Borde and Sheila Malovany-Chevallier (New York: Alfred A. Knopf, 2010), pp. 721–723, 735–736, 751.

of a job and masculine protection. For the married woman, her salary usually only means extra income; for the "woman who is helped," it is the man's protection that seems inessential; but neither woman buys total independence through her own efforts.

However, there are quite a lot of privileged women today who have gained economic and social autonomy in their professions. They are the ones who are at issue when the question of women's possibilities and their future is raised. While they are still only a minority, it is particularly interesting to study their situation closely; they are the subject of continuing debate between feminists and antifeminists. The latter maintain that today's emancipated women do not accomplish anything important, and that besides they have trouble finding their inner balance. The former exaggerate the emancipated women's achievements and are blind to their frustrations. . . .

There is one female function that is still almost impossible to undertake in complete freedom, and that is motherhood; in England and in America, the woman can at least refuse it at will, thanks to the practice of birth control; we have seen that in France she is often compelled to have painful and costly abortions;[1] she often finds herself burdened with a child she did not want, ruining her professional life. If this burden is a heavy one, it is because, inversely, social norms do not allow the woman to procreate as she pleases: the unwed mother causes scandal, and for the child an illegitimate birth is a stain; it is rare for a woman to become a mother without accepting the chains of marriage or lowering herself. If the idea of artificial insemination interests women so much, it is not because they wish to avoid male lovemaking: it is because they hope that voluntary motherhood will finally be accepted by society. It must be added that given the lack of well-organized day nurseries and kindergartens, even one child is enough to entirely paralyze a woman's activity; she can continue to work only by abandoning the child to her parents, friends, or servants. She has to choose between sterility, often experienced as a painful frustration, and burdens hardly compatible with a career.

Thus the independent woman today is divided between her professional interests and the concerns of her sexual vocation; she has trouble finding her balance; if she does, it is at the price of concessions, sacrifices, and juggling that keep her in constant tension. . . .

The free woman is just being born; when she conquers herself, she will perhaps justify Rimbaud's[2] prophecy: "Poets will be. When woman's infinite servitude is broken, when she lives for herself and by herself, man—abominable until now—giving her her freedom, she too will be a poet! Woman will find the unknown! Will her worlds of ideas differ from ours? She will find strange,

---

[1]**birth control . . . costly abortions**: French women did not gain legal access to contraceptives until 1967, whereas Americans gained full access in 1936. Abortion was illegal in both countries in 1949, becoming legal in the United States in 1973 and in France in 1975.

[2]**Rimbaud**: Arthur Rimbaud (1854–1891); radical French poet.

unfathomable, repugnant, delicious things, we will take them, we will understand them." Her "worlds of ideas" are not necessarily different from men's, because she will free herself by assimilating them; to know how singular she will remain and how important these singularities will continue to be, one would have to make some foolhardy predictions. What is beyond doubt is that until now women's possibilities have been stifled and lost to humanity, and in her and everyone's interest it is high time she be left to take her own chances.

READING QUESTIONS

1. Based on this excerpt, what does "equality" mean to Simone de Beauvoir?

2. What problems does de Beauvoir anticipate for women attempting to achieve her definition of equality?

3. What reasons could women have for not wanting to achieve the sort of liberation de Beauvoir promotes?

4. Based on your reading, what would de Beauvoir like to see change?

■ COMPARATIVE AND DISCUSSION QUESTIONS ■

1. Given his response to Churchill's "iron curtain" speech, how might Stalin have characterized the Marshall Plan? How might Marshall have responded to Stalin's position?

2. What connections can you make between the writings of Simone de Beauvoir and Frantz Fanon? How did the war shape the perspectives of both authors?

3. Compare Fanon's perspective to those of the documents of Chapter 24. How does his vision of the West compare to the ones found there?

4. How did ideas about feminism and women's rights change from the time that Mary Wollstonecraft wrote her *A Vindication of the Rights of Woman* (Document 19-6) to when de Beauvoir wrote *The Second Sex*? What continuities in thinking can you discern?

5. How might Churchill have used accounts like that of Solzhenitsyn to bolster his argument about division of the world?

29

Challenging the Postwar Order

1960–1991

The West and the Soviets both faced identity crises in the 1970s and 1980s. Economic difficulties in the seventies, West and East, underscored the tensions and conflicts within both capitalist and communist systems. As western European economies slowed and then contracted, discontent grew with the American-style consumer society that had emerged after World War II. Increasingly resentful of American influence on European economics, foreign policy, and culture, many Europeans came to believe that it was time to make a sharper distinction between American and European interests. In the East, workers began to grow restless, as the widening gap between communist ideals and realities became ever more difficult to disguise or ignore. In the communist world the growing tide of protest proved difficult to stop, and by the early 1990s communist regimes across eastern Europe had been toppled and the Soviet Union had collapsed.

SOURCES IN CONVERSATION

Reforming Socialist Societies

The Soviet decision to allow limited, cautious reform in the Eastern bloc in the 1960s encouraged reformers in Czechoslovakia to initiate much more dramatic changes in 1968. Frightened by the possibility of similar movements erupting elsewhere in eastern Europe, the Soviets moved in and forcefully reasserted their control. Soviet leaders took a stark lesson away from the events of 1968. Communist rule was to be maintained at any cost.

There would be no more "reform from within." Pressure for change, however, continued to build, and the 1980s would see dramatic challenges to Soviet rule, challenges that would culminate in the collapse of communism.

29-1 | SOLIDARITY UNION, *Twenty-One Demands: A Call for Workers' Rights and Freedoms* (1980)

Polish resistance to Soviet domination in the 1980s found a point of focus in the activities of the anticommunist shipbuilder's union *Solidarność* (Solidarity). Labor unions and strikes were illegal in the Soviet empire, but Solidarity, headed by worker Lech Walesa, successfully directed a group of ex-communist ally parties in broad resistance to the Soviets. In 1980 workers hung a pair of wooden boards with "Twenty-One Demands" at the entrance to a shipyard. The demands reflected a key aspect of Solidarity's program, a determination to link the specific concerns of shipyard workers to broad-based reform. As you read the demands, think about the kinds of changes the workers wanted. What kind of future did they hope to create for their country?

1. Acceptance of Free Trade Unions independent of both the Party and employers, in accordance with the International Labor Organization's Convention number 87 on the freedom to form unions, which was ratified by the Polish government.
2. A guarantee of the right to strike and guarantees of security for strikers and their supporters.
3. Compliance with the freedoms of press and publishing guaranteed in the Polish constitution. A halt to repression of independent publications and access to the mass media for representatives of all faiths.
4. (a) Reinstatement to their former positions for: people fired for defending workers' rights, in particular those participating in the strikes of 1970 and 1976; students dismissed from school for their convictions.
   (b) The release of all political prisoners. . . .
   (c) A halt to repression for one's convictions.
5. The broadcasting on the mass media of information about the establishment of the Interfactory Strike Committee (MKS) and publication of the list of demands.
6. The undertaking of real measures to get the country out of its present crisis by:
   (a) providing comprehensive, public information about the socioeconomic situation;
   (b) making it possible for people from every social class and stratum of society to participate in open discussions concerning the reform program.

"The Twenty-One Demands," in *The Passion of Poland*, by Lawrence Weschler (New York: Pantheon, 1984), pp. 206–208.

7. Compensation of all workers taking part in the strike for its duration with holiday pay from the Central Council of Trade Unions.[1]

8. Raise the base pay of every worker 2,000 zlotys[2] per month to compensate for price rises to date.

9. Guaranteed automatic pay raises indexed to price inflation and to decline in real income.

10. Meeting the requirements of the domestic market for food products: only surplus goods to be exported.

11. The rationing of meat and meat products through food coupons (until the market is stabilized).

12. Abolition of "commercial prices" and hard currency sales in so-called "internal export" shops.[3]

13. A system of merit selection for management positions on the basis of qualifications rather than [Communist] Party membership. Abolition of the privileged status of MO[4], SB[5] and the party apparatus through: equalizing all family subsidies; eliminating special stores; etc.

14. Reduction of retirement age for women to 50 and for men to 55. Anyone who has worked in the PRL [Polish People's Republic] for 30 years, for women, or 35 years for men, without regard to age, should be entitled to retirement benefits.

15. Bringing pensions and retirement benefits of the "old portfolio" to the level of those paid currently.

16. Improvement in the working conditions of the Health Service, which would assure full medical care to working people.

17. Provision for sufficient openings in daycare nurseries and preschools for the children of working people.

18. Establishment of three-year paid maternity leaves for the raising of children.

19. Reduce the waiting time for apartments.

20. Raise per diem [allowance for work-related travel] from 40 zlotys to 100 zlotys and provide cost-of-living increases.

21. Saturdays to be days off from work. Those who work on round-the-clock jobs or three-shift systems should have the lack of free Saturdays compensated by increased holiday leaves or through other paid holidays off from work.

---

[1]**Central Council of Trade Unions**: Official Soviet union organization, state-run and officially responsible for preventing the sorts of situations about which the workers complained in Gdansk.

[2]**zloty**: Basic unit of Polish currency; not convertible into Western currency at the time. It was losing value due to rising inflation.

[3]**"internal export" shops**: State-run shops where people with Western currency could buy consumer goods not available to workers paid in zlotys (the government had introduced a special type of currency), as part of the communist government's efforts to keep its economy afloat.

[4]**MO**: *Milicja Obywatelska* ("People's Militia"); the main Polish police force.

[5]**SB**: *Służba Bezpieczeństwa*, literally "Security Service," the communist secret police; roughly analogous to the Russian KGB.

READING QUESTIONS

1. What sort of problems do Solidarity's leaders see with their workplace?

2. What does the document reveal about the relationship between the current Polish governance and the reality of everyday life in Soviet-occupied Europe? What do the workers consider the standard of care?

3. Although these demands were made against a communist state, in what ways do the authors accept the premise that the state has a responsibility to its citizens?

29-2 | MIKHAIL GORBACHEV, *Perestroika: A Soviet Leader Calls for Change* (1987)

Throughout the 1970s, Soviet leaders resisted pressure for political and economic reform, refusing to acknowledge the inequities, inefficiencies, and injustices of the Soviet system. The party leaders that controlled the government were insulated and inflexible. Years of focus on military production and heavy industry had created a shortage of consumer goods, a situation that led the West German chancellor to liken the Soviet Union to an abysmally poor African country, but with rockets. Soviet leaders could not, however, ignore reality forever. In 1985 Mikhail Gorbachev became head of the Communist Party. Convinced that the survival of the Soviet Union was at stake, Gorbachev committed himself to the reform of the Soviet economy and the apparatus by which the party controlled information. These changes were referred to, respectively, as *perestroika*— "restructuring" —and *glasnost*— "openness."

Perestroika is an urgent necessity arising from the profound processes of development in our socialist society. This society is ripe for change. It has long been yearning for it. Any delay in beginning perestroika could have led to an exacerbated internal situation in the near future, which, to put it bluntly, would have been fraught with serious social, economic and political crises. . . .

In the latter half of the seventies—something happened that was at first sight inexplicable. The country began to lose momentum. Economic failures became more frequent. Difficulties began to accumulate and deteriorate, and unresolved problems to multiply. Elements of what we call stagnation and other phenomena alien to socialism began to appear in the life of society. A kind of "braking mechanism" affecting social and economic development formed. And all this happened at a time when scientific and technological revolution opened up new prospects for economic and social progress. . . .

An absurd situation was developing. The Soviet Union, the world's biggest producer of steel, raw materials, fuel and energy, has shortfalls in them due to wasteful or inefficient use. One of the biggest producers of grain for food, it nevertheless has to buy millions of tons of grain a year for fodder. We have the largest number of doctors and hospital beds per thousand of the population and,

From Mikhail Gorbachev, *Perestroika: New Thinking for Our Country and the World* (New York: Harper & Row, 1987), pp. 3–5, 7–8, 10, 22–24.

at the same time, there are glaring shortcomings in our health services. Our rockets can find Halley's comet and fly to Venus with amazing accuracy, but side by side with these scientific and technological triumphs is an obvious lack of efficiency in using scientific achievements for economic needs, and many Soviet household appliances are of poor quality.

This, unfortunately, is not all. A gradual erosion of the ideological and moral values of our people began.

It was obvious to everyone that the growth rates were sharply dropping and that the entire mechanism of quality control was not working properly; there was a lack of receptivity to the advances in science and technology; the improvement in living standards was slowing down and there were difficulties in the supply of foodstuffs, housing, consumer goods and services.

On the ideological plane as well, the braking mechanism brought about ever greater resistance to the attempts to constructively scrutinize the problems that were emerging and to the new ideas. Propaganda of success—real or imagined—was gaining the upper hand. Eulogizing and servility were encouraged; the needs and opinions of ordinary working people, of the public at large, were ignored. . . .

The presentation of a "problem-free" reality backfired: a breach had formed between word and deed, which bred public passivity and disbelief in the slogans being proclaimed. It was only natural that this situation resulted in a credibility gap: everything that was proclaimed from the rostrums and printed in newspapers and textbooks was put in question. Decay began in public morals; the great feeling of solidarity with each other that was forged during the heroic times of the Revolution [1917], the first five-year plans,[1] the Great Patriotic War[2] and postwar rehabilitation was weakening; alcoholism, drug addiction and crime were growing; and the penetration of the stereotypes of mass culture alien to us, which bred vulgarity and low tastes and brought about ideological barrenness increased. . . .

An unbiased and honest approach led us to the only logical conclusion that the country was verging on crisis. . . .

I would like to emphasize here that this analysis began a long time before the April Plenary Meeting[3] and that therefore its conclusions were well thought out. It was not something out of the blue, but a balanced judgment. It would be a mistake to think that a month after the Central Committee Plenary Meeting in March 1985, which elected me General Secretary, there suddenly appeared a group of people who understood everything and knew everything, and that these people gave clear-cut answers to all questions. Such miracles do not exist.

The need for change was brewing not only in the material sphere of life but also in public consciousness. People who had practical experience, a sense of

---

[1]**five-year plans**: Stalin's attempts to transform the rural, agrarian Soviet Union into an industrial state. The first plan began in 1928, the second in 1932 (a year early), and succeeded but at tremendous human cost.

[2]**Great Patriotic War**: Soviet name for World War II, in which the Soviets lost at least twenty million people.

[3]**April Plenary Meeting**: Regular meeting of the Communist Party's officials.

justice and commitment to the ideals of Bolshevism[4] criticized the established practice of doing things and noted with anxiety the symptoms of moral degradation and erosion of revolutionary ideals and socialist values. . . .

Perestroika is closely connected with socialism as a system. That side of the matter is being widely discussed, especially abroad, and our talk about perestroika won't be entirely clear if we don't touch upon that aspect.

Does perestroika mean that we are giving up socialism or at least some of its foundations? Some ask this question with hope, others with misgiving.

There are people in the West who would like to tell us that socialism is in a deep crisis and has brought our society to a dead end. That's how they interpret our critical analysis of the situation at the end of the seventies and beginning of the eighties. We have only one way out, they say: to adopt capitalist methods of economic management and social patterns, to drift toward capitalism.

They tell us that nothing will come of perestroika within the framework of our system. They say we should change this system and borrow from the experience of another socio-political system. To this they add that, if the Soviet Union takes this path and gives up its socialist choice, close links with the West will supposedly become possible. They go so far as to claim that the October 1917 Revolution was a mistake which almost completely cut off our country from world social progress.

To put an end to all the rumors and speculations that abound in the West about this, I would like to point out once again that we are conducting all our reforms in accordance with the socialist choice. We are looking within socialism, rather than outside it, for the answers to all the questions that arise. We assess our successes and errors alike by socialist standards. Those who hope that we shall move away from the socialist path will be greatly disappointed. Every part of our program of perestroika—and the program as a whole, for that matter—is fully based on the principle of more socialism and more democracy. . . .

We will proceed toward better socialism rather than away from it. We are saying this honestly, without trying to fool our own people or the world. Any hopes that we will begin to build a different, nonsocialist society and go over to the other camp are unrealistic and futile. Those in the West who expect us to give up socialism will be disappointed. It is high time they understood this, and, even more importantly, proceeded from that understanding in practical relations with the Soviet Union. . . .

We want more socialism and, therefore, more democracy.

READING QUESTIONS

1. What attitudes does Gorbachev seem to hold toward the West, particularly Western culture, as gleaned from this document?

---

[4]**Bolshevism**: Vladimir Lenin's—the first Soviet leader—interpretation of Marx's ideas; named after the Bolshevik faction of the prerevolutionary Social Democratic Party.

2. In what ways might this document be seen as a refutation of the policies of former Soviet leaders? In what ways does it seek to continue them?

3. Based on this document, what is Mikhail Gorbachev's relationship with Western free-market ideology?

4. To whom does Gorbachev ascribe the blame for the Soviet Union's recent economic failures? What solutions does he propose?

29-3 | Tiananmen Square: Resistance to the Power of the State
JEFF WIDENER, *Tank Man* (1989)

In 1989 prodemocracy demonstrations were not confined to Europe. Chinese students camped out in Tiananmen Square for weeks in the same sort of protests that seemed to have worked in Czechoslovakia and Poland. Unlike the communist governments of eastern Europe, however, the Chinese government proved willing to use force to maintain itself, and the Chinese army proved willing to obey orders to suppress the demonstrations. As the tanks rolled toward the square, they were held up by a single man, apparently with his shopping purchases, who blocked their path. Photojournalist Jeff Widener snapped this picture of the scene, which came to symbolize resistance—albeit ultimately futile—to state power.

"The Unknown Rebel," June 5, 1989. AP Photo/Jeff Widener.

READING QUESTIONS

1. To what use might this image be put by advocates of nonviolent revolution? How effective would those uses be, given the ultimate fate of the Tiananmen Square demonstrators?

2. What sort of reaction might this image provoke in a supporter of strong state power?

3. What reasons might the tank commander have for not running down the man in his way? What could this suggest about the limits of military power?

29-4 | Women Demand Fundamental Change

BETTY FRIEDAN, *Statement of Purpose of the National Organization for Women: Defining Full Equality* (1966)

Women's rights activists of the late nineteenth and early twentieth century focused their attention on the right to vote. The "second-wave" feminists of the 1960s and 1970s pursued a much broader agenda. Rejecting biological determinism, second-wave feminists attacked both discrimination against women and the social structures and patterns that established and reinforced male dominance. This statement of purpose, written in 1966 for the National Organization for Women by Betty Friedan, one of the organization's founders, captures much of the outlook and objectives of this new generation of activists. As you read it, think about how it differs from earlier efforts to define and defend women's rights.

We, men and women who hereby constitute ourselves as the National Organization for Women, believe that the time has come for a new movement toward true equality for all women in America, and toward a fully equal partnership of the sexes, as part of the world-wide revolution of human rights now taking place within and beyond our national borders.

The purpose of NOW is to take action to bring women into full participation in the mainstream of American society now, exercising all the privileges and responsibilities thereof in truly equal partnership with men. . . .

NOW is dedicated to the proposition that women, first and foremost, are human beings, who, like all other people in our society, must have the chance to develop their fullest human potential. We believe that women can achieve such equality only by accepting to the full the challenges and responsibilities they share with all other people in our society, as part of the decision-making mainstream of American political, economic and social life. . . .

Enormous changes taking place in our society make it both possible and urgently necessary to advance the unfinished revolution of women toward true equality, now. With a life span lengthened to nearly 75 years it is no longer either

Betty Friedan, *The National Organization for Women's 1966 Statement of Purpose*. From *The National Organization for Women*, http://now.org/history/purpos66.html.

necessary or possible for women to devote the greater part of their lives to child-rearing; yet childbearing and rearing which continues to be a most important part of most women's lives—still is used to justify barring women from equal professional and economic participation and advance.

Today's technology has reduced most of the productive chores which women once performed in the home and in mass-production industries based upon routine unskilled labor. This same technology has virtually eliminated the quality of muscular strength as a criterion for filling most jobs, while intensifying American industry's need for creative intelligence. In view of this new industrial revolution created by automation in the mid-twentieth century, women can and must participate in old and new fields of society in full equality—or become permanent outsiders.

Despite all the talk about the status of American women in recent years, the actual position of women in the United States has declined, and is declining, to an alarming degree throughout the 1950's and 60's. Although 46.4% of all American women between the ages of 18 and 65 now work outside the home, the overwhelming majority—75%—are in routine clerical, sales, or factory jobs, or they are household workers, cleaning women, hospital attendants. About two-thirds of Negro women workers are in the lowest paid service occupations. Working women are becoming increasingly—not less—concentrated on the bottom of the job ladder. As a consequence full-time women workers today earn on the average only 60% of what men earn, and that wage gap has been increasing over the past twenty-five years in every major industry group. In 1964, of all women with a yearly income, 89% earned under $5,000 a year; half of all full-time year round women workers earned less than $3,690; only 1.4% of full-time year round women workers had an annual income of $10,000 or more.

Further, with higher education increasingly essential in today's society, too few women are entering and finishing college or going on to graduate or professional school. Today, women earn only one in three of the B.A.'s and M.A.'s granted, and one in ten of the Ph.D.'s.

In all the professions considered of importance to society, and in the executive ranks of industry and government, women are losing ground. Where they are present it is only a token handful. Women comprise less than 1% of federal judges; less than 4% of all lawyers; 7% of doctors. Yet women represent 51% of the U.S. population. And, increasingly, men are replacing women in the top positions in secondary and elementary schools, in social work, and in libraries—once thought to be women's fields. . . .

WE BELIEVE that the power of American law, and the protection guaranteed by the U.S. Constitution to the civil rights of all individuals, must be effectively applied and enforced to isolate and remove patterns of sex discrimination, to ensure equality of opportunity in employment and education, and equality of civil and political rights and responsibilities on behalf of women, as well as for Negroes and other deprived groups.

We realize that women's problems are linked to many broader questions of social justice; their solution will require concerted action by many groups.

Therefore, convinced that human rights for all are indivisible, we expect to give active support to the common cause of equal rights for all those who suffer discrimination and deprivation, and we call upon other organizations committed to such goals to support our efforts toward equality for women. . . .

WE BELIEVE that this nation has a capacity at least as great as other nations, to innovate new social institutions which will enable women to enjoy the true equality of opportunity and responsibility in society, without conflict with their responsibilities as mothers and homemakers. In such innovations, America does not lead the Western world, but lags by decades behind many European countries. We do not accept the traditional assumption that a woman has to choose between marriage and motherhood, on the one hand, and serious participation in industry or the professions on the other. We question the present expectation that all normal women will retire from job or profession for 10 or 15 years, to devote their full time to raising children, only to reenter the job market at a relatively minor level. This, in itself, is a deterrent to the aspirations of women, to their acceptance into management or professional training courses, and to the very possibility of equality of opportunity or real choice, for all but a few women. Above all, we reject the assumption that these problems are the unique responsibility of each individual woman, rather than a basic social dilemma which society must solve. True equality of opportunity and freedom of choice for women requires such practical, and possible innovations as a nationwide network of child-care centers, which will make it unnecessary for women to retire completely from society until their children are grown, and national programs to provide retraining for women who have chosen to care for their children full-time.

WE BELIEVE that it is as essential for every girl to be educated to her full potential of human ability as it is for every boy—with the knowledge that such education is the key to effective participation in today's economy and that, for a girl as for a boy, education can only be serious where there is expectation that it will be used in society. We believe that American educators are capable of devising means of imparting such expectations to girl students. Moreover, we consider the decline in the proportion of women receiving higher and professional education to be evidence of discrimination. This discrimination may take the form of quotas against the admission of women to colleges, and professional schools; lack of encouragement by parents, counselors and educators; denial of loans or fellowships; or the traditional or arbitrary procedures in graduate and professional training geared in terms of men, which inadvertently discriminate against women. We believe that the same serious attention must be given to high school dropouts who are girls as to boys.

WE REJECT the current assumptions that a man must carry the sole burden of supporting himself, his wife, and family, and that a woman is automatically entitled to lifelong support by a man upon her marriage, or that marriage, home and family are primarily woman's world and responsibility—hers, to dominate—his to support. We believe that a true partnership between the sexes demands a different concept of marriage, an equitable sharing of the responsibilities of home and children and of the economic burdens of their support. We believe that proper recognition should be given to the economic and social value of home-making and child-care. To these ends, we will seek to open a reexamination of laws and mores governing marriage and divorce, for we believe that the current state of "half-equity" between the sexes discriminates against both men and women, and is the cause of much unnecessary hostility between the sexes.

WE BELIEVE that women must now exercise their political rights and responsibilities as American citizens. They must refuse to be segregated on the basis of sex into separate-and-not-equal ladies' auxiliaries in the political parties, and they must demand representation according to their numbers in the regu-larly constituted party committees — at local, state, and national levels — and in the informal power structure, participating fully in the selection of candidates and political decision-making, and running for office themselves.

IN THE INTERESTS OF THE HUMAN DIGNITY OF WOMEN, we will pro-test, and endeavor to change, the false image of women now prevalent in the mass media, and in the texts, ceremonies, laws, and practices of our major social institutions. Such images perpetuate contempt for women by society and by women for themselves. We are similarly opposed to all policies and prac-tices — in church, state, college, factory, or office — which, in the guise of protec-tiveness, not only deny opportunities but also foster in women self-denigration, dependence, and evasion of responsibility, undermine their confidence in their own abilities and foster contempt for women. . . .

WE BELIEVE THAT women will do most to create a new image of women by acting now, and by speaking out in behalf of their own equality, freedom, and human dignity — not in pleas for special privilege, nor in enmity toward men, who are also victims of the current, half-equality between the sexes — but in an active, self-respecting partnership with men. By so doing, women will develop confidence in their own ability to determine actively, in partnership with men, the conditions of their life, their choices, their future and their society.

READING QUESTIONS

1. What was the purpose of NOW? How does its agenda differ from that of earlier women's rights organizations?

2. Why did NOW believe that a push for full equality was particularly urgent in 1966?

3. How was the statement of purpose shaped by the larger context of social and political change in the mid-1960s?

29-5 | The Challenges of the Post-Communist Era

VACLAV HAVEL, *New Year's Address to the Nation* (1990)

One of the last countries to fall under Soviet influence after the World War II was Czechoslovakia. In 1968 an attempt to escape that influence led to Soviet tanks on the streets of Prague. After Gorbachev announced in 1989 that he would no longer enforce membership in the Soviet bloc, the Czechs and Slovaks retreated from one-party rule in a revolution so bloodless it became known as the "Velvet Revolution." Simply escaping from communism did not solve all their problems, however, and here the newly elected president, playwright Vaclav Havel (VAH-slav HAH-vel), muses on the nature of the past and potential of the future.

My dear fellow citizens,

For forty years you heard from my predecessors on this day different variations on the same theme: how our country was flourishing, how many million tons of steel we produced, how happy we all were, how we trusted our government, and what bright perspectives were unfolding in front of us.

I assume you did not propose me for this office so that I, too, would lie to you.

Our country is not flourishing. The enormous creative and spiritual potential of our nation is not being used sensibly. Entire branches of industry are producing goods that are of no interest to anyone, while we are lacking the things we need. A state which calls itself a workers' state humiliates and exploits workers. Our obsolete economy is wasting the little energy we have available. A country that once could be proud of the educational level of its citizens spends so little on education that it ranks today as seventy-second in the world. We have polluted the soil, rivers, and forests bequeathed to us by our ancestors, and we have today the most contaminated environment in Europe. Adults in our country die earlier than in most other European countries.

Allow me a small personal observation. When I flew recently to Bratislava, I found some time during discussions to look out of the plane window. I saw the industrial complex of Slovnaft chemical factory and the giant Petr'alka housing estate right behind it. The view was enough for me to understand that for decades our statesmen and political leaders did not look or did not want to look out of the windows of their planes. No study of statistics available to me would enable me to understand faster and better the situation in which we find ourselves.

But all this is still not the main problem. The worst thing is that we live in a contaminated moral environment. We fell morally ill because we became used to saying something different from what we thought. We learned not to believe in anything, to ignore one another, to care only about ourselves. Concepts such as love, friendship, compassion, humility, or forgiveness lost their depth and

Prague Castle Administration, archival Web page, http://old.hrad.cz/president/Havel/speeches/1990/0101_uk.html.

dimension, and for many of us they represented only psychological peculiarities, or they resembled gone-astray greetings from ancient times, a little ridiculous in the era of computers and spaceships. Only a few of us were able to cry out loudly that the powers that be should not be all-powerful and that the special farms, which produced ecologically pure and top-quality food just for them, should send their produce to schools, children's homes, and hospitals if our agriculture was unable to offer them to all.

The previous regime—armed with its arrogant and intolerant ideology—reduced man to a force of production, and nature to a tool of production. In this it attacked both their very substance and their mutual relationship. It reduced gifted and autonomous people, skillfully working in their own country, to the nuts and bolts of some monstrously huge, noisy, and stinking machine, whose real meaning was not clear to anyone. It could not do more than slowly but inexorably wear out itself and all its nuts and bolts.

When I talk about the contaminated moral atmosphere, I am not talking just about the gentlemen who eat organic vegetables and do not look out of the plane windows. I am talking about all of us. We had all become used to the totalitarian system and accepted it as an unchangeable fact and thus helped to perpetuate it. In other words, we are all—though naturally to differing extents—responsible for the operation of the totalitarian machinery. None of us is just its victim. We are all also its co-creators.

Why do I say this? It would be very unreasonable to understand the sad legacy of the last forty years as something alien, which some distant relative bequeathed to us. On the contrary, we have to accept this legacy as a sin we committed against ourselves. If we accept it as such, we will understand that it is up to us all, and up to us alone to do something about it. We cannot blame the previous rulers for everything, not only because it would be untrue, but also because it would blunt the duty that each of us faces today: namely, the obligation to act independently, freely, reasonably, and quickly. Let us not be mistaken: the best government in the world, the best parliament and the best president, cannot achieve much on their own. And it would be wrong to expect a general remedy from them alone. Freedom and democracy include participation and therefore responsibility from us all.

If we realize this, then all the horrors that the new Czechoslovak democracy inherited will cease to appear so terrible. If we realize this, hope will return to our hearts.

In the effort to rectify matters of common concern, we have something to lean on. The recent period—and in particular the last six weeks of our peaceful revolution—has shown the enormous human, moral and spiritual potential, and the civic culture that slumbered in our society under the enforced mask of apathy. Whenever someone categorically claimed that we were this or that, I always objected that society is a very mysterious creature and that it is unwise to trust only the face it presents to you. I am happy that I was not mistaken. Everywhere in the world people wonder where those meek, humiliated, skeptical, and seemingly cynical citizens of Czechoslovakia found the marvelous strength to shake the totalitarian yoke from their shoulders in several weeks, and in a decent and peaceful way. And let us ask: Where did the young people who never knew another system get their desire for truth, their love of free thought, their political ideas, their civic courage and civic prudence? How did it happen that their parents—the very generation that had been considered lost—joined them? How is it that so many people immediately knew what to do and none needed any advice or instruction?

I think there are two main reasons for the hopeful face of our present situation. First of all, people are never just a product of the external world; they are also able to relate themselves to something superior, however systematically the external world tries to kill that ability in them. Secondly, the humanistic and democratic traditions, about which there had been so much idle talk, did after all slumber in the unconsciousness of our nations and ethnic minorities, and were inconspicuously passed from one generation to another, so that each of us could discover them at the right time and transform them into deeds.

We had to pay, however, for our present freedom. Many citizens perished in jails in the 1950s, many were executed, thousands of human lives were destroyed, hundreds of thousands of talented people were forced to leave the country. Those who defended the honor of our nations during the Second World War, those who rebelled against totalitarian rule and those who simply managed to remain themselves and think freely, were all persecuted. We should not forget any of those who paid for our present freedom in one way or another. Independent courts should impartially consider the possible guilt of those who were responsible for the persecutions, so that the truth about our recent past might be fully revealed.

We must also bear in mind that other nations have paid even more dearly for their present freedom, and that indirectly they have also paid for ours. The rivers of blood that have flowed in Hungary, Poland, Germany, and recently in such a horrific manner in Romania, as well as the sea of blood shed by the nations of the Soviet Union, must not be forgotten. First of all because all human suffering concerns every other human being. But more than this, they must also not be forgotten because it is these great sacrifices that form the tragic background of today's freedom or the gradual emancipation of the nations of the Soviet Bloc, and thus the background of our own newfound freedom. Without the changes in the Soviet Union, Poland, Hungary, and the German Democratic Republic, what has happened in our country would have scarcely happened. And if it did, it certainly would not have followed such a peaceful course.

The fact that we enjoyed optimal international conditions does not mean that anyone else has directly helped us during the recent weeks. In fact, after hundreds of years, both our nations have raised their heads high of their own initiative without relying on the help of stronger nations or powers. It seems to me that this constitutes the great moral asset of the present moment. This moment holds within itself the hope that in the future we will no longer suffer from the complex of those who must always express their gratitude to somebody. It now depends only on us whether this hope will be realized and whether our civic, national, and political self-confidence will be awakened in a historically new way.

Self-confidence is not pride. Just the contrary: only a person or a nation that is self-confident, in the best sense of the word, is capable of listening to others, accepting them as equals, forgiving its enemies and regretting its own guilt. Let us try to introduce this kind of self-confidence into the life of our community and, as nations, into our behavior on the international stage. Only thus can we restore our self-respect and our respect for one another as well as the respect of other nations.

Our state should never again be an appendage or a poor relative of anyone else. It is true that we must accept and learn many things from others, but we must do this in the future as their equal partners, who also have something to offer.

Our first president[1] wrote: "Jesus, not Caesar." In this he followed our philosophers Chelick[2] and Komensk.[3] I dare to say that we may even have an opportunity to spread this idea further and introduce a new element into European and global politics. Our country, if that is what we want, can now permanently radiate love, understanding, the power of the spirit and of ideas. It is precisely this glow that we can offer as our specific contribution to international politics.

Masaryk based his politics on morality. Let us try, in a new time and in a new way, to restore this concept of politics. Let us teach ourselves and others that politics should be an expression of a desire to contribute to the happiness of the community rather than of a need to cheat or rape the community. Let us teach ourselves and others that politics can be not simply the art of the possible, especially if this means the art of speculation, calculation, intrigue, secret deals, and pragmatic maneuvering, but that it can also be the art of the impossible, that is, the art of improving ourselves and the world.

We are a small country, yet at one time we were the spiritual crossroads of Europe. Is there a reason why we could not again become one? Would it not be another asset with which to repay the help of others that we are going to need?

Our homegrown Mafia, those who do not look out of the plane windows and who eat specially fed pigs, may still be around and at times may muddy the waters, but they are no longer our main enemy. Even less so is our main enemy any kind of international Mafia. Our main enemy today is our own bad traits: indifference to the common good, vanity, personal ambition, selfishness, and rivalry. The main struggle will have to be fought on this field.

---

[1]**our first president**: Thomas Garrigue Masaryk, the first president of Czechoslovakia (1918–1935); a humanist and democrat.

[2]**Chelick**: Petr Chelčický; Bohemian author who lived roughly between 1390 and 1460, and who decried secular power and war as being in opposition to Christianity.

[3]**Komensk**: J. A. Komensky (1592–1670); Bohemian (Czech) religious reformer who valued education as a way to universal humanity, and who became a Czech national symbol in the nineteenth century.

There are free elections and an election campaign ahead of us. Let us not allow this struggle to dirty the so-far clean face of our gentle revolution. Let us not allow the sympathies of the world, which we have won so fast, to be equally rapidly lost through our becoming entangled in the jungle of skirmishes for power. Let us not allow the desire to serve oneself to bloom once again under the stately garb of the desire to serve the common good. It is not really important now which party, club or group prevails in the elections. The important thing is that the winners will be the best of us, in the moral, civic, political and professional sense, regardless of their political affiliations. The future policies and prestige of our state will depend on the personalities we select, and later, elect to our representative bodies.

My dear fellow citizens!

Three days ago I became the president of the republic as a consequence of your will, expressed through the deputies of the Federal Assembly. You have a right to expect me to mention the tasks I see before me as president.

The first of these is to use all my power and influence to ensure that we soon step up to the ballot boxes in a free election, and that our path toward this historic milestone will be dignified and peaceful.

My second task is to guarantee that we approach these elections as two self-governing nations who respect each other's interests, national identity, religious traditions, and symbols. As a Czech who has given his presidential oath to an important Slovak who is personally close to him, I feel a special obligation—after the bitter experiences that Slovaks had in the past—to see that all the interests of the Slovak nation are respected and that no state office, including the highest one, will ever be barred to it in the future.

My third task is to support everything that will lead to better circumstances for our children, the elderly, women, the sick, the hardworking laborers, the national minorities, and all citizens who are for any reason worse off than others. High-quality food or hospitals must no longer be a prerogative of the powerful; they must be available to those who need them the most.

As supreme commander of the armed forces I want to guarantee that the defensive capability of our country will no longer be used as a pretext for anyone to stand in the way of courageous peace initiatives, the reduction of military service, the establishment of alternative military service, and the overall humanization of military life.

In our country there are many prisoners who, though they may have committed serious crimes and have been punished for them, have had to submit—despite the goodwill of some investigators, judges, and above all defense lawyers—to a debased judiciary process that curtailed their rights. They now have to live in prisons that do not strive to awaken the better qualities contained in every person, but rather humiliate them and destroy them physically and mentally. In a view of this fact, I have decided to declare a relatively extensive amnesty. At the same time I call on the prisoners to understand that forty years of unjust investigations, trials, and imprisonments cannot be put right overnight, and to understand that the changes that are being speedily prepared still require time to implement. By rebelling, the prisoners would help neither society nor themselves. I also call on the public not to fear the prisoners once they are released, not to make their lives difficult, to help them, in the Christian spirit, after their return among us to find within themselves that which jails could not find in them: the capacity to repent and the desire to live a respectable life.

My honorable task is to strengthen the authority of our country in the world. I would be glad if other states respected us for showing understanding, tolerance, and love for peace. I would be happy if Pope John Paul II and the Dalai Lama of Tibet could visit our country before the elections, if only for a day. I would be happy if our friendly relations with all nations were strengthened. I would be happy if we succeeded before the elections in establishing diplomatic relations with the Vatican and Israel. I would also like to contribute to peace by briefly visiting our close neighbors, the German Democratic Republic and the Federal Republic of Germany. Neither shall I forget our other neighbors—fraternal Poland and the ever-closer countries of Hungary and Austria.

In conclusion, I would like to say that I want to be a president who will speak less and work more. To be a president who will not only look out of the windows of his airplane but who, first and foremost, will always be present among his fellow citizens and listen to them well.

You may ask what kind of republic I dream of. Let me reply: I dream of a republic independent, free, and democratic, of a republic economically prosperous and yet socially just; in short, of a humane republic that serves the individual and that therefore holds the hope that the individual will serve it in turn. Of a republic of well-rounded people, because without such people it is impossible to solve any of our problems—human, economic, ecological, social, or political.

The most distinguished of my predecessors opened his first speech with a quotation from the great Czech educator Komensk. Allow me to conclude my first speech with my own paraphrase of the same statement:

People, your government has returned to you!

READING QUESTIONS

1. What were the successes and failures of the communist system as Havel describes them?

2. How does Havel appear to apportion responsibility for the system he has succeeded? Are the average citizens exempt from these criticisms?

3. What are the problems Havel sees for the future? How does he approach solving them?

■ COMPARATIVE AND DISCUSSION QUESTIONS ■

1. On what priorities and reforms do the leaders of Solidarity and Mikhail Gorbachev seem to agree? About which priorities do they disagree?

2. Compare and contrast Havel's New Year's message with the Solidarity Union's "Twenty-One Demands." What similarities and differences do you see in their analysis of the causes of the economic and social problems faced by eastern Europe?

3. How do Havel's thoughts on the nature of unfree society compare with the photograph from China of a single man holding up four tanks? Based on what happened to the Tiananmen demonstrators, are Havel's beliefs about the future justified?

4. Compare and contrast NOW's statement of purpose with the excerpt from Simone de Beauvoir's *The Second Sex* (Document 28-5). What similarities do you see in Friedan's and de Beauvoir's analyses of the place of women in modern society? What differences do you note?

30

Life in an Age of Globalization

1990 to the Present

Although global relationships have impacted the world's economy at least since the time of the Crusades, in the years after the collapse of the Soviet Union triumphal narratives of the expansion of Western ideals of democracy and capitalism began to speak of globalization. Europe's economy was unified as it had never been before, and the interchange of peoples, products, and ideas seemed to be proceeding on Western terms. In the late 1990s opposition emerged to the cultural and economic domination of the West, among both activists in the West and traditionalists in other parts of the world. The skeptical rationalist world that the Enlightenment had created was not welcoming for everyone, and some discontented groups began to return to and reinterpret their traditional identities in opposition to the West. A new dimension was added to the opposition to economic globalization in 2008 when an economic crisis in the United States triggered a global economic downturn. The resulting economic upheaval in Europe threatened to reverse the decades-long trend toward European unity.

SOURCES IN CONVERSATION

Islam Versus the West?

The end of the Cold War gave rise to the hope that a new era of international cooperation was about to begin. With the world no longer divided into rival camps along ideological lines, nations would be free to find common interests and to work together to achieve common objectives. How-

ever, little more than a decade after the end of the Cold War, many observers were convinced that a new global dividing line had emerged, this time
with the West pitted against militant Islam. The two documents included
here challenged the validity of this claim. In the first, Amartya Sen examines the proposition that the terrorist attacks of September 11, 2001, were
part of a larger "clash of civilizations." In the second, Tariq Ramadan maps
out a vision of the future of Muslims in the West, one that did not involve
either the abandonment of Islamic principles or the isolation of Muslims
from their non-Muslim neighbors.

30-1 | AMARTYA SEN, *A World Not Neatly Divided* (November 23, 2001)

The widely held assumption that the fall of the Soviet Union had made the world safer was
shattered by the terrorist attacks of September 11, 2001. In the wake of the al-Qaeda terrorist
attack on the Pentagon and World Trade Center towers, leaders and ordinary individuals alike
cast about for an explanation of the horror they had witnessed. Many focused their attention
on the fact that the plane hijackers were Muslim, positing a connection between the tenets
of Islam and terrorism, and suggesting that Islam and the West were locked in a battle for
cultural and ideological supremacy. Amartya Sen, an Indian academic then at Cambridge
University, argued six weeks after the attacks that this rhetoric of "clashing civilizations" was
ill-equipped to capture the complexity of a diverse world.

When people talk about clashing civilizations, as so many politicians and aca-
demics do now, they can sometimes miss the central issue. The inadequacy of
this thesis begins well before we get to the question of whether civilizations must
clash. The basic weakness of the theory lies in its program of categorizing people
of the world according to a unique, allegedly commanding system of classification. This is problematic because civilizational categories are crude and inconsistent and also because there are other ways of seeing people (linked to politics,
language, literature, class, occupation, or other affiliations).

   The befuddling influence of a singular classification also traps those who
dispute the thesis of a clash: To talk about "the Islamic world" or "the Western
world" is already to adopt an impoverished vision of humanity as unalterably
divided. In fact, civilizations are hard to partition in this way, given the diversi-
ties within each society as well as the linkages among different countries
and cultures. For example, describing India as a "Hindu civilization" misses
the fact that India has more Muslims than any other country except Indonesia
and possibly Pakistan. It is futile to try to understand Indian art, literature,
music, food, or politics without seeing the extensive interactions across barriers
of religious communities. These include Hindus and Muslims, Buddhists,

Amartya Sen, "A World Not Neatly Divided," *The New York Times*, November 23, 2001.

Jains,[1] Sikhs,[2] Parsees,[3] Christians (who have been in India since at least the fourth century, well before England's conversion to Christianity [sixth century C.E.]), Jews (present since the fall of Jerusalem [70 C.E.]), and even atheists and agnostics. Sanskrit has a larger atheistic literature than exists in any other classical language. Speaking of India as a Hindu civilization may be comforting to the Hindu fundamentalist, but it is an odd reading of India.

A similar coarseness can be seen in the other categories invoked, like "the Islamic world." Consider Akbar and Aurangzeb, two Muslim emperors of the Mogul[4] dynasty in India. Aurangzeb tried hard to convert Hindus into Muslims and instituted various policies in that direction, of which taxing the non-Muslims was only one example. In contrast, Akbar reveled in his multiethnic court and pluralist laws, and issued official proclamations insisting that no one "should be interfered with on account of religion" and that "anyone is to be allowed to go over to a religion that pleases him."

If a homogeneous view of Islam were to be taken, then only one of these emperors could count as a true Muslim. The Islamic fundamentalist would have no time for Akbar; Prime Minister Tony Blair, given his insistence that tolerance is a defining characteristic of Islam, would have to consider excommunicating Aurangzeb. I expect both Akbar and Aurangzeb would protest, and so would I. A similar crudity is present in the characterization of what is called "Western civilization." Tolerance and individual freedom have certainly been present in European history. But there is no dearth of diversity here, either. When Akbar was making his pronouncements on religious tolerance in Agra [in northern India, near Nepal], in the 1590s, the Inquisitions were still going on; in 1600, Giordano Bruno[5] was burned at the stake, for heresy, in Campo dei Fiori in Rome.

Dividing the world into discrete civilizations is not just crude. It propels us into the absurd belief that this partitioning is natural and necessary and must overwhelm all other ways of identifying people. That imperious view goes not only against the sentiment that "we human beings are all much the same," but also against the more plausible understanding that we are diversely different. For example, Bangladesh's split from Pakistan was not connected with religion, but with language and politics.

Each of us has many features in our self-conception. Our religion, important as it may be, cannot be an all-engulfing identity. Even a shared poverty can be a

---

[1]**Jains**: Followers of one of the oldest religions in India, which encompasses several ancient religions, who believe in the potential of each individual soul. Jains have many beliefs similar to Hindus.

[2]**Sikhs**: Followers of another Indian religion, founded in the fifteenth century but only becoming prominent in the seventeenth. Sikhs were once persecuted by both Hindus and Muslims.

[3]**Parsees**: Members of a branch of Zoroastrianism, the religion of the ancient Persians, believed to have been in India for at least a thousand years.

[4]**Mogul**: Descendants of the Mongols in central India who converted to Islam. Akbar ruled from 1556 to 1605, and Aurangzeb from 1658 to 1707.

[5]**Giordano Bruno**: An Italian who argued that the earth went around the sun, though some of his unusual theological beliefs were the reason why he was burned in a Roman plaza.

source of solidarity across the borders. The kind of division highlighted by, say, the so-called "antiglobalization" protesters—whose movement is, incidentally, one of the most globalized in the world—tries to unite the underdogs of the world economy and goes firmly against religious, national or "civilizational" lines of division.

The main hope of harmony lies not in any imagined uniformity, but in the plurality of our identities, which cut across each other and work against sharp divisions into impenetrable civilizational camps. Political leaders who think and act in terms of sectioning off humanity into various "worlds" stand to make the world more flammable—even when their intentions are very different. They also end up, in the case of civilizations defined by religion, lending authority to religious leaders seen as spokesmen for their "worlds." In the process, other voices are muffled and other concerns silenced. The robbing of our plural identities not only reduces us; it impoverishes the world.

READING QUESTIONS

1. According to Sen, when are generalizations about the world possible? In what ways are they necessary in talking about a complex world?

2. Why might Sen's argument challenge the worldview of both the extremists behind the September 11 attacks and the leaders of the governments who oppose them?

3. What advantages did Sen believe would result from embracing the "plurality of our identities"?

30-2 | TARIQ RAMADAN, *Western Muslims and the Future of Islam* (2004)

In the aftermath of World War II and the Algerian revolt of 1956–1963, large numbers of North African Muslims emigrated to France searching for economic opportunity (a process also at work for different reasons in Germany and Britain). Assimilation proved problematic for many of these immigrants, and many in their host countries were disinclined to accept them. Tariq Ramadan, a prominent Muslim scholar, has written several books that attempt to provide a way to reconcile the traditional, universalist claims of Islam with the skeptical, post-Enlightenment European society. Here, Ramadan sets out the basic issues his work attempts to address.

When I wrote *To Be a European Muslim: A Study of the Islamic Sources in Light of the European Context* in 1997, many readers were surprised and challenged by the approach to the Islamic textual sources (the Qur'an and the Sunna) that I was proposing, and by the propositions I was trying to articulate with regard to reading our sources. Their questions were usually aimed in the same direction: where would it lead *in practice*? For I had said that this was only a first step and that more work would have to follow to formulate the vision of the whole and to apply these reflections in practical terms on the ground. These past years have been fed by a constant threefold work of deepening my reflection on the sources, bringing them face to face with the realities on the ground, and analyzing the local dynamics in accordance with meetings and exchanges with Muslim association groups (and consequently a number of partners) in Europe and North America (not forgetting the very Western circumstances of Mauritius, Reunion, or Singapore). This has made it possible for me to take up the work begun five years ago and to synthesize it into a more global and coherent vision of Islamic principles, the available juridical instruments, and the means of employing them. This work makes up the whole of the first part of this present volume. I have not included all the elements of reflection contained in *To Be a European Muslim*, but I have restricted myself to those that had a direct link with my purpose here: to understand the universality of the message of Islam, and to highlight the means we are given to help us live in our own time, in the West, with respect for ourselves and for others. The approach I propose is anchored in the Islamic tradition and amplified from within it: in this sense it is both deeply classical and radically new. Beginning with the Qur'an and the Sunna and the methodologies set down by the ulama[1] throughout the history of the Islamic sciences, I have tried to immerse myself again in reading these sources in the light of our new Western context; even though the methodology adopted is classical, I have not hesitated sometimes to question certain definitions and categorizations and to suggest others. It is especially in my suggestions and my replies that one will doubtless find some new perspectives, which I hope may be useful. My conviction in elaborating on this work is that the movement toward reform, which was once intrinsic to the juridical compass of Islam, can take place effectively only from within, in, and through a rigorous faithfulness to the sources and the norms of reading them. This is the requirement I have laid upon myself.

The second part of my study concentrates on the practical application of these reflections in Western society. Questions as essential as the spiritual life, or education in industrialized, more or less postmodern, more or less secularized societies, are studied with an attempt, wherever possible, to approach the subject from three perspectives: the principles to respect, the reality of the situation, and the reforms that seem to me necessary to face the challenges of life in Europe or North America. I have tried to follow the same stages in each chapter. Following on from spirituality and education, social engagement and political participation, economic resistance, interreligious dialogue, and the cultural equivalent are some of the subjects I have felt needed to be addressed at this precise juncture of our history in the West.

---

[1]**ulama**: Sometimes spelled *ulemma*, the community of Muslim scholars who interpret Islamic law.

We are currently living through a veritable silent revolution in Muslim communities in the West: more and more young people and intellectuals are actively looking for a way to live in harmony with their faith while participating in the societies that are their societies, whether they like it or not. French, English, German, Canadian, and American Muslims, women as well as men, are constructing a "Muslim personality" that will soon surprise many of their fellow citizens. Far from media attention, going through the risks of a process of maturation that is necessarily slow, they are drawing the shape of European and American Islam: faithful to the principles of Islam, dressed in European and American cultures, and definitively rooted in Western societies. This grassroots movement will soon exert considerable influence over worldwide Islam: in view of globalization and the Westernization of the world, these are the same questions as those already being raised from Morocco to Indonesia.

Globalization contains the paradox that at the same time that it causes the old traditional points of reference to disappear, it reawakens passionate affirmations of identity that often verge on withdrawal and self-exclusion. The Muslim world is not exempt from such phenomena: from Africa to Asia, via America and Europe, this kind of discourse is multiplied. It is about self-protection, self-preservation, and sometimes even self-definition over and against the "Western megamachine," to use the formulation of Serge Latouche: "Whatever is Western is anti-Islamic" or "Islam has nothing in common with the West." This bipolar vision is widespread and gives some Muslims a sense of power, might, and legitimacy in Otherness. But not only is this bipolar and simplistic vision a decoy (and the claims that justify it are untruths) but the power that it bestows is a pure illusion: in practice, the Muslims who maintain these theses only isolate themselves, and sometimes, by their excessive emotional, intellectual, and social isolation, even strengthen the logic of the dominant system whose power, by contrast, lies in always appearing open, pluralistic, and rational.

The approach I propose here is the exact opposite of this attitude. Beginning with the message of Islam and its universal principles, I have investigated the tools that can give an impetus, from the inside, to a movement of reform and integration into the new environments. The power and effectiveness of the "principle of integration," which is the foundation upon which all the juridical instruments for adaptation must depend, lie in the fact that it comes with an entirely opposite perspective; instead of being sensitive, obsessed by self-protection and withdrawal and attempts to integrate *oneself* by "the little door," on the margin, or "as a minority" it is, on the contrary, a matter of *integrating*, making one's own all that people have produced that is good, just, humane — intellectually, scientifically, politically, economically, culturally, and so on. While our fellow-citizens speak of this "integration" of Muslims "among us," the question for the Muslims presents itself differently: their universal principles teach them that wherever the law respects their integrity and their freedom of conscience and worship, they are at home, and must consider the attainments of these societies as their own and must involve themselves, with their fellow-citizens, in making it good and better. No withdrawal, no obsession with identity — on the contrary, it is a question of entering into an authentic dialogue, as between equals, with all our fellow-citizens with respect for the identical universality of our respective values, willingly open to mutual enrichment and eventually to becoming true partners in action.

I know these ideas are frightening and that they appear new and "offensive," to use the expression of a questioner who heard them at one of my lectures in the United Kingdom. Let me say that my reading of the scriptural sources and the study of our Western environment have led me to lay down two fundamental theses that involve the determined rejection of certain intellectual positions. First, for me it is not a question of relativizing the universal principles of Islam in order to give the impression that we are integrating ourselves into the rational order. In my view, the issue is to find out how the Islamic universal accepts and respects pluralism and the belief of the Other: it is one thing to relativize what I believe and another to respect fully the conventions of the Other. The postmodernist spirit would lead us unconsciously to confuse the second proposition with the first. I refuse: it is in the very name of the universality of my principle that my conscience is summoned to respect diversity and the relative, and that is why, even in the West (especially in the West), we have not to think of our presence in terms of "minority." What seems to be a given in our thinking: "the Muslim minority," "the law of minorities" (*fiqh al-aqalliyyat*), must, I believe, be rethought. We shall do a little of this in the following pages. Second, I defend fiercely the idea that Western Muslims must be intellectually, politically, and financially independent. Of course, this does not imply that exchanges and discussions with Muslim countries should cease—rather the contrary. We have more need than ever to maintain spaces for meeting and debate (especially since there are not yet any ulama we can refer to who were born and formed in the West). In this period of transition, links between Muslims of West and East are essential. What I mean exactly by the idea of "independence" is that Western citizens of the Muslim faith must think for themselves, develop theses appropriate to their situation, and put forward new and concrete ideas. They must refuse to remain dependent, either on the intellectual level, or more damagingly, on the political or financial levels. These types of dependences are the worst because they prevent the acquisition of responsibility and the liberation of heart and minds. In the same way, as a citizen, I refuse to support the colonialist reaction found among certain governments and commentators that consists of wanting to keep Muslims in these old (or other new) dependences and in wanting to "speak for them," as we reject the insidious new "paternalism" of some who "help" "young" Muslims eternally destined in their spirits never to become adults.

These two positions of principle are ultimately nothing but the reflection of the dynamics that are slowly coming into place in the West. I have consciously decided not to deal specifically with the problems of political security faced by European and American states, or with Islamophobia or social discrimination—not because I think these problems are secondary but because my thinking is based at a higher level. It is by acquiring the conviction that they can be faithful to their principles while being totally involved in the life of their society that

Muslims will find the means to confront these difficulties and act to resolve them. It is an established and unacceptable fact that the governments of the United States (particularly after the outrages of 11 September 2001) and Europe maintain relations that are sometimes disrespectful of and even clearly discriminatory against citizens and residents of their countries who are of Muslim faith. It is no less true that they apply a security policy including constant surveillance: distrust is maintained, and the image of the "Muslim" often remains suspect. The general picture conceived by the Western population in general is so negative that one could call it Islamophobia, and this is a fact that many Muslims have lived with on a daily basis. One could extend the list of difficulties, complaints, and criticism at will. My response to all these phenomena is to insist to Muslims that they stay in the higher reaches, in awareness of their principles, values, and responsibilities. By developing a global vision of their points of reference and their objectives, by studying their situation and being reconciled with themselves, they have the responsibility to become engaged in all the areas we shall study in this book. Muslims will get what they deserve: if, as watchful and participating citizens, they study the machinery of their society, demand their rights to equality with others, struggle against all kinds of discrimination and injustice, establish real partnerships beyond their own community and what concerns themselves alone, it will be an achievement that will make political security measures, discrimination, Islamophobic behavior, and so on drift away downstream. In the end, the ball is in their court . . . unless they are determined to remain forever on the margins.

This book is only one step toward the building of the Muslim personality in the West and doubtless in the modern era, too. It will not be the last. Other works, *in sha Allah,*[2] must continue to trace the path back to the beginning. I have humbly tried to draw the theoretical and practical outlines of a vision for the future, full on. I want to engage with this in practice, and already, across all the countries of the West, this vision is being accomplished. The road is still long, but indwelt by this humble "need of Him," one must not be afraid or apologize for needing time.

READING QUESTIONS

1. In what ways does Ramadan seem to reject Western thinking, and in what ways does he embrace it?

2. Ramadan seeks to solve the problem of retreating into isolation in the face of globalization. Is he convincing, or is his position a more sophisticated retreat into tradition?

---

[2] *in sha Allah*: "God willing."

30-3 | Protesting Globalization

A Greenpeace Activist at the G8 Summit (2001)

The creation of the global economy sped up in the 1990s with the development of the Internet and the accompanying economic boom. As triumphal narratives of a global West emerged, a counternarrative of exploitation of the developing world for the comfort of the world's wealthiest nations emerged as well. Since 2001, every gathering of the G8 (the leaders of the eight largest economies in the world: France, Germany, Italy, Japan, the United Kingdom, the United States, Canada, and Russia) has been met with organized, sometimes violent, protests. The marchers decry the consumerism and materialism of the West, and the use of poorly paid labor in Africa and Asia to sustain Western economies, as suggested by this Greenpeace protester at the 2001 G8 summit in Genoa, Italy.

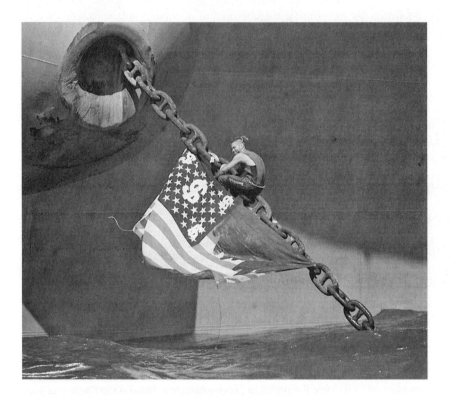

READING QUESTIONS

1. What criticism is the protester making of American policy? How might the people who benefit from those policies respond?

2. Is there any irony in the ability of the protesters to use the products of the globalized society to protest it? Does that compromise their message or strengthen it?

Reuters/Stefano Rellandini, July 17, 2001. © Reuters/Corbis.

30-4 | Arab Spring
A Tunisian Woman Casts Her Vote (2011)

In 2011, revolution in Tunisia triggered a chain reaction that led to the fall of the Mubarak regime in Egypt and the outbreak of civil war in Syria. Dubbed the "Arab Spring," a term that recalled prodemocracy uprisings in eastern Europe decades earlier, the events gave hope to many that the era of authoritarian government in North Africa and the Middle East would someday come to an end. In this photograph taken in October 2011, a Tunisian woman casts her vote in the elections that followed the overthrow of the Tunisian dictatorship.

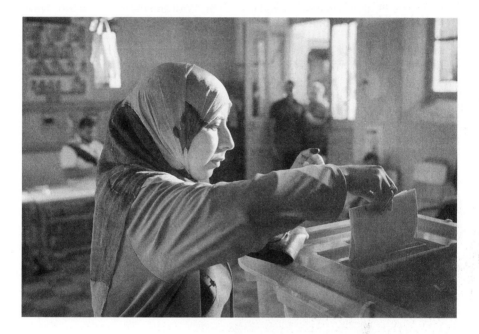

READING QUESTIONS

1. Why might the photographer have chosen to represent the Tunisian election with an image of a woman voting? What implications might this image have had for Western viewers?

2. In your opinion, what are the long-term implications of the Arab Spring for the political development of the Islamic world?

Ezequiel Scagnetti / Invision / Aurora Photos.

▪ COMPARATIVE AND DISCUSSION QUESTIONS ▪

1. How might Sen and Ramadan disagree about the basis of personal identity in the globalized society? On what points might they agree?

2. Does Ramadan support the process of globalization? What reaction do you think he would have to the protesters against the G8?

3. Based on the documents in this chapter, what are the bases for individual and group identity in the globalizing world?

4. In your opinion, can an appropriate analogy be made between the Cold War (see Chapter 28) and current relations between the West and the Islamic world? How do recent events in Tunisia, Egypt, and Syria fit into your analysis?